50% OFF
Online PECT PreK-4 Prep Course!

By Mometrix

Dear Customer,

We consider it an honor and a privilege that you chose our PECT PreK-4 Study Guide. As a way of showing our appreciation and to help us better serve you, we are offering **50% off our online PECT PreK-4 Prep Course**. Many PECT PreK-4 courses are needlessly expensive and don't deliver enough value. With our course, you get access to the best PECT PreK-4 prep material, and **you only pay half price**.

We have structured our online course to perfectly complement your printed study guide. The PECT PreK-4 Prep Course contains **in-depth lessons** that cover all the most important topics, **40+ video reviews** that explain difficult concepts, over **350 practice questions** to ensure you feel prepared, and more than **350 digital flashcards**, so you can study while you're on the go.

Online PECT PreK-4 Prep Course

Topics Included:

- Child Development, Learning, and Assessment

- Collaboration and Professionalism

- Language and Literacy Development

- Social Studies, Arts, and Humanities

- Mathematics, Science, and Health

Course Features:

- PECT PreK-4 Study Guide
  - Get content that complements our best-selling study guide.
- Full-Length Practice Tests
  - With over 350 practice questions, you can test yourself again and again.
- Mobile Friendly
  - If you need to study on the go, the course is easily accessible from your mobile device.
- PECT PreK-4 Flashcards
  - Our course includes a flashcard mode with over 350 content cards to help you study.

To receive this discount, visit us at mometrix.com/university/pectprek/ or simply scan this QR code with your smartphone. At the checkout page, enter the discount code: **PECTK50off**

If you have any questions or concerns, please contact us at support@mometrix.com.

FREE Study Skills Videos/DVD Offer

Dear Customer,

Thank you for your purchase from Mometrix! We consider it an honor and a privilege that you have purchased our product and we want to ensure your satisfaction.

As part of our ongoing effort to meet the needs of test takers, we have developed a set of Study Skills Videos that we would like to give you for <u>FREE</u>. These videos cover our *best practices* for getting ready for your exam, from how to use our study materials to how to best prepare for the day of the test.

All that we ask is that you email us with feedback that would describe your experience so far with our product. Good, bad, or indifferent, we want to know what you think!

To get your FREE Study Skills Videos, you can use the **QR code** below, or send us an **email** at studyvideos@mometrix.com with *FREE VIDEOS* in the subject line and the following information in the body of the email:

- The name of the product you purchased.
- Your product rating on a scale of 1-5, with 5 being the highest rating.
- Your feedback. It can be long, short, or anything in between. We just want to know your impressions and experience so far with our product. (Good feedback might include how our study material met your needs and ways we might be able to make it even better. You could highlight features that you found helpful or features that you think we should add.)

If you have any questions or concerns, please don't hesitate to contact me directly.

Thanks again!

Sincerely,

Jay Willis
Vice President
jay.willis@mometrix.com
1-800-673-8175

PECT
PreK-4
Secrets Study Guide

Exam Review and PECT Practice Test
for the Pennsylvania Educator
Certification Tests

Written and edited by Mometrix Test Prep

Printed in the United States of America

This paper meets the requirements of ANSI/NISO Z39.48-1992 (Permanence of Paper).

Mometrix offers volume discount pricing to institutions. For more information or a price quote, please contact our sales department at sales@mometrix.com or 888-248-1219.

Mometrix Media LLC is not affiliated with or endorsed by any official testing organization. All organizational and test names are trademarks of their respective owners.

Paperback
ISBN 13: 978-1-5167-3694-2
ISBN 10: 1-5167-3694-X

DEAR FUTURE EXAM SUCCESS STORY

First of all, **THANK YOU** for purchasing Mometrix study materials!

Second, congratulations! You are one of the few determined test-takers who are committed to doing whatever it takes to excel on your exam. **You have come to the right place.** We developed these study materials with one goal in mind: to deliver you the information you need in a format that's concise and easy to use.

In addition to optimizing your guide for the content of the test, we've outlined our recommended steps for breaking down the preparation process into small, attainable goals so you can make sure you stay on track.

We've also analyzed the entire test-taking process, identifying the most common pitfalls and showing how you can overcome them and be ready for any curveball the test throws you.

Standardized testing is one of the biggest obstacles on your road to success, which only increases the importance of doing well in the high-pressure, high-stakes environment of test day. Your results on this test could have a significant impact on your future, and this guide provides the information and practical advice to help you achieve your full potential on test day.

Your success is our success

We would love to hear from you! If you would like to share the story of your exam success or if you have any questions or comments in regard to our products, please contact us at **800-673-8175** or **support@mometrix.com**.

Thanks again for your business and we wish you continued success!

Sincerely,
The Mometrix Test Preparation Team

Need more help? Check out our flashcards at:
http://MometrixFlashcards.com/PECT

TABLE OF CONTENTS

Introduction

Thank you for purchasing this resource! You have made the choice to prepare yourself for a test that could have a huge impact on your future, and this guide is designed to help you be fully ready for test day. Obviously, it's important to have a solid understanding of the test material, but you also need to be prepared for the unique environment and stressors of the test, so that you can perform to the best of your abilities.

For this purpose, the first section that appears in this guide is the **Secret Keys**. We've devoted countless hours to meticulously researching what works and what doesn't, and we've boiled down our findings to the five most impactful steps you can take to improve your performance on the test. We start at the beginning with study planning and move through the preparation process, all the way to the testing strategies that will help you get the most out of what you know when you're finally sitting in front of the test.

We recommend that you start preparing for your test as far in advance as possible. However, if you've bought this guide as a last-minute study resource and only have a few days before your test, we recommend that you skip over the first two Secret Keys since they address a long-term study plan.

If you struggle with **test anxiety**, we strongly encourage you to check out our recommendations for how you can overcome it. Test anxiety is a formidable foe, but it can be beaten, and we want to make sure you have the tools you need to defeat it.

Review Video Directory

As you work your way through this guide, you will see numerous review video links interspersed with the written content. If you would like to access all of these review videos in one place, click on the video directory link found on the bonus page: **mometrix.com/bonus948/pectprek4**

1

Secret Key #1 – Plan Big, Study Small

There's a lot riding on your performance. If you want to ace this test, you're going to need to keep your skills sharp and the material fresh in your mind. You need a plan that lets you review everything you need to know while still fitting in your schedule. We'll break this strategy down into three categories.

Information Organization

Start with the information you already have: the official test outline. From this, you can make a complete list of all the concepts you need to cover before the test. Organize these concepts into groups that can be studied together, and create a list of any related vocabulary you need to learn so you can brush up on any difficult terms. You'll want to keep this vocabulary list handy once you actually start studying since you may need to add to it along the way.

Time Management

Once you have your set of study concepts, decide how to spread them out over the time you have left before the test. Break your study plan into small, clear goals so you have a manageable task for each day and know exactly what you're doing. Then just focus on one small step at a time. When you manage your time this way, you don't need to spend hours at a time studying. Studying a small block of content for a short period each day helps you retain information better and avoid stressing over how much you have left to do. You can relax knowing that you have a plan to cover everything in time. In order for this strategy to be effective though, you have to start studying early and stick to your schedule. Avoid the exhaustion and futility that comes from last-minute cramming!

Study Environment

The environment you study in has a big impact on your learning. Studying in a coffee shop, while probably more enjoyable, is not likely to be as fruitful as studying in a quiet room. It's important to keep distractions to a minimum. You're only planning to study for a short block of time, so make the most of it. Don't pause to check your phone or get up to find a snack. It's also important to **avoid multitasking**. Research has consistently shown that multitasking will make your studying dramatically less effective. Your study area should also be comfortable and well-lit so you don't have the distraction of straining your eyes or sitting on an uncomfortable chair.

 The time of day you study is also important. You want to be rested and alert. Don't wait until just before bedtime. Study when you'll be most likely to comprehend and remember. Even better, if you know what time of day your test will be, set that time aside for study. That way your brain will be used to working on that subject at that specific time and you'll have a better chance of recalling information.

Finally, it can be helpful to team up with others who are studying for the same test. Your actual studying should be done in as isolated an environment as possible, but the work of organizing the information and setting up the study plan can be divided up. In between study sessions, you can discuss with your teammates the concepts that you're all studying and quiz each other on the details. Just be sure that your teammates are as serious about the test as you are. If you find that your study time is being replaced with social time, you might need to find a new team.

Secret Key #2 – Make Your Studying Count

You're devoting a lot of time and effort to preparing for this test, so you want to be absolutely certain it will pay off. This means doing more than just reading the content and hoping you can remember it on test day. It's important to make every minute of study count. There are two main areas you can focus on to make your studying count.

Retention

It doesn't matter how much time you study if you can't remember the material. You need to make sure you are retaining the concepts. To check your retention of the information you're learning, try recalling it at later times with minimal prompting. Try carrying around flashcards and glance at one or two from time to time or ask a friend who's also studying for the test to quiz you.

To enhance your retention, look for ways to put the information into practice so that you can apply it rather than simply recalling it. If you're using the information in practical ways, it will be much easier to remember. Similarly, it helps to solidify a concept in your mind if you're not only reading it to yourself but also explaining it to someone else. Ask a friend to let you teach them about a concept you're a little shaky on (or speak aloud to an imaginary audience if necessary). As you try to summarize, define, give examples, and answer your friend's questions, you'll understand the concepts better and they will stay with you longer. Finally, step back for a big picture view and ask yourself how each piece of information fits with the whole subject. When you link the different concepts together and see them working together as a whole, it's easier to remember the individual components.

Finally, practice showing your work on any multi-step problems, even if you're just studying. Writing out each step you take to solve a problem will help solidify the process in your mind, and you'll be more likely to remember it during the test.

Modality

Modality simply refers to the means or method by which you study. Choosing a study modality that fits your own individual learning style is crucial. No two people learn best in exactly the same way, so it's important to know your strengths and use them to your advantage.

For example, if you learn best by visualization, focus on visualizing a concept in your mind and draw an image or a diagram. Try color-coding your notes, illustrating them, or creating symbols that will trigger your mind to recall a learned concept. If you learn best by hearing or discussing information, find a study partner who learns the same way or read aloud to yourself. Think about how to put the information in your own words. Imagine that you are giving a lecture on the topic and record yourself so you can listen to it later.

For any learning style, flashcards can be helpful. Organize the information so you can take advantage of spare moments to review. Underline key words or phrases. Use different colors for different categories. Mnemonic devices (such as creating a short list in which every item starts with the same letter) can also help with retention. Find what works best for you and use it to store the information in your mind most effectively and easily.

Secret Key #3 – Practice the Right Way

Your success on test day depends not only on how many hours you put into preparing, but also on whether you prepared the right way. It's good to check along the way to see if your studying is paying off. One of the most effective ways to do this is by taking practice tests to evaluate your progress. Practice tests are useful because they show exactly where you need to improve. Every time you take a practice test, pay special attention to these three groups of questions:

- The questions you got wrong
- The questions you had to guess on, even if you guessed right
- The questions you found difficult or slow to work through

This will show you exactly what your weak areas are, and where you need to devote more study time. Ask yourself why each of these questions gave you trouble. Was it because you didn't understand the material? Was it because you didn't remember the vocabulary? Do you need more repetitions on this type of question to build speed and confidence? Dig into those questions and figure out how you can strengthen your weak areas as you go back to review the material.

Additionally, many practice tests have a section explaining the answer choices. It can be tempting to read the explanation and think that you now have a good understanding of the concept. However, an explanation likely only covers part of the question's broader context. Even if the explanation makes perfect sense, **go back and investigate** every concept related to the question until you're positive you have a thorough understanding.

As you go along, keep in mind that the practice test is just that: practice. Memorizing these questions and answers will not be very helpful on the actual test because it is unlikely to have any of the same exact questions. If you only know the right answers to the sample questions, you won't be prepared for the real thing. **Study the concepts** until you understand them fully, and then you'll be able to answer any question that shows up on the test.

It's important to wait on the practice tests until you're ready. If you take a test on your first day of study, you may be overwhelmed by the amount of material covered and how much you need to learn. Work up to it gradually.

On test day, you'll need to be prepared for answering questions, managing your time, and using the test-taking strategies you've learned. It's a lot to balance, like a mental marathon that will have a big impact on your future. Like training for a marathon, you'll need to start slowly and work your way up. When test day arrives, you'll be ready.

Start with the strategies you've read in the first two Secret Keys—plan your course and study in the way that works best for you. If you have time, consider using multiple study resources to get different approaches to the same concepts. It can be helpful to see difficult concepts from more than one angle. Then find a good source for practice tests. Many times, the test website will suggest potential study resources or provide sample tests.

Practice Test Strategy

If you're able to find at least three practice tests, we recommend this strategy:

UNTIMED AND OPEN-BOOK PRACTICE

Take the first test with no time constraints and with your notes and study guide handy. Take your time and focus on applying the strategies you've learned.

TIMED AND OPEN-BOOK PRACTICE

Take the second practice test open-book as well, but set a timer and practice pacing yourself to finish in time.

TIMED AND CLOSED-BOOK PRACTICE

Take any other practice tests as if it were test day. Set a timer and put away your study materials. Sit at a table or desk in a quiet room, imagine yourself at the testing center, and answer questions as quickly and accurately as possible.

Keep repeating timed and closed-book tests on a regular basis until you run out of practice tests or it's time for the actual test. Your mind will be ready for the schedule and stress of test day, and you'll be able to focus on recalling the material you've learned.

Secret Key #4 – Pace Yourself

Once you're fully prepared for the material on the test, your biggest challenge on test day will be managing your time. Just knowing that the clock is ticking can make you panic even if you have plenty of time left. Work on pacing yourself so you can build confidence against the time constraints of the exam. Pacing is a difficult skill to master, especially in a high-pressure environment, so **practice is vital**.

Set time expectations for your pace based on how much time is available. For example, if a section has 60 questions and the time limit is 30 minutes, you know you have to average 30 seconds or less per question in order to answer them all. Although 30 seconds is the hard limit, set 25 seconds per question as your goal, so you reserve extra time to spend on harder questions. When you budget extra time for the harder questions, you no longer have any reason to stress when those questions take longer to answer.

Don't let this time expectation distract you from working through the test at a calm, steady pace, but keep it in mind so you don't spend too much time on any one question. Recognize that taking extra time on one question you don't understand may keep you from answering two that you do understand later in the test. If your time limit for a question is up and you're still not sure of the answer, mark it and move on, and come back to it later if the time and the test format allow. If the testing format doesn't allow you to return to earlier questions, just make an educated guess; then put it out of your mind and move on.

On the easier questions, be careful not to rush. It may seem wise to hurry through them so you have more time for the challenging ones, but it's not worth missing one if you know the concept and just didn't take the time to read the question fully. Work efficiently but make sure you understand the question and have looked at all of the answer choices, since more than one may seem right at first.

Even if you're paying attention to the time, you may find yourself a little behind at some point. You should speed up to get back on track, but do so wisely. Don't panic; just take a few seconds less on each question until you're caught up. Don't guess without thinking, but do look through the answer choices and eliminate any you know are wrong. If you can get down to two choices, it is often worthwhile to guess from those. Once you've chosen an answer, move on and don't dwell on any that you skipped or had to hurry through. If a question was taking too long, chances are it was one of the harder ones, so you weren't as likely to get it right anyway.

On the other hand, if you find yourself getting ahead of schedule, it may be beneficial to slow down a little. The more quickly you work, the more likely you are to make a careless mistake that will affect your score. You've budgeted time for each question, so don't be afraid to spend that time. Practice an efficient but careful pace to get the most out of the time you have.

Secret Key #5 – Have a Plan for Guessing

When you're taking the test, you may find yourself stuck on a question. Some of the answer choices seem better than others, but you don't see the one answer choice that is obviously correct. What do you do?

The scenario described above is very common, yet most test takers have not effectively prepared for it. Developing and practicing a plan for guessing may be one of the single most effective uses of your time as you get ready for the exam.

In developing your plan for guessing, there are three questions to address:

- When should you start the guessing process?
- How should you narrow down the choices?
- Which answer should you choose?

When to Start the Guessing Process

Unless your plan for guessing is to select C every time (which, despite its merits, is not what we recommend), you need to leave yourself enough time to apply your answer elimination strategies. Since you have a limited amount of time for each question, that means that if you're going to give yourself the best shot at guessing correctly, you have to decide quickly whether or not you will guess.

Of course, the best-case scenario is that you don't have to guess at all, so first, see if you can answer the question based on your knowledge of the subject and basic reasoning skills. Focus on the key words in the question and try to jog your memory of related topics. Give yourself a chance to bring the knowledge to mind, but once you realize that you don't have (or you can't access) the knowledge you need to answer the question, it's time to start the guessing process.

It's almost always better to start the guessing process too early than too late. It only takes a few seconds to remember something and answer the question from knowledge. Carefully eliminating wrong answer choices takes longer. Plus, going through the process of eliminating answer choices can actually help jog your memory.

Summary: Start the guessing process as soon as you decide that you can't answer the question based on your knowledge.

7

How to Narrow Down the Choices

The next chapter in this book (**Test-Taking Strategies**) includes a wide range of strategies for how to approach questions and how to look for answer choices to eliminate. You will definitely want to read those carefully, practice them, and figure out which ones work best for you. Here though, we're going to address a mindset rather than a particular strategy.

Your odds of guessing an answer correctly depend on how many options you are choosing from.

Number of options left	5	4	3	2	1
Odds of guessing correctly	20%	25%	33%	50%	100%

You can see from this chart just how valuable it is to be able to eliminate incorrect answers and make an educated guess, but there are two things that many test takers do that cause them to miss out on the benefits of guessing:

- Accidentally eliminating the correct answer
- Selecting an answer based on an impression

We'll look at the first one here, and the second one in the next section.

To avoid accidentally eliminating the correct answer, we recommend a thought exercise called **the $5 challenge**. In this challenge, you only eliminate an answer choice from contention if you are willing to bet $5 on it being wrong. Why $5? Five dollars is a small but not insignificant amount of money. It's an amount you could afford to lose but wouldn't want to throw away. And while losing $5 once might not hurt too much, doing it twenty times will set you back $100. In the same way, each small decision you make—eliminating a choice here, guessing on a question there—won't by itself impact your score very much, but when you put them all together, they can make a big difference. By holding each answer choice elimination decision to a higher standard, you can reduce the risk of accidentally eliminating the correct answer.

The $5 challenge can also be applied in a positive sense: If you are willing to bet $5 that an answer choice *is* correct, go ahead and mark it as correct.

Summary: Only eliminate an answer choice if you are willing to bet $5 that it is wrong.

Which Answer to Choose

You're taking the test. You've run into a hard question and decided you'll have to guess. You've eliminated all the answer choices you're willing to bet $5 on. Now you have to pick an answer. Why do we even need to talk about this? Why can't you just pick whichever one you feel like when the time comes?

The answer to these questions is that if you don't come into the test with a plan, you'll rely on your impression to select an answer choice, and if you do that, you risk falling into a trap. The test writers know that everyone who takes their test will be guessing on some of the questions, so they intentionally write wrong answer choices to seem plausible. You still have to pick an answer though, and if the wrong answer choices are designed to look right, how can you ever be sure that you're not falling for their trap? The best solution we've found to this dilemma is to take the decision out of your hands entirely. Here is the process we recommend:

Once you've eliminated any choices that you are confident (willing to bet $5) are wrong, select the first remaining choice as your answer.

Whether you choose to select the first remaining choice, the second, or the last, the important thing is that you use some preselected standard. Using this approach guarantees that you will not be enticed into selecting an answer choice that looks right, because you are not basing your decision on how the answer choices look.

This is not meant to make you question your knowledge. Instead, it is to help you recognize the difference between your knowledge and your impressions. There's a huge difference between thinking an answer is right because of what you know, and thinking an answer is right because it looks or sounds like it should be right.

Summary: To ensure that your selection is appropriately random, make a predetermined selection from among all answer choices you have not eliminated.

Test-Taking Strategies

This section contains a list of test-taking strategies that you may find helpful as you work through the test. By taking what you know and applying logical thought, you can maximize your chances of answering any question correctly!

It is very important to realize that every question is different and every person is different: no single strategy will work on every question, and no single strategy will work for every person. That's why we've included all of them here, so you can try them out and determine which ones work best for different types of questions and which ones work best for you.

Question Strategies

☑ READ CAREFULLY

Read the question and the answer choices carefully. Don't miss the question because you misread the terms. You have plenty of time to read each question thoroughly and make sure you understand what is being asked. Yet a happy medium must be attained, so don't waste too much time. You must read carefully and efficiently.

☑ CONTEXTUAL CLUES

Look for contextual clues. If the question includes a word you are not familiar with, look at the immediate context for some indication of what the word might mean. Contextual clues can often give you all the information you need to decipher the meaning of an unfamiliar word. Even if you can't determine the meaning, you may be able to narrow down the possibilities enough to make a solid guess at the answer to the question.

☑ PREFIXES

If you're having trouble with a word in the question or answer choices, try dissecting it. Take advantage of every clue that the word might include. Prefixes can be a huge help. Usually, they allow you to determine a basic meaning. *Pre-* means before, *post-* means after, *pro-* is positive, *de-* is negative. From prefixes, you can get an idea of the general meaning of the word and try to put it into context.

☑ HEDGE WORDS

Watch out for critical hedge words, such as *likely, may, can, sometimes, often, almost, mostly, usually, generally, rarely,* and *sometimes*. Question writers insert these hedge phrases to cover every possibility. Often an answer choice will be wrong simply because it leaves no room for exception. Be on guard for answer choices that have definitive words such as *exactly* and *always*.

☑ SWITCHBACK WORDS

Stay alert for *switchbacks*. These are the words and phrases frequently used to alert you to shifts in thought. The most common switchback words are *but, although,* and *however*. Others include *nevertheless, on the other hand, even though, while, in spite of, despite,* and *regardless of*. Switchback words are important to catch because they can change the direction of the question or an answer choice.

☑ FACE VALUE

When in doubt, use common sense. Accept the situation in the problem at face value. Don't read too much into it. These problems will not require you to make wild assumptions. If you have to go beyond creativity and warp time or space in order to have an answer choice fit the question, then you should move on and consider the other answer choices. These are normal problems rooted in reality. The applicable relationship or explanation may not be readily apparent, but it is there for you to figure out. Use your common sense to interpret anything that isn't clear.

Answer Choice Strategies

⊘ ANSWER SELECTION

The most thorough way to pick an answer choice is to identify and eliminate wrong answers until only one is left, then confirm it is the correct answer. Sometimes an answer choice may immediately seem right, but be careful. The test writers will usually put more than one reasonable answer choice on each question, so take a second to read all of them and make sure that the other choices are not equally obvious. As long as you have time left, it is better to read every answer choice than to pick the first one that looks right without checking the others.

⊘ ANSWER CHOICE FAMILIES

An answer choice family consists of two (in rare cases, three) answer choices that are very similar in construction and cannot all be true at the same time. If you see two answer choices that are direct opposites or parallels, one of them is usually the correct answer. For instance, if one answer choice says that quantity x increases and another either says that quantity x decreases (opposite) or says that quantity y increases (parallel), then those answer choices would fall into the same family. An answer choice that doesn't match the construction of the answer choice family is more likely to be incorrect. Most questions will not have answer choice families, but when they do appear, you should be prepared to recognize them.

⊘ ELIMINATE ANSWERS

Eliminate answer choices as soon as you realize they are wrong, but make sure you consider all possibilities. If you are eliminating answer choices and realize that the last one you are left with is also wrong, don't panic. Start over and consider each choice again. There may be something you missed the first time that you will realize on the second pass.

⊘ AVOID FACT TRAPS

Don't be distracted by an answer choice that is factually true but doesn't answer the question. You are looking for the choice that answers the question. Stay focused on what the question is asking for so you don't accidentally pick an answer that is true but incorrect. Always go back to the question and make sure the answer choice you've selected actually answers the question and is not merely a true statement.

⊘ EXTREME STATEMENTS

In general, you should avoid answers that put forth extreme actions as standard practice or proclaim controversial ideas as established fact. An answer choice that states the "process should be used in certain situations, if..." is much more likely to be correct than one that states the "process should be discontinued completely." The first is a calm rational statement and doesn't even make a definitive, uncompromising stance, using a hedge word *if* to provide wiggle room, whereas the second choice is far more extreme.

⊘ BENCHMARK

As you read through the answer choices and you come across one that seems to answer the question well, mentally select that answer choice. This is not your final answer, but it's the one that will help you evaluate the other answer choices. The one that you selected is your benchmark or standard for judging each of the other answer choices. Every other answer choice must be compared to your benchmark. That choice is correct until proven otherwise by another answer choice beating it. If you find a better answer, then that one becomes your new benchmark. Once you've decided that no other choice answers the question as well as your benchmark, you have your final answer.

⊘ Predict the Answer

Before you even start looking at the answer choices, it is often best to try to predict the answer. When you come up with the answer on your own, it is easier to avoid distractions and traps because you will know exactly what to look for. The right answer choice is unlikely to be word-for-word what you came up with, but it should be a close match. Even if you are confident that you have the right answer, you should still take the time to read each option before moving on.

General Strategies

⊘ Tough Questions

If you are stumped on a problem or it appears too hard or too difficult, don't waste time. Move on! Remember though, if you can quickly check for obviously incorrect answer choices, your chances of guessing correctly are greatly improved. Before you completely give up, at least try to knock out a couple of possible answers. Eliminate what you can and then guess at the remaining answer choices before moving on.

⊘ Check Your Work

Since you will probably not know every term listed and the answer to every question, it is important that you get credit for the ones that you do know. Don't miss any questions through careless mistakes. If at all possible, try to take a second to look back over your answer selection and make sure you've selected the correct answer choice and haven't made a costly careless mistake (such as marking an answer choice that you didn't mean to mark). This quick double check should more than pay for itself in caught mistakes for the time it costs.

⊘ Pace Yourself

It's easy to be overwhelmed when you're looking at a page full of questions; your mind is confused and full of random thoughts, and the clock is ticking down faster than you would like. Calm down and maintain the pace that you have set for yourself. Especially as you get down to the last few minutes of the test, don't let the small numbers on the clock make you panic. As long as you are on track by monitoring your pace, you are guaranteed to have time for each question.

⊘ Don't Rush

It is very easy to make errors when you are in a hurry. Maintaining a fast pace in answering questions is pointless if it makes you miss questions that you would have gotten right otherwise. Test writers like to include distracting information and wrong answers that seem right. Taking a little extra time to avoid careless mistakes can make all the difference in your test score. Find a pace that allows you to be confident in the answers that you select.

⊘ Keep Moving

Panicking will not help you pass the test, so do your best to stay calm and keep moving. Taking deep breaths and going through the answer elimination steps you practiced can help to break through a stress barrier and keep your pace.

12

Final Notes

The combination of a solid foundation of content knowledge and the confidence that comes from practicing your plan for applying that knowledge is the key to maximizing your performance on test day. As your foundation of content knowledge is built up and strengthened, you'll find that the strategies included in this chapter become more and more effective in helping you quickly sift through the distractions and traps of the test to isolate the correct answer.

Now that you're preparing to move forward into the test content chapters of this book, be sure to keep your goal in mind. As you read, think about how you will be able to apply this information on the test. If you've already seen sample questions for the test and you have an idea of the question format and style, try to come up with questions of your own that you can answer based on what you're reading. This will give you valuable practice applying your knowledge in the same ways you can expect to on test day.

Good luck and good studying!

Child Development, Learning, and Assessment

Transform passive reading into active learning! After immersing yourself in this chapter, put your comprehension to the test by taking a quiz. The insights you gained will stay with you longer this way. Scan the QR code to go directly to the chapter quiz interface for this study guide. If you're using a computer, simply visit the bonus page at **mometrix.com/bonus948/pectprek4** and click the Chapter Quizzes link.

Overview of Human Developmental Theories

ISSUES OF HUMAN DEVELOPMENT

Historically, there have been a number of arguments that theories of human development seek to address. These ideas generally lie on a spectrum, but are often essential concepts involved in developmental theories. For instance, the nature vs. nurture debate is a key concept involved in behaviorist camps of development, insisting that a substantial portion of a child's development may be attributed to his or her social environment.

- **Universality vs. context specificity**: Universality implies that all individuals will develop in the same way, no matter what culture they live in. Context specificity implies that development will be influenced by the culture in which the individual lives.
- **Assumptions about human nature** (3 doctrines: original sin, innate purity, and tabula rasa):
  - Original sin says that children are inherently bad and must be taught to be good.
  - Innate purity says that children are inherently good.
  - Tabula rasa says that children are born as "blank slates," without good or bad tendencies, and can be taught right vs. wrong.
- **Behavioral consistency**: Children either behave in the same manner no matter what the situation or setting, or they change their behavior depending on the setting and who is interacting with them.
- **Nature vs. nurture**: Nature is the genetic influences on development. Nurture is the environment and social influences on development.
- **Continuity vs. discontinuity**: Continuity states that development progresses at a steady rate and the effects of change are cumulative. Discontinuity states that development progresses in a stair-step fashion and the effects of early development have no bearing on later development.
- **Passivity vs. activity**: Passivity refers to development being influenced by outside forces. Activity refers to development influenced by the child himself and how he responds to external forces.
- **Critical vs. sensitive period**: The critical period is that window of time when the child will be able to acquire new skills and behaviors. The sensitive period refers to a flexible time period when a child will be receptive to learning new skills, even if it is later than the norm.

THEORETICAL SCHOOLS OF THOUGHT ON HUMAN DEVELOPMENT

- **Behaviorist Theory** – This philosophy discusses development in terms of conditioning. As children interact with their environments, they learn what behaviors result in rewards or punishments and develop patterns of behaviors as a result. This school of thought lies heavily within the nurture side of the nature/nurture debate, arguing that children's personalities and behaviors are a product of their environments.

15

- **Constructivist Theory** – This philosophy describes the process of learning as one in which individuals build or construct their understanding from their prior knowledge and experiences in an environment. In constructivist thought, individuals can synthesize their old information to generate new ideas. This school of thought is similar to behaviorism in that the social environment plays a large role in learning. Constructivism, however, places greater emphasis on the individual's active role in the learning process, such as the ability to generate ideas about something an individual has not experienced directly.
- **Ecological Systems Theory** – This philosophy focuses on the social environments in and throughout a person's life. Ecological systems theorists attempt to account for all of the complexities of various aspects of a person's life, starting with close relationships, such as family and friends, and zooming out into broader social contexts, including interactions with school, communities, and media. Alongside these various social levels, ecological systems discuss the roles of ethnicity, geography, and socioeconomic status in development across a person's lifespan.
- **Maturationist Theory** – This philosophy largely focuses on the natural disposition of a child to learn. Maturationists lean heavily into the nature side of the nature/nurture argument and say that humans are predisposed to learning and development. As a result, maturationists propose that early development should only be passively supported.
- **Psychoanalytic Theory** – Psychoanalytic theorists generally argue that beneath the conscious interaction with the world, individuals have underlying, subconscious thoughts that affect their active emotions and behaviors. These subconscious thoughts are built from previous experiences, including developmental milestones and also past traumas. These subconscious thoughts, along with the conscious, interplay with one another to form a person's desires, personality, attitudes, and habits.

FREUD'S PSYCHOSEXUAL DEVELOPMENTAL THEORY

Sigmund Freud was a neurologist who founded the psychoanalytic school of thought. He described the distinction between the conscious and unconscious mind and the effects of the unconscious mind on personality and behavior. He also developed a concept of stages of development, in which an individual encounters various conflicts or crises, called psychosexual stages of development. The way in which an individual handles these crises were thought to shape the individual's personality over the course of life. This general formula heavily influenced other psychoanalytic theories.

ERIKSON'S PSYCHOSOCIAL DEVELOPMENTAL THEORY

Eric Erikson's psychosocial development theory was an expansion and revision of Freud's psychosexual stages. Erikson describes eight stages in which an individual is presented with a crisis, such as an infant learning to trust or mistrust his or her parents to provide. The choice to trust or mistrust is not binary, but is on a spectrum. According to the theory, the individual's resolution of the crisis largely carries through the rest of his or her life. Handling each of the eight conflicts well theoretically leads to a healthy development of personality. The conflicts are spaced out throughout life, beginning at infancy and ending at death.

KOHLBERG'S STAGES OF MORAL DEVELOPMENT

Kohlberg's stages of moral development are heavily influenced by Erikson's stages. He describes three larger levels of moral development with substages. In the first level, the **preconventional level**, morality is fully externally controlled by authorities and is motivated by avoidance of punishment and pursuit of rewards. In the second level, the **conventional level**, the focus shifts to laws and social factors and the pursuit of being seen by others as good or nice. In the third and final level, the **postconventional** or **principled level**, the individual looks beyond laws and social obligations to more complex situational considerations. A person in this stage might consider that a law may not always be the best for individuals or society and a particular situation may warrant breaking the rule for the true good.

GEORGE HERBERT MEAD'S PLAY AND GAME STAGE DEVELOPMENT THEORY

George Herbert Mead was a sociologist and psychologist who described learning by stepping into **social roles**. According to his theory, children first interact with the world by imitating and playing by themselves, in which a child can experiment with concepts. Mead describes this development in terms of three stages characterized by increasing complexity of play. A child in the **preparatory stage** can **play** pretend and learn cooking concepts by pretending to cook. As a child develops socially, they learn to step in and out of increasingly abstract and complex **roles** and include more interaction. This is known as the **play stage**, including early interactive roles. For instance, children may play "cops and robbers," which are more symbolically significant roles as they are not natural roles for children to play in society. As social understanding develops, children enter the **game stage**, in which the child can understand their own role and the roles of others in a game. In this stage, children can participate in more complex activities with highly structured rules. An example of a complex game is baseball, in which each individual playing has a unique and complex role to play. These stages are thought to contribute to an individual's ability to understand complex social roles in adulthood.

IVAN PAVLOV

Ivan Pavlov was a predecessor to the behaviorist school and is credited with being the first to observe the process of classical conditioning, also known as Pavlovian conditioning. Pavlov observed that dogs would begin salivating at the sound of a bell because they were conditioned to expect food when they heard a bell ring. According to classical conditioning, by introducing a neutral stimulus (such as a bell) to a naturally significant stimulus (such as the sight of food), the neutral stimulus will begin to create a conditioned response on its own.

JOHN B. WATSON

Watson is credited as the founder of behaviorism and worked to expand the knowledge base of conditioning. He is famous for his experiments, including highly unethical experiments such as the "Little Albert" experiment in which he used classical conditioning to cause an infant to fear animals that he was unfamiliar with. Watson proposed that psychology should focus only on observable behaviors.

B.F. SKINNER

Skinner expanded on Watson's work in behaviorism. His primary contributions to behaviorism included studying the effect of **reinforcement** and **punishment** on particular behaviors. He noted that stimuli can be both additive or subtractive may be used to either increase or decrease behavior frequency and strengths.

LEV VYGOTSKY

Vygotsky's sociocultural theory describes development as a social process, in which individuals mediate knowledge through social interactions and can learn by interacting with and watching others. Vygotsky's ideas have been widely adopted in the field of education, most notably his theory of the "**zone of proximal development**." This theory describes three levels of an individual's ability to do tasks, including completely incapable of performing a task, capable with assistance, and independently capable. As an individual's experience grows, they should progress from less capable and independent to more capable and independent.

> **Review Video: Instructional Scaffolding**
> Visit mometrix.com/academy and enter code: 989759

BANDURA'S SOCIAL LEARNING THEORY

Albert Bandura's social learning theory argues against some of the behaviorist thoughts that a person has to experience stimulus and response to learn behaviors, and instead posits that an individual can learn from other peoples' social interactions. Bandura would say that most learning takes place from observing and predicting social behavior, and not through direct experience. This becomes a more efficient system for learning because people are able to learn information more synthetically.

BOWLBY'S ATTACHMENT THEORY

Bowlby's attachment theory describes the impact that early connections have on lifelong development. Working from an evolutionary framework, Bowlby described how infants are predisposed to be attached to their caregivers as this increases chance of survival. According to Bowlby's theory, infants are predisposed to stay close to known caregivers and use them as a frame of reference to help with learning what is socially acceptable and what is safe.

PIAGET'S COGNITIVE DEVELOPMENT THEORY

Piaget's theory of cognitive development describes how as individuals develop, their cognitive processes are able to become more complex and abstract. In the early stages, an infant may be able to recognize an item, such as a glass of water, on sight only. As that individual grows, they are able to think, compare, and eventually develop abstract thoughts about that concept. According to Piaget, this development takes place in all individuals in predictable stages.

MASLOW'S HIERARCHY OF NEEDS

Maslow defined human motivation in terms of needs and wants. His **hierarchy of needs** is classically portrayed as a pyramid sitting on its base divided into horizontal layers. He theorized that, as humans fulfill the needs of one layer, their motivation turns to the layer above. The layers consist of (from bottom to top):

- **Physiological**: The need for air, fluid, food, shelter, warmth, and sleep.
- **Safety**: A safe place to live, a steady job, a society with rules and laws, protection from harm, and insurance or savings for the future.
- **Love/Belonging**: A network consisting of a significant other, family, friends, co-workers, religion, and community.
- **Esteem or self-respect**: The knowledge that you are a person who is successful and worthy of esteem, attention, status, and admiration.
- **Self-actualization**: The acceptance of your life, choices, and situation in life and the empathetic acceptance of others, as well as the feeling of independence and the joy of being able to express yourself freely and competently.

Review Video: Maslow's Hierarchy of Needs
Visit mometrix.com/academy and enter code: 461825

Cognitive Development

PIAGET'S THEORY OF COGNITIVE DEVELOPMENT

Jean Piaget's theory of cognitive development consists of four stages that a child moves through throughout life. The four stages are the **sensorimotor stage** (birth-2 years), **preoperational stage** (2-7 years), **concrete operational stage** (7-11 years), and **formal operational stage** (12 years and beyond). Piaget believed that the way children think changes as they pass through these stages. In the **sensorimotor stage**, infants exist in the present moment and investigate their world for the first time through their five senses, reflexes, and actions. Key skills infants acquire during this stage include object permanence and self-recognition. In the **preoperational stage**, children learn to express ideas symbolically, including through language and pretend play. Markers of this stage include engaging in animism, egocentrism, and the inability to understand conservation (the knowledge that the quantity of something does not change when its appearance does). In the **concrete operational stage**, children develop logical thought and begin understanding conservation. The **formal operational stage** brings the ability to think abstractly and hypothetically. Piaget believed that children learn through experimenting and building upon knowledge from experiences. He asserted that educators should be highly qualified and trained to create experiences that support development in each of these stages.

SKILLS TYPICALLY ACQUIRED AT EACH STAGE OF COGNITIVE DEVELOPMENT

- **Sensorimotor:** As children in the sensorimotor stage gain an increasing awareness of their bodies and the world around them, a wide range of skills are acquired as they mature from infancy to toddlerhood. Early skills at this stage include sucking, tasting, smiling, basic vocalizations, and **gross motor skills** such as kicking and grasping. These skills increase in complexity over time and come to include abilities such as throwing and dropping objects, crawling, walking, and using simple words or phrases to communicate. As children near the end of this stage, they are typically able to exhibit such skills as stacking, basic problem solving, planning methods to achieve a task, and attempting to engage in daily routines such as dressing themselves or brushing their hair.
- **Preoperational:** This stage is marked by significant leaps in **cognition** and **gross motor skills**. Children in the preoperational stage are able to use increasingly complex language to communicate, and develop such skills as jumping, running, and climbing as they gain increasing control over their bodies. Preoperational children begin learning the basic categorization of alike objects, such as animals, flowers, or foods. This stage is also characterized by the development of pretend play and includes such skills as creating imaginary friends, role playing, and using toys or objects to symbolize something else, such as using a box as a pretend house.
- **Concrete Operational:** In this stage, children begin developing **logical reasoning** skills that allow them to perform increasingly complex tasks. Concrete operational children are able to distinguish subcategories, including types of animals, foods, or flowers, and can organize items in ascending or descending order based upon such characteristics as height, weight, or size. Children at this stage develop the understanding that altering the appearance of an object or substance does not change the amount of it. A classic example of this is the understanding that liquid transferred from one container to another retains its volume. This concept is known as **conservation**.
- **Formal Operational:** The formal operational stage is characterized by the development of **abstract** and **hypothetical** cognitive skills. Children at this stage are able to solve increasingly complex math equations, hypothesize and strategically devise a plan for engaging in science experiments, and develop creative solutions to problems. They are also able to theorize potential outcomes to hypothetical situations, as well as consider the nuances of differing values, beliefs, morals, and ethics.

SUBSTAGES OF THE SENSORIMOTOR STAGE

Piaget's sensorimotor stage is divided into six substages. In each, infants develop new skills for representing and interacting with their world. In the first substage, infants interact **reflexively** and involuntarily to stimuli in the form of muscle jerking when startled, sucking, and gripping. Subsequent stages are circular, or repetitive, in nature, and are based on interactions with the self and, increasingly, the environment. **Primary circular reactions**, or intentionally repeated actions, comprise the second substage. Infants notice their actions and sounds and purposefully repeat them, but these actions do not extend past the infant's body. Interaction with the environment begins in the third substage as infants engage in **secondary circular reactions**. Here, infants learn that they can interact with and manipulate objects within their environment to create an effect, such as a sound from pressing a button. They then repeat the action and experience joy in this ability. In the fourth substage, secondary circular reactions become coordinated as infants begin planning movements and actions to create an effect. **Tertiary circular reactions** allow for exploration in the fifth substage, as infants start experimenting with cause and effect. In the sixth substage, infants begin engaging in **representational thought** and recall information from memory.

EXAMPLES OF PRIMARY, SECONDARY, AND TERTIARY CIRCULAR REACTIONS

The following are some common examples of primary, secondary, and tertiary circular reactions:

- **Primary:** Primary circular reactions are comprised of repeated **bodily** actions that the infant finds enjoyable. Such actions include thumb sucking, placing hands or feet in the mouth, kicking, and making basic vocalizations.
- **Secondary:** Secondary circular reactions refer to repeated enjoyable interactions between the infant and objects within their **environment** in order to elicit a specific response. Such actions include grasping objects, rattling toys, hitting buttons to hear specific sounds, banging two objects together, or reaching out to touch various items.
- **Tertiary:** Tertiary circular reactions are comprised of intentional and planned actions using objects within the environment to **achieve a particular outcome**. Examples include stacking blocks and knocking them down, taking toys out of a bin and putting them back, or engaging in a repeated behavior to gauge a caretaker's reaction each time.

DEFINING CHARACTERISTICS OF THE PREOPERATIONAL STAGE OF DEVELOPMENT

The preoperational stage of development refers to the stage before a child can exercise operational thought and is associated with several defining characteristics including **pretend play**, **animism**, and **egocentrism**. As children learn to think and express themselves symbolically, they engage in pretend play as a means of organizing, understanding, and representing the world around them as they experience it. During this stage, children do not understand the difference between inanimate and animate objects, and thus demonstrate animism, or the attribution of lifelike qualities to inanimate objects. Egocentrism refers to the child's inability to understand the distinction between themselves and others, and consequentially, the inability to understand the thoughts, perspectives, and feelings of others. During the preoperational stage, the brain is not developed enough to understand **conservation**, which is the understanding that the quantity of something does not change just because its appearance changes. Thus, children in this stage exhibit **centration**, or the focusing on only one aspect of something at a time at. Additionally, children struggle with **classification** during this stage, as they are not cognitively developed enough to understand that an object can be classified in multiple ways.

MILESTONES ACHIEVED DURING THE CONCRETE OPERATIONAL STAGE OF DEVELOPMENT

The concrete operational stage marks the beginning of a child's ability to think logically about the concrete world. In this stage, children develop many of the skills they lacked in the preoperational phase. For example, egocentrism fades as children in this stage begin to develop empathy and understand others' perspectives. Additionally, they develop an understanding of conservation, or the idea that the quantity of something does not change with its appearance. Children in this stage begin to learn to classify objects in more than one way and can categorize them based on a variety of characteristics. This allows them to practice **seriation**, or the arranging of objects based on quantitative measures.

DEVELOPMENT OF COGNITIVE ABILITIES IN THE FORMAL OPERATIONAL STAGE

In the formal operational stage, children can think beyond the concrete world and in terms of abstract thoughts and hypothetical situations. They develop the ability to consider various outcomes of events and can think more creatively about solutions to problems than in previous stages. This advanced cognitive ability contributes to the development of personal identity. In considering abstract and hypothetical ideas, children begin to formulate opinions and develop personal stances on intangible concepts, thus establishing individual character. The formal operational stage continues to develop through adulthood as individuals gain knowledge and experience.

Lev Vygotsky's Theory of Cognitive Development

Lev Vygotsky's theory on cognitive development is heavily rooted in a **sociocultural** perspective. He argued that the most important factors for a child's cognitive development reside in the cultural context in which the child grows up and social interactions that they have with adults, mentors, and more advanced peers. He believed that children learn best from the people around them, as their social interactions, even basic ones such as smiling, waving, or facial expressions, foster the beginning of more complex cognitive development. He is well-known for his concept of the **Zone of Proximal Development (ZPD)**, which is the idea that as children mature, there are tasks they can perform when they receive help from a more advanced individual. He believed that children could move through the ZPD and complete increasingly complicated tasks when receiving assistance from more cognitively advanced mentors. According to Vygotsky, children develop the most when passing through the ZPD. Vygotsky's contributions are heavily embedded in modern education, and often take the form of teacher-led instruction and scaffolding to assist learners as they move through the ZPD.

Zone of Proximal Development

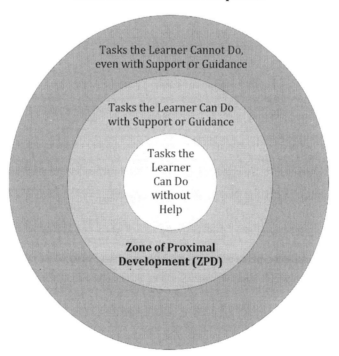

Review Video: **Zone of Proximal Development (ZPD)**
Visit mometrix.com/academy and enter code: 555594

Social and Emotional Development

Erik Erikson's Eight Stages of Psychosocial Development

Erik Erikson defined eight predetermined stages of psychosocial development from birth to late adulthood in which an individual encounters a crisis that must be resolved to successfully transition to the next stage. The first is **trust vs. mistrust** (0-18 months), where the infant learns that the world around them is safe and they can trust caregivers to tend to their basic needs. The next stage is **autonomy vs. shame** (18 months-3 years), where children learn to control their actions and establish independence. In the **initiative vs. guilt stage** (3-5 years), children acquire a sense of purpose and initiative through social interactions. Next, children enter the **industry vs. inferiority stage** (6-11 years), where they develop mastery and pride in completing a task. The next stage is **identity vs. role confusion** (12-18 years), in which children explore and develop characteristics that will comprise their identity and determine their role in society. The sixth stage is **intimacy vs. isolation** (19-40 years), where one forms relationships by sharing the identity developed in the previous stage with others. **Generativity vs. stagnation** (40-65 years) occurs in middle adulthood and focuses on contributing to society's next generation through finding one's life purpose. The last stage is **ego integrity vs. despair** (65 to death), in which one reflects on the productivity and success of their life.

EXPECTED BEHAVIORS AT EACH STAGE OF PSYCHOSOCIAL DEVELOPMENT

Stage	Examples of expected behaviors
Trust vs. mistrust	In this stage, the infant's primary goal is ensuring the fulfillment of their **basic needs**. Infants will cry or make other vocalizations to indicate to caregivers when they want something, such as to be fed or picked up. Separation anxiety from parents is also typical during this stage.
Autonomy vs. shame	Children in this stage begin attempting to perform daily tasks **independently**, such as making food, dressing themselves, bathing, or combing their hair. As children in this stage begin to realize they have a separate identity, they often begin attempting to assert themselves to parents and caregivers.
Initiative vs. guilt	Children at this stage often begin actively engaging and playing with other children. In play settings, these children will often assume **leadership roles** among a group of peers, create new games or activities, and devise their own rules for them. The initiative vs. guilt stage is also characterized by the development of feelings of sadness or guilt when making a mistake or hurting another's feelings.
Industry vs. inferiority	In this stage, children begin attempting to master concepts or skills with the intention of seeking **approval** and **acceptance** from others, particularly those older than themselves, in order to secure a feeling of competency. Children in this stage often become more involved in striving to succeed academically, extracurricular activities, and competitive sports.
Identity vs. role confusion	This stage is characterized by experimentation and uncertainty as young adolescents strive to establish an **independent identity**. Typical behaviors include interacting with new peer groups, trying new styles of dress, engaging in new activities, and considering new beliefs, values, and morals. As young adolescents in this stage are impressionable, they may potentially engage in risky or rebellious behavior as a result of peer pressure.
Intimacy vs. isolation	Individuals in this stage have typically established their identities and are ready to seek **long-term relationships**. This stage marks the development of a social network comprised of close friends and long-term romantic partners.
Generativity vs. stagnation	During this stage, individuals begin engaging in **productive** activities to benefit others and elicit personal fulfillment. Such activities include advancing in a career, parenting, or participating in community service projects.

Stage	Examples of expected behaviors
Integrity vs. despair	This stage occurs at the end of one's life and is characterized by **reflection** upon lifetime accomplishments and positive contributions to society. Doing so allows the individual to assess whether their life purpose was fulfilled and begin accepting death.

INCORPORATING LIFE SKILLS INTO CURRICULUM

In addition to academic achievement, the ultimate goal of education is to develop the whole child and provide a successful transition to independence and adulthood. Incorporating such valuable life skills as decision-making, goal setting, organization, self-direction, and workplace communication in early childhood through grade 12 curriculum is vital in ensuring students become productive contributors to society. Furthermore, the implementation of these life skills in early childhood is integral in allowing children to successfully progress in independence and maturity. The acquisition of such skills instills in students the self-motivation and ability to set goals, make decisions on how to effectively organize and manage time to complete them, and overcome obstacles. Additionally, teaching students to apply these skills promotes effective communication when working with others toward a goal. Through incorporating life skills into curriculum, teachers instill a growth mindset and foster self-empowered, confident lifelong learners with the necessary tools to navigate real-life situations and achieve success as they transition to adulthood. In the classroom, activities that promote leadership skills, cooperative learning, goal setting, self-monitoring, and social interaction foster an increasing sense of independence as children develop.

EFFECT OF EXTERNAL ENVIRONMENTAL FACTORS ON SOCIAL AND EMOTIONAL DEVELOPMENT

Social and emotional development is heavily influenced by a child's home environment. Children learn social and emotional skills such as self-regulation, self-awareness, coping, and relationship building through modeling from parents and caregivers. A positive and supportive home environment is integral for proper social and emotional development. External factors, including lack of affection and attention, parental divorce, and homelessness, pose profound negative impacts on this development. In terms of social development, such external factors could lead to attachment or abandonment issues, as well as distrust. Furthermore, children exposed to negative environmental factors could struggle forging relationships, cooperating, and following societal rules. Emotionally, negative impacts on development cause aggression, poor self-regulation, insecurity, anxiety, isolation, and depression. Since developmental domains are interconnected, the impacts that external factors have on social and emotional development ultimately damage cognitive and physical development. Underdeveloped social skills impair cognitive development because the inability to properly interact with peers impedes the ability to learn from them. Additionally, inadequate emotional skills can inhibit concentration and understanding in school, thus inhibiting cognitive development. Physically, struggling to interact with others leads to impaired development of gross and fine motor skills as well as large muscle development that would be achieved through play.

Physical Development

PHYSICAL CHANGES OCCURRING IN EARLY CHILDHOOD THROUGH ADOLESCENCE

As children pass through stages of development from early childhood through middle childhood and adolescence, they experience significant physical changes. Children in early childhood experience rapid growth in height and weight as they transition away from physical characteristics of infancy. In this stage, children begin to gain independence as they develop and improve upon gross and fine motor skills. By early childhood, children develop the ability to walk, run, hop, and as they mature through this stage, learn to throw, catch, and climb. They learn to hold and manipulate small objects such as zippers and buttons, and can grasp writing utensils to create shapes, letters, and drawings with increasing accuracy. Physical growth varies for individual children in middle childhood as some children begin experiencing prepubescent bodily changes. Children in middle childhood experience further improvements and refinements of gross and fine motor skills and coordination. Significant physical and appearance changes occur in adolescence as children enter puberty. These changes often occur quickly, resulting in a period of awkwardness and lack of coordination as adolescents adjust to this rapid development.

IMPACT OF EXTERNAL FACTORS ON PHYSICAL DEVELOPMENT

As children pass through physical development stages from early childhood to adolescence, it is important that environmental factors are supportive of proper growth and health. Physical development can be hindered by external factors, such as poor nutrition, lack of sleep, prenatal exposure to drugs, and abuse, as these can cause significant and long-lasting negative consequences. Exposure to such factors can lead to stunted physical growth, impaired brain development and function, poor bone and muscle development, and obesity. Furthermore, the negative impacts from such external factors ultimately impedes cognitive, social, and emotional development. Impaired brain development and function negatively affect cognitive development by impacting the ability to concentrate and grasp new concepts. In terms of emotional development, physical impairments due to external factors can cause a child to become depressed, withdrawn, aggressive, have low self-esteem, and unable to self-regulate. Improper physical growth and health impacts social development in that physical limitations could hinder a child's ability to properly interact with and play with others. Impacted brain development and function can limit a child's ability to understand social cues and norms.

Language Development

STAGES OF LANGUAGE DEVELOPMENT

The first stage of language development and acquisition, the **pre-linguistic stage**, occurs during an infant's first year of life. It is characterized by the development of gestures, making eye contact, and sounds like cooing and crying. The **holophrase** or **one-word sentence stage** develops in infants between 10 and 13 months of age. In this stage, young children use one-word sentences to communicate meaning in language. The **two-word sentence stage** typically develops by the time a child is 18 months old. Each two-word sentence usually contains a noun or a verb and a modifier, such as "big balloon" or "green grass." Children in this stage use their two-word sentences to communicate wants and needs. **Multiple-word sentences** form by the time a child is two to two and a half years old. In this stage, children begin forming sentences with subjects and predicates, such as "tree is tall" or "rope is long." Grammatical errors are present, but children in this stage begin demonstrating how to use words in appropriate context. Children ages two and a half to three years typically begin using more **complex grammatical structures**. They begin to include grammatical structures that were not present before, such as conjunctions and prepositions. By the age of five or six, children reach a stage of **adult-like language development**. They begin to use words in appropriate context and can move words around in sentences while maintaining appropriate sentence structure. Language development and acquisition has a wide range of what is considered normal development. Some children do not attempt to speak for up to two years and then may experience an explosion of language development at a later time. In these cases, children often emerge from their silent stage with equivalent language development to babies who were more expressive early on. A child who does not speak after two years, however, may be exhibiting signs of a developmental delay.

ORAL LANGUAGE DEVELOPMENT

Oral language development begins well before students enter educational environments. It is learned first without formal instruction, with **environmental factors** being a heavy influence. Children tend to develop their own linguistic rules as a result of genetic disposition, their environments, and how their individual thinking processes develop. Oral language refers to both speaking and listening. Components of oral language development include phonology, syntax, semantics, morphology, and pragmatics. **Phonology** refers to the production and recognition of sounds. **Morphology** refers to how words are formed from smaller pieces, called morphemes. **Semantics** refers to meaning of words and phrases and has overlap with morphology and syntax, as morphemes and word order can both change the meaning of words. Semantic studies generally focus on learning and understanding vocabulary. **Syntax** refers to how words and morphemes are combined to

24

make up meaningful phrases. In English, word order is the primary way that many components of grammar are communicated. Finally, **pragmatics** refers to the practical application of language based on various social situations. For instance, a college student is likely to use different vocabulary, complexity, and formality of language when speaking with a professor than when speaking with his or her peer group. Each of these five components of language are applied in oral language. Awareness and application of these components develops over time as students gain experience and education in language use. **Oral language development** can be nurtured by caregivers and teachers well before children enter educational environments. Caregivers and teachers can promote oral language development by providing environments full of language development opportunities. Additionally, teaching children how conversation works, encouraging interaction among children, and demonstrating good listening and speaking skills are good strategies for nurturing oral language development.

> **Review Video: Components of Oral Language Development**
> Visit mometrix.com/academy and enter code: 480589

HELPING STUDENTS DEVELOP ORAL LANGUAGE ABILITIES

Children pick up oral language skills in their home environments and build upon these skills as they grow. Early language development is influenced by a combination of genetic disposition, environment, and individual thinking processes. Children with **oral language acquisition difficulties** often experience difficulties in their **literacy skills**, so activities that promote good oral language skills also improve literacy skills. **Strategies** that help students develop oral language abilities include developing appropriate speaking and listening skills; providing instruction that emphasizes vocabulary development; providing students with opportunities to communicate wants, needs, ideas, and information; creating language learning environments; and promoting auditory memory. Developing appropriate speaking and listening skills includes teaching turn-taking, awareness of social norms, and basic rules for speaking and listening. Emphasizing **vocabulary development** is a strategy that familiarizes early learners with word meanings. Providing students with opportunities to **communicate** is beneficial for developing early social skills. Teachers can create **language learning environments** by promoting literacy in their classrooms with word walls, reading circles, or other strategies that introduce language skills to students. Promoting **auditory memory** means teaching students to listen to, process, and recall information.

> **Review Video: Types of Vocabulary Learning (Broad and Specific)**
> Visit mometrix.com/academy and enter code: 258753

HELPING STUDENTS MONITOR ERRORS IN ORAL LANGUAGE

Oral language is the primary way people communicate and express their knowledge, ideas, and feelings. As oral language generally develops, their **speaking and listening skills** become more refined. This refinement of a person's language is called fluency, which can be broken down into the subdisciplines of language, reading, writing, speaking, and listening. **Speaking fluency** usually describes the components of rate, accuracy, and prosody. **Rate** describes how fast a person can speak and **prosody** describes the inflection and expressions that a person puts into their speech. **Accuracy** describes how often a person makes an error in language production. In early stages of language development, individuals generally do not have enough language knowledge to be able to monitor their own speech production for errors and require input from others to notice and correct their mistakes. As an individual becomes more proficient, they will be able to monitor their own language usage and make corrections to help improve their own fluency. In the classroom, the teacher needs to be an active component of language monitoring to help facilitate growth. Teachers can monitor **oral language errors** with progress-monitoring strategies. Teachers can also help students monitor their own **oral language development** as they progress through the reading curriculum. Students can monitor their oral language by listening to spoken words in their school and home environments, learning and practicing self-correction skills, and participating in reading comprehension and writing activities. Students can also monitor oral language errors by learning oral language rules for phonics, semantics, syntax, and pragmatics. These rules typically generalize to developing appropriate oral language skills.

EXPRESSIVE AND RECEPTIVE LANGUAGE

Expressive language refers to the aspects of language that an individual produces, generally referring to writing and speaking. **Receptive language** refers to the aspects of language that an individual encounters or receives, and generally refers to reading and listening. Both expressive and receptive language are needed for communication from one person to another.

	Expressive	Receptive
Written	Writing	Reading
Oral	Speaking	Listening

EXPRESSIVE LANGUAGE SKILLS

Expressive language skills include the ability to use vocabulary, sentences, gestures, and writing. People with good **expressive language skills** can label objects in their environments, put words in sentences, use appropriate grammar, demonstrate comprehension verbally by retelling stories, and more. This type of language is important because it allows people to express feelings, wants and needs, thoughts and ideas, and individual points of view. Strong expressive language skills include pragmatic knowledge, such as using gestures and facial expressions or using appropriate vocabulary for the listener or reader and soft skills, such as checks for comprehension, use of analogies, and grouping of ideas to help with clarity. Well-expressed language should be relatively easy for someone else to comprehend.

RECEPTIVE LANGUAGE SKILLS

Receptive language refers to a person's ability to perceive and understand language. Good receptive language skills involve gathering information from the environment and processing it into meaning. People with good **receptive language skills** perceive gestures, sounds and words, and written information well. Receptive language is important for developing appropriate communication skills. Instruction that targets receptive language skills can include tasks that require sustained attention and focus, recognizing emotions and gestures, and listening and reading comprehension. Games that challenge the players to communicate carefully, such as charades or catchphrase, can be a great way to target receptive language skills. As one student tries to accurately express an idea with words or gestures, the rest of the class must exercise their receptive language skills. Lastly, focusing on **social skills and play skills instruction** encourages opportunities for children to interact with their peers or adults. This fosters receptive language skills and targets deficits in these skills.

STAGES OF LITERACY DEVELOPMENT

The development of literacy in young children is separated into five stages. Names and ranges of these stages sometimes vary slightly, but the stage milestones are similar. Stage 1 is the **Emergent Reader stage**. In this stage, children ages 6 months to 6 years demonstrate skills like pretend reading, recognizing letters of the alphabet, retelling stories, and printing their names. Stage 2 is the **Novice/Early Reader stage** (ages 6–7 years). Children begin to understand the relationships between letters and sounds and written and spoken words, and they read texts containing high-frequency words. Children in this stage should develop orthographic conventions and semantic knowledge. In Stage 3, the **Decoding Reader stage**, children ages 7–9 develop decoding skills in order to read simple stories. They also demonstrate increased fluency. Stage 4 (ages

26

8–15 years) is called the **Fluent, Comprehending/Transitional Reader stage**. In this stage, fourth to eighth graders read to learn new ideas and information. In Stage 5, the **Expert/Fluent Reader stage**, children ages 16 years and older read more complex information. They also read expository and narrative texts with multiple viewpoints.

Review Video: Stages of Reading Development
Visit mometrix.com/academy and enter code: 121184

RELATIONSHIP BETWEEN LANGUAGE DEVELOPMENT AND EARLY LITERACY SKILLS

Language development and early literacy skills are interconnected. **Language concepts** begin and develop shortly after birth with infant/parent interactions, cooing, and then babbling. These are the earliest attempts at language acquisition for infants. Young children begin interacting with written and spoken words before they enter their grade school years. Before they enter formal classrooms, children begin to make **connections** between speaking and listening and reading and writing. Children with strong speaking and listening skills demonstrate strong literacy skills in early grade school. The development of **phonological awareness** is connected to early literacy skills. Children with good phonological awareness recognize that words are made up of different speech sounds. For example, children with appropriate phonological awareness can break words (e.g., "bat" into separate speech sounds, "b-a-t"). Examples of phonological awareness include rhyming (when the ending parts of words have the same or similar sounds) and alliteration (when words all have the same beginning sound). Success with phonological awareness (oral language) activities depends on adequate development of speech and language skills.

PROMOTING LITERACY DURING THE EARLY STAGES OF LITERACY DEVELOPMENT

Teachers and parents can implement strategies at different stages of literacy development in order to build **good reading skills** in children with and without disabilities. During the **Emergent Reader stage**, teachers and parents can introduce children to the conventions of reading with picture books. They can model turning the pages, reading from left to right, and other reading conventions. Book reading at this stage helps children begin to identify letters, letter sounds, and simple words. Repetitive reading of familiar texts also helps children begin to make predictions about what they are reading. During the **Novice/Early Reader** and **Decoding Reader stages**, parents and teachers can help children form the building blocks of decoding and fluency skills by reading for meaning and emphasizing letter-sound relationships, visual cues, and language patterns. In these stages, increasing familiarity with sight words is essential. In the **Fluent, Comprehending/Transitional Reader stage**, children should be encouraged to read book series, as the shared characters, settings, and plots help develop their comprehension skills. At this stage, a good reading rate (fluency) is an indicator of comprehension skills. **Expert/Fluent readers** can independently read multiple texts and comprehend their meanings. Teachers and parents can begin exposing children to a variety of fiction and non-fiction texts before this stage in order to promote good fluency skills.

Review Video: Phonics (Encoding and Decoding)
Visit mometrix.com/academy and enter code: 821361

Review Video: Fluency
Visit mometrix.com/academy and enter code: 531179

Health Needs in Early Childhood

EFFECT OF MATURATIONAL FACTORS ON THE DEVELOPMENT AND LEARNING

Many physiological factors affect the development of babies and young children. These dictate which kinds of learning activities are appropriate or ineffective for certain ages. For example, providing a newborn with visual stimuli from several feet away is wasted, as newborns cannot yet focus on distant objects. Adults cannot expect infants younger than about 5 months to sit up unsupported, as they have not yet developed the strength for it.

Adults cannot expect toddlers who have not yet attained stable walking gaits to hop or balance upon one foot successfully. It is not coincidental that first grade begins at around 6 years: younger children cannot physically sit still for long periods and have not developed long enough attention spans to prevent distraction. This is also why kindergarten classes feature varieties of shorter-term activities and more physical movement. Younger children also have not yet developed the self-regulation to keep from shouting out on impulse, getting up and running around, etc.—behaviors disruptive to formal schooling but developmentally normal.

NUTRITIONAL FACTORS IN DIET AFFECTING EARLY CHILDHOOD DEVELOPMENT

Babies are typically nourished via the mother's milk or infant formula, and then with baby food; however, young children mostly eat the same foods as adults by the age of 2 years. Though they eat smaller quantities, young children have similar nutritional needs to those of adults. Calcium can be more important in early childhood to support the rapid bone growth occurring during this period; young children should receive 2–3 servings of dairy products and/or other calcium-rich foods. For all ages, whole-grain foods are nutritionally superior for their fiber and nutrients than refined flours, which have had these removed. Refined flours provide "empty calories," causing wider blood-sugar fluctuations and insulin resistance—type 2 diabetes risks—than whole grains, which stabilize blood sugar and offer more naturally occurring vitamins and minerals. Darkly and brightly colored produce are most nutritious. Adults should cut foods into small, bite-sized pieces to prevent choking in young children, who have not yet perfected their biting, chewing, and swallowing skills.

CONSIDERATIONS FOR EARLY CHILDHOOD NUTRITION

Raw or lightly steamed vegetables are best because excess heat destroys nutrients and frying adds fat calories. Fresh, in-season and flash-frozen fruits are more nutritious and less processed than canned. Adults should monitor young children's diets to limit highly processed produce, which can have excessive sugar, salt, or preservatives. Good protein sources include legumes, nuts, lean poultry, and fish. Serving nut butters instead of whole nuts is safer, but spread thinly on whole-grain breads, crackers, or vegetable pieces, because young children can choke on large globs of nut butter as well. Omega-3 fatty acids from salmon, mackerel, herring, flaxseeds, and walnuts control inflammation, prevent heart arrhythmias, and lower blood pressure. Monounsaturated fats from avocados, olives, peanuts, and their oils, as well as canola oil, prevent heart disease, lower bad cholesterol, and raise good cholesterol. Polyunsaturated fats from nuts and seeds and from corn, soy, sesame, sunflower, and safflower oils lower cholesterol. These fats/oils should be served in moderation, and saturated fats should be avoided.

CONSIDERATIONS FOR FEEDING YOUNG CHILDREN

Saturated fats from meats and full-fat dairy should be limited; they can cause health problems like high cholesterol, cardiovascular disease, obesity, and diabetes. Trans fats are produced chemically by hydrogenating normally liquid unsaturated fats and converting them to solid, saturated fats as in margarine and shortening used in many baked goods. These are considered even unhealthier than regular saturated fats and should be avoided. (The words *partially hydrogenated* in the ingredients signal trans fats.) Infants derive enough water from their mother's milk or from formula, but young children should be given plenty of water and/or milk in "sippy cups" to stay hydrated. The common practice of giving young children fruit juice should be avoided. Even without added sugars, fruit juices crowd out room in small stomachs for food nutrients and cause dental cavities and weaken permanent teeth before they erupt. Children can also gain weight, as juice calories do not replace food calories the way actual fruit does with its fiber and solids. Young children should eat two-thirds of adult-sized portions.

CHARACTERISTICS OF YOUNG CHILDREN'S NUTRITIONAL NEEDS

Young children have smaller stomachs than adults and cannot eat as much at one time as teens or adults. However, it is common practice for today's restaurants to provide oversized portions. The historical tradition of encouraging young children to "clean their plates" is ill-advised, considering these excessive portions and the abundance of food in America today. Adults can help young children by teaching them instead to respond to their own bodies' signals and eat only until they are satisfied. Adults can also place smaller portions of food on young children's plates and request to-go containers at restaurants to take leftovers home. Because young children cannot eat a lot at once, they must maintain their blood sugar and energy throughout the day by snacking between meals. However, "snack foods" need not be high in sugar, salt, and unhealthy fats. Cut pieces of fresh fruits and vegetables, whole-grain crackers and low-fat cheeses, and portable yogurt tubes make good snacks for young children.

DEVELOPMENT OF NUTRITIOUS EATING HABITS AND ATTITUDES

Early childhood is an age range often associated with "finicky" eaters. Adults can experiment by substituting different foods that are similar sources of protein or other nutrients to foods young children dislike. Preparing meals to look like happy faces or animals or to have appealing designs can entice young children to eat varied foods. Engaging children age-appropriately in selecting and preparing meals with supervision can also motivate them to consume foods when they have participated in their preparation. Adults should model healthy eating habits for young children, who imitate admired adults' behaviors. Early childhood is when children form basic food-related attitudes and habits and so is an important time for influencing these. Children are exposed to unhealthy foods in advertising, at school, in restaurants, and with friends, so adult modeling and guidance regarding healthy choices are important to counteract these influences. However, adults should also impart the message early that no foods are "bad" or forbidden, allowing some occasional indulgences in small amounts to prevent the development of eating disorders.

RELATIONSHIP OF SLEEP QUALITY TO BLOOD SUGAR CONTROL IN CHILDREN WITH TYPE 1 DIABETES

Researchers find blood sugar stability problematic for many children with type 1 (juvenile) diabetes, despite all efforts by parents and children to follow diabetic health care rules, because of sleep differences. Diabetic children spend more time in lighter than deeper stages of sleep compared to nondiabetic children. This results in higher levels of blood sugar and poorer school performance. Lighter sleep and resulting daytime sleepiness tend to increase blood sugar levels. Sleep apnea is a sleep disorder that causes a person's breathing to be interrupted often during sleeping. These breathing interruptions result in poorer sleep quality, fatigue, and daytime sleepiness. Sleep apnea has previously been associated with type 2 diabetes—historically adult-onset, though now children are developing it, too. It is now known that apnea is also associated with type 1 diabetes in children: roughly one-third of diabetic children studied have sleep apnea, regardless of their weight (being overweight can contribute to apnea). Sleep apnea is additionally associated with much higher blood sugars in diabetic children.

GENERAL SLEEP NEEDS AND BEHAVIORS OF YOUNG CHILDREN

Sleep allows the body to become repaired and recharged for the day and is vital for young children's growth and development. Children aged 2–5 years generally need 10–12 hours of sleep daily. Children 5–7 years old typically need 9–11 hours of sleep. Their sleep schedules should be fairly regular. While occasionally staying up later or missing naps for special events is not serious, overall inconsistent/disorganized schedules cause lost sleep and lethargic and/or cranky children. Some young children sleep fewer hours at night but need long daytime naps, while others need longer, uninterrupted nighttime sleep but seldom nap. Young children are busy exploring and discovering new things; they have a lot of energy and are often excited even when tired. Because they have not developed much self-regulation, they need adult guidance to calm down enough to go to sleep and will often resist bedtimes. Adults should plan bedtime routines. These can vary, but their most important aspect is consistency. Children then expect routines' familiar steps, and anticipating these steps comfort them.

COMPONENTS AND CHARACTERISTICS OF GOOD BEDTIME ROUTINES

Bedtime routines serve as transitions from young children's exciting, adventurous daytime activities to the tranquility needed for healthful rest. Adults should begin routines by establishing and enforcing a rule that daytime activities like rough-and-tumble physical play or TV-watching stop at a specific time. While preschoolers may be less interested in video games than older children, establishing limits early will help parents enforce stopping these activities at bedtime when they are older, too. Bath time is one good way to begin bedtime routines. Toys and games make baths fun, and bath washes with lavender and other soothing ingredients are now available to relax young children. Also, since young children eat smaller meals, healthy bedtime snacks are important. Too much or too little food will disrupt sleep, and too much liquid can cause bedwetting. Adults should plan nighttime snacks appropriately for the individual child. Bedtime reading promotes interest in books and learning and adult-child/family bonding, and calms children. Singing lullabies, hugging, and cuddling also support bonding, relax children, and make them feel safe and secure.

HELPING YOUNG CHILDREN TRANSITION FROM CRIBS TO REGULAR BEDS

One of young children's significant transitions from infancy is moving from a crib to a "big bed." Some become very motivated to escape cribs. For example, some bright, adventurous toddlers and even babies have untied padded crib bumpers, stacked them, and climbed out of the crib. For such children, injury is a greater danger from a crib than a bed. Others, whose cognitive and verbal skills are more developed than motor skills, may stand or jump up and down, repeatedly calling, "Hey, I'm up!" until a parent comes. These children should be moved to regular beds, with guardrails and/or body pillows to prevent rolling and falling-out accidents. If a child is moved to a bed to free the crib for a new baby, this should be done weeks ahead of the infant's arrival if possible, to separate these two significant life events. Most young children are excited about "grown-up" beds. Some, if hesitant, can sleep in the crib and nap in the bed for a gradual transition until ready for the bed full-time.

CONSIDERATIONS IN CHILDREN'S BEDROOMS AND FAMILY BEDS

The majority of early childhood experts think young children should not have adults in their rooms every night while they fall asleep. They believe this can interfere with young children's capacity for "self-soothing" and falling asleep on their own, making them dependent on an adult presence to fall asleep. Parents/caregivers are advised to help children relax until sleepy, and then leave, saying "Good night" and "I love you." Young children frequently feel more comfortable going to bed with a favorite blanket or stuffed animal and/or a night light. Regardless, fears and nightmares are still fairly common in early childhood. "Family beds" (i.e., children sleeping in the same bed or adjacent beds with parents) are subject to controversy. However, this is traditional in many developing countries and was historically so in America. Whatever the individual family choice, it should be consistent, as young children will be frustrated by inconsistent practices and less likely to develop good sleeping habits.

HYGIENE IN EARLY CHILDHOOD
IMPORTANCE OF HAND-WASHING

A major change during early childhood is that hygiene transforms from something adults do for children to something children learn to do themselves. Toddlers are typically learning toilet-training, getting many germs on their hands. Preschoolers today are also often exposed to germs in daycare or school settings. Adults must explain to young children using concrete, easily understood terms how germs spread, how hand-washing removes germs, and when and how to wash their hands. Adults also need to remind children frequently to wash their hands until it becomes a habit. Hand-washing should be required before eating, after toileting, after being outdoors, after sneezing/coughing, and after playing with pets. Because young children have short attention spans and can be impatient, they are unlikely to wash long or thoroughly enough. Adults can encourage this by teaching children to sing "Happy Birthday" or other 15- to 20-second songs/verses while washing, both assuring optimal hand-washing duration and making the process more fun.

BATHING

While infants are bathed by adults, by the time they are toddlers or preschoolers, they generally have learned to sit in a bathtub and wash themselves. However, regardless of their ability to bathe, young children should never be left unsupervised by adults in the bath. Young children can drown very quickly, even in an inch of water; an adult should always be in the bathroom. Also, adults should not let young children run bathwater: they are likely to make it too cold or hot. Adults can prevent scalding accidents by turning down the water heater temperature. The adult should adjust water temperature and test it on his or her own inner arm (an area with more sensitive skin). Parents/caregivers should choose baby shampoos, soaps, and washes that do not irritate young eyes or skin, and keep adult bath products out of children's reach and sight. Very active children may need to bathe daily; others suffering dry, itchy skin should bathe every other day and/or have parents/caregivers apply mild moisturizing lotion.

PROMOTING AND TEACHING DENTAL HYGIENE

Even while young children still have their deciduous teeth ("baby" teeth), dental hygiene practices can affect their permanent adult teeth before they erupt. For example, excessive sugar can weaken adult teeth before they even appear above the gumline. Adults should not only teach young children how important it is to brush their teeth twice and floss once daily at a minimum, they should also model these behaviors. Children are far more likely to imitate parents' dental hygiene practices than do what parents only tell them but do not do themselves. Integrating tooth brushing into morning and bedtime routines promotes the habit. Adults can help motivate resistant children with entertaining toothbrushes that play music, spin, light up, and/or have cartoon illustrations. Young children have not developed the fine motor skills sufficient for flossing independently and will need adult supervision until they are older. Individual flossers are easier for them to use with help than traditional string dental floss.

EXERCISE BENEFITS FOR YOUNG CHILDREN

Young children need daily physical exercise to strengthen their bones, lungs, hearts, and other muscles. Throwing, catching, running, jumping, kicking, and swinging actions develop young children's gross motor skills. Children sleep better with regular physical activity and are at less risk for obesity. Playing actively with other children also develops social skills, including empathy, sharing, cooperation, and communication. Family playtimes strengthen bonding and let parents model positive exercise habits. Outdoor play is fun for youngsters; running and laughing lift children's moods. Pride at physical attainments moreover boosts children's self-images and self-esteem. At least 60 minutes of physical activity most days is recommended for children. This includes jungle gyms, slides, swings, and other playground equipment; family walks, bike-riding, playing backyard catch, baseball, football, or basketball; adult-supervised races or obstacle courses; and age-appropriate community sports activities/leagues. Adults should plan and supervise activities to prevent injuries. They should also provide repeated sunscreen applications for outdoor activities to prevent sunburn and long-term skin damage.

EXPOSURE TO TV/OTHER MEDIA AND OPTIMAL ENVIRONMENTAL CONDITIONS FOR LEISURE ACTIVITIES

Preschool-aged children are not yet cognitively able to distinguish between reality and fantasy. Therefore, overly violent or intense content in TV or other media can frighten them. Additionally, exposure to video violence has been proven to increase aggressive behaviors in young children. Moreover, using TV as a babysitter for long times excludes more cognitively stimulating and interactive pursuits. Parents/caregivers can provide young children with paints, crayons, and modeling clay. They can play board games and simple card games, do puzzles, sing songs, and read stories with young children. Pretend/make-believe play develops during early childhood, so adults can encourage their playing "house," "dress-up," or "auto shop." Park/playground trips afford outdoor play and physical activity/exercise. Visiting local museums, zoos, or planetariums combine education and entertainment with outings. In multiple-child families, it is important for each child to get some one-on-one time with parents regularly, even in unstructured activities like going to the hardware store with Daddy or keeping Mommy company while she washes dishes.

DISADVANTAGES/ADVANTAGES AND RISK/PROTECTIVE FACTORS IN ECONOMICALLY DEPRIVED AND CULTURALLY DIVERSE ENVIRONMENTS

Historically, research on the effects of poverty has been focused on the disadvantages coming from a lack of necessary resources and the presence of risk factors. Due to the lack of resources, children in economically deprived communities commonly have fewer stimulating toys, less diverse verbal interaction, and commonly inadequate nutrition. Other risk factors often include unhealthy family environments, medical illness without treatment, and insufficient social-services, such as education, policing, and medical care. However, more recent

31

research also identifies poverty's advantages, including opportunities for young children to play with peers and older children with little adult intervention, promoting empathy, cooperation, self-control, self-reliance, and sense of belonging; experience with multiple teaching styles, especially modeling, observation, and imitation; and language acquisition within a culturally-specific context through rich cultural traditions of stories, songs, games, and toys. These findings illuminate the resiliency or stress resistance of some children. Recent research also identifies protective factors against risk factors. These protections contribute to child resiliency, including the child's personality traits; having stable, supportive, cohesive family units; and having external support systems promoting positive values and coping skills.

INFLUENCE OF CULTURES AND CULTURAL VALUES ON EARLY CHILDHOOD DEVELOPMENT

The culture in a society influences and determines one's individual values, as do both historical and current social and political occurrences. One's values then influence the ways in which children are valued and raised. American educators can understand the "American" perspective on early childhood better through understanding cultural diversity. Americans tend to fixate on their own culture's beliefs of truth as the only existing reality, but depending on personal histories and values and current conditions, there can actually be multiple right ways of doing things. For example, Western cultures value children's early attainment of independence and individuality, but Eastern cultures value interdependence and group harmony more than individualism. In affluent societies, letting children explore the environment early and freely is valued, but in poor and/or developing societies, parents protect children, keeping them close and even carrying them while working, and thus do not value early freedom and exploration.

EFFECT OF AGE, ETHNICITY, AND INCOME ON HEALTH AND SCHOOL OUTCOMES

Research traces many variations in well-being and health to early childhood. These differences come from inequities in service access and treatment, congenital health problems, and early exposure to greater familial and community risk factors. Child groups at risk that are overrepresented in the American population include young children, low-income children, and minority children. These risk factors also carry a high correlation with one another as minority groups tend to be overrepresented below the **federal poverty level (FPL)** and low-income families statistically carry the highest birth rate. Childhood poverty has long-lasting effects on students' developmental, socioeconomic, and academic success. Furthermore, the earlier a student is in poverty, the more likely they are to encounter the adverse effects of poverty, as they may miss certain milestones or lack the support needed to keep up with their peers.

ENVIRONMENT, SOCIAL AND EMOTIONAL SUPPORT, SELF-IMAGE, AND SUCCESS

Researchers have recently found that a child's sense of self is significant in predicting success in life. Even when a child's family environment involves multiple stressors, having a good relationship with one parent mitigates a child's psychosocial risks. As a child grows older, a close, supportive, lasting relationship with an adult outside the family can confer similar protection. Such relationships promote self-esteem in a child. Children with positive self-esteem are more able to develop feelings of control, mastery, and self-efficacy to achieve tasks, and they are more able to manage stressful life experiences. Such children demonstrate more initiative in forming relationships and accomplishing tasks. They reciprocally derive more positive experiences from their environments. Children with positive self-concepts pursue, develop, and sustain experiences and relationships that support success. Their positive self-images are further enhanced by these successes, generating additional supportive relationships and experiences. While we often hear about negative cycles of poverty, abuse, or failure, positive cycles of success can be equally as self-perpetuating.

INDIVIDUALISTIC VERSUS COLLECTIVISTIC CULTURES

Anthropologists have classified various world cultures along a continuum of how individualistic or interdependent their structures and values are. Investigating these differences is found to afford much insight and application for early childhood education. The predominant culture in America is considered very individualistic. Children are encouraged to assert themselves and make their own choices to realize their highest potentials, with the ultimate goal of individual self-fulfillment. Collectivistic/sociocentric cultures, however, place the highest importance on group well-being; if collective harmony is disrupted by individual assertiveness, such self-assertion is devalued. Some educators characterize this contrast as the difference between standing out (individualist) and fitting in (collectivist). Researchers note that when asked to finish "I am…" statements, members of interdependent cultures tend to supply a family role, religion, or organization (e.g., "a father/a Buddhist"), whereas members of individualistic cultures cite personal qualities (e.g., "intelligent/hardworking"). Research finds American culture most individualistic, Latin American and Asian cultures most interdependent, and European cultures in the middle.

HEALTH STATISTICS RELATED TO RACE AND ETHNICITY

Children are at higher risk for inadequate development when they are born prematurely or with low birth weights. Recent research found racial and ethnic disparities in these birth conditions. For example, average rates of low birth weights between 2018 and 2020 were almost double for African Americans as for whites (14 percent versus 6.9 percent). Latinos had similar but slightly higher risk than whites for low birth weight (7.5 percent versus 6.9 percent). Native American/Alaska Natives had slightly higher risk than whites (8.1 percent versus 6.9 percent), as did Asian/Pacific Islanders (8.6 percent versus 6.9 percent). The CDC reported that in 2017 and 2018, the prevalence of obesity among different racial groups varied greatly. Non-Hispanic Asians reported the lowest average 17.4 percent of obesity, whereas non-Hispanic White demonstrated a 42.2 percent obesity rate, followed by 44.8 percent for Hispanic and 49.6 percent for Non-Hispanic Black adults. These two statistics demonstrate a sample of correlated health risks present among varied socioeconomic groups.

Learning Across the Curriculum

USING INTEGRATED CURRICULA

Integrating subject/domain content across the curriculum has been used for years at every educational level, from higher education to early childhood education. However, recent demands for accountability, as exemplified and escalated by No Child Left Behind, can distract educators from holistic and overall learning toward preoccupation with developing isolated skills and using test scores to measure achievement. But rather than discarding teaching methods proven effective, early childhood educators need to integrate newer, mandate-related practices into existing plans and methods. Teaching integrated curricula in early childhood classrooms has proven effective for both children and teachers. Integrating learning domains and subject content, in turn, integrates the child's developing skills with the whole child. When teachers use topics children find interesting and exciting, in-depth projects focusing on particular themes, and good children's literature, they give children motivation to learn the important concepts and skills they need for school and life success. Children should bring home from preschool not only further developed skills but also knowledge useful and meaningful in life.

USING MANIPULATIVES FOR PRESCHOOL MATH LEARNING

Young children learn primarily through visually inspecting, touching, holding, and manipulating concrete objects. While they are less likely to understand abstract concepts presented abstractly, such concepts are likelier accessible to preschoolers through the medium of real things they can see, feel, and manipulate. **Manipulatives** are proven as effective learning devices; some early math curricula (e.g., Horizons) even require them. They are also particularly useful for children with tactile or visual learning styles. Many math manipulatives are available for sale, such as linking cubes; 3-dimensional geometric shapes and "geoboards"; large magnetized numbers for whiteboards; weights, scales, and balances for measurements; math blocks; math games; number boards and color tiles; flashcards; play money and toy cash registers, and activities; objects for sorting and patterning; or tangrams for recognizing shapes, reproducing and designing patterns, and spatial problem-solving. Teachers can create homemade math manipulatives using bottle caps/lids; seashells, pebbles/stones; buttons; keys; variously sized, shaped, and colored balls; coffee stirrers; or cardboard tubes from paper products.

HELPING YOUNG CHILDREN USE INQUIRY AND DISCOVERY IN SCIENCE

Early childhood teachers are advised to "teach what they know," meaning use materials with which they are familiar. For example, teachers who like plants can have young children plant beans, water them, and watch them grow, moreover incorporating this activity with the story "Jack and the Beanstalk." Teachers can bring in plants, leaves, and flowers for children to observe and measure their sizes, shapes, or textures. Experts recommend teachers utilize their everyday environments to procure learning materials, such as pine needles and cones, loose feathers and leaves found outdoors, animal fur from pets or groomers, and/or snakeskins or turtle shells from local pet stores. Experts advise teachers to use their observational skills during inquiry and discovery activities: if children apply nonstandard and/or unusual uses of some materials, teachers should observe what could be a new discovery, wherein students teach adults new learning, too. Teachers should let children play with and explore new materials to understand their purposes, uses, and care before using them in structured activities.

PROCESS SKILLS DEVELOPED BY PRESCHOOL SCIENCE PROGRAMS

Experts find three process skills that good early childhood science programs help develop are **observation**, **classification**, and **communication**. Young children are inherently curious about the world and hence enjoy many activities involving inquiry and discovery. Teachers can uncover science in many existing preschool activities. For example, since young children relate to activities focusing on themselves, teachers can have them construct skeletons of dry pasta, using their pictures as heads. Cooking activities involve science, as do art activities. Teachers can have children explore various substances' solubility in water and which colors are produced by mixing which other colors. They can have them compare and contrast different objects. They can create inexpensive science centers using animal puppets; models; thematically-related games, puzzles, books, and writing materials; mirrors, prisms, and magnifiers; scales; magnets; and various observable, measurable objects. Teachers should regularly vary materials to sustain children's interest.

PRESCHOOL ACTIVITIES FOR DEVELOPING PHYSICAL COORDINATION, FINE MOTOR SKILLS, AND LARGE MUSCLE SKILLS

Preschoolers are more likely to fall because their lower bodies are not yet developed equally to their upper bodies, giving them higher centers of gravity. Therefore, seeing how long they can balance on one foot and hopping exercises help improve balance and coordination. Hopping races let preschoolers participate in groups and observe peer outcomes, which can also enhance self-confidence and supporting others. "Freeze dancing" (like musical chairs without the chair-sitting), without eliminations, provides physical activity and improves coordination. Using writing implements, tying shoes, and playing with small items develop fine motor skills. With preschoolers, it is more effective and developmentally appropriate to incorporate fine motor activities into playtime than to separate quiet activity from play. For example, on nature walks, teachers can have children collect pebbles and twigs and throw them into a stream, developing coordination and various muscles. Running, skipping, and playing tag develop large muscle skills. Kicking, throwing, and catching balls give good unstructured exercise without game rules preschoolers cannot understand. Preschoolers' short attention spans preclude long activity durations.

BENEFITS OF AESTHETIC EXPERIENCES

To help children learn color names and develop sensory discrimination and classification abilities, some art museums offer preschool lessons, which teachers can also use as models. For example, a teacher can read a children's story or sing a song about color, then present artwork for children to examine, and then a separate display with different shapes of different colors used by the artist, asking children to name these and any other colors they know, and identify any other colors the artist used not represented in the second display. The teacher then demonstrates how mixing produces other colors. After this demonstration with children's discussion, the teacher gives each child a piece of heavy-duty paper and a brush. The teacher pours about an inch-sized puddle of each of the three primary colors—red, blue, and yellow—in the middle of each child's paper. The teacher then tells the children to use their brushes to explore mixing colors and see the variety of other colors they can create.

BENEFITS OF THE LINE IN VISUAL ARTS

Activities focusing on lines in art help young children expand their symbol recognition, develop their comparison-making ability, and facilitate shape recognition. Teachers can begin by singing a song or reading a children's story about lines. Then they can present one painting, drawing, or other artwork and help children point at various kinds of lines that the artist used. The teacher can draw various line types on a separate piece of paper (e.g. wavy, pointy, spiral) and ask children to find similar lines in the artwork. Then the teacher can ask children to try drawing these different lines themselves. Teachers should also inform children of various tools for drawing lines, such as crayons, pencils, markers, chalk, and paint, and let them experiment with these. An early childhood teacher can also supply butcher paper or other roll paper for each child to lie down on in whatever creative body positions they can make. The teacher outlines their body shapes with a marker. Then the teacher has the children explore drawing different kinds of lines, using various kinds of drawing tools, to enhance and personalize their individual body outlines.

AESTHETIC EXPERIENCES INVOLVING SHAPE

Giving young children learning activities that focus on shapes used in art helps them develop their abilities to form concepts and identify discrepancies. Manipulating basic geometric shapes also stimulates their creative thinking skills and imaginations, as well as developing early geometric math skills. For example, an early childhood teacher can first read aloud a children's book about shapes, of which many are available. After reading it through, the teacher can go back through the story, asking children to point to and name shapes they recognize. Then the teacher can show children an artwork. Using line drawings and/or solid geometric shapes, they discuss what shapes the artist used. The teacher can help children arrange solid shapes to form different images (people, flowers, houses). The teacher can then give children paper pulp trays, heavy paper, and/or board; assorted wooden, cardboard, and/or plastic shapes; and instructions to think and arrange shapes they can make with them, and then give them glue to affix the shapes to their trays, paper, and/or board. They can paint their creations after the glue dries.

EXPLORING TEXTURE IN ART

Preschoolers learn much through looking at and touching concrete materials. Activities involving visual and tactile examination and manipulation plus verbal discussion enhance young children's representational/symbolic thinking abilities. Such activities also enable children to explore various ways of representing different textures visually. Teachers can provide "feely bags or boxes"—bags or boxes with variously textured items inside, such as sandpaper, fleece, clay, wool, or tree bark—for children to feel and describe textures before seeing them, and identify objects based on feel. A teacher can then show children a selected artwork, and they can discuss together which textures are included(e.g., smooth, rough, jagged, bumpy, sharp, prickly, soft, or slippery). The teacher can then demonstrate using plaster, thickened paste, or clay how to create various textures using assorted tools (e.g., tongue depressors, plastic tableware, chopsticks, small toys, or child-safe pottery tools) and have children experiment with discovering and producing as many different textures as they can. After children's products dry, they can paint them the next day.

PROVIDING AFFECTIVE LEARNING EXPERIENCES

Providing affective experiences supports young children's emotional development, including understanding and expressing their emotions. These enable development of emotional self-regulation/self-control. Emotional development is also prerequisite to and supportive of social interactions and development. Affective activities also help teachers understand how children feel, which activities they find most fascinating, and/or why they are not participating. "Feelings and Faces" activities are useful. For example, a teacher can have each child draw four different "feeling" faces on paper plates (e.g., happy, sad, angry, confused, excited) and discuss each. A teacher can offer various scenarios, like learning a new song, painting a picture, getting a new pet, or feeling sick, and ask children how they feel about each. Then the teacher can give them new paper plates, having them draw faces showing feelings they often have. Gluing Popsicle sticks to the plates turns them into "masks." The teacher can prompt the children on later days to hold up their masks to illustrate how they feel on a given day and about specific activities/experiences.

MOST IMPORTANT SOCIAL SKILLS

Experts find it crucial for young children's later success in school and life to have experiences that develop understanding of their own and others' emotions, constructive management of their strong feelings, and skills in forming and maintaining relationships. Young children use earlier developed motor skills like pushing/shoving, biting, hitting, or kicking, to get what they want rather than later developing verbal skills. Since physical aggression is antisocial, social development includes learning more acceptable, verbal emotional expressions. "Punch and Judy"–type puppet-shows depicting aggression's failures entertain preschoolers; discussing puppet behavior develops social skills. Teachers have children say which puppets they liked or disliked and considered good or bad, what happened, what might happen next, and how puppets could act differently. Teachers can reinforce children's discussion of meeting needs using words, not violence. Many read-aloud stories explain why people behave certain ways in social contexts; discussion/question-and-answer groups promote empathy, understanding, and listening skills. Assigning collaborative projects, like scrapbooking in small groups, helps young children learn cooperation, turn-taking, listening, and verbally expressing what they want.

PROVIDING AFFECTIVE EXPERIENCES AND PROMOTING EMOTIONAL DEVELOPMENT, PHYSICAL ACTIVITY, AND CREATIVITY

Early childhood teachers can help children understand their feelings and others' feelings, express their emotions, engage in physical exercise, use creative thinking, and have fun by using emotional movement activities. For example, the teacher can begin with prompting the children to demonstrate various types of body movements and postures, like crawling, walking, tiptoeing, skipping, hopping, crouching, slouching, limping, or dancing. Then the teacher can ask the children which feelings they associate with each type of movement and body position. The teacher can play some music for children to move to, and give them instructions such as "Move like you are happy… like you are sad… like you are scared… like you are surprised… like you are angry…" Teachers can also use "freeze"/"statue" dances or games, wherein children move to music and must freeze in position like statues when the music stops; for affective practice, teachers instruct children to depict a certain emotion each time they freeze in place.

Learning Environments in Early Childhood

GUIDELINES FOR INDOOR AND OUTDOOR SPACE USE

Indoor and outdoor early childhood learning environments should be safe, clean, and attractive. They should include at least 35 square feet indoors and 75 square feet outdoors of usable play space per child. Staff must have access to prepare spaces before children's arrival. Gyms or other larger indoor spaces can substitute if outdoor spaces are smaller. The youngest children should be given separate outdoor times/places. Outdoor scheduling should ensure enough room and prevent altercations/competition among different age groups. Teachers can assess if enough space exists by observing children's interactions and engagement in activities. Children's products and other visuals should be displayed at child's-eye level. Spaces should be arranged to allow individual, small-group, and large-group activity. Space organization should create clear pathways enabling children to move easily among activities without overly disturbing others, and should promote positive social interactions and behaviors; activities in each area should not distract children in other areas.

ARRANGEMENT OF LEARNING ENVIRONMENTS
ARRANGING INDOOR LEARNING ENVIRONMENTS ACCORDING TO CURRICULAR ACTIVITIES

EC experts indicate that rooms should be organized to enable various activities, but not necessarily to limit activities to certain areas. For example, mathematical and scientific preschool activities may occur in multiple parts of a classroom, though the room should still be laid out to facilitate their occurrence. Sufficient space for infants to crawl and toddlers to toddle is necessary, as are both hard and carpeted floors. Bolted-down/heavy, sturdy furniture is needed for infants and toddlers to use for pulling up, balancing, and cruising. Art and cooking activities should be positioned near sinks/water sources for cleanup. Designating separate areas for activities like block-building, book-reading, musical activities, and dramatic play facilitates engaging in each of these. To allow ongoing project work and other age-appropriate activities, school-aged children should have separate areas. Materials should be appropriate for each age group and varied. Books, recordings, art supplies, and equipment and materials for sensory stimulation, manipulation, construction, active play, and dramatic play, all arranged for easy, independent child access and rotated for variety, are needed.

ARRANGING LEARNING ENVIRONMENTS TO CHILDREN'S PERSONAL, PRIVACY, AND SENSORY NEEDS

In any early childhood learning environment, the indoor space should include easily identifiable places where children and adults can store their personal belongings. Since early childhood involves children in groups for long time periods, they should be given indoor and outdoor areas allowing solitude and privacy while still easily permitting adult supervision. Playhouses and tunnels can be used outdoors, while small interior rooms and partitions can be used indoors. Environments should include softness in various forms like grass outdoors; carpet, pillows, and soft chairs indoors; adult laps to sit in and be cuddled; and soft play materials like clay, Play-Doh, finger paints, water, and sand. While noise is predictable, even desirable in early childhood environments, undue noise causing fatigue and stress should be controlled by noise-absorbing elements like rugs, carpets, drapes, acoustic ceilings, and other building materials. Outdoor play areas supplied by a school or community should be separated from roadways and other hazards by fencing and/or natural barriers. Awnings can substitute for shade, and inclines/ramps for hills, when these are not naturally available. Surfaces and equipment should be varied.

Developmentally Appropriate Practices

DEVELOPMENTALLY APPROPRIATE PRACTICE

Developmentally Appropriate Practice **(DAP)** is an approach to teaching grounded in theories of child development. It is derived from the belief that children are naturally curious to learn, and when provided a stimulating environment, are encouraged to take initiative in their own learning. This approach allows for a great deal of choice in learning experiences. The teacher's role is to facilitate active learning by creating developmentally appropriate activities based on the awareness of similarities between children in various developmental stages and the knowledge that each child develops at their own rate. With this knowledge, the teacher can then adjust the curriculum, activities, and assessments to fit the needs of individual students based on an awareness of age, cultural, social, and individual expectations.

CREATING INSTRUCTION TAILORED TO COGNITIVE DEVELOPMENT

A developmentally responsive teacher understands that the needs of students change as they mature through the stages of cognitive development. Furthermore, an effective teacher uses this knowledge to plan instruction that coincides with each developmental level. The early childhood teacher understands the needs and abilities of preoperational children, and designs instruction that focuses on interacting with the world around them through hands-on activities and pretend play. Such activities foster exploration of the environment, roles, and connections. Developmentally responsive elementary school teachers are aware of the logical thinking patterns that occur during the concrete operational stage. Thus, they create instruction that allows children to interact with tangible materials to help them draw logical conclusions about their environment and understand abstract ideas. As children reach adolescence, a developmentally responsive teacher understands the increased ability to think abstractly, hypothetically, and reflectively in the formal operational stage. They use this knowledge to create instruction that encourages discussion, debate, creative problem solving, and opportunities to develop opinions, beliefs, and values.

COGNITIVE DEVELOPMENT

IMPORTANCE IN DESIGN OF APPROPRIATE LEARNING EXPERIENCES THAT FACILITATE GROWTH

The teacher must understand their students' cognitive developmental ability relative to their grade level in order to create effective, engaging learning experiences that facilitate growth. This understanding allows teachers to develop age-appropriate instruction, activities, and assessment that challenges students based on their skills and abilities but is attainable based on their cognitive developmental level. In knowing how students in a given grade level think and learn, the teacher can develop instruction that effectively facilitates learning and growth, such as creating opportunities for purposeful play with young children, opportunities for middle-school aged students to engage in logical problem solving, or activities that promote the development of abstract thinking and reasoning with adolescents. In addition, understanding students' cognitive abilities of each developmental level allow the teacher to better understand the nuances that exist within them, as students ultimately develop at their own pace and have individual learning needs.

IMPACT ON TEACHING AND LEARNING

Students' thinking and learning develops as they mature, as their thought processes and worldview changes. Consequently, teaching and learning must adapt to accommodate these changes and facilitate growth. In the early years of cognitive development, children learn through interacting with the surrounding environment using their physical senses and engage in independent play. To facilitate this, young children need learning experiences that stimulate their development through exploration. As children reach early elementary school, they begin to think symbolically and play with others. Purposeful play and interaction with learning materials becomes an important part of learning at this stage. Teachers should act as facilitators and provide multiple opportunities for children to engage in purposeful, self-directed play with interactive materials as they learn to categorize the world around them. By later childhood, children think concretely and logically, and thus, need hands-on learning experiences that provide opportunities for classification, experimentation, and problem-solving skills to facilitate their level of cognition and promote development. As children reach adolescence, they are increasingly able to think abstractly and consider hypothetical situations beyond what is concretely present. To enhance learning, teachers must provide opportunities for exploring different perspectives, values, and synthesizing information to engage in creative problem solving.

APPROPRIATE INSTRUCTIONAL ACTIVITIES

The following are some examples of appropriate instructional activities for early childhood, middle-level, and high school students:

- **Early childhood:** Activities that allow for exploration, play, and movement while teaching young children to function and cooperate in a group setting are most valuable in early childhood classrooms. **Movement activities** such as dancing, jumping rope, using outdoor play equipment, as well as structured and unstructured play, are beneficial in developing gross motor skills and teaching young children to properly interact with others. **Whole-group** activities such as circle time, class songs, and read-aloud sessions are also valuable in teaching young children appropriate communication skills within a group. **Thematic learning stations**, such as a science center, dramatic play area, library corner, block area, art center, and technology center, allow young children to explore their own interests on a variety of topics while developing creative and imaginative skills. **Sensory play** stations that include such items as a sand box or water table, are beneficial in further developing motor skills and allowing young children to explore and experiment with a variety of textures. Young children also require opportunities for quiet activities, such as naptime, self-selected reading, or meditation throughout the day in order to process information, reflect, and rest after active movement.

- **Middle-level**: Students at this age are best supported by the implementation of **hands-on** learning activities that develop **logical reasoning** and **collaboration** skills. Collaborative activities such as science experiments, mathematical word problems, the use of manipulatives, and projects that allow opportunities for building, creating, disassembling, and exploring, are beneficial in facilitating such a learning experience. Social and emotional learning activities are also important in developing middle school students' skills in these domains. Incorporating such activities as class meetings, community building activities, and self-reflection activities, are valuable methods for teaching social and emotional skills. In addition, cooperative learning opportunities should be implemented frequently across subject areas to further develop students' ability to work productively with others. Examples include literacy circles, creating teams for class review games, or group presentations.

38

- **High School:** Instructional activities for high school students should be designed to foster the development of **abstract** and **hypothetical** thinking abilities while preparing them to become productive members of society as they enter adulthood. Activities such as debates, class discussions, and mock trials are beneficial in providing high school students the opportunity to employ abstract reasoning, consider solutions to hypothetical situations, and develop empathy for opposing viewpoints. Assignments that require students to engage in the research process are valuable opportunities for developing higher-order thinking skills, as they encourage students to analyze, compare, and interpret information, as well as seek evidence to support their claims. In addition, incorporating activities that benefit the community, such as fundraisers or food and clothing drives, are beneficial in teaching high school students the importance of positively contributing to society.

EFFECTIVE AND DEVELOPMENTALLY APPROPRIATE LEARNING EXPERIENCES AND ASSESSMENTS

Effective developmentally appropriate instruction requires careful consideration when planning to ensure that students' individual needs across domains are supported to facilitate growth and a positive learning experience. The teacher must consider the developmental stage of their students based upon their age group, as well as students' individual differences. With this knowledge in mind, teachers must ensure that they provide an inclusive learning environment that fosters growth and development by creating challenging, yet attainable activities based on students' needs. Likewise, teachers must evaluate whether learning experiences and assessments are age, developmentally, and culturally appropriate while ensuring that they are tailored to students' unique learning differences. Learning experiences must provide opportunities for hands-on, cooperative, and self-directed learning, exploration, and participation to allow students to interact with their environment and build experiences. Additionally, lessons and activities should be flexible in nature to allow for inquiry and build upon students' prior experiences. Effective developmentally appropriate assessments are aimed at monitoring student progress and allow for flexibility based on students' learning differences. They should be intended to provide feedback to the teacher on how to better adapt instruction to meet students' individual needs and foster developmental growth.

FACILITATING DEVELOPMENT OF LIFE SKILLS AND ATTITUDES IN MIDDLE SCHOOL-AGE CHILDREN

Middle school-age children are at a pivotal development point in which they experience rapid and profound change. In this transition, they often demonstrate characteristics of younger and older children and are therefore at a critical stage for developing the beliefs, attitudes, and habits that will be the foundation for their future. Teachers must understand the implications of these changes and design instruction that addresses students' learning needs and facilitates the development of such important life skills as working and getting along with others, appreciating diversity, and committing to continued schooling. Cooperative learning and team building strategies instill the importance of working together positively to problem solve, building on one another's strengths, and valuing other's perspectives. These strategies also teach students to appreciate diversity through encouraging them to work with peers with different backgrounds and experiences. Additionally, teachers can teach students to embrace diversity through creating a culturally responsive classroom environment that models acceptance and incorporates elements of students' differences into instruction to demonstrate the value of diverse perspectives. Teachers promote positive attitudes toward academics that encourage a commitment to continued schooling by teaching organization, time management, and goal-setting skills that instill a growth mindset and provide a foundation for success.

IMPACT OF STUDENT CHARACTERISTICS ON TEACHING AND LEARNING

YOUNG CHILDREN

The developmental level of young children is characterized by defining attributes that impact teaching and learning, and for which several considerations must be made to design and implement effective instruction. As the attention span of young children is limited, the teacher must think about how to effectively act as a facilitator for learning more often than directly instructing students. **Direct instruction** must be delivered in small, manageable chunks to accommodate students' attention spans and ensure they retain and understand new concepts. Thus, the teacher must evaluate which elements of the curriculum require structured learning, while allowing for flexibility within instruction to accommodate student inquiry. Young children also need frequent **movement**, **physical activity**, and **social interaction**, as they learn and build experiences concretely through moving, playing, interacting with, and exploring their environment. To create a learning environment that accommodates these characteristics, the teacher must consider the physical arrangement of the classroom, and whether it adequately allows for movement. Additionally, teachers must incorporate **structured** and **unstructured activities** that foster and promote exploration, inquiry, play, cooperative learning, and hands-on interactions with the learning environment. With these considerations in mind, the teacher enhances students' learning experience by tailoring instruction to their developmental characteristics.

MIDDLE SCHOOL-AGED CHILDREN

As middle school-age children transition from childhood to adolescence, they experience vast changes across all developmental domains. Consequently, they exhibit characteristics that affect teaching and learning that require careful consideration when adapting instruction to their unique learning needs. While these students require increasing independence as they mature, they still need a structured, predictable environment to ease the transition into high school. The teacher must create a balance between fostering independence and growth while providing a schedule and routine. Opportunities for self-directed learning and student choice, as well as strategies for self-assessment and reflection foster autonomy and self-responsibility over learning while the teacher facilitates and monitors progress. Strategies to teach effective organizational and time management skills further promote independence and prepare students for success upon entering high school. As middle school-age students develop, the importance of peers becomes increasingly prevalent as they begin to search for their identity and shape their own values and beliefs. Teachers must ensure to provide opportunities for cooperative and small group learning to facilitate students' social development while considering the importance of promoting positive peer relationships at this impressionable developmental level.

ADOLESCENT CHILDREN

The developmental changes that occur in adolescence result in distinct characteristics as students in this age group transition into young adulthood. During this stage, students are discovering their identities, values, and beliefs and begin to explore long-term career and life choices. As they navigate their development and shape the person they will become, social relationships come to be increasingly important. Teachers must consider the impact of these characteristics when developing instruction to effectively address the unique needs of this age group and establish foundational attitudes, habits, and skills necessary for success in life. Effective instruction encourages adolescents to consider different perspectives, morals, and values to broaden their worldview and foster the development of their own beliefs. Lessons and activities should allow for exploration of personal interests, skills, and abilities as students shape their personalities and begin to consider long-term life goals. Moreover, the teacher should incorporate strategies that assist adolescents in goal setting to successfully foster a growth mindset and provide a foundation for success. Additionally, as socialization is highly influential at this stage, teachers must consider the importance of incorporating cooperative learning strategies and opportunities for socialization within instruction to encourage healthy peer relationships and foster positive identity development.

INTERCONNECTION OF DEVELOPMENTAL DOMAINS

Developmental domains are deeply interconnected. If one area of a child's development is negatively impacted, it is likely to pose negative consequences on other developmental areas. Proper physical development is key to developing cognitively, socially, and emotionally in that physical development allows children to acquire the necessary gross and fine motor skills to explore and experiment with the world around them, as well as interact with others. Physical development includes development of the brain, and factors such as poor nutrition, sleep, or prenatal exposure to drugs potentially hinder brain development. Consequentially, this may result in cognitive delays, and ultimately lead to social or emotional developmental delays through negatively impacting the child's ability to interact with others, build relationships, emotionally regulate, or communicate effectively.

FACTORS TO CONSIDER WHEN SELECTING MATERIALS FOR LEARNING AND PLAY

To plan meaningful, integrated, and active learning and play experiences, the teacher must have a deep understanding of both the developmental stage of the students and an understanding of students' individual needs. With this knowledge in mind, there are several factors that the teacher must consider when choosing materials that support active learning and play experiences, and ultimately, the development of the whole child. Materials should be adaptable in use to facilitate development in multiple areas. Versatility is also important in fostering imagination and creativity. The teacher must consider how the chosen materials will support understanding of concepts covered in instruction, as well as how they will support conceptual, perceptual, and language development. Furthermore, the teacher must ensure that materials are age-appropriate, stimulating, and encourage active participation both independently and cooperatively.

CHARACTERISTICS OF A DEVELOPMENTALLY RESPONSIVE CLASSROOM

A developmentally responsive classroom is one in which the teacher understands the cognitive, physical, social, and emotional developmental stages of students while recognizing nuances and individual developmental differences within these stages. The teacher understands that developmental domains are interconnected, and effectively responds to unique developmental differences by designing a learner-centered curriculum and classroom environment that caters to each students' abilities, needs, and developmental levels to develop the whole child. The developmentally responsive classroom is engaging, supportive, and provides challenging learning opportunities based on individual learner abilities. There are several factors the teacher must consider in the developmentally responsive classroom when planning an appropriate, engaging, and challenging learning experience. The teacher must have a deep understanding of which teaching strategies will most effectively appeal to students of varying developmental levels and be prepared to teach content in multiple ways. Furthermore, the teacher must consider how to plan and organize activities, lessons, breaks, and the overall classroom environment. This would include considering how to arrange the classroom, which activity areas to include, spacing, and classroom equipment. The developmentally responsive classroom should promote positivity and productivity through creating a supportive yet challenging learning atmosphere that welcomes and respects differences, thus encouraging students' curiosity and excitement for learning.

Role of Play in Learning and Development

CHARACTERISTICS OF THE DEVELOPMENTAL PLAY STAGES

As children develop, so do their styles of play. Developmental play stages are divided into five primary phases: **solitary play** (Birth-2 years), **onlooker play** (2 years), **parallel play** (2-3 years), **associative play** (3-4 years) and **cooperative play** (4 years and beyond). During the **solitary play** stage, children play alone and are uninterested in playing with others, or what other children around them are doing. When they reach the **onlooker play** stage, children will watch other children play, but will not actively engage in playing with others. In **parallel play**, children do not play with one another, but will often play next to each other and will use similar materials. They may be curious about what other children are doing, and may copy them, but will not directly play with them. Children begin to intentionally play with others in the **associative play** stage, but the play is unorganized and still largely individual in its goals. In **cooperative play**, children begin to intentionally play and share materials in organized groups, and often have a common purpose or goal when playing.

Parallel Play

Cooperative Play

PURPOSES AND BENEFITS OF PLAY IN EARLY CHILDHOOD EDUCATION

Purposeful play is an integral part of learning and development in the early childhood classroom. Its purpose is to aid and allow children to incorporate all aspects of development and thus provides cognitive, social, emotional, and physical benefits. Purposeful play deepens children's understanding of new concepts through allowing them to explore and experiment in the world around them using imagination and creativity. Integrating purposeful play into the early childhood classroom is further beneficial in that it allows children to construct and build on knowledge through experiences and helps develop divergent and convergent thinking. The socialization children get from play strengthens their language skills through speaking to one another, using new vocabulary, and listening to others. Purposeful play strengthens physical-motor development in that it calls for children to move their bodies in games, running, jumping, etc. Play is necessary for building important emotional and social skills that are necessary for being a successful member of society later in life.

Schedules, Routines, and Activities for Young Children

IDEAL SCHEDULE FOR YOUNG CHILDREN

An ideal schedule for young children reflects their developmental characteristics and capabilities to maximize their learning. A **predictable** routine is necessary for young children to feel secure in their learning environment, and therefore, each day should follow a similar schedule while allowing room for **flexibility** if an activity takes longer than expected. Each day should begin with a clear routine, such as unpacking, a "warm-up" activity, and a class meeting to allow students to share thoughts, ask questions, and allow the teacher to discuss what will occur that day. This establishes a positive tone for the day while focusing the attention on learning. Similarly, the end of the day should have a specific routine, such as cleaning up materials and packing up for dismissal. Young children learn best by physically interacting with and exploring their environment. As such, each day should include large blocks of time for **active movement** throughout the day in the form of play, projects, and learning centers. Periods of **rest** must follow such activities, as this enables young children to process and internalize what they learned. **Direct instruction** should occur before active movement periods and last approximately 15-20 minutes to sustain engagement and attention on learning.

Example Daily Schedule for the Early Childhood Education Classroom	
8:00-8:30	Welcome, unpack, morning work
8:30-8:45	Circle time, review class calendar
8:45-9:30	Literacy/Language Arts
9:30-10:15	Learning Stations

10:15-11:00	Math
11:00-11:30	Music/Dance/Movement
11:30-12:15	Lunch
12:15-1:00	Recess/Unstructured play
1:00-1:20	Rest/Quiet time
1:20-2:00	Science
2:00-2:45	Creative Arts
2:45-3:15	Daily reflection, pack up, dismissal

Some examples of restful and active movement activities for young children are discussed below:

- **Restful:** Incorporating restful activities into the early childhood classroom are beneficial in helping young children process and retain new concepts and providing them the opportunity to unwind after active movement activities. Examples of such activities include nap time, class meditation, self-reflection activities, independent art projects, or self-selected reading time. Teachers can also read aloud to students or play an audiobook during these periods.
- **Active:** Providing young children with multiple opportunities for active movement throughout the day is beneficial in promoting the development of gross motor skills, connections to learning, and the ability to function in a group setting. Active movement opportunities should include whole-class, small group, and independent activities. Examples include class dances, songs, or games, nature walks, or total participation activities such as gallery walks or four corners. Physical education activities, such as jump rope, tag, sports, or using playground equipment are also beneficial. Young children should also be provided with ample time for both structured and unstructured play throughout the day.

BALANCING RESTFUL AND ACTIVE MOVEMENT ACTIVITIES

A schedule that balances **rest** and **active movement** is necessary for positive cognitive, physical, emotional, and social development in young children. Connecting learning to active movement strengthens students' understanding of new concepts, as it allows them to physically explore and interact with their environment, experiment with new ideas, and gain new experiences for healthy **cognitive development**. In addition, incorporating active movement encourages the use of **gross motor skills** and provides students with the space to physically express themselves in an appropriate setting, thus promoting physical and emotional development. Active movement also encourages the development of positive **interpersonal skills** as young children interact and explore with one another. Restful periods are equally as important to young children's development. Incorporating rest after a period of active movement further strengthens young children's connection to learning by providing them the opportunity to reflect, process, and internalize new information.

PROVIDING LARGE BLOCKS OF TIME FOR PLAY, PROJECTS, AND LEARNING CENTERS

Providing young children with ample time for play, projects, and learning centers throughout the school day is integral to fostering their development across domains. Young children learn most effectively through active movement as they physically interact with their environment, and incorporating large blocks of time for such activities allows them to do so. Significant time dedicated to active play, projects, and learning centers on a variety of topics allows young children to explore and experiment with the world around them, test new ideas, draw conclusions, and acquire new knowledge. This supports healthy **physical** and **cognitive development**, as it provides young children the opportunity to engage in learning across subject areas while connecting it to active movement for strengthened understanding. In addition, allowing large blocks of time for these activities is necessary for **social** and **emotional development**, as it provides young children the space to interact with one another and develop important skills such as cooperation, sharing, conflict resolution, and emotional self-regulation. Dedicating large blocks of time to play, projects, and learning centers establishes a student-led, hands-on learning environment that is reflective of the developmental characteristics and needs of young children.

DEVELOPMENTAL CHARACTERISTICS OF YOUNG CHILDREN IN RELATION TO INTERACTIONS WITH OTHERS

Designing group activities that align with young children's ability to collaborate while supporting social development requires a realistic understanding of their capacity to do so. This entails understanding the **developmental characteristics** of young children at varying stages, including how the nature of their interactions with others evolves. Young children learn by exploring and interacting with their environment, so they need ample opportunities for play and active movement to do so. However, the teacher must recognize that the way young children play and collaborate develops over time. Young children typically exhibit little interest in actively playing with others until approximately age four. Until then, they progress through stages of solitary play, observing their peers, playing independently alongside others, and eventually, loosely interacting, perhaps with the same toys, while still primarily engaging in independent play. During these stages, it is important that the teacher foster **collaboration** by providing multiple opportunities for play as well as learning materials that encourage **cooperation** and **sharing**. The teacher must, however, maintain the understanding that these children have yet to develop the capacity to intentionally work with others. Once this ability is developed, the teacher can integrate coordinated group activities that encourage collaboration toward a common goal.

CONSIDERATIONS WHEN DESIGNING GROUP ACTIVITIES FOR YOUNG CHILDREN

For young children, thoughtfully designed group activities are integral in promoting development across domains. These opportunities facilitate social and emotional development by encouraging collaboration and positive communication, as well as physical and cognitive growth as children play, explore, and interact with others in the learning environment. It is therefore important that the teacher carefully consider the particulars of group activities when planning to ensure maximized learning and development. The teacher must consider the **developmental characteristics** of their students' age group, including their capacity to collaborate with others. This enables the teacher to plan group activities that align with students' abilities while promoting collaboration and development. All **learning materials** must be carefully selected to encourage collaboration, sharing, and the development of positive social skills at a developmentally appropriate level. The teacher must also consider **desired learning outcomes** and the nature of the learning taking place to determine whether group activities should be structured or unstructured. Unstructured play is valuable in allowing students to develop their social and emotional skills in a natural setting, whereas structured, teacher-led group activities allow for more focused learning. Desired outcomes also determine the size of groups for the activity to best promote collaboration and learning.

GROUP ACTIVITIES THAT REFLECT AND DEVELOP YOUNG CHILDREN'S ABILITY TO COLLABORATE

Young children benefit from a variety of **whole-class** and **small-group** activities designed to reflect and develop their collaborative skills. When the teacher incorporates group activities to encourage cooperation, sharing, and positive interactions, young children gain important social and emotional skills necessary for development across domains. Whole-group activities such as **circle time** provide young children with the opportunity to interact with others, express ideas, and ask questions in a developmentally appropriate setting. This activity develops important collaborative skills, such as taking turns, active listening, and respectful communication. Other **whole-group activities**, such as reading aloud, group songs, dances, games, or class nature walks, are effective in teaching young children how to productively contribute to and function in a group setting. **Small-group activities** can be incorporated throughout all aspects of structured and unstructured learning to develop young children's collaborative skills. Learning centers, such as a science area, pretend play area, or building block center, provide materials that encourage collaboration while allowing students to interact with others according to their abilities in a student-led setting. Problem-solving activities, such as puzzles, games, age-appropriate science experiments, or scavenger hunts, are effective in teaching young children how to work together toward a common goal.

ORGANIZING AND MANAGING GROUP ACTIVITIES TO PROMOTE COLLABORATIVE SKILLS AND INDIVIDUAL ACCOUNTABILITY

Well-planned group activities are beneficial in developing students' collaborative skills and sense of individual accountability. Such group activities are well-organized, effectively managed, and intentionally structured with a **clear goal** or problem that must be solved while allowing room for creativity to enhance the collaborative process. When designing these activities, the teacher must incorporate enough **significant components** to ensure all students within the group can productively contribute. If the assignment is too simple, students can easily complete it on their own, whereas a multifaceted activity instills a sense of interdependence within the group that fosters the development of collaborative skills. To promote individual accountability, **meaningful roles** and responsibilities should be assigned to each group member because when students feel others are relying on their contributions to complete a task, they develop a sense of ownership that motivates active participation. To further develop collaborative skills and individual accountability, students should be graded both as a **whole-group** and **individually**. This encourages group cooperation while ensuring that students' individual contributions are recognized. Including **self-assessments** at the end of group activities is beneficial in allowing students to reflect on the quality of their contributions to the group and ways they could improve their collaborative skills.

Thoughtful consideration of how to best organize and manage collaborative activities helps establish an environment that supports students in learning to work together productively and assume responsible roles within a group. When planning group activities, the teacher must consider the **desired learning outcomes** and the **nature of the task** to determine whether there are enough significant components that would benefit from collaboration. **Group size** must also be considered to most effectively foster collaboration and individual accountability when assuming responsible roles. Groups with too few students may be inadequate for addressing all the components of a complex task, whereas grouping too many students together limits productive collaboration and makes it difficult for each member to assume a significant, responsible role. The teacher must be selective regarding which students are grouped together to best facilitate productive collaboration. This includes determining which students will work well together, as well as grouping students that may need support with others that can provide scaffolding. It is also important to consider how **responsibilities** will be divided to ensure each member is given a significant role that allows them to contribute productively to the group, as well how their contributions will be monitored and **assessed**.

The Learning Environment

ESTABLISHING A POSITIVE, PRODUCTIVE CLASSROOM ENVIRONMENT
UNIQUE CHARACTERISTICS AND NEEDS OF STUDENTS AT VARYING DEVELOPMENTAL LEVELS

Students at each developmental level possess unique characteristics and needs that must be met in the classroom to ensure productivity and a positive classroom environment. For successful learning, the teacher must recognize the nuances of varying developmental levels to properly understand their students' abilities and design instruction accordingly. When the teacher is attuned to the distinct characteristics and needs of their students, they can align **curriculum**, **instructional strategies**, **activities**, and **assessments** in a way that is accessible and comprehensible to all students. This understanding enables the teacher to deliver instruction at a **pace** appropriate to students' developmental stage while ensuring they are challenged across domains based upon their ability for continuous whole-child development. In addition, knowledge of the general characteristics and needs of developmental stages enables the teacher to effectively identify and accommodate individual variances that occur within these stages for **student-centered** learning. When instruction is tailored to address the needs of varying developmental stages and individual differences, students feel supported in their learning. This ultimately fosters increased self-esteem, student engagement, and positive attitudes toward learning that contribute to an overall productive and successful classroom environment.

ADDRESSING DEVELOPMENTAL CHARACTERISTICS AND NEEDS OF YOUNGER STUDENTS

A positive and productive classroom environment for younger children requires the teacher to understand the intricacies of this developmental stage and implement strategies accordingly to promote success in learning. Younger students learn by **exploring** and **interacting** with the world around them and must be provided with multiple opportunities to do so. **Play** is integral to young students' development across domains. Therefore, both planned and free play should be incorporated throughout instruction. Play enables students to explore their environment and make connections that strengthen their learning while promoting the development of problem-solving and higher-order thinking skills. In addition, allowing frequent opportunities for play facilitates the acquisition of important social and emotional skills, such as cooperation, conflict resolution, and sharing. Likewise, incorporating frequent **movement** throughout lessons allows young students to explore their physical space and actively engage in learning for deeper understanding. Additionally, **cooperative learning** strategies encourage the development of necessary social and emotional skills and are important in teaching young children how to effectively work with others to solve a problem. When the teacher implements strategies appropriate to younger students' developmental levels, it enhances motivation, active engagement, and promotes positive attitudes toward learning for a productive classroom environment.

COLLABORATIVE OPPORTUNITIES IN ADDRESSING DEVELOPMENTAL CHARACTERISTICS AND NEEDS OF MIDDLE-LEVEL STUDENTS

Middle-level students experience significant developmental changes as they approach adolescence and therefore, have unique characteristics and needs that must be met to ensure a positive and productive learning environment. **Collaborative opportunities** are beneficial in supporting the development of cognitive, social, and emotional skills of middle-level students and should be implemented frequently. This strategy enables these students to work productively with others and promotes the development of positive **interpersonal** and **communication** skills. This is especially important in middle-level education, as students at this developmental stage begin forming their identities, attitudes toward learning, and influential peer relationships. Middle-level students build **self-confidence** through collaborative learning, as it enables them to develop positive leadership skills. Additionally, collaborative opportunities expose students to the varying backgrounds and perspectives of their classmates, thus fostering appreciation for individual differences and contributing to a positive classroom climate. Collaborative learning is also beneficial for **cognitive development**, as it allows students to build upon one another's background knowledge for enhanced learning and encourages critical and higher-order thinking while working together to solve a problem. Providing middle-level students with collaborative opportunities increases overall engagement for a positive and productive classroom environment, as well as develops necessary skills for successful transition into adolescence.

PROMOTING RESPECT FOR THE COMMUNITY AND PEOPLE IN IT AMONG OLDER STUDENTS

As older students prepare for adulthood, it is important that they develop a respect for their community and the people in it. Implementing strategies to facilitate this is vital in equipping older students with **real-world skills** necessary to become productive contributors to society. By self-educating and modeling respect for the community and its people, the teacher can influence students to adopt the same sentiment. Establishing a positive community within the classroom through such activities as class meetings, discussions, and cultural activities promotes respect for others that extends to real-world situations. Strategies that demonstrate connection to the community strengthen students' overall respect and responsibility for it. This can be achieved by incorporating **authentic materials**, including news stories, art, music, and relevant speakers, to develop students' understanding and insight regarding the characteristics and needs of the community. Encouraging students to bring items from home to share fosters appreciation for their community by exposing them to the backgrounds and perspectives within it. **Community service** projects such as fundraisers, food drives, and service field trips further promote students' respect for their community while demonstrating the real-world applications of their learning. This ultimately makes learning meaningful and contributes to a positive, productive learning environment.

POSITIVE CLASSROOM CLIMATE

Classroom climate refers to the overall atmosphere that the teacher establishes and is powerful in determining the nature of the learning experience. Students are most successful in their learning when the climate is positive, encouraging, and focused on creating a collaborative, supportive community. A positive classroom climate is **welcoming**, **inclusive**, and **respectful** of all individuals. Instruction is delivered in an engaging, comprehensible way in a structured, orderly, and safe environment. The atmosphere is **visually appealing** and stimulating, yet not overwhelming, and is physically arranged in a way that maximizes learning. **Collaboration** and **supportive interactions** are encouraged throughout the learning process to enhance engagement and develop positive social and emotional skills. Such an environment builds students' self-esteem and confidence by ensuring they feel safe and empowered to participate and work with others in the learning process. In addition, it encourages positive attitudes toward learning that are necessary for active student engagement and productivity. When the classroom climate is positive, students are more self-motivated, thus strengthening their learning and promoting academic achievement.

COLLABORATION AND SUPPORTIVE INTERACTIONS

Collaboration and **supportive interactions** are key components of a positive classroom climate and should be integrated throughout instruction to promote active engagement and success in learning for all students. To achieve this, the teacher must establish a classroom community focused on respect, inclusiveness, and open dialogue. This ensures students feel safe and empowered to express themselves and interact constructively. By teaching and **modeling** active listening skills, the teacher can demonstrate and influence respectful communication in the classroom. **Team-building activities**, including class meetings, games, and discussions, are valuable strategies for creating a community that encourages productive collaboration and supportive interactions. In addition, establishing **clear expectations** for positive communication and involving students in their creation instills a sense of personal responsibility to adhere to them when working with others. Once expectations are understood, students must be provided with multiple and varied **collaborative learning** opportunities to continuously practice developing positive interpersonal skills. As students participate in learning, the teacher must be sure to consistently praise cooperation and positive interactions to reinforce the standards of communication. When the teacher promotes collaboration and supportive interactions, they create a positive classroom climate that increases students' productivity and self-motivation to actively participate in learning for maximized achievement.

RESPECT FOR DIVERSITY AND INDIVIDUAL DIFFERENCES

An emphasis on respect for **diversity** and **individual differences** in the classroom is necessary to establish a positive, productive learning atmosphere. Teaching and modeling this sentiment to students instills the notion that everyone has unique and valuable experiences, perspectives, and characteristics to contribute to the classroom community. Emphasizing respect for all individuals ensures students feel validated and secure in their own identities while teaching them to appreciate diversities among their classmates. Such an environment promotes collaboration and supportive interactions, as it is built on a foundation of welcoming, inclusiveness, and acceptance that empowers students to confidently interact with peers as they engage in learning. When students feel respected, it increases their self-esteem and positive self-concept. Students that feel confident in the classroom are more likely to develop positive attitudes toward learning. This ultimately fosters a positive classroom climate in which students are motivated to actively engage in instruction and achieve academic success.

IMPACT OF INTERACTIONS ON CLASSROOM CLIMATE
TEACHER-STUDENT INTERACTIONS

Interactions between teachers and their students play a significant role in determining overall classroom climate and the quality of the learning experience. The way in which the teacher interacts with students influences their **social**, **emotional**, and **cognitive development**, as well as sets the tone for how students interact with each other. This ultimately shapes students' **self-esteem** and contributes to their level of engagement, attitude toward learning, and academic achievement. Therefore, it is important that the teacher

47

ensure all interactions with students on a whole-class and individual level are positive, unbiased, encouraging, and respectful of each individual. Working to build relationships with students demonstrates a genuine interest in their lives that contributes to a positive, productive classroom climate in which students feel welcomed, accepted, and empowered to actively engage in learning. Positive interactions between the teacher and students support a healthy sense of self-esteem as well as positive social and emotional skills that contribute to cognitive development. Students with greater self-esteem are more likely to develop positive attitudes toward learning that foster increased self-motivation to actively participate in learning, thus contributing to enhanced academic achievement.

STUDENTS' INTERACTIONS WITH ONE ANOTHER

The classroom climate is dependent on the nature of **students' interactions** with one another. These interactions largely determine the quality of student learning as well as development across domains. Positive communication facilitates the development of healthy **social** and emotional skills that serve to enhance cognitive development. Students with strong social and **emotional skills** are often more motivated to actively participate in learning and are more productive in collaborative situations, as they can build upon one another's knowledge. Therefore, the teacher must implement a variety of strategies to ensure interactions among students are positive, respectful, and supportive to establish a classroom climate focused on productive learning. **Community building** exercises establish a climate built on positive and supportive communication while demonstrating the benefits of productive cooperation in achieving a goal. Teaching and **modeling** positive communication skills sets the tone and expectations for how students will interact with one another. Students should be given **frequent opportunities** to interact both during and outside of instructional time to promote the development of necessary interpersonal skills for healthy social development. In addition, **strategic student groupings** during collaborative work and consistent monitoring help ensure maximized productivity and that the standards for communication are reinforced.

COMMUNICATING AN ENTHUSIASM FOR LEARNING
ESTABLISHING ENVIRONMENTS PROMOTING POSITIVE ATTITUDES TOWARD LEARNING

The nature of the classroom environment is reliant on the **efforts**, **behaviors**, and **attitudes** of the teacher. The teacher is responsible for setting the tone of the classroom, which determines the overall climate and has significant impacts on the quality and effectiveness of the learning experience. The classroom environment influences students' engagement, positive communication, and attitudes toward learning, which contribute to their overall academic achievement. Successful teaching and learning require the teacher to intentionally take measures to establish a welcoming, accepting, and encouraging classroom environment that promotes excitement and positive attitudes toward learning. Teachers must model genuine respect for their students and enthusiasm for learning, as well as present instruction in a way that is engaging, comprehensible, and responsive to students' needs and interests. The physical classroom must be arranged in such a way that is visually appealing, safe, and facilitative of productive learning. It is also important that the teacher establish and consistently reinforce structured routines, procedures, and behavioral expectations to contribute to an overall positive climate and ensure students feel secure and willing to participate in learning. When the classroom environment is exciting, positive, and engaging, it encourages positive attitudes toward learning that increase motivation to succeed.

INFLUENCE ON STUDENTS' MOTIVATION, PRODUCTIVITY, AND ACADEMIC ACHIEVEMENT

Modeling is perhaps one of the most powerful strategies in influencing students' attitudes, behaviors, and actions in the classroom. As students spend a great deal of time with their teachers, the level of enthusiasm for learning demonstrated by the teacher inevitably influences their own excitement in the classroom. Therefore, the teacher must conscientiously model enthusiasm for teaching and learning to positively influence students' internal motivation for productivity, learning, and achievement. Students are highly perceptive, and as such, if the teacher appears unmotivated in their practice or disinterested in the content, students will likely adopt the same sentiment and become disengaged or apathetic toward learning. The enthusiasm modeled by the teacher must be **authentic** to elicit the same genuine interest in learning from students. When the teacher demonstrates sincere excitement about the content they are teaching, it prompts curiosity for learning among students that enhances their motivation and attitudes toward learning. In addition, modeling enthusiasm for teaching and learning enhances the relationship between the teacher and students, thus contributing to a positive classroom climate that makes students excited to learn. When students have a positive attitude toward learning, they are more motivated to productively engage in learning and achieve academic success.

METHODS AND IMPACT ON CLASSROOM CLIMATE AND STUDENT ENGAGEMENT

Communicating sincere enthusiasm for teaching and learning is essential to establishing a positive, productive classroom climate focused on student engagement and achievement. Students' interest and excitement for learning are directly reflective of the sentiments exhibited by the teacher. As such, it is important that the teacher intentionally and consistently communicate excitement for their practice and content. To achieve this, the teacher must ensure that their **behaviors**, **actions**, **language**, **tone of voice**, and **interactions** with students are positive in nature. By working to build positive **interpersonal relationships** with students and demonstrating genuine interest in their lives, experiences, interests, and needs, the teacher can effectively communicate enthusiasm for their practice that motivates students to engage in learning. This is further reflected in the physical **classroom arrangement**. A classroom that is visually appealing, stimulating, and reflective of students' interests and achievements illustrates the teacher's enthusiasm and promotes a positive classroom climate in which students are excited and motivated to engage in learning.

CONVEYING HIGH EXPECTATIONS FOR ALL STUDENTS

SIGNIFICANCE IN PROMOTING PRODUCTIVITY, ACTIVE ENGAGEMENT, AND SUCCESS IN LEARNING

Communicating **high academic** and **behavioral expectations** is necessary for establishing a classroom climate focused on productivity, active engagement, and achievement. Students are heavily influenced by the teacher's expectations for them, and therefore, when high learning standards are set, students will more likely strive to achieve them. High expectations increase the **relevancy** of learning by focusing instruction and providing a clear purpose that motivates students to participate. In addition, by conveying high expectations, the teacher demonstrates a **belief in their students' abilities** to overcome personal challenges and achieve success. This notion promotes a **growth mindset** among students, which is the belief that intelligence is not inherent, but rather, can be attained and consistently improved upon. This enhances students' self-esteem and confidence, which promotes positive attitudes toward learning that foster active engagement, productivity, and success. Communicating high expectations while providing necessary supports motivates students to challenge themselves academically and gives them a sense of self-responsibility over their learning that encourages them to work to their highest potential. This ultimately creates a positive classroom climate in which students feel supported and empowered to productively engage in learning and achieve success.

STRATEGIES AND IMPACT ON CLASSROOM CLIMATE AND STUDENT ACHIEVEMENT

Communicating **high academic** and **behavioral expectations** is most effective when done so through a variety of means. This ensures that students are aware of the teacher's expectations of them and consistently reinforces high standards to establish a positive classroom climate focused on student motivation, productivity, and achievement. Expectations must always be **clear** and **visible** in the classroom, and the teacher must frequently remind students by restating them throughout instruction. Establishing learning goals and objectives that are challenging, yet attainable based on students' abilities effectively communicates high expectations and the teacher's belief that students can achieve them. This is further iterated when students encounter challenges and rather than lowering expectations, the teacher maintains the same high standards while providing necessary supports for achievement. The teacher can also communicate high expectations by ensuring they provide students with timely, clear, and constructive **feedback** on their progress and ways in which they can improve to meet them. Frequent **communication with families** is beneficial in reinforcing academic and behavioral expectations at home to ensure student awareness and maximize their effectiveness in the classroom.

LITERACY-RICH ENVIRONMENT

A **literacy-rich** classroom focuses on the development of all literacy components by immersing students in reading, writing, speaking, and listening skills across subject areas. While all students benefit from such an environment, it is especially important for **ELL students** and students with **developmental disabilities** in acquiring the literacy and language skills necessary for success. In a literacy-rich environment, the teacher provides multiple opportunities to engage in teacher-led and student-selected reading, writing, speaking, and listening activities in all areas of instruction. Students may be asked to solve word problems in math, write a report on a famous artist in art, or keep an observation log in science to encourage literacy development across content areas. Students are provided with multiple print and digital literacy materials on a variety of topics with varying levels of complexity to accommodate individual developmental levels while encouraging reading, vocabulary acquisition, and listening skills. Additionally, the teacher surrounds students with **print-rich** materials, including posters, word walls, labels, and bulletin boards on a variety of topics to further promote literacy development. A literacy-rich environment continuously promotes and emphasizes the importance of literacy skills in all areas of life that serve as a necessary foundation for academic and real-world success.

> **Review Video: Importance of Promoting Literacy in the Home**
> Visit mometrix.com/academy and enter code: 862347
>
> **Review Video: Characteristics of Literacy-Rich, Content-Area Classrooms**
> Visit mometrix.com/academy and enter code: 571455

SAFE, NURTURING, AND INCLUSIVE CLASSROOM ENVIRONMENT

A safe, nurturing, and inclusive classroom environment focuses on meeting students' emotional needs for healthy development in this domain. The overall climate in such an environment is welcoming and emphasizes **respect**, **acceptance**, and **positive communication** among the teacher and students. The classroom is brightly decorated and reflective of students' diversities, interests, and achievements to promote a sense of security and inclusivity that motivates active participation in learning. Instructional activities are also reflective of students' differences, learning styles, and interests, with necessary supports instilled to accommodate individual learning needs. This establishes an **equitable environment** that ensures all students feel respected, nurtured, and supported both academically and emotionally. Such an environment is **structured** and orderly with clear expectations, procedures, and routines to foster a sense of security as students engage in learning. Collaboration and supportive interactions among students are encouraged to create a positive, productive classroom community in which students feel confident to express themselves and participate in learning. A classroom environment that is safe, nurturing, and inclusive develops students' sense of self-concept that contributes to positive communication, relationships, and attitudes necessary for emotional development.

DEVELOPING STUDENTS' EMOTIONAL INTELLIGENCE

Emotional intelligence refers to the ability to recognize and regulate one's own emotions as well as identify and empathetically respond to the emotions of others. Developing this skill through a variety of strategies is integral to successful development across other domains. By **modeling** such skills as empathy and active listening, the teacher can influence students' abilities to identify and properly respond to their own and other's emotions. Teaching **coping strategies**, including journaling, breathing, or counting techniques, promotes students' self-regulation to manage emotions when faced with a conflict or challenge. Teaching emotional intelligence can also be integrated throughout instruction, such as prompting students to describe the feelings of a character in a book, or discuss emotions evoked from a painting. Students with strong emotional intelligence are likely to develop positive interpersonal relationships for healthy social development. This contributes to improved cognitive development in that when students collaborate productively, they build upon one another's knowledge. Emotionally intelligent students are also likely to have positive attitudes

50

toward learning, as they have the capacity to self-regulate when faced with obstacles and properly engage in instruction for enhanced cognitive development.

MEETING AND RESPECTING STUDENTS' EMOTIONAL NEEDS, INDIVIDUAL RIGHTS, AND DIGNITY

Successful learning and **whole-child** development are reliant on the degree to which students' emotional needs, individual rights, and dignity are met and respected in the classroom. This establishes the tone of the overall classroom climate that determines students' sense of safety, nurturing, and inclusion when interacting with others and engaging in learning. By taking measures to prioritize students' emotional needs and create a respectful, accepting classroom community, the teacher establishes a positive learning atmosphere that promotes cognitive, social, and emotional growth for whole-child development. When students feel emotionally supported and respected in their identities, they develop a healthy sense of self-esteem that positively influences their attitude toward learning and motivation to participate. This ultimately impacts **cognitive development**, as students that actively and confidently engage in learning are more likely to be academically successful. These students are also more effectively able to develop important interpersonal communication skills necessary for healthy **social development**, as students that feel secure and accepted are more likely to be supportive of others. By meeting students' emotional needs and respecting their individual rights and dignities, the teacher effectively prepares students with the skills necessary for academic and real-world success.

Behavior in Early Childhood

PRINCIPLES RELATED TO EARLY CHILDHOOD BEHAVIOR MANAGEMENT

Repetition and consistency are two major elements for managing young children's behavior. Adults must always follow and enforce whichever rules they designate. They must also remember that they will need to repeat their rules over and over to make them effective. Behaviorism has shown it is more powerful to reward good behaviors than punish bad behaviors. Consistently rewarding desired behaviors enables young children to make the association between behavior and reward. Functional behavior analysis can inform adults: knowing the function of a behavior is necessary to changing it. For example, if a toddler throws a tantrum out of frustration, providing support/scaffolding for a difficult task, breaking it down to more manageable increments via task analysis, and giving encouragement would be appropriate strategies. If the tantrum was a bid for attention, adults would only reinforce/strengthen tantrum recurrence by paying attention. Feeling valued and loved within a positive relationship greatly supports young children's compliance with rules. The **"10:1 Rule"** prescribes at least 10 positive comments per 1 negative comment/correction.

AGGRESSION

Preschoolers typically demonstrate some aggressive behavior, which tends to peak around age 4. **Instrumental aggression** is one basic type: younger preschoolers frequently shout, hit, or kick others to get concrete objects they want. Middle preschoolers are more likely to exhibit **hostile aggression**, including getting even for wrongs or injuries they feel others have done to them. Hostile aggression occurs in two subtypes: overt and relational. **Overt aggression** involves physically harming others or threatening to do so, while **relational aggression** involves emotional/social harm, such as rejecting or excluding another from a group of friends or spreading malicious rumors about another. Young boys are more likely to engage in **overt aggression**, while young girls are more likely to engage in relational aggression. These gender preferences in aggressive behaviors tend to remain the same at all ages if aggression exists. While most young children eventually phase out aggression as they learn other ways of resolving social conflicts, some persist in verbally and/or physically aggressive behavior, causing problems.

MINIMIZING AGGRESSIVE BEHAVIOR

While it is normal for preschoolers to exhibit some physical and verbal aggression until they have learned more mature ways of expressing feelings, getting what they want, and settling disputes, there are things adults can do to influence them such that aggressive behavior does not develop into a predominant method of social interaction. Adults set examples for children, and children learn by observing and imitating those examples. Therefore, parents, caregivers, and teachers should not model verbally and/or physically aggressive behaviors such as calling others names, yelling at others, or punishing others' undesirable behaviors using physical force. Not only should adults avoid disciplining children physically, but they should also avoid physically and/or verbally violent interactions with other adults. Social learning theorist Albert Bandura proved that children who viewed violent videos imitated what they observed and engaged in more aggressive behavior, so adults should also prevent young children's exposure to violent TV programming and video games.

MANAGING THE NORMAL BEHAVIOR OF YOUNG CHILDREN

Before reacting to young children's behaviors, adults should make sure children understand the situation. They should state rules simply and clearly, repeat them frequently for a long time for young children to remember and follow them, and state and enforce rules very consistently to avoid confusion. Adults should tell children clearly what they expect of them. They should never assume they need do nothing when children follow rules; they should consistently give rewards for compliance. Adults should also explain to young children why they are or are not receiving rewards by citing the rule they did or did not follow. Adults can arrange the environment to promote success. For example, if a child throws things that break windows, adults can remove such objects and substitute softer/more lightweight items. Organization is also important. Adults should begin with a simple, easy-to-implement plan and adhere to it. They should record children's progress; analyzing the records shows what does and does not work and why, enabling new/revised plans.

> **Review Video: Promoting Appropriate Behavior**
> Visit mometrix.com/academy and enter code: 321015

GENETIC AND ENVIRONMENTAL INFLUENCES ON BEHAVIOR

Research into factors influencing early childhood behavior identifies both genetic variables and environmental ones, like corporal punishment, affecting young children's propensities toward antisocial behavior. Children experiencing more corporal punishment and children who are at greater genetic risk display greater behavior problems. However, boys at higher genetic risk for behavior problems who also experience more corporal punishment exhibit the most antisocial behavior. Therefore, both genetic risk factors and corporal punishment significantly predict preschoolers' antisocial behavior. Additionally, the nature-nurture interaction of genetic risk factors and environmental punishment is statistically significant for young boys but not young girls. Such evidence shows that environmental learning is not wholly responsible for antisocial behavior: genetic variables predispose some young children to antisocial behaviors more than others.

Behavior Management Theory

MANAGING AND MONITORING STUDENT BEHAVIOR

BEHAVIORISM AND CONDITIONING

The theoretical school of **behaviorism** was established by John B. Watson and further developed by Ivan Pavlov and B.F. Skinner. Behaviorism emphasizes the role of environmental and experiential learning in the behavior of animals and humans. Simply put, if a person experiences a desirable result from a particular behavior, that person is more likely to perform the behavior in pursuit of the result. Likewise, undesirable results cause a person to avoid performing an associated behavior. This process of **reinforcing** or rewarding good behaviors and **punishing** unwanted behaviors is known as conditioning. Behaviorists use the terms positive and negative to refer to the mode of conditioning. The term **positive** refers to an added stimulus, such as giving a child a treat as positive reinforcement or giving added homework as positive punishment. **Negative**, on the other hand refers to removing a stimulus, such as taking recess away as a negative punishment, or taking away extra classwork as negative reinforcement for students performing their homework independently. In the classroom, the teacher has the opportunity to help students learn to meet specific behavioral expectations. The tools of behaviorism may be carefully employed in the classrooms through positive and negative punishments and rewards. Classroom rules and expectations should be made clear as soon as possible and reinforced through verbal praise, prizes, or special privileges. Likewise, negative behaviors should be discouraged through verbal warnings, loss of privileges, and communication with the family or administrators when necessary.

CHOICE THEORY

Choice theory, developed by **William Glasser**, states that behavior is chosen, either consciously or unconsciously, to meet the **five basic needs** of survival, love and belonging, power, freedom, and fun. Rather than implement positive and negative reinforcements to drive behavior, the teacher must aim to teach students self-responsibility for their actions. This includes encouraging students to reflect and consider the reasons for their actions and attempt to rectify any misbehavior. This method relies on the notion that if students understand how their desire to meet certain needs impacts their actions, they are more likely to engage in positive behavior. In the classroom, the teacher focuses on meeting students' **five basic needs** to encourage positive behavior by creating a classroom climate that emphasizes **communication, relationship building**, and **self-reflection**. This includes establishing positive relationships with students, holding class discussions, and teaching conflict resolution skills to create a safe, welcoming learning environment. Instructional activities are tailored to individual needs, and students have a great deal of choice in their own learning with the intention of promoting positive behavior by meeting their needs for power and freedom.

ASSERTIVE DISCIPLINE THEORY

The **Assertive Discipline theory** was developed by **Lee** and **Marlene Canter**. This theory states that the teacher is in charge of **instruction, the classroom**, and **students' behavior**. The expectation is that the teacher establishes clear behavioral standards that protect their right to teach and students' right to learn without distraction or disruption. Negative consequences for unwanted behavior are instilled to deter students from deviating from behavioral expectations. This theory argues that if teachers are viewed as firm and consistent, students will have a greater respect for them and ultimately engage in positive behavior. In the classroom, the teacher is in control of **establishing** and **consistently reinforcing** standards for student behavior. This establishes a sense of predictability, as students are clear on what is expected of them as they engage in learning. Students are expected to comply with the teacher's expectations, and a system of **negative consequences** are in place to discourage unwanted behavior. Positive behavior is rewarded to further reinforce desired behavior. The teacher in this classroom believes that creating such an environment enhances students' ability to focus on learning without disruption.

STUDENT-DIRECTED LEARNING THEORY

The **Student-Directed Learning theory**, or the idea of the **Democratic Classroom**, was founded by **Alfie Kohn** and emphasizes the importance of **student choice** and **classroom community** in influencing behavior. This includes having students contribute to the development of behavioral expectations, as this helps students understand their purpose while instilling a sense of ownership and accountability. Instructional activities are tailored to accommodate students' individual interests and natural curiosity while emphasizing cooperation to foster an engaging learning environment that promotes positive behavior. This theory focuses on eliciting students' intrinsic motivation to engage in positive behavior, rather than relying on positive and negative reinforcements. In the classroom, students primarily direct their own learning based upon their **natural curiosity** while the teacher acts as a **facilitator**. Students contribute to the development of behavioral expectations that are instilled to promote respect and focus on learning. **Active engagement, cooperation**, and **collaborative learning** are emphasized over direct instruction. Students may be engaging in differing activities simultaneously as the teacher moves around the classroom to monitor progress and assist as necessary.

SOCIAL LEARNING THEORY AND BEHAVIOR MANAGEMENT

The **Social Learning theory**, developed by **Albert Bandura**, asserts that one's **environment** and the **people** within it heavily influence behavior. As humans are social creatures, they learn a great deal by **observing** and **imitating** one another. This theory is also rooted in the importance of **self-efficacy** in achieving desired behavior, as students must be motivated and confident that they can effectively imitate what they observe. In the classroom, the teacher establishes behavioral expectations and focuses on **modeling** positive behaviors, attitudes, and interactions with the intention of encouraging students to do the same. The teacher recognizes and praises positive behavior from students to elicit the same behavior from others. The teacher also emphasizes a growth mindset in the classroom to promote students' sense of self-efficacy.

BEHAVIOR STANDARDS AND EXPECTATIONS FOR STUDENTS AT DEVELOPMENTAL LEVELS

Behavioral standards that emphasize respect for oneself, others, and property are necessary in creating a safe, positive, and productive learning environment for students of all ages. However, as students at varying developmental levels differ in their capabilities across domains, behavioral expectations must be **realistic**, **applicable**, and reflect an **awareness** of these **differences** while encouraging growth. Young children, for example, are learning to interact with others and function in a group setting. Behavioral expectations must be attuned to this understanding while promoting the development of positive interpersonal skills. Young children also require ample opportunities for active movement and cannot reasonably be expected to sit still for long periods of time. Middle level students are at a unique transitional period in their development and often exhibit characteristics of both young children and adolescents. Behavioral standards for these students must recognize the significant social, emotional, cognitive, and physical changes occurring at this stage by emphasizing self-control, emotional regulation, and positive interactions. As older students prepare for adulthood, they can generally be expected to conduct themselves with a degree of maturity and responsibility in a variety of settings. Appropriate behavioral standards for these students emphasize self-responsibility, respectful interactions, and independently completing necessary tasks.

EFFECTIVE MANAGEMENT OF STUDENT BEHAVIOR
MANAGEMENT PROCEDURES AND SIGNIFICANCE IN POSITIVE, PRODUCTIVE, AND ORGANIZED LEARNING ENVIRONMENT

Promoting **appropriate behavior** and **ethical work habits** while taking specific measures to **manage student behavior** creates a safe, organized, and productive classroom. Such an environment is beneficial for students' motivation, engagement, and ability to focus on learning. This is achieved by communicating and consistently reinforcing **high**, yet **realistic behavioral expectations** for all students. This, when combined with **relationship building** strategies, establishes a positive rapport between the teacher and students that encourages appropriate behavior and ethical work habits. Students are more inclined to adhere to expectations for behavior and work habits when their relationship with the teacher is founded on mutual understanding and respect. In addition, students that feel they are a part of developing academic and behavioral expectations feel a greater sense of **ownership** and responsibility to follow them, and, therefore, it is beneficial to include students in this process. Encouraging students to **self-monitor** their behavior and utilize conflict resolution strategies furthers this sense of accountability, as it prompts students to positively manage their own actions and work habits. Misbehavior must be addressed appropriately and in a timely manner, and consequences must follow a logical sequence, such as a verbal warning, followed by loss of privileges or communication with family.

> **Review Video: <u>Student Behavior Management Approaches</u>**
> Visit mometrix.com/academy and enter code: 843846
>
> **Review Video: <u>Promoting Appropriate Behavior</u>**
> Visit mometrix.com/academy and enter code: 321015

STRATEGIES

Proactively implementing effective behavior management strategies is beneficial to establishing and maintaining a positive, productive learning environment. The **physical environment** should be arranged in such a way that facilitates ease of movement while limiting the amount of free space that could encourage student disruption. Planning for **smooth transitions** from one activity to the next further discourages behavioral disruptions. Desks should be arranged so that students can easily view the teacher, projector, chalkboard, or other information pertinent to learning. Expectations for behavior, procedures, and routines, including consequences, should be predictable, consistent, succinct, and visible at all times. Allowing students to participate in the development of classroom procedures and routines is valuable in providing students with a sense of personal accountability that increases the likelihood that they will follow them. Students also often respond well to incentives for modeling appropriate behavior, such as a **PBIS reward system**, verbal praise, or a positive phone call home. Nonverbal strategies are valuable in subtly managing student behavior throughout instruction, such as hand gestures, proximity, or eye contact. Misbehavior should be addressed discreetly and privately so as to avoid embarrassing the student or encouraging further disruption.

IMPORTANCE OF CONSISTENCY

Standards for behavior must be enforced consistently in order to establish a well-managed classroom in which students can focus on learning. This includes communicating **clear expectations**, holding all students equally accountable with specific **positive and negative consequences**, and **following through** on implementing them. In doing so, the teacher ensures that students are always aware of the behavior expected from them, and what will happen if they do not adhere to the standards. When students are clear regarding behavioral expectations and assured that they will be enforced, they are more inclined to demonstrate appropriate conduct. This creates a predictable, secure environment that promotes student motivation, engagement, and focused productivity in learning. Consistently enforcing behavior standards gives the teacher a sense of credibility among students, and therefore, students are more likely to respect and adhere to these expectations. In addition, holding all students to the same high behavioral standards contributes to a positive classroom climate in which all students feel they are treated fairly.

Diverse Student Populations

UNDERSTANDING STUDENTS' DIVERSE BACKGROUNDS AND NEEDS
SELF-EDUCATION

Educating oneself on students' diverse backgrounds and needs enhances one's overall understanding of their students and creates a culturally sensitive, accepting classroom environment tailored to students' individual needs. There are several avenues through which teachers should educate themselves in an effort to build an accepting and respectful classroom climate. Communication is key for learning about diversities; thus, it is important for teachers to foster and maintain positive communications with students' families to deepen understanding of cultures, beliefs, lifestyles, and needs that exist within their classroom. This could include learning some language of students with different cultural backgrounds, attending family nights at school, or participating in social events within their students' communities to integrate themselves into the culture. Furthermore, teachers can learn more about their students' backgrounds and needs through gaining an understanding of student differences, incorporating these diversities into the curriculum, and encouraging students to participate in learning by sharing aspects of their lives with the class.

TEACHING, LEARNING, AND CLASSROOM CLIMATE BENEFITS

A deep understanding of students' diverse backgrounds and needs provides multiple benefits for teaching, learning, and overall classroom climate. Knowledge of students' diversities allows teachers to understand the individual needs and abilities of their students, and tailor instruction accordingly to maximize student development and achievement. Additionally, it allows teachers to know which authentic materials to incorporate in lessons and instructions to best create an engaging, relevant, and respectful learning experience that fosters student interest in learning and promotes success. Furthermore, by enhancing understanding of students' diverse backgrounds and needs, teachers consequently begin to model an attitude of inclusivity, acceptance, and respect for differences, which is then reflected by students and achieves a positive, welcoming classroom climate that promotes diversity.

Copyright © Mometrix Media. You have been licensed one copy of this document for personal use only. Any other reproduction or redistribution is strictly prohibited. All rights reserved. This content is provided for test preparation purposes only and does not imply an endorsement by Mometrix of any particular political, scientific, or religious point of view.

IMPLICATIONS FOR TEACHING, LEARNING, AND ASSESSMENT IN DIVERSE CLASSROOMS

In any classroom, a teacher will encounter a wide range of variances among individual students that inevitably will influence teaching, learning, and assessment. Diversities in ethnicity, gender, language background, and learning exceptionality will likely exist simultaneously in a single classroom. Educators must be prepared to teach to these diversities while concurrently teaching students the value and importance of diversity. The curriculum and classroom environment must be adjusted to meet individual student needs and create an **inclusive**, **respectful**, and **equitable** environment that welcomes differences and allows for success in learning. This begins with the teacher developing an understanding of the unique diversities that exist within their students and using this knowledge to **differentiate** curriculum, materials, activities, and assessments in such a way that students of all needs, interests, backgrounds, and abilities feel encouraged and included. Furthermore, the teacher must understand how to instill appropriate supports to accommodate the diverse needs of students, as well as how to modify the classroom environment in such a way that is reflective of the diversity of the students.

CONSIDERATIONS FOR TEACHING IN DIVERSE CLASSROOMS

ETHNICALLY-DIVERSE CLASSROOMS

As society becomes increasingly diverse, teachers will certainly encounter classrooms with students of multiple ethnicities. Thus, to create an accepting and respectful classroom environment that allows for success in learning for all students, there are several factors to consider. Teachers must educate themselves on the various ethnicities within their classroom. This includes being mindful of **social norms, values, beliefs, traditions,** and **lifestyles** of different ethnic groups, and learning to communicate with students and families in a respectful, culturally sensitive manner. Additionally, the teacher must make a conscious effort to incorporate aspects of each ethnicity into the curriculum, activities, and classroom environment to create an inclusive atmosphere that teaches the acceptance, respect for, and celebration of differences. Teachers must be **culturally competent** and ensure that all materials are accurate, relevant, authentic, and portray the different ethnicities within the classroom in a respectful, unbiased manner. Furthermore, teachers must consider how their own ethnicity impacts their teaching style and interactions with students, how they may be perceived by other ethnic groups, and how to respond in a manner that fosters respect and inclusivity.

GENDER-DIVERSE CLASSROOMS

When approaching a gender-diverse classroom, teachers need to consider their perceptions, interactions with, and expectations of different genders, as well as how the classroom environment and materials portray gender differences. Teachers must work to eliminate possible stereotypical beliefs so all students feel respected, accepted, and encouraged to participate. Furthermore, teachers must consider how their behavior acts as a model for how students perceive gender roles and should act in a way that eliminates gender divisiveness. Teachers should use gender-neutral language when addressing students and ensure that all students receive equal attention. Teachers must maintain equal academic and behavioral expectations between genders and be sure to equally praise and discipline students so that neither gender feels superior or inferior to another. Regarding curriculum and classroom materials, teachers must ensure that the classroom environment encourages equal participation in, access to, and choice of all activities and procedures. Activities and materials should provide equal opportunities and foster collaboration between genders. Furthermore, teachers must ensure that curriculum materials avoid gender stereotypes, and highlight each gender equally in order to create an accepting and respectful learning environment that provides equal opportunities for students of all genders to develop their individual identities and abilities.

LINGUISTICALLY DIVERSE CLASSROOMS

In a **linguistically diverse** classroom, teachers must consider how to effectively demonstrate value for students' native languages while simultaneously supporting the development of necessary language skills to thrive in the school setting. By accepting and encouraging students to use their native languages, teachers can establish an inclusive learning environment that celebrates linguistic differences, and therefore, encourages students to want to build upon their language skills. Through this, teachers create an equitable learning environment that allows for academic success. To develop English language skills, the teacher must first consider each students' language ability and level of exposure to English prior to entering the classroom, as well as the level of language learning support each student has at home. Teachers can then implement effective instructional strategies and supports to modify curriculum in a way that addresses students' language needs. Teachers must also consider the implications of the classroom environment on language acquisition. By creating an atmosphere that encourages language acquisition through **literacy-rich resources** and **cooperative learning**, teachers promote the use of language skills and ultimately provide opportunities for success for all students.

LINGUISTIC SUPPORTS AND INSTRUCTIONAL STRATEGIES PROMOTING ENGLISH LANGUAGE PROFICIENCY

Incorporating a variety of linguistic aids and instructional strategies is beneficial in supporting ELL students of varying levels of English language proficiency. **Visual representations** to accompany instruction, such as posters, charts, pictures, slide shows, videos, tables, or anchor charts, are valuable in providing clarification and reference while promoting vocabulary acquisition. When delivering instruction, **body language** such as hand gestures, eye contact, and movement to mimic verbal directions and explanations can provide clarification to enhance understanding. These students may also require **translation devices** for clarification, an interpreter to help with understanding instructions and new concepts, alternate assignments with simplified language, or **individualized instruction** from an ESL teacher. Frequently checking for understanding and providing clarification as necessary throughout instruction are necessary to ensuring ELL students understand learning materials, instructions, and assessments. In addition, creating a print and literacy-rich environment by including word walls for new vocabulary, reading materials that vary in complexity, labels, and opportunities for speaking, reading, and writing within instruction are valuable in promoting English language acquisition.

LEARNING DISABILITIES AND OTHER EXCEPTIONALITIES

In a classroom where learning disabilities and exceptionalities are present, teachers must consider accommodations for students of various learning needs while fostering an atmosphere of respect and acceptance. Teachers must understand the individual learning needs of each student and differentiate instruction accordingly to create an equitable and inclusive learning atmosphere. For **learning disabled** students, teachers must consider accommodations that allow for inclusion in all areas of curriculum and instruction. Such considerations may include extended work time, individualized instruction, and cooperative learning activities to ensure that learning disabled students are provided the necessary supports to achieve academic success. For students with other exceptionalities, such as **gifted and talented** students, teachers need to consider ways to provide challenging and stimulating opportunities for expansion and enrichment of curriculum. Furthermore, the teacher must be aware of their own interactions with students in order to demonstrate and encourage respect and acceptance among students. By providing supports for individual student success, teachers can effectively highlight students' strengths and therefore, teach students to accept and celebrate differences in learning abilities.

Educating Students about Diversity

GOALS OF TEACHING DIVERSITY IN THE CLASSROOM

Teaching diversity in the classroom aims to establish a welcoming and inclusive classroom environment that encourages academic achievement and whole-child development. Diversity education works to develop students' understanding, acceptance, and respect for others' perspectives while instilling the concept that people are ultimately more alike than different, and that diversities should be celebrated. Teaching the importance of differences creates a positive, inclusive classroom atmosphere in which all students feel respected, safe, and valued by their teacher and peers. Such an environment promotes academic achievement among students in that it encourages participation in learning and builds the self-esteem necessary for positive growth and development. Furthermore, teaching diversity has a significant role in **whole-child development** in that it instills the ability to understand and respect multiple frames of reference, thus increasing their ability to problem solve, cooperate with others, and develop a broader global perspective. Additionally, it allows for the development of cultural competency and ultimately creates accepting and respectful contributors to society.

> **Review Video: <u>Multiculturalism/Celebrating All Cultures</u>**
> Visit mometrix.com/academy and enter code: 708545

RECOGNIZING AND ELIMINATING PERSONAL BIASES

Personal biases are often subtle and unconscious, yet it is essential that teachers work to recognize and eliminate them to create an accepting and respectful classroom environment. Personal biases may negatively impact teaching style, interactions with students, and ultimately, student learning and self-esteem. In eliminating personal bias, teachers ensure that they establish an inclusive classroom environment where each student is treated fairly. Furthermore, students' beliefs toward diversity are influenced by the attitudes and behaviors modeled by their teacher, and therefore, eradicating personal bias is vital in positively influencing students to accept and respect differences. To eliminate personal bias, teachers must **reflect** on their own culture's attitudes toward diversity, as well as how these attitudes influence their interactions toward other groups, and work to make positive changes. Teachers must **educate** themselves on the diversities among their students and work to deepen their understanding of different groups through **communicating** with families, **integrating** themselves into students' communities, and participating in **professional development** that focuses on **cultural competency** and the importance of teaching diversity. Through making positive changes against personal biases, teachers foster a classroom environment that promotes diversity and empowers all students to be successful.

IMPACT OF DIVERSE CULTURAL CLIMATE IN THE CLASSROOM

Creating a diverse cultural climate in the classroom results in an empowering and engaging learning environment that facilitates academic success. An atmosphere that respects and accepts differences fosters a sense of inclusivity and welcoming among teachers and students, which allows students to feel comfortable with differences, safe in their own identities, and consequently, comfortable to engage in learning. This fosters a positive attitude toward learning that promotes academic achievement. Additionally, when students accept one another's differences in a diverse cultural climate, they are better able to work together and adopt creative problem-solving solutions through others' perspectives, which results in success in learning. Furthermore, a successfully diverse cultural climate reflects the diversity of the students within it, which ultimately creates a more engaging and relevant academic environment that sparks motivation and curiosity toward learning. Learning environments that reflect students' diversity create a sense of unity and belonging in the classroom and positively contribute to success in learning through building students' self-esteem and self-concept to empower them in believing they can achieve academic success.

AUTHENTIC CLASSROOM MATERIALS

Authentic classroom materials are artifacts from various cultures, events, or periods of time. These items enhance the relevancy of instruction by promoting students' real-world connection to learning and may also be used to incorporate students' backgrounds and experiences into the classroom to increase engagement. Such materials include magazines, newspapers, advertisements, restaurant menus, and recipes. In addition, resources such as video clips, films, television shows, documentaries, news segments, and music serve as authentic media sources to incorporate into instruction. Original works or documents, including art pieces, literature, poetry, maps, or historical records, are also valuable authentic resources for providing students with a real-world learning experience.

LOCATING AND IMPLEMENTING

Authentic classroom materials and resources are integral in creating a classroom environment that fosters engaging, relevant, and positive learning experiences. Teachers must work to develop an understanding of the diversities among their students and use this knowledge to locate and implement authentic classroom

58

materials into daily instruction. In doing so, teachers create a positive learning environment that accepts and respects differences through incorporating **relevant** and **familiar** materials that make students from all backgrounds feel valued and included in instruction. When students can see aspects of their culture reflected in authentic learning materials, they can make **personal connections** between what they are learning and their own lives, and learning becomes more valuable, engaging, and relevant, thereby promoting success in learning.

INCORPORATING DIVERSITY EDUCATION INTO THE CLASSROOM

Incorporating diversity into the classroom maximizes student opportunities for academic success through creating a welcoming, empowering, and inclusive atmosphere. Teachers can implement multiple strategies to incorporate **diversity education** into the curriculum both as its own unit and woven into content instruction once they develop an understanding of the diversities among their own students. Through **building relationships** with students, teachers can use their knowledge of students' lives to incorporate aspects of their backgrounds into the curriculum by creating specific **cultural lessons** on food, music, language, art, and history. Additionally, **cultural comparison** studies are an effective method of teaching students the value of diversity, as well as highlighting the fact that people from different backgrounds often have more similarities than differences. Teachers can further implement diversity education by encouraging students to participate in learning through having them share elements of their culture and background with the class through activities such as show and tell or hosting family nights. Furthermore, integrating **cooperative learning** activities into instruction allow and encourage students from different backgrounds to work together and gain an understanding of the perspectives and backgrounds of others.

INCORPORATING DIVERSITY IN THE CURRICULUM

Incorporating diversity into the curriculum is vital for teaching the value and importance of differences and for contributing to a respectful and accepting environment. Additionally, it is imperative that diversity education extend from the curriculum to the entire classroom environment to maximize student growth and opportunity to reach potential. When students learn in an atmosphere that celebrates diversity and identifies strengths in differences, they feel a sense of belonging and confidence that encourages them to engage in learning, thus maximizing the potential for academic success. Teachers can effectively integrate diversity into the classroom environment through making authentic cultural materials such as texts, music, and art readily accessible for students. Additionally, providing several opportunities for students to collaborate and socialize in a natural setting allows them to gain an understanding and respect for their peers' backgrounds. By encouraging students to share aspects of their own lives and backgrounds with the class through cultural activities, teachers facilitate a diverse climate that celebrates differences.

CULTURALLY RESPONSIVE TEACHING

Culturally responsive teaching is an instructional approach in which the teacher practices awareness, inclusivity, and sensitivity regarding the social and cultural diversities that are present within the classroom. With this awareness in mind, the culturally responsive teacher designs curriculum, instruction, activities, and assessments that are inclusive and reflective of students' social and cultural backgrounds and experiences. When planning instruction and learning experiences, the teacher can demonstrate awareness of social and cultural norms through consciously educating themselves on the beliefs, values, and norms of their students. This is achieved through connecting with students and building positive relationships to learn about their individual backgrounds and locate authentic learning materials that are reflective of their experiences. Through communicating with students' parents, family members, and members of the community, the teacher can practice and build awareness of the diverse social and cultural norms of their students to gain an understanding of how to design culturally responsive instruction. By educating themselves on the social and cultural norms of their students, the teacher can effectively ensure that students' diversities are reflected in all areas of instruction in a culturally sensitive manner to create an empowering learning environment that engages all students.

	Practices for Culturally Responsive Teaching
1	Create an inclusive classroom environment
2	Recognize personal biases and work to eliminate them
3	Self-educate on the community and students' social and cultural backgrounds
4	Use curriculum that reflects students' diversities using authentic materials
5	Frequently communicate with students' families
6	Build positive interpersonal relationships with students
7	Be involved in the community

Supporting Students with Varied Learning Needs

PLANNING AND ADAPTING LESSONS TO ADDRESS STUDENTS' NEEDS

VARIED BACKGROUNDS

Effectively planning lessons and adapting instruction to address students' varied backgrounds requires teachers to gain an understanding of individual students, and educate themselves on **customs, norms**, and **values** of the cultures in their classroom. This allows teachers to effectively plan **culturally responsive** lessons with **authentic materials** to make learning valuable, interesting, relevant, and allow students to feel included. Understanding students' backgrounds means teachers recognize variances in their knowledge and experiences on different topics and can effectively plan engaging and inclusive lessons that build upon it. Teachers must assess students' knowledge on material prior to creating lessons to effectively plan instruction that adapts to the needs of students' varied backgrounds and reflects students' experiences. Teachers must plan lesson materials such as texts, art, music, and language that accurately and sensitively reflect students' diverse backgrounds. Cooperative learning strategies should be incorporated to facilitate communication among students with varying backgrounds, as it helps them build knowledge from others' experiences, as well as teaches them to respect and value differences among their peers. Teachers must plan instruction that communicates high academic expectations for all students and adapt instruction as necessary by implementing supports to create equity and address the needs of varying backgrounds.

> **Review Video: Adapting and Modifying Lessons or Activities**
> Visit mometrix.com/academy and enter code: 834946

DIFFERENCES IN INDIVIDUAL STUDENTS' SKILLS

Teachers must use their knowledge of differences in students' skills to plan multifaceted, adaptable lessons that highlight students' strengths while providing instructional supports where needed based on individual skill level. To effectively plan, teachers must incorporate multiple strategies and mediums for instruction, activities, and assessments to allow students of all skill levels equitable and enriching access to content material. This includes allowing multiple opportunities for **student choice** in learning and demonstration of understanding through such strategies as choice boards, learning centers, project menus, and digital resources that allow students to approach content in multiple ways. In doing so, teachers effectively plan instruction that allows students to grasp new material and demonstrate learning in a way that best suits their skill level. Additionally, teachers must plan to incorporate **scaffolds** into their lessons and plan to adapt instruction as needed through continuous **formative assessments** to provide additional support for students of lower skill levels, while adding opportunities for enrichment and acceleration for gifted students. Supports can also be effectively planned into lessons through providing several opportunities for small-group activities in which students of various skill levels can work together, provide peer tutoring, and build upon one another's knowledge.

DIFFERENCES IN STUDENTS' INDIVIDUAL INTERESTS

In order to plan engaging instruction that fosters success in learning, teachers must plan lessons and adapt instruction to address differences in students' individual interests. To accomplish this, teachers first need to work to build relationships with students and develop an understanding of their unique interests to effectively tailor instruction that taps into these interests. Through **differentiated instruction** and the incorporation of **student-choice** opportunities for learning and assessment, teachers can effectively plan **student-centered** lessons that teach content in multiple ways that appeal to varying interests. Additionally, interest centers in the classroom foster engagement in learning, are easily adaptable, and can be planned into daily instruction. By frequently conducting **formative assessments**, teachers can gauge student interest in activities and adjust as necessary. This ultimately promotes self-direction, motivation, and curiosity in learning through providing students the opportunity to build content knowledge based on their individual interests.

DIFFERENCES IN STUDENTS' INDIVIDUAL LEARNING NEEDS

Differences in backgrounds, abilities, skills, and interests results in a wide spectrum of student learning needs that must be addressed when planning effective and adaptable instruction. Teachers must recognize the individual learning needs of students to plan lessons that are accommodating, equitable, and promote success in learning. Through **student-centered** and **differentiated** instruction, teachers can effectively provide multiple avenues for content instruction, learning, and assessment based on individual need. Planning for **student-choice** and **self-directed learning** allows teachers to successfully address all learning styles and needs. Additionally, teachers must incorporate scaffolds into their lessons to adapt instruction. This can be done through incorporating such supports as graphic organizers, outlines, charts, and visuals, as well as planning for small, mixed-ability group instruction based on learning needs to provide scaffolding. Teachers should plan to check frequently for understanding during instruction in order to adapt activities and adjust instruction to meet individual learning needs.

ELL STUDENTS

English language learners (ELLs) need support in both understanding content material and building their English proficiency levels. To effectively plan and adapt instruction to accommodate them and facilitate success in learning, it is important that teachers demonstrate respect for the student's native language while encouraging the acquisition of English language skills. Teachers should plan for some content instruction to be in the student's native language to begin to build knowledge. To effectively assist ELLs in building vocabulary on specific content areas, lessons should be planned around **themed units**. Additionally, planning multiple cooperative learning and peer-tutoring activities allows ELLs to practice and develop their English skills in a natural setting, as well provides support for understanding new instructional concepts. Teachers must plan to scaffold content material, texts, and writing assignments to align with students' proficiency levels through adding such supports as graphic organizers, labels, and charts. Incorporating **linguistic aids** such as verbal cues, gestures, pictures, and digital resources allow teachers to effectively adapt instruction as necessary to support understanding and develop English language skills.

STUDENTS WITH DISABILITIES

Students with disabilities may require **instructional or physical supports** in order to have an equitable learning experience that facilitates their academic success. Teachers must be cognizant of any student disabilities and work to effectively plan instruction in a subtle, sensitive, and inclusive manner. Students with learning disabilities may require the planning of supports such as preferential seating, extra time for work and assessments, graphic organizers, and shorter or chunked assignments. These students may need to be paired with others that can provide scaffolding and peer-tutoring or may require individualized instruction or small focused groups. Students with physical disabilities may require such supports as a modified classroom environment to address their physical needs, audiovisual supplements, enlarged font, or braille texts. Teachers

61

must work to incorporate these supports into their lesson planning to ensure that all students are included and empowered to learn, while allowing for flexibility in their lesson plans to allow for necessary adaptations.

CULTURAL AND SOCIOECONOMIC DIFFERENCES

ADDRESSING DIFFERENCES IN AN INCLUSIVE AND EQUITABLE CLASSROOM ENVIRONMENT

In a **culturally responsive** classroom, the teacher recognizes and is sensitive to the importance of planning instruction that addresses cultural and socioeconomic differences among students for creating an **inclusive** and **equitable** learning environment. The teacher responds to differences in norms, values, interests, and lifestyles through designing relevant instruction that builds on students' experiences and facilitates personal connections that foster engagement in learning. This is important in conveying to students the value of their diverse experiences and highlighting their strengths in a manner that empowers them to achieve academic success while providing support where needed. It is important that the teacher incorporate supports in instructional planning to address academic, social, behavioral, and emotional needs of students from different cultural and socioeconomic backgrounds to provide all students an equitable opportunity for success in learning while maintaining high academic expectations.

POSSIBLE IMPACTS ON ACADEMIC ACHIEVEMENT

If not properly addressed, cultural and socioeconomic differences among students pose potentially negative impacts on academic achievement. It is vital that teachers recognize and accommodate these differences to instill the proper supports for engagement and success in learning. Students from different cultural or socioeconomic backgrounds may feel excluded from curriculum and instruction, which may result in lowered self-concept, self-esteem, and ultimately, disengagement toward learning. Thus, teachers must practice **culturally responsive teaching** to create instruction in which all students feel valued and included. These students may lack the support or resources for education at home due to various cultural and social challenges, and students from low socioeconomic backgrounds may face health, behavioral, or emotional challenges that impact their development and ability to learn. It is important that the teacher recognize these challenges and subtly address them in the classroom to establish an inclusive, equitable, and empowering environment that fosters engagement in learning. Some strategies for addressing these differences include providing community classroom materials, extra time for tutoring and assistance outside of classroom hours, individualized instruction, or opportunities to use the internet at school for students who lack access at home.

SIGNIFICANCE OF VARIED STUDENT LEARNING NEEDS AND PREFERENCES

IMPLICATIONS ON INSTRUCTION

Variances in students' learning needs and preferences implies that instruction must be **differentiated**, flexible, and allow for adaptations as necessary to accommodate students' individual needs, abilities, and interests. Furthermore, it means that teachers must work to build relationships with their students to develop an understanding of their different needs and preferences. This allows teachers to design instruction that emphasizes individual strengths while challenging students academically based on their abilities and providing instructional supports where necessary to ensure student success. To accomplish this, teachers must plan and deliver instructional material in multiple ways to address differences in learning needs and preferences, as well as allow for student choice in learning, processing, and demonstrating understanding of content.

POSSIBLE VARIANCES THAT MAY BE ENCOUNTERED

Teachers will inevitably encounter an array of learning needs and preferences among their students. As students have varying **learning styles**, including but not limited to visual, auditory, or kinesthetic, their methods for acquiring, processing, and retaining information will differ, as well as their **preferred modalities** for doing so. Some students may prefer written assignments in which they work independently, while others may prefer activities that involve active movement within a group. Similarly, some students require more individualized attention, while others may function better in a small group or whole-class setting. Students will also come to the classroom with differing **academic abilities**, and therefore, will require varying levels of assistance, support, and guidance to facilitate their success in learning. In addition, students may have specific learning, physical, social, or emotional **disabilities**, and as such, will need varying degrees of supports and accommodations to support their ability to learn effectively.

IMPORTANCE OF TAILORING CURRICULUM, INSTRUCTION, AND ASSESSMENTS

Through tailoring curriculum, instruction, and assessments according to student learning needs and preferences, teachers create a **student-centered** learning environment. This motivates and empowers students to take ownership of their learning and allows every student an equal opportunity to achieve academic success. By creating a flexible curriculum and presenting instruction through multiple methods, teachers ensure that the learning needs and preferences of all students are met by facilitating a dynamic and engaging learning environment in which students can learn in the way that best suits their needs. Furthermore, in adapting assessments based upon students' learning needs and preferences by allowing **student choice**, teachers maximize student understanding of content material, allowing them to demonstrate learning according to their interests and abilities.

Types of Disabilities and Exceptionalities and their Implications

CAUSES OF INTELLECTUAL DISABILITIES IN BABIES AND YOUNG CHILDREN
INFECTIONS

Congenital cytomegalovirus (CMV) is passed to fetuses from mothers, who may be asymptomatic. About 90% of newborns are also asymptomatic; 5–10% of these have later problems. Of the 10% born with symptoms, 90% will have later neurological abnormalities, including intellectual disabilities. **Congenital rubella**, or German measles, is also passed to fetuses from unvaccinated and exposed mothers, causing neurological damage, including blindness or other eye disorders, deafness, heart defects, and intellectual disabilities. **Congenital toxoplasmosis** is passed to fetuses by infected mothers, who can be asymptomatic, with a parasite from raw or undercooked meat that causes intellectual disabilities, vision or hearing loss, and other conditions. Encephalitis is brain inflammation caused by infection, most often viral. **Meningitis** is inflammation of the meninges, or membranes, covering the brain and is caused by viral or bacterial infection; the bacterial form is more serious. Both encephalitis and meningitis can cause intellectual disabilities. Maternal **human immunodeficiency virus** (HIV) and **acquired immunodeficiency syndrome** (AIDS) can be passed to fetuses, destroying immunity to infections, which can cause intellectual disabilities. **Maternal listeriosis**, a bacterial infection from contaminated food, animals, soil, or water, can cause meningitis and intellectual disabilities in surviving fetuses and infants.

ENVIRONMENTAL, NUTRITIONAL, AND METABOLIC INFLUENCES

Environmental deprivation syndrome results when developing children are deprived of necessary environmental elements—physical, including adequate nourishment (malnutrition); climate or temperature control (extremes of heat or cold); hygiene, like changing and bathing; and so on. It also includes lack of adequate cognitive stimulation, which can stunt a child's intellectual development, and neglect in general. Malnutrition results from starvation; vitamin, mineral, or nutrient deficiency; deficiencies in digesting or absorbing foods; and some other medical conditions. **Environmental radiation**, depending on dosage and time of exposure, can cause intellectual disabilities. **Congenital hypothyroidism** (underactive thyroid) can cause intellectual disabilities, as can hypoglycemia (low blood sugar) from inadequately controlled diabetes or occurring independently and infant **hyperbilirubinemia**. Bilirubin, a waste product of old red blood cells, is found in bile made by the liver and is normally removed by the liver; excessive bilirubin buildup in babies can cause intellectual disabilities. **Reye's syndrome**, caused by aspirin given to children with flu or chicken pox, or following these viruses or other upper respiratory infections, or from unknown causes, produces sudden liver and brain damage and can result in intellectual disabilities.

GENETIC ABNORMALITIES AND SYNDROMES AFFECTING THE NERVOUS SYSTEM

Rett syndrome is a nervous system disorder causing developmental regression, particularly severe in expressive language and hand function. It is associated with a defective protein gene on an X chromosome. Having two X chromosomes, females with the defect on one of them can survive; with only one X chromosome, males are either miscarried, stillborn, or die early in infancy. Rett syndrome produces many symptoms, including intellectual disabilities.**Tay-Sachs disease**, an autosomal recessive disorder, is a nervous system disease caused by a defective gene on chromosome 15, resulting in a missing protein for breaking down gangliosides, chemicals in nerve tissues that build up in cells, particularly brain neurons, causing damage. Tay-Sachs is more prevalent in Ashkenazi Jews. The adult form is rare; the infantile form is commonest, with nerve damage starting in utero. Many symptoms, including intellectual disabilities, appear at 3 to 6 months, and death occurs by 4 to 5 years. Tuberous sclerosis, caused by genetic mutations, produces tumors damaging the kidneys, heart, skin, brain, and central nervous system. Symptoms include intellectual disabilities, seizures, and developmental delays.

GENETIC OR INHERITED METABOLIC DISORDERS

- **Adrenoleukodystrophy** is an X-linked genetic trait. Some female carriers have mild forms, but it affects more males more seriously. It impairs metabolism of very long-chain fatty acids, which build up in the nervous system (as well as adrenal glands and male testes). The childhood cerebral form, manifesting at ages 4 to 8, causes seizures, visual and hearing impairments, receptive aphasia, dysgraphia, dysphagia, intellectual disabilities, and other effects.
- **Galactosemia** is an inability to process galactose, a simple sugar in lactose, or milk sugar. By-product buildup damages the liver, kidneys, eyes, and brain.
- **Hunter syndrome, Hurler syndrome, and Sanfilippo syndrome** each cause the lack of different enzymes; all cause an inability to process mucopolysaccharides or glycosaminoglycans (long sugar-molecule chains). Hurler and Sanfilippo (but not Hunter) syndromes are autosomal recessive traits, meaning both parents must pass on the defect. All cause progressive intellectual disabilities.
- **Lesch Nyhan syndrome**, affecting males, is a metabolic deficiency in processing purines. It causes hemiplegia, varying degrees of intellectual disabilities, and self-injurious behaviors.
- **Phenylketonuria** (PKU), an autosomal recessive trait, causes lack of the enzyme to process dietary phenylalanine, resulting in intellectual disabilities.

PRESCRIPTION DRUGS, SUBSTANCES OF ABUSE, SOCIAL DRUGS, AND DISEASES

- **Warfarin**, a prescription anticoagulant drug to thin the blood and prevent excessive clotting, can cause microcephaly (undersized head) and intellectual disabilities in an infant when the mother has taken it during pregnancy.
- **Trimethadione**, the prescription antiseizure drug, can cause developmental delays in babies when it has been taken by pregnant mothers.
- **Maternal abuse of solvent chemicals** during pregnancy can also cause microcephaly and intellectual disabilities.
- **Maternal crack cocaine abuse** during pregnancy can cause severe and profound intellectual disabilities and many other developmental defects in fetuses, which become evident when they are newborns.
- **Maternal alcohol abuse** can cause fetal alcohol syndrome, which often includes intellectual disabilities, among many other symptoms.
- **Maternal rubella** (German measles) virus can cause intellectual disabilities as well as visual and hearing impairments and heart defects.
- **Maternal herpes simplex virus** can cause microcephaly, intellectual disabilities, and microphthalmia (small or no eyes).
- **The varicella** (chicken pox) **virus** in pregnant mothers can also cause intellectual disabilities as well as muscle atrophy in babies.

Characteristics of Infants and Young Children with Intellectual Disabilities

Newborns with intellectual disabilities, especially of greater severity, may not demonstrate normal reflexes, such as rooting and sucking reflexes, necessary for nursing. They may not show other temporary infant reflexes such as the Moro, Babinski, swimming, stepping, or labyrinthine reflexes, or they may demonstrate weaker versions of some of these. In some babies, these reflexes will exist but persist past the age when they normally disappear. Babies with intellectual disabilities are likely to display developmental milestones at later-than-typical ages. The ages when they do display milestones vary according to the severity of the disability and by individual. Young children with intellectual disabilities are likely to walk, self-feed, and speak later than normally developing children. Those who learn to read and write do so at later ages. Children with mild intellectual disabilities may lack curiosity and have quiet demeanors; those with profound intellectual disabilities are likely to remain infantile in abilities and behaviors throughout life. Intellectually disabled children will score below normal on standardized IQ tests and adaptive behavior rating scales.

Potential Variables Causing Learning Disabilities

LDs are basically neurological disorders. Though they are more specific to particular areas of learning than global disorders like intellectual disabilities, scientific research has found correlations between LDs and many of the same factors that cause intellectual disabilities, including prenatal influences like excessive alcohol or other drug consumption, diseases, and so on. Once babies are born, glandular disorders, brain injuries, exposure to secondhand smoke or other toxins, infections of the central nervous system, physical trauma, or malnutrition can cause neurological damage resulting in LDs. Hypoxia and anoxia (oxygen loss) before, during, or after birth is a cause, as are radiation and chemotherapy. These same influences often cause behavioral disorders as well as LDs. Another factor is genetic: Both LDs and behavior disorders have been observed to run in families. While research has not yet identified specific genetic factors, heritability does appear to be a component in influencing learning and behavioral disorders.

Types of Neurological Damage Found in Children with LDs and ADHD

Various neurological research studies have revealed that children diagnosed with LDs and ADHD have at least one of several kinds of structural damage to their brains. Scientists have found smaller numbers of cells in certain important regions of the brains of some children with learning and behavioral disorders. Some of these children are found to have brain cells of smaller than normal size. In some cases, dysplasia is discovered; that is, some brain cells migrate into the wrong area of the brain. In some children with learning and behavioral disorders, blood flow is found to be lower than normal to certain regions in the brain. Also, the brain cells of some children with learning and behavioral disabilities show lower levels of glucose metabolism; glucose (blood sugar) is the brain's main source of fuel, so inadequate utilization of glucose can affect the brain's ability to perform some functions related to cognitive processing, as in LDs, and to attention and impulse control, as in ADHD.

Behavioral Variations and Characteristics of ADHD

While the chief symptoms associated with ADHD are inattentiveness, impulsive behavior, distractibility, and excessive physical activity, there is considerable variation among individual children having ADHD. For example, the degree of severity of this condition can vary widely from one child to the next. In addition, each child can vary in how much he or she exhibits each of these primary characteristics. Some children might not appear to behave very impulsively but show severe deficits in attention. Some may focus better, but only for short periods, and are very easily distracted. Some display very disruptive behavior, while others do not but may daydream excessively, not attending to programming. In general, children who have ADHD can show deficits in following rules and directions. Also, when their developmental skills are evaluated or observed, they are likely to demonstrate inconsistencies in performance over time. To identify or select specific intervention methods and strategies, professionals should use a comprehensive evaluation to obtain information about the child's specific behaviors in his or her natural environment that need remediation.

65

TYPES AND CHARACTERISTICS OF LEARNING DISABILITIES

Dyslexia is the most common subcategory of specific learning disability that primarily affects reading but can also interfere with writing and speaking. Characteristics include reversing letters and words, for example, confusing *b* and *d* in reading and writing; reading *won* as *now*, confusing similar speech sounds like /p/ and /b/, and perceiving spaces between words in the wrong places when reading. **Dyscalculia** is difficulty doing mathematical calculations; it can also affect using money and telling time. Dysgraphia means difficulties specifically with writing, including omitting words in writing sentences or leaving sentences unfinished, difficulty putting one's thoughts into writing, and poor handwriting. **Central auditory processing disorder** causes difficulty perceiving small differences in words despite normal hearing acuity; for example, *couch* and *chair* may be perceived as *cow* and *hair*. Background noise and information overloads exacerbate the effects. Visual processing disorders affect visual perception despite normal visual acuity, causing difficulty finding information in printed text or from maps, charts, pictures, graphs, and so on; synthesizing information from various sources into one place; and remembering directions to locations.

ATTACHMENT STYLES IDENTIFIED IN TODDLERS BY MARY AINSWORTH

Mary Ainsworth worked with **John Bowlby**, discovering the first empirical evidence supporting his attachment theory. From her "strange situation" experiments, she identified secure, insecure and avoidant, insecure and resistant, and insecure and disorganized attachment styles. Securely attached children show normal separation anxiety when their mother leaves and happiness when she returns, avoid strangers when alone but are friendly when their mother is present, and use their mother as a safe base for environmental exploring. Insecure and resistant children show exaggerated separation anxiety, ambivalence, and resistance to their mother upon reuniting, fear strangers, cry more, and explore less than secure or avoidant babies. Insecure and avoidant children show no separation anxiety or stranger anxiety and little interest on reunions with their mother and are comforted equally by their mother or strangers. Insecure and disorganized types seem dazed and confused, respond inconsistently, and may mix resistant and ambivalent and avoidant behaviors. Secure styles are associated with sensitive, responsive caregiving and children's positive self-images and other images, resistant and ambivalent styles with inconsistent caregiving, and avoidant with unresponsive caregivers. Avoidant, resistant, and disorganized styles, associated with negative self-images and low self-esteem, are most predictive of emotional disturbances.

EMOTIONAL DISTURBANCES IN YOUNG CHILDREN CLASSIFIED AS ANXIETY DISORDERS

Anxiety disorders all share a common characteristic of overwhelming, irrational, and unrealistic fears and include:

- **Generalized anxiety disorder** (GAD) involves excessive worrying about anything or everything and free-floating anxiety.
- **Obsessive-compulsive disorder** (OCD) involves obsessive and preoccupied thoughts and compulsive or irresistible actions, including often bizarre rituals. Germ phobia, constant hand washing, repeatedly checking whether tasks are done or undone, and collecting things excessively are common.
- **Posttraumatic stress disorder** (PTSD) follows traumatic experiences/events. Children have frequent, extreme nightmares, crying, flashbacks wherein they vividly perceive or believe they are experiencing the traumatic event again, insomnia, depression, anxiety, and social withdrawal.
- **Panic Disorder** symptoms include panic attacks involving extreme fear and physical symptoms like a racing heart, cold hands and feet, pallor, hyperventilation, and feeling unable to move
- **Social phobia** includes fear and avoidance of day care, preschool, or other social settings
- **Specific phobias** are associated with specific objects, animals, or persons and are often triggered by traumatic experiences involving these

FACTORS CONTRIBUTING TO EMOTIONAL DISTURBANCES

Researchers have investigated **emotional disturbances** but have not yet established known causes for any. Some disturbances, for example, the major mental illness **schizophrenia**, seem to run in families and hence include a genetic component; childhood schizophrenia exists as a specific diagnosis. Factors contributing to emotional disturbances can be biological or environmental but more often are likely a combination of both. Dysfunctional family dynamics can often contribute to emotional disorders in children. Physical and psychological stressors on children can also contribute to the development of emotional problems. Some people have attributed emotional disturbances to diet, and scientists have also researched this but have not discovered proof of cause and effect. **Bipolar disorder** is often successfully treated with the chemical lithium, which affects sodium flow through nerve cells, so chemical imbalance may be implicated as an etiology. Pediatric bipolar disorder, which has different symptoms than adult bipolar disorder, correlates highly with histories of bipolar and other mood disorders or alcoholism in both parents.

SYMPTOMS OF PEDIATRIC BIPOLAR DISORDER

Bipolar disorder, formerly called manic-depressive disorder, has similar depressive symptoms in children as adults. However, children's mood swings often occur much faster, and children show more symptoms of anger and irritability than other adult manic symptoms. Bipolar children's most common symptoms include:

- Frequent mood swings
- Extreme irritability
- Protracted (up to several hours) tantrums or rages
- Separation anxiety
- Oppositional behavior
- Hyperactivity
- Impulsivity, and distractibility
- Restlessness and fidgetiness
- Silly, giddy, or goofy behavior
- Aggression
- Racing thoughts
- Grandiose beliefs or behaviors
- Risk-taking
- Depressed moods
- Lethargy
- Low self-esteem
- Social anxiety
- Hypersensitivity to environmental or emotional triggers
- Carbohydrate (sugar or starch) cravings
- Trouble getting up in the morning

Other common symptoms include bed-wetting (especially in boys), night terrors, pressured or fast speech, obsessive or compulsive behaviors, motor and vocal tics, excessive daydreaming, poor short-term memory, poor organization, learning disabilities, morbid fascinations, hypersexuality, bossiness and manipulative behavior, lying, property destruction, paranoia, hallucinations, delusions, and suicidal ideations. Less common symptoms include migraines, bingeing, self-injurious behaviors, and animal cruelty.

CONDUCT DISORDER IN CHILDREN

Factors contributing to conduct disorders in children include genetic predispositions, neurological damage, child abuse, and other traumatic experiences. Children with conduct disorders display characteristic emotional and behavioral patterns. These include aggression: They bully or intimidate others, often start physical fights, will use dangerous objects as weapons, exhibit physical cruelty to animals or humans, and assault and steal from others. Deliberate property destruction is another characteristic—breaking things or setting fires. Young children are limited in some of these activities by their smaller size, lesser strength, and lack of access; however, they show the same types of behaviors against smaller, younger, weaker, or more vulnerable children and animals, along with oppositional and defiant behaviors against adults. Also, while truancy is impossible or unlikely in preschoolers, and running away from home is less likely, young children with conduct disorders are likely to demonstrate some forms of seriously violating rules, another symptom of this disorder.

SYMPTOMS OF CHILDHOOD-ONSET SCHIZOPHRENIA

The incidence of childhood-onset schizophrenia is rare, but it does exist. One example of differential diagnosis involves distinguishing qualitatively between true auditory hallucinations and young children's "hearing voices" otherwise: in the latter case, a child hears his or her own or a familiar adult's voice in his or her head and does not seem upset by it, while in the former, a child may hear other voices, seemingly in his or her ears, and is frightened and confused by them. Tantrums, defiance, aggression, and other acting-out, externalized behaviors are less frequent in childhood-onset schizophrenia than internalized developmental differences, for example, isolation, shyness, awkwardness, fickleness, strange facial expressions, mistrust, paranoia, anxiety, and depression. Children demonstrate nonpsychotic symptoms earlier than psychotic ones. However, it is difficult to use prepsychotic symptoms as predictors due to variance among developmental peculiarities. While psychiatrists find the course of childhood-onset schizophrenia somewhat more variable than in adults, child symptoms resemble adult symptoms. Childhood-onset schizophrenia is typically chronic and severe, responds less to medication, and has a more guarded prognosis than adolescent- or adult-onset schizophrenia.

DIAGNOSING THE EMOTIONAL DISTURBANCES IN CHILDREN CLASSIFIED AS PSYCHOTIC DISORDERS

Psychosis is a general psychiatric category referring to thought disturbances or disorders. The most common symptoms are delusions (believing things that are not true) and hallucinations (seeing, hearing, feeling, tasting, or smelling things that are not there). While early childhood psychosis is rarer than at later ages, psychiatrists confirm it does occur. Moreover, prognosis is poorer for psychosis with onset in early childhood than in adolescence or adulthood. Causes can be from known metabolic or brain disorders or unknown. Younger children are more vulnerable to environmental stressors. Also, in young children, thoughts distorted by fantasy can be from normal cognitive immaturity, due to lack of experience and a larger range of normal functioning, or pathology; where they lie on this continuum must be determined by clinicians. Believing one is a superhero who can fly can be vivid imagination or delusional; having imaginary friends can be pretend play or hallucinatory. Other developmental disorders can also cloud differential diagnosis.

VISUAL IMPAIRMENTS
DEVELOPMENTAL CHARACTERISTICS OF INFANTS AND YOUNG CHILDREN WITH VISUAL IMPAIRMENTS

Historically, it was thought that visually impaired children developed more slowly than normal; however, it is now known that ages for reaching developmental milestones are equally variable in visually impaired babies as in others and that they acquire milestones within equal age ranges. One developmental difference is in sequence: visually impaired children tend to utter their first words or subject-verb two-word sentences earlier than other children. Some visually impaired children also demonstrate higher levels of language development at younger-than-typical ages. For example, they may sing songs from memory or recall events from the past at earlier ages than other children. This is a logical development in children who must rely more on input to their hearing and other senses than to their vision when the latter is impaired. Totally blind babies reach for objects later, hence explore the environment later; hand use, eye-hand coordination, and gross and fine motor skills are delayed. Blind infants' posture control develops normally (rolling, sitting, all-fours, and standing), but mobility (raising on arms, pulling up, and walking) is delayed.

CAUSES OF VISUAL IMPAIRMENTS IN BABIES AND YOUNG CHILDREN

Syndrome-related and other malformations like cleft iris or lens dislocation causing visual impairment can have prenatal origins. Cataracts clouding the eye's lens can be congenital, traumatic, or due to maternal rubella. Eyes can be normal, but impairment in the brain's visual cortex can cause visual impairment. Infantile glaucoma, like adult glaucoma, causes intraocular fluid buildup pressure and visual impairment. Conjunctivitis and other infections cause visual impairment. Strabismus and nystagmus are ocular-muscle conditions, respectively causing eye misalignments and involuntary eye movements. Trauma damaging the eyeball(s) is another visual impairment cause. The optic nerve can suffer from atrophy (dysfunction) or hypoplasia, that is, developmental regression, usually prenatally due to neurological trauma; acuity cannot be corrected. Refractive errors like nearsightedness, farsightedness, and astigmatism are correctable. Retinoblastoma, or behind-the-eye tumors, can cause blindness and fatality; surgical or chemotherapeutic treatment is usually required before age 2. Premature infants can have retinopathy of prematurity or retrolental fibroplasia. Cryotherapeutic treatment seems to stop disease progression. Its effects range from none to severe visual impairment (approximately 25% of children) to complete blindness.

IMPACTS OF BLINDNESS UPON COGNITIVE DEVELOPMENT

Blind children have more difficulty determining and confirming characteristics of things, hence defining concepts and organizing them into more abstract levels; their problem-solving is active but harder, and they construct different realities than sighted children. Blind babies typically acquire object permanence (the understanding that unseen objects still exist) a year later than normal; they learn to reach for objects only by hearing. Understanding cause-and-effect relationships is difficult without visual evidence. Blind babies and toddlers take longer to understand an object's constancy regardless of their orientation in space, affecting their ability to orient toys and their own hands. Blind children can identify object size differences and similarities, but classifying object differences and similarities in other attributes requires longer times and more exposures to various similar objects. Blind children's development of the abilities to conserve object properties like material or substance, weight, amount and volume, length, and liquid volume is later than normal.

EFFECTS OF BLINDNESS ON EMOTIONAL AND SOCIAL DEVELOPMENT

Blind babies and children are more dependent than others on adults, affecting development. With control of their inner realities but not of their outer environments, blind children may withdraw, seeking and responding less to social interaction. They may not readily develop concepts of the external world or self-concepts as beings separate from the world and the understanding that they can be both agents and recipients of actions relative to the environment. Mother-infant smiling initiates recognition, attachment, and communication in sighted babies; blind infants smile on hearing mother's voice at 2 months. Only tactile stimuli like tickling and nuzzling evoke regular smiling in blind babies. Missing facial expressions and other visual cues, blind children have more complicated social interactions. They often do not understand the basics of playing with others and seem emotionally ambivalent or uninterested and uncommunicative. Peers may reject or avoid them; adults often overprotect them. Self-help skills like chewing, scooping, self-feeding, teeth brushing, grooming, and toilet training are delayed in blind children.

HEARING IMPAIRMENTS
PREVALENCE AND ETIOLOGIES OF HEARING IMPAIRMENTS

Half or more (50% to 60%) of infant hearing losses have genetic origins—Down and other genetically based syndromes or the existence of parental hearing loss. About 25% or more of infant hearing losses are caused by maternal infections during pregnancy, such as cytomegalovirus (CMV), postnatal complications like blood transfusions or infection with meningitis, or traumatic head injuries. Included in this 25% or more are babies having nongenetic neurological disorders or conditions that affect their hearing. Malformations of the ears, head, or face can cause hearing loss in babies. Babies spending five days or longer in neonatal intensive care units (NICUs) or having complications while in the NICU are also more likely to suffer hearing loss. Around 25% of babies are diagnosed with hearing loss whose etiology is unknown.

SIGNS OF HEARING IMPAIRMENTS

If an infant does not display a startle response to loud noises, this is a potential sign of hearing loss. This can also indicate other developmental disabilities, but because hearing loss is the most prevalent disability among newborns, hearing screening is a priority. Between birth and 3 or 4 months old, babies should turn toward the source of a sound; if they do not, it could indicate hearing loss. A child who does not utter first words like *mama* or *dada* by age 1 could have hearing impairment. When babies or young children do not turn their heads when their names are called, adults may mistake this for inattention or ignoring; however, children turning upon seeing adults, but not upon hearing their names, can indicate hearing loss. Babies and children who seem to hear certain sounds but not others may have partial hearing losses. Delayed speech-language development or unclear speech, not following directions, saying "Huh?" often, and wanting higher TV or music volumes can indicate hearing loss in children.

SPEECH AND LANGUAGE IMPAIRMENTS
FACTORS CONTRIBUTING TO SPEECH AND LANGUAGE IMPAIRMENTS

Some speech and language disorders in children have unknown causes. Others have known causes such as hearing loss: speech and language are normally acquired primarily through the auditory sense, so children with impaired hearing have delayed and impaired development of speech and language. Brain injuries, neurological disorders, viral diseases, and some medications can also cause problems with developing language or speech. Children with intellectual disabilities are more likely to have delayed language development, and their speech is also more likely to develop more slowly and to be distorted. Cerebral palsy causes neuromuscular weakness and incoordination of speech. When severe, it can cause the inability to produce recognizable speech sounds; some children without speech can still vocalize, and some cannot. A cleft palate or lip and other physical impairments affect speech. Inadequate speech-language modeling at home inhibits speech-language development. Vocal abuse in children (screaming, coughing, throat clearing, or excessive talking) can cause vocal nodules or polyps, causing voice disorders. Stuttering can be related to maturation, anxiety or stress, auditory feedback defects, or unknown causes.

CHARACTERISTICS

In speech, most phonological disorders are articulatory; that is, children fail to pronounce specific speech sounds or phonemes correctly beyond the normal developmental age for achieving accuracy. Stuttering, disfluency, and rate and rhythm disorders cause children to repeat phonemes, especially initial word sounds; to repeat words; to prolong vowels or consonants; or to block, straining so hard to produce a sound that, pressure builds, but no sound issues. Their speech rates may also increase and decrease irregularly. Children with voice disorders can have voices that sound hoarse, raspy, overly nasal, higher- or lower-pitched than normal, overly weak or strident, and whispery or harsh. Hoarseness is common with vocal nodules and polyps. Cleft palate commonly causes hypernasality. In language, one of the most common impairments is delayed language development due to environmental deprivation, intellectual disabilities, neurological damage or defects, hearing loss, visual impairment, and so on. Children with neurological damage or disorders may exhibit aphasias, language disorders characterized by receptive difficulty with understanding spoken or written language, or expressive difficulty constructing spoken or written language.

PHYSICAL AND HEALTH IMPAIRMENTS
EXAMPLES OF PHYSICAL AND HEALTH IMPAIRMENTS

In the special education field of early childhood education, "other health impairment" is a term referring to health and physical conditions that rob a child of strength, vitality, or alertness or that cause excessive alertness to environmental stimuli, all having the end result of impeding the child's ability to attend or respond to the educational environment. Health problems can be acute(short-term or temporary but serious) or chronic (long-term, persistent, or recurrent). Some examples of such health and physical impairments include cerebral palsy, spina bifida, amputations or missing limbs, muscular dystrophy, cystic fibrosis, asthma, rheumatic fever, sickle-cell anemia, nephritis or kidney disease, leukemia, Tourette syndrome, hemophilia, diabetes, heart disease, AIDS, and lead poisoning. All these conditions and others can interfere with a child's development and ability to attend and learn. In addition to seizure disorders, which often cause neurological damage, seizure-controlling medications also frequently cause drowsiness, interfering with attention and cognition. Attention deficit and attention deficit hyperactivity disorders (ADD and ADHD) limit attention span, focus, and concentration and thus are sometimes classified as health impairments requiring special education services.

CHARACTERISTICS OF BABIES AND CHILDREN WITH PHYSICAL AND HEALTH IMPAIRMENTS

The characteristics of children having various physical or health impairments can range from having no limitations to severe limitations in their activities. Children with cerebral palsy, for example, usually have deficiencies in gross and fine motor development and deficits in speech-language development. Physical and health conditions causing severe debilitation in some children not only seriously limit their daily activities but also cause multiple primary disabilities and impair their intellectual functioning. Other children with physical or health impairments function at average, above-average, or gifted intellectual and academic levels. An important consideration when working with babies and young children having physical or health impairments is handling and positioning them physically. Correctly picking up, holding, carrying, giving assistance, and physically supporting younger children and arranging play materials for them based on their impairment is not only important for preventing injury, pain, and discomfort; it also enables them to receive instruction better and to manipulate materials and perform most efficiently. Preschoolers with physical impairments also tend to have difficulty with communication skills, so educators should give particular attention to facilitating and developing these.

DEVELOPMENTAL DELAYS

FACTORS LEADING TO DEVELOPMENTAL DELAYS

Developmental delays can come from genetic or environmental causes or both. Infants and young children with intellectual disabilities are most likely to exhibit developmental delays. Their development generally proceeds similarly to that of normal children but at slower rates; milestones are manifested at later-than-typical ages. Sensory impairments such as with hearing and vision can also delay many aspects of children's development. Children with physical and health impairments are likely to exhibit delays in their motor development and performance of physical activities. Another factor is environmental: children deprived of adequate environmental stimulation commonly show delays in cognitive, speech-language, and emotional and social development. Children with autism spectrum disorders often have markedly delayed language and speech development; many are nonverbal. Autistic children also typically have impaired social development, caused by an inability or difficulty with understanding others' emotional and social nonverbal communications. When they cannot interpret these, they do not know how to respond and also cannot imitate them; however, they can often learn these skills with special instruction.

CHARACTERISTICS INDICATING DEVELOPMENTAL DELAYS

Developmental delays mean that a child does not reach developmental milestones at the expected ages. For example, if most babies normally learn to walk between 12 and 15 months of age, a 20-month-old who is not beginning to walk is considered as having a developmental delay. Delays can occur in cognitive, speech-language, social-emotional, gross motor skill, or fine motor skill development. Signs of delayed motor development include stiff or rigid limbs, floppy or limp body posture for the child's age, using one side of the body more than the other, and clumsiness unusual for the child's age. Behavioral signs of children's developmental delays include inattention or shorter-than-normal attention span for the age, avoiding or infrequent eye contact, focusing on unusual objects for long times or preferring objects over social interaction, excessive frustration when attempting tasks normally simple for children their age, unusual stubbornness; aggressive and acting-out behaviors; daily violent behaviors, rocking, excessive talking to oneself, and not soliciting love or approval from parents.

TRAUMATIC BRAIN INJURY (TBI)

IDEA'S LEGAL DEFINITION OF TRAUMATIC BRAIN INJURY

TBI is defined by the **IDEA law** (the Individuals with Disabilities Education Act) as "an acquired injury to the brain from external physical force, resulting in total or partial functional disability or psychosocial impairment, or both, that adversely affect a child's educational performance." This definition excludes injuries from birth trauma, congenital injuries, and degenerative conditions. TBI is the foremost cause of death and disability in children (and teens) in the USA. The most common causes of TBI in children include falls, motor vehicle accidents, and physical abuse. In spite of the IDEA's definition, aneurysms and strokes are three examples of internal traumas that can also cause TBI in babies and young children. External head injuries that can result in TBI include both open and closed head injuries. Shaken baby syndrome is caused by forcibly shaking an infant. This causes the brain literally to bounce against the insides of the skull, causing rebound injuries, resulting in TBI and even death.

> **Review Video: <u>Medical Conditions in Education</u>**
> Visit mometrix.com/academy and enter code: 531058

CHARACTERISTICS

TBI can impair a child's cognitive development and processing. It can impede the language development of children, which is dependent upon cognitive development. Children who have sustained TBI often have difficulties with attention, retention, and memory; reasoning, judgment, understanding abstract concepts, and thinking abstractly; and problem-solving abilities. TBIs can also impair a child's motor functions and physical abilities. The sensory and perceptual functions of children with TBI can be abnormal. Their ability to process information is often compromised. Their speech can also be affected. In addition, TBIs can impair a child's psychosocial behaviors. Memory deficits are commonest, tend to be more long-lasting, and are often area-specific; for example, a child may recall personal experiences but not factual information. Other common characteristics of TBI include cognitive inflexibility or rigidity, damaged conceptualization and reasoning, language loss or poor verbal fluency, problems with paying attention and concentrating, inadequate problem solving, and problems with reading and writing.

ETIOLOGIES AND CHARACTERISTICS OF MULTIPLE DISABILITIES

The term ***multiple disabilities*** refers to any combination of more than one disabling condition. For example, a child may be both blind and deaf due to causes such as having rheumatic fever in infancy or early childhood. Anything causing neurological damage before, during, or shortly after birth can result in multiple disabilities, particularly if it is widespread rather than localized. For example, infants deprived of oxygen or suffering traumatic brain injuries in utero, during labor or delivery, or postnatally can sustain severe brain damage. So can babies having encephalitis or meningitis and those whose mothers abused drugs prenatally. Infants with this type of extensive damage can often present with multiple disabilities, including intellectual disabilities, cerebral palsy, physical paralysis, mobility impairment, visual impairment, hearing impairment, and speech-language disorders. They may have any combination of or all of these disabilities as well as others. In addition to a difficulty or inability with normal physical performance, multiple disabled children often have difficulty acquiring and retaining cognitive skills and transferring or generalizing skills among settings and situations.

PREMATURITY OR PRETERM BIRTH

Babies born before 37 weeks' gestation are classified as **premature** or **preterm**. Premature infants can have difficulty with breathing, as their lungs are not fully developed, and with regulating their body temperatures. Premature infants may be born with pneumonia, respiratory distress, extra air or bleeding in the lungs, jaundice, sepsis or infection, hypoglycemia (low blood sugar), severe intestinal inflammation, bleeding into the brain or white-matter brain damage, or anemia. They have lower-than-normal birth weights, body fat, muscle tone, and activity. Additional typical characteristics of premature infants include apnea (interrupted breathing); lanugo (a coating of body hair that full-term infants no longer have); thin, smooth, shiny, translucent skin through which veins are visible; soft, flexible ear cartilage; cryptorchidism (undescended testicles) and small, non-ridged scrotums in males; enlarged clitorises in females; and feeding difficulties caused by weak or defective sucking reflexes or incoordination of swallowing with breathing.

DISABLING CONDITIONS RESULTING FROM PREMATURE BIRTHS

Physicians find it impossible to predict the long-term results of prematurity for any individual baby based on an infant's gestational age and birth weight. However, some related immediate and long-term effects can be identified. Generally, the lower the birth weight and the more prematurely a child is born, the greater the risk is for complications. Infants born at less than 34 weeks of gestation typically cannot coordinate their sucking and swallowing and may temporarily need feeding or breathing tubes or oxygen. They also need special nursery care until able to maintain their body temperatures and weights. Long-term complications of prematurity can include bronchopulmonary dysplasia, a chronic lung condition; delayed physical growth and development; delayed cognitive development; mental or physical delays or disabilities; and blindness, vision loss, or retinopathy of prematurity (formerly called retrolental fibroplasia). While some premature infants sustain long-term disabilities, some severe, other babies born prematurely grow up to show no effects at all; any results within this range can also occur.

Screening in Early Childhood

SCREENING FOR PARTICULAR DELAY CRITERION

Initial screenings are required, but if a young child has been screened for developmental disorders or delays within the past 6 months and no changes have been observed or reported, repeat screening may be waived. Hearing and vision screenings are mandatory when screening young children. Formal developmental measures are also required, which may include screening tests of motor skills development, cognitive development, social-emotional development, and self-help skills development. Formal screening tests of speech-language development are also required. Additional tests recommended during screening include informal measures. For example, checklists, rating scales, and inventories may be used to screen a child's behavior, mood, and performance of motor skills, cognitive skills, self-help skills, and social and emotional skills. On checklists, parents or caregivers check whether the child does or does not demonstrate listed behaviors, or assessors may complete them via parent or caregiver interviews or interviewing and observing the child. Rating scales ask parents, caregivers, and assessors to rate a child's behaviors, affect, mood, and so on, within a range of numbered and labeled descriptions. Inventories list demonstrated skills and needs. Behavioral observations and existing records and information are also used.

FEATURES OF DEVELOPMENTAL SCREENINGS AND EVALUATIONS

If a child's development is suspected of being delayed—for example, the child is not reaching developmental milestones during expected age ranges—a developmental screening may be administered. Screening tests are quickly performed and yield more general results. The hospital or doctor's office may give a questionnaire to the parent or caregiver to complete for a screening. Alternatively, a health or education professional may administer a screening test to the child. Screening tests are not intended to diagnose specific conditions or give details; they are meant to identify children who may have some problem. Screenings can overidentify or under-identify developmental delays in children. Hence, if the screening identifies a child as having developmental delays, the child is then referred for a developmental evaluation—a much longer, more thorough, comprehensive, in-depth assessment using multiple tests, administered by a psychologist or other highly-trained professional. Evaluation provides a profile of a child's strengths and weaknesses in all developmental domains. Determination of needs for early intervention services or treatment plans is based on evaluation results.

DEVELOPMENTAL EVALUATION DATA TYPES

The child's social history should be obtained, which is typically done by a social worker. Details of the child's developmental progress up until present day; the family's composition, socioeconomic status, and situation; and the child's and family's health and medical histories and status should be emphasized. A physician's or nurse's medical assessment is required, including a **physical examination** and, if indicated, a specialist's examination. A psychologist typically assesses intellectual and **cognitive development**; at least one such test is generally required. At least one test of adaptive behavior is also required to assess **emotional-social development**. **Self-help skills** are evaluated; this may be included within cognitive, adaptive behavior, or programming assessments. **Communication skills** are typically evaluated by a speech-language pathologist. Both receptive and expressive language must be tested comprehensively rather than simply by single-word vocabulary tests. As indicated, **speech articulation** is also tested. At least one test of **motor skills**, typically administered by a physical or occupational therapist, is required. **Programming** evaluation requires at least one criterion-referenced or curriculum-based measure, typically administered by an educator.

CHILD FIND

Child Find is an ongoing process with the aim of locating, identifying, and referring young children with disabilities and their families as early as possible for service programs. This process consists of activities designed to raise public awareness and screenings and evaluations to identify and diagnose disabilities. The federal IDEA law mandates under Part B that disabled children are guaranteed early childhood special education services and under Part C that infants and toddlers at risk for developmental delays are guaranteed early intervention programs. (Eligibility guidelines vary by US state.) The IDEA requires school districts to find, identify, and evaluate children with disabilities in their attendance areas. School districts have facilitated this Child Find process by establishing community-informed referral networks whose members refer children who may have exceptional educational needs (EENs). Network members typically include parents, doctors, birth-to-3 programs, child care programs, Head Start programs, public health agencies, social service agencies, and any other community members with whom the young children come into contact.

CURRENT COLLABORATIVE APPROACHES AND MODELS OF SCREENING

Historically, the tradition was to conduct kindergarten screenings of children entering schools around age 5. However, in recent years, school districts have developed community referral networks to assist in the processes of Child Find, screening, evaluation, and referral for early intervention and early childhood special education and related services. Current models are more informal, proactive, and collaborative. Cooperative educational interagency service efforts give parents information about normal early childhood development and available community resources and offer opportunities for developmental screenings of their young children. Specific procedures are governed by individual US state laws. Generally, district networks implementing current models send developmental review forms to parents to complete in advance, and then they attend a developmental screening at a community site. Parents discuss normal early childhood growth and development with program staff, while, in the same room, trained professionals observe their children as they play. Children's vision and hearing are also screened. Parents can discuss their children's current development with psychologists, early childhood educators, or counselors. Thereafter, they can learn about community resources.

DEFINING DEVELOPMENTAL DELAYS IN INFANTS AND TODDLERS

The IDEA Part C specifies the areas of development that states must include in **defining developmental delays**. However, individual states must identify the criteria they use to determine eligibility, including pertinent diagnostic instruments, procedures, and functional levels. States currently use quantitative and qualitative measures. Quantitative criteria for developmental delay include the difference between chronological age and performance level, expressed as a percentage of chronological age; performance at a given number of months below chronological age; or number of standard deviations (SDs) below mean of performance on a norm-referenced test. Qualitative criteria include the development considered atypical or delayed for established norms or observed behaviors considered atypical. At least one state differentially defines delay according to a child's age in months, with the rationale that a 25% delay, for example, is very different for a 1-year-old than a 3-year-old. Quantitative criteria for defining delay and determining eligibility vary widely among states. A 25% or 20% delay (2 SDs below mean in 1+ areas or 1.5 SD below mean in 2+ areas) is some common state criteria.

RISK FACTORS IN INFANTS AND TODDLERS

Scientists find that developmental outcomes for children are not reliably predicted by any one risk factor or event. **Developmental risk** increases with increased biological, medical, or environmental risk factors. However, researchers have found some variables that afford resiliency in children to offset risk factors. These can include the child's basic temperament, the child having high self-esteem, the child having a good emotional relationship with at least one parent, and the child having experiences of successful learning. These findings indicate that assessments should include criteria for multiple biological and environmental risk factors, for cumulative biological and environmental risk factors, and for protective or resilience factors, considering all of these in the context of change occurring over time. Under the IDEA, US states have the option to provide early intervention services to children considered at risk for adverse developmental outcomes as well as those already identified with them. Some states apply multiple-risk models, requiring three to five risk factors for service eligibility. Some states also determine eligibility with less DD when biological, medical, or environmental risk factors also exist.

INFORMATION SOURCES ON EARLY INTERVENTION AND PRESCHOOL SPECIAL EDUCATION SERVICES

Military families stationed both in the United States and overseas who have young special needs children can seek information and assistance from the federally funded organization Specialized Training of Military Families (STOMP). The staff of STOMP is composed of parents having special needs children themselves, who also have been trained to work with other parents of special needs children. STOMP staff members are spouses of military personnel who thus understand the unique, specialized circumstances and needs of military families. Another government agency, the US Department of Defense, includes the office of the Department of Defense Education Activity (DoDEA) and provides comprehensive guidance to military families with special needs children who are eligible to receive, or are receiving, free appropriate public education (FAPE) as mandated by the IDEA law, whether that education is located in the United States or in other countries.

PROVIDING SPECIAL EDUCATION SERVICES FOR PRESCHOOLERS

If parents observe that their preschooler is not attaining developmental milestones within the expected age ranges or does not seem to be developing in the same way as most other children, they should seek **evaluation** for possible developmental delay or disability. Although 3-to-5-year-olds are likely not in elementary school yet, the elementary school in a family's school district is still the best first contact because the IDEA law specifies that school districts must provide special education services at no family cost to eligible children, including preschoolers. Another excellent source of more information about special education is the National Dissemination Center for Children with Disabilities (NICHCY) of the US Department of Education's Office of Special Education Programs. They partner with nonprofit organizations like the Academy for Educational Development (AED) to produce useful documents for families with special needs children. NICHCY supplies state resource sheets listing main contacts regarding special education services in each US state. Families can obtain these sheets at NICHCY's website or by telephone.

INFORMATION SOURCES FOR EVALUATION

Under the IDEA (Individuals with Disabilities Education Act), evaluation information sources include: physicians' reports, the child's medical history, developmental test results, current classroom observations and assessments (when applicable), completed developmental and behavioral checklists, feedback and observations from parents and all other members of the evaluation team, and any other significant records, reports, and observations regarding the child. Under the IDEA, the parents are involved in the evaluation, along with at least one regular education teacher and special education teacher, if the child has these, and any special education service provider working with the child—for children receiving early intervention services from birth through age 2 and transitioning to preschool special education, it may be an early intervention service provider; a school administrator knowledgeable about children with disabilities, special education policies, regular education curriculum, and resources available; a psychologist or educator who can interpret evaluation results and discuss indicated instruction; individuals with special expertise or knowledge regarding the child (recruited by school or parents); when appropriate, the child; and other professionals, for example, physical or occupational therapists, speech therapists, medical specialists, and so on.

INFORMAL ASSESSMENT INSTRUMENTS

Early childhood teachers assess pre-K children's performance in individual, small-group, and whole-class activities throughout the day using informal tools that are teacher-made, school-, program-, or district-furnished, or procured by school systems from commercial educational resources. For classroom observations, teachers might complete a form based on their observations during class story or circle time, organized using three themes per day, each targeting different skills—social-emotional, math, alphabet knowledge, oral language, or emergent writing. They note the names of children demonstrating the specified skill and those who might need follow-up, and provide needed one on one interventions daily. For individual observations, teachers might fill out a chart divided into domains like physical development, oral language development,

75

math, emergent reading, emergent writing, science and health, fine arts, technology and media, social studies, social-emotional development, and approaches to learning, noting one child's strengths and needs in each area per chart. In addition to guided observation records, teachers complete checklists, keep anecdotal and running records, and assemble portfolio assessments of children's work. Tracking children's progress informs responsive instructional planning.

> **Review Video: <u>Assessment Reliability and Validity</u>**
> Visit mometrix.com/academy and enter code: 424680

DIFFERENCES BETWEEN SCREENING AND ASSESSMENT INSTRUMENTS

A variety of screening and assessment instruments exist for early childhood measurement. Some key areas where they differ include which developmental domains are measured by an instrument; for which applications an instrument is meant to be used; to which age ranges an instrument applies; the methods by which a test or tool is administered; the requirements for scoring and interpreting a test, scale, or checklist; whether an instrument is appropriate for use with ethnically diverse populations; and whether a tool is statistically found to have good validity and reliability. Early childhood program administrators should choose instruments that can measure the developmental areas pertinent to their program; support their program's established goals; and include all early childhood ages served in their program. Instruments' administration, scoring, and interpretation methods should be congruent with program personnel's skills. Test/measure administration should involve realistic time durations. Instruments/tools should be appropriate to use with ethnically diverse and non-English-speaking children and families. Tests should also be proven psychometrically accurate and dependable enough.

TYPICAL APPLICATIONS OF SCREENING AND ASSESSMENT INSTRUMENTS

The ways in which screening and assessment instruments applicable to early childhood education are used include a wide range of variations. For example, early childhood education programs typically need to identify children who might have developmental disorders or delays. Screening instruments are used to identify those children showing signs of possible problems who need assessments, not to diagnose problems. Assessment instruments are used to develop and/or confirm diagnoses of developmental disorders or delays. Assessment tools are also used to help educators and therapists plan curricular and treatment programs. Another important function of assessment instruments is to determine a child's eligibility for a given program. In addition, once children are placed in early childhood education programs, assessment tools can be used to monitor their progress and other changes occurring over time. Moreover, program administrators can use assessment instruments to evaluate children's achievement of the learning outcomes that define their program goals, and, by extension, the teachers' effectiveness in furthering children's achievement of those outcomes.

FORMAL ASSESSMENT INSTRUMENTS

Formal assessment instruments are typically standardized tests, administered to groups. They give norms for age groups/developmental levels for comparison. They are designed to avoid administrator bias and capture children's responses only. Their data can be scaled and be reported in aggregate to school/program administrators and policymakers. The Scholastic Early Childhood Inventory (SECI) is a formal one-on-one instrument to assess children's progress in four domains found to predict kindergarten readiness: phonological awareness, oral language development, alphabet knowledge, and mathematics. Other instruments measuring multiple developmental domains include:

- **The Assessment, Evaluation, and Programming System** (0–6 years) for planning intervention
- **The Bayley Scale for Infant Development** (1–42 months) for assessing developmental delays
- **The Brigance Diagnostic Inventory of Early Development** (0–7 years) for planning instruction
- **The Developmental Profile II** (0–6 years) to assess special needs and support IEP development
- **The Early Coping Inventory** (4–36 months)

- **Early Learning Accomplishment Profile** (0–36 months), both for planning interventions
- **The Infant-Toddler Developmental Assessment** (0–42 months) to screen for developmental delays

SCREENING AND ASSESSMENT INSTRUMENTS MEASURING DEVELOPMENT

The available screening and assessment instruments for early childhood development cover a wide range in scope and areas of focus. Some measures are comprehensive, assessing young children's progress in many developmental domains, including sensory, motor, physical, cognitive, linguistic, emotional, and social. Some other instruments focus exclusively on only one domain, such as language development or emotional-social development. Some instruments even focus within a domain upon only one of its facets, (e.g., upon attachment or temperament within the domain of emotional-social development). In addition, some tools measure risk and resiliency factors influencing developmental delays and disorders. Programs like Head Start that promote general early childhood development should select comprehensive assessment instruments. Outreach programs targeting better identification of children having untreated and/or undetected mental health problems should choose instruments assessing social-emotional development. Clinics treating children with regulatory disorders might select an instrument measuring temperament. Prevention programs helping multiple-needs families access supports and services could use a measure for risk and resiliency factors. Multifaceted early childhood programs often benefit most from using several instruments in combination.

AGE RANGES INCLUDED IN VARIOUS SCREENING AND ASSESSMENT INSTRUMENTS

An important consideration for screening and assessment in early childhood is that early childhood development is very dynamic and occurs rapidly. Hence, screening and assessment instruments must be sensitive to such frequent and pronounced developmental changes. Some instruments target specific age ranges like 0–36 months. Others cover wider ranges, such as children aged 2–16 years. The latter may have internal means of application to smaller age ranges; for example, sections respectively for 3-6-month-old babies, 7–12-month-olds, and 12–18-month-olds. Or they indicate different scoring and interpretation criteria by age; for example, some screening tools specify different numbers of test items depending on the child's age to indicate a need for assessment. Choosing screening and assessment instruments covering the entire age range served in an early childhood education program is advantageous—not only because they can be used with all child ages in the program but also because they can be administered and readministered at the beginning and end of programs and/or in between, to compare and monitor changes, which is difficult with separate, age-specific tests.

Special Education Services in Early Childhood

SPECIAL EDUCATION SERVICES FOR PRESCHOOL CHILDREN

Special education for preschoolers is education specifically designed to meet the individual needs of a child aged 3 to 5 years with a disability or developmental delay. The specialized design of this instruction can include adaptations to the content, the teaching methods, and the way instruction is delivered to meet a disabled child's unique needs. Special education for preschoolers includes various settings, such as in the home, classrooms, hospitals, institutions, and others. It also includes a range of related services, such as speech-language pathology services, specialized physical education instruction, early vocational training, and training in travel skills. The school district's special education system provides evaluation and services to eligible preschoolers free of charge. Evaluation's purposes are to determine whether a child has a disability under the IDEA's definitions and determine that child's present educational needs.

POST-EVALUATION AND THE INDIVIDUALIZED EDUCATION PROGRAM

After a preschool child is evaluated, the parents and involved school personnel meet to discuss the evaluation results. Parents are included in the group that decides whether the child is eligible for special education services based on those results. For eligible children, the parents and school personnel will develop an IEP. Every child who will receive special education services must have an IEP. The main purposes of the IEP are (1) to establish reasonable educational goals for the individual child and (2) to indicate what services the school district will provide to the child. The IEP includes a statement of the child's present levels of functioning and performance. It also includes a list of more general instructional goals for the child to achieve through school and parental support along with more specific learning objectives reflecting those goals and specifying exactly what the child will be able to demonstrate, under what circumstances, how much of the time—for example, a percentage of recorded instances—and within what time period (e.g., 1 year).

INDIVIDUALIZED EDUCATION PROGRAM GOALS AND OBJECTIVES

In an IEP, the goals are more global, describing a skill for the child to acquire or a task to master. The objectives are more specific articulations of achievements that will demonstrate the child's mastery of the goal. For example, if a goal is for the child to increase his or her functional communicative vocabulary, a related objective might be for the child to acquire x number of new words in x length of time; another related objective could be for the child to use the words acquired in 90% of recorded relevant situations. If the goal is for the child to demonstrate knowledge and discrimination of colors, one objective might be for the child to identify correctly a red, yellow, and blue block 95% of the time when asked to point out each color within a group of blocks. Progress toward or achievement of some objectives may be measured via formal tests; with preschoolers, many others are measured via observational data collection.

PROGRESS MONITORING, UPDATING, AND REVISING IEPS

Once a child has been identified with a disability, has been determined eligible for special education and related services under the IDEA, and has had an IEP developed and implemented, the child's progress must be monitored. Monitoring methods may be related to evaluation methods. For example, if a child identified with problem behaviors was initially evaluated using a behavioral checklist, school personnel can use the same checklist periodically, comparing its results to the baseline levels of frequency and severity originally obtained. If an affective disorder or disturbance was identified and instruments like the Beck Depression Inventory or Anxiety Inventory were used, these can be used again periodically; reduced symptoms would indicate progress. If progress with IEP goals and objectives is less or greater than expected, the IEP team meets and may revise the program. This can include specifying shorter or longer times to achieve some goals and objectives; lowering or raising requirements proving too difficult or easy; resetting successive objective criteria in smaller or larger increments; changing teaching methods, content, or materials used; and so on.

Assessment Methodology

ASSESSMENT METHODS

Effective teaching requires multiple methods of assessment to evaluate student comprehension and instructional effectiveness. Assessments are typically categorized as diagnostic, formative, summative, and benchmark, and are applicable at varying stages of instruction. **Diagnostic** assessments are administered before instruction and indicate students' prior knowledge and areas of misunderstanding to determine the path of instruction. **Formative** assessments occur continuously to measure student engagement, comprehension, and instructional effectiveness. These assessments indicate instructional strategies that require adjustment to meet students' needs in facilitating successful learning, and include such strategies as checking for understanding, observations, total participation activities, and exit tickets. **Summative** assessments are given at the end of a lesson or unit to evaluate student progress in reaching learning targets and identify areas of misconception for reteaching. Such assessments can be given in the form of exams and quizzes, or project-based activities in which students demonstrate their learning through hands-on, personalized methods. Additionally, portfolios serve as valuable summative assessments in allowing students to demonstrate their progress over time and provide insight regarding individual achievement. **Benchmark** assessments occur less frequently and encompass large portions of curriculum. These assessments are intended to evaluate the progress of groups of students in achieving state and district academic standards.

Assessment Types

- **Diagnostic:** These assessments can either be formal or informal and are intended to provide teachers with information regarding students' level of understanding prior to beginning a unit of instruction. Examples include pretests, KWL charts, anticipation guides, and brainstorming activities. Digital resources, such as online polls, surveys, and quizzes are also valuable resources for gathering diagnostic feedback.
- **Formative:** These assessments occur throughout instruction to provide the teacher with feedback regarding student understanding. Examples include warm-up and closure activities, checking frequently for understanding, student reflection activities, and providing students with color-coded cards to indicate their level of understanding. Short quizzes and total participation activities, such as four corners, are also valuable formative assessments. Numerous digital resources, including polls, surveys, and review games, are also beneficial in providing teachers with formative feedback to indicate instructional effectiveness.
- **Summative:** Summative assessments are intended to indicate students' level of mastery and progress toward reaching academic learning standards. These assessments may take the form of written or digital exams and include multiple choice, short answer, or long answer questions. Examples also include projects, final essays, presentations, or portfolios to demonstrate student progress over time.
- **Benchmark:** Benchmark assessments measure students' progress in achieving academic standards. These assessments are typically standardized to ensure uniformity, objectivity, and accuracy. Benchmark assessments are typically given as a written multiple choice or short answer exam, or as a digital exam in which students answer questions on the computer.

> **Review Video: Formative and Summative Assessments**
> Visit mometrix.com/academy and enter code: 804991

Determining Appropriate Assessment Strategies

As varying assessment methods provide different information regarding student performance and achievement, the teacher must consider the most applicable and effective assessment strategy in each stage of instruction. This includes determining the **desired outcomes** of assessment, as well as the information the teacher intends to ascertain and how they will apply the results to further instruction. **Age** and **grade level** appropriateness must be considered when selecting which assessment strategies will enable students to successfully demonstrate their learning. Additionally, the teacher must be cognizant of students' individual differences and learning needs to determine which assessment model is most **accommodating** and reflective of their progress. It is also important that the teacher consider the practicality of assessment strategies, as well as methods they will use to implement the assessment for maximized feedback regarding individual and whole-class progress in achieving learning goals.

Assessments That Reflect Real-World Applications

Assessments that reflect **real-world applications** enhance relevancy and students' ability to establish personal connections to learning that deepen understanding. Implementing such assessments provides authenticity and enhances engagement by defining a clear and practical purpose for learning. These assessments often allow for hands-on opportunities for demonstrating learning and can be adjusted to accommodate students' varying learning styles and needs while measuring individual progress. However, assessments that focus on real-world applications can be subjective, thus making it difficult to extract concrete data and quantify student progress to guide future instructional decisions. In addition, teachers may have difficulty analyzing assessment results on a large scale and comparing student performance with other schools and districts, as individual assessments may vary.

Diagnostic Tests

Diagnostic tests are integral to planning and delivering effective instruction. These tests are typically administered prior to beginning a unit or lesson and provide valuable feedback for guiding and planning instruction. Diagnostic tests provide **preliminary information** regarding students' level of understanding and prior knowledge. This serves as a baseline for instructional planning that connects and builds upon students' background knowledge and experiences to enhance success in learning. Diagnostic tests allow the teacher to identify and clarify areas of student misconception prior to engaging in instruction to ensure continued comprehension and avoid the need for remediation. They indicate areas of student strength and need, as well as individual instructional aids that may need to be incorporated into lessons to support student achievement. In addition, these tests enable the teacher to determine which instructional strategies, activities, groupings, and materials will be most valuable in maximizing engagement and learning. Diagnostic tests can be **formal** or **informal**, and include such formats as pre-tests, pre-reading activities, surveys, vocabulary inventories, and graphic organizers such as KWL charts to assess student understanding prior to engaging in learning. Diagnostic tests are generally not graded as there is little expectation that all students in a class possess the same baseline of proficiency at the start of a unit.

FORMATIVE ASSESSMENTS

Formative assessments are any assessments that take place in the **middle of a unit of instruction**. The goals of formative assessments are to help teachers understand where a student is in their progress toward **mastering** the current unit's content and to provide the students with **ongoing feedback** throughout the unit. The advantage of relying heavily on formative assessments in instruction is that it allows the teacher to continuously **check for comprehension** and adjust instruction as needed to ensure that the whole class is adequately prepared to proceed at the end of the unit. To understand formative assessments well, teachers need to understand that any interaction that can provide information about the student's comprehension is a type of formative assessment which can be used to inform future instruction.

Formative assessments are often a mixture of formal and informal assessments. **Formal formative assessments** often include classwork, homework, and quizzes. Examples of **informal formative assessments** include simple comprehension checks during instruction, class-wide discussions of the current topic, and exit slips, which are written questions posed by teachers at the end of class, which helps the teacher quickly review which students are struggling with the concepts.

SUMMATIVE ASSESSMENTS

Summative assessment refers to an evaluation at the end of a discrete unit of instruction, such as the end of a course, end of a unit, or end of a semester. Classic examples of summative assessments include end of course assessments, final exams, or even qualifying standardized tests such as the SAT or ACT. Most summative assessments are created to measure student mastery of particular **academic standards**. Whereas formative assessment generally informs current instruction, summative assessments are used to objectively demonstrate that each individual has achieved adequate mastery of the standards in question. If a student has not met the benchmark, they may need extra instruction or may need to repeat the course.

These assessments usually take the form of **tests** or formal portfolios with rubrics and clearly defined goals. Whatever form a summative takes, they are almost always high-stakes, heavily-weighted, and they should always be formally graded. These types of assessments often feature a narrower range of question types, such as multiple choice, short answer, and essay questions to help with systematic grading. Examples of summative assessments include state tests, end-of-unit or chapter tests, end-of-semester exams, and assessments that formally measure student mastery of topics against a established benchmarks.

Project-based assessments are beneficial in evaluating achievement, as they incorporate several elements of instruction and highlight real-world applications of learning. This allows students to demonstrate understanding through a hands-on, individualized approach that reinforces connections to learning and increases retainment. **Portfolios** of student work over time serve as a valuable method for assessing individual progress toward reaching learning targets. Summative assessments provide insight regarding overall instructional effectiveness and are necessary for guiding future instruction in subsequent years but are not usually used to modify current instruction.

> **Review Video: Assessment Reliability and Validity**
> Visit mometrix.com/academy and enter code: 424680

BENCHMARK ASSESSMENTS

Benchmark assessments are intended to quantify, evaluate, and compare individual and groups of students' achievement of school-wide, district, and state **academic standards.** They are typically administered in specific intervals throughout the school year and encompass entire or large units of curriculum to determine student mastery and readiness for academic advancement. Benchmark assessments provide data that enable the teacher to determine students' progress toward reaching academic goals to guide current and continued instruction. This data can be utilized by the school and individual teachers to create learning goals and objectives aligned with academic standards, as well as plan instructional strategies, activities, and assessments to support students in achieving them. In addition, benchmark assessments provide feedback regarding understanding and the potential need for remediation to allow the teacher to instill necessary supports in future instruction that prepare students for success in achieving learning targets.

ALIGNMENT OF ASSESSMENTS WITH INSTRUCTIONAL GOALS AND OBJECTIVES

To effectively monitor student progress, assessments must align with **instructional goals** and **objectives**. This allows the teacher to determine whether students are advancing at an appropriate pace to achieve state and district academic standards. When assessments are aligned with specific learning targets, the teacher ensures that students are learning relevant material to establish a foundation of knowledge necessary for growth and academic achievement. To achieve this, the teacher must determine which instructional goals and objectives their students must achieve and derive instruction, content, and activities from these specifications. Instruction must reflect and reinforce learning targets, and the teacher must select the most effective strategies for addressing students' needs as they work to achieve them. Assessments must be reflective of content instruction to ensure they are aligned with learning goals and objectives, as well as to enable the teacher to evaluate student progress in mastering them. The teacher must clearly communicate learning goals and objectives throughout all stages of instruction to provide students with clarity on expectations. This establishes a clear purpose and focus for learning that enhances relevancy and strengthens connections to support student achievement.

CLEARLY COMMUNICATING ASSESSMENT CRITERIA AND STANDARDS

Students must be clear on the purpose of learning throughout all stages of instruction to enhance understanding and facilitate success. When assessment **criteria** and **standards** are clearly communicated, the purpose of learning is established, and students are able to effectively connect instructional activities to learning goals and criteria for assessment. Communicating assessment criteria and standards provides students with clarity on tasks and learning goals they are expected to accomplish as they prepare themselves for assessment. This allows for more **focused instruction** and engagement in learning, as it enhances relevancy and student motivation. Utilizing appropriate forms of **rubrics** is an effective strategy in specifying assessment criteria and standards, as it informs students about learning goals they are working toward, the quality of work they are expected to achieve, and skills they must master to succeed on the assessment. Rubrics indicate to students exactly how they will be evaluated, thus supporting their understanding and focus as they engage in learning to promote academic success.

RUBRICS FOR COMMUNICATING STANDARDS

The following are varying styles of rubrics that can be used to communicate criteria and standards:

- **Analytic:** Analytic rubrics break down criteria for an assignment into several categories and provide an explanation of the varying levels of performance in each one. This style of rubric is beneficial for detailing the characteristics of quality work, as well as providing students with feedback regarding specific components of their performance. Analytic rubrics are most effective when used for summative assessments, such as long-term projects or essays.
- **Holistic:** Holistic rubrics evaluate the quality of the student's assignment as a whole, rather than scoring individual components. Students' score is determined based upon their performance across multiple performance indicators. This style of rubric is beneficial for providing a comprehensive evaluation but limits the amount of feedback that students receive regarding their performance in specific areas.
- **Single-Point:** Single point rubrics outline criteria for assignments into several categories. Rather than providing a numeric score to each category, however, the teacher provides written feedback regarding the students' strengths and ways in which they can improve their performance. This style of rubric is beneficial in providing student-centered feedback that focuses on their overall progress.
- **Checklist:** Checklists typically outline a set of criteria that is scored using a binary approach based upon completion of each component. This style increases the efficiency of grading assignments and is often easy for students to comprehend but does not provide detailed feedback. This method of grading should generally be reserved for shorter assignments.

COMMUNICATING HIGH ACADEMIC EXPECTATIONS IN ASSESSMENTS

The attitudes and behaviors exhibited by the teacher are highly influential on students' attitudes toward learning. Teachers demonstrate belief in students' abilities to be successful in learning when they communicate **high academic expectations**. This promotes students' **self-concept** and establishes a **growth mindset** to create confident, empowered learners that are motivated to achieve. High expectations for assessments and reaching academic standards communicates to students the quality of work that is expected of them and encourages them to overcome obstacles as they engage in learning. When communicating expectations for student achievement, it is important that the teacher is aware of students' individual learning needs to provide the necessary support that establishes equitable opportunities for success in meeting assessment criteria and standards. Setting high expectations through assessment criteria and standards while supporting students in their learning enhances overall achievement and establishes a foundation for continuous academic success.

EFFECTIVE COMMUNICATION AND IMPACT ON STUDENT LEARNING

Communicating high academic expectations enhances students' self-concept and increases personal motivation for success in learning. To maximize student achievement, it is important that the teacher set high academic expectations that are **clearly** communicated through **age-appropriate** terms and consistently reinforced. Expectations must be reflected through learning goals and objectives, and **visible** at all times to ensure student awareness. The teacher must be **specific** in communicating what they want students to accomplish and clearly detail necessary steps for achievement while assuming the role of facilitator to guide learning and provide support. Providing constructive **feedback** throughout instruction is integral in reminding students of academic expectations and ensuring they are making adequate progress toward reaching learning goals. When high academic expectations are communicated and reinforced, students are empowered with a sense of confidence and self-responsibility for their own learning that promotes their desire to learn. This ultimately enhances achievement and equips them with the tools necessary for future academic success.

ANALYZING AND INTERPRETING ASSESSMENT DATA

Teachers can utilize multiple techniques to effectively analyze and interpret assessment data. This typically involves creating charts and graphs outlining different data subsets. They can list each learning standard that was assessed, determine how many students overall demonstrated proficiency on the standard, and identify individual students who did not demonstrate proficiency on each standard. This information can be used to differentiate instruction. Additionally, they can track individual student performance and progress on each standard over time.

Teachers can take note of overall patterns and trends in assessment data. For example, they can determine if any subgroups of students did not meet expectations. They can consider whether the data confirms or challenges any existing beliefs, implications this may have on instructional planning and what, if any, conclusions can be drawn from this data.

Analyzing and interpreting assessment data may raise new questions for educators, so they can also determine if additional data collection is needed.

USING ASSESSMENT DATA TO DIFFERENTIATE INSTRUCTION FOR INDIVIDUAL LEARNERS

By analyzing and interpreting assessment data, teachers can determine if there are any specific learning standards that need to be retaught to their entire classes. This may be necessary if the data shows that all students struggled in these specific areas. Teachers may consider reteaching these standards using different methods if the initial methods were unsuccessful.

Teachers can also form groups of students who did not demonstrate proficiency on the same learning standards. Targeted instruction can be planned for these groups to help them make progress in these areas. Interventions can also be planned for individual students who did not show proficiency in certain areas. If interventions have already been in place and have not led to increased learning outcomes, the interventions may be redesigned. If interventions have been in place and assessment data now shows proficiency, the interventions may be discontinued.

If assessment data shows that certain students have met or exceeded expectations in certain areas, enrichment activities can be planned to challenge these students and meet their learning needs.

ALIGNING ASSESSMENTS WITH INSTRUCTIONAL GOALS AND OBJECTIVES

Assessments that are congruent to instructional goals and objectives provide a **clear purpose** for learning that enhances student understanding and motivation. When learning targets are reflected in assessments, instructional activities and materials become more **relevant**, as they are derived from these specifications. Such clarity in purpose allows for more focus and productivity as students engage in instruction and fosters connections that strengthen overall understanding for maximized success in learning. Aligning assessments with instructional goals and objectives ensures that students are learning material that is relevant to the curriculum and academic standards to ensure **preparedness** as they advance in their academic careers. In addition, it enables the teacher to evaluate and monitor student progress to determine whether they are progressing at an ideal pace for achieving academic standards. With this information, the teacher can effectively modify instruction as necessary to support students' needs in reaching desired learning outcomes.

NORM-REFERENCED TESTS

On **norm-referenced tests**, students' performances are compared to the performances of sample groups of similar students. Norm-referenced tests identify students who score above and below the average. To ensure reliability, the tests must be given in a standardized manner to all students.

Norm-referenced tests usually cover a broad range of skills, such as the entire grade-level curriculum for a subject. They typically contain a few questions per skill. Whereas scores in component areas of the tests may be calculated, usually overall test scores are reported. Scores are often reported using percentile ranks, which indicate what percentage of test takers scored lower than the student being assessed. For example, a student's score in the 75th percentile means the student scored better than 75% of other test takers. Other times, scores may be reported using grade-level equivalency.

One advantage of norm-referenced tests is their objectivity. They also allow educators to compare large groups of students at once. This may be helpful for making decisions regarding class placements and groupings. A disadvantage of norm-referenced tests is that they only indicate how well students perform in comparison to one another. They do not indicate whether or not students have mastered certain skills.

CRITERION-REFERENCED TESTS

Criterion-referenced tests measure how well students perform on certain skills or standards. The goal of these tests is to indicate whether or not students have mastered certain skills and which skills require additional instruction. Scores are typically reported using the percentage of questions answered correctly or students' performance levels. Performance levels are outlined using terms such as below expectations, met expectations, and exceeded expectations.

One advantage of criterion-referenced tests is they provide teachers with useful information to guide instruction. They can identify which specific skills students have mastered and which skills need additional practice. Teachers can use this information to plan whole-class, small-group, and individualized instruction. Analyzing results of criterion-referenced tests over time can also help teachers track student progress on certain skills. A disadvantage of criterion-referenced tests is they do not allow educators to compare students' performances to samples of their peers.

WAYS THAT STANDARDIZED TEST RESULTS ARE REPORTED

- **Raw scores** are sometimes reported and indicate how many questions students answered correctly on a test. By themselves, they do not provide much useful information. They do not indicate how students performed in comparison to other students or to grade-level expectations.
- **Grade-level equivalents** are also sometimes reported. A grade-level equivalent score of 3.4 indicates that a student performed as well as an average third grader in the fourth month of school. It can indicate whether a student is performing above or below grade-level expectations, but it does not indicate that the student should be moved to a different grade level.
- **Standard scores** are used to compare students' performances on tests to standardized samples of their peers. Standard deviation refers to the amount that a set of scores differs from the mean score on a test.
- **Percentile ranks** are used on criterion-referenced tests to indicate what percentage of test takers scored lower than the student whose score is being reported.
- **Cutoff scores** refer to predetermined scores students must obtain in order to be considered proficient in certain areas. Scores below the cutoff level indicate improvement is needed and may result in interventions or instructional changes.

FORMAL AND INFORMAL ASSESSMENTS

Assessments are any method a teacher uses to gather information about student comprehension of curriculum, including improvised questions for the class and highly-structured tests. **Formal assessments** are assessments that have **clearly defined standards and methodology**, and which are applied consistently to all students. Formal tests should be objective and the test itself should be scrutinized for validity and reliability since it tends to carry higher weight for the student. Summative assessments, such as end-of-unit tests, lend themselves to being formal tests because it is necessary that a teacher test the comprehension of all students in a consistent and thorough way.

Although formal assessments can provide useful data about student performance and progress, they can be costly and time-consuming to implement. Administering formal assessments often interrupts classroom instruction, and may cause testing anxiety.

Informal assessments are assessments that do not adhere to formal objectives and they do not have to be administered consistently to all students. As a result, they do not have to be scored or recorded as a grade and generally act as a **subjective measure** of class comprehension. Informal assessments can be as simple as asking a whole class to raise their hand if they are ready to proceed to the next step or asking a particular question of an individual student.

Informal assessments do not provide objective data for analysis, but they can be implemented quickly and inexpensively. Informal assessments can also be incorporated into regular classroom instruction and activities, making them more authentic and less stressful for students.

USING VARIOUS ASSESSMENTS

The goal of **assessment** in education is to gather data that, when evaluated, can be used to further student learning and achievement. **Standardized tests** are helpful for placement purposes and to reflect student progress toward goals set by a school district or state. If a textbook is chosen to align with district learning standards, the textbook assessments can provide teachers with convenient, small-scale, regular checks of student knowledge against the target standard.

In order be effective, teachers must know where their students are in the learning process. Teachers use a multitude of **formal and informal assessment methods** to do this. Posing differentiated discussion questions is an example of an informal assessment method that allows teachers to gauge individual student progress rather than their standing in relation to a universal benchmark.

Effective teachers employ a variety of assessments, as different formats assess different skills, promote different learning experiences, and appeal to different learners. A portfolio is an example of an assessment that gauges student progress in multiple skills and through multiple media. Teachers can use authentic or performance-based assessments to stimulate student interest and provide visible connections between language-learning and the real world.

ASSESSMENT RELIABILITY

Assessment reliability refers to how well an assessment is constructed and is made up of a variety of measures. An assessment is generally considered **reliable** if it yields similar results across multiple administrations of the assessment. A test should perform similarly with different test administrators, graders, and test-takers and perform consistently over multiple iterations. Factors that affect reliability include the day-to-day wellbeing of the student (students can sometimes underperform), the physical environment of the test, the way it is administered, and the subjectivity of the scorer (with written-response assessments).

Perhaps the most important threat to assessment reliability is the nature of the **exam questions** themselves. An assessment question is designed to test student knowledge of a certain construct. A question is reliable in this sense if students who understand the content answer the question correctly. Statisticians look for patterns in student marks, both within the single test and over multiple tests, as a way of measuring reliability. Teachers should watch out for circumstances in which a student or students answer correctly a series of questions about a given concept (demonstrating their understanding) but then answer a related question incorrectly. The latter question may be an unreliable indicator of concept knowledge.

MEASURES OF ASSESSMENT RELIABILITY

- **Test-retest reliability** refers to an assessment's consistency of results with the same test-taker over multiple retests. If one student shows inconsistent results over time, the test is not considered to have test-retest reliability.
- **Intertester reliability** refers to an assessment's consistency of results between multiple test-takers at the same level. Students at similar levels of proficiency should show similar results.
- **Interrater reliability** refers to an assessment's consistency of results between different administrators of the test. This plays an especially critical role in tests with interactive or subjective responses, such as Likert-scales, cloze tests, and short answer tests. Different raters of the same test need to have a consistent means of evaluating the test-takers' performance. Clear rubrics can help keep two or more raters consistent in scoring.

- **Intra-rater reliability** refers to an assessment's consistency of results with one rater over time. One test rater should be able to score different students objectively to rate subjective test formats fairly.
- **Parallel-forms reliability** refers to an assessment's consistency between multiple different forms. For instance, end-of-course assessments may have many distinctive test forms, with different questions or question orders. If the different forms of a test do not provide the same results, it is said to be lacking in parallel-forms reliability.
- **Internal consistency reliability** refers to the consistency of results of similar questions on a particular assessment. If there are two or more questions targeted at the same standard and at the same level, they should show the same results across each question.

ASSESSMENT VALIDITY

Assessment validity is a measure of the relevancy that an assessment has to the skill or ability being evaluated, and the degree to which students' performance is representative of their mastery of the topic of assessment. In other words, a teacher should ask how well an assessment's results correlate to what it is looking to assess. Assessments should be evaluated for validity on both the **individual question** level and as a **test overall**. This can be especially helpful in refining tests for future classes. The overall validity of an assessment is determined by several types of validity measures.

An assessment is considered **valid** if it measures what it is intended to measure. One common error that can reduce the validity of a test (or a question on a test) occurs if the instructions are written at a reading level the students can't understand. In this case, it is not valid to take the student's failed answer as a true indication of his or her knowledge of the subject. Factors internal to the student might also affect exam validity: anxiety and a lack of self-esteem often lower assessments results, reducing their validity of a measure of student knowledge.

An assessment has content validity if it includes all the **relevant aspects** of the subject being tested—if it is comprehensive, in other words. An assessment has **predictive validity** if a score on the test is an accurate predictor of future success in the same domain. For example, SAT exams purport to have validity in predicting student success in a college. An assessment has construct validity if it accurately measures student knowledge of the subject being tested.

MEASURES OF ASSESSMENT VALIDITY

- **Face validity** refers to the initial impression of whether an assessment seems to be fit for the task. As this method is subjective to interpretation and unquantifiable, it should not be used singularly as a measurement of validity.
- **Construct validity** asks if an assessment actually assesses what it is intended to assess. Some topics are more straightforward, such as assessing if a student can perform two-digit multiplication. This can be directly tested, which gives the assessment a strong content validity. Other measures, such as a person's overall happiness, must be measured indirectly. If an assessment asserted that a person is generally happy if they smile frequently, it would be fair to question the construct validity of that assessment because smiling is unlikely to be a consistent measure of all peoples' general happiness.
- **Content validity** indicates whether the assessment is comprehensive of all aspects of the content being assessed. If a test leaves out an important topic, then the teacher will not have a full picture as a result of the assessment.
- **Criterion validity** refers to whether the results of an assessment can be used to **predict** a related value, known as **criterion**. An example of this is the hypothesis that IQ tests would predict a person's success later in life, but many critics believe that IQ tests are not valid predictors of success because intelligence is not the only predictor of success in life. IQ tests have shown validity toward predicting academic success, however. The measure of an assessment's criterion validity depends on how closely related the criterion is.

- **Discriminant validity** refers to how well an assessment tests only that which it is intended to test and successfully discriminates one piece of information from another. For instance, a student who is exceptional in mathematics should not be able to put that information into use on a science test and gain an unfair advantage. If they are able to score well due to their mathematics knowledge, the science test did not adequately discriminate science knowledge from mathematics knowledge.
- **Convergent validity** is related to discriminant validity, but takes into account that two measures may be distinct, but can be correlated. For instance, a personality test should distinguish self-esteem from extraversion so that they can be measured independently, but if an assessment has convergent validity, it should show a correlation between related measures.

PRACTICALITY

An assessment is **practical** if it uses an appropriate amount of human and budgetary resources. A practical exam doesn't take very long to design or score, nor does it take students very long to complete in relation to other learning objectives and priorities. Teachers often need to balance a desire to construct comprehensive or content-valid tests with a need for practicality: lengthy exams consume large amounts of instruction time and may return unreliable results if students become tired and lose focus.

ASSESSMENT BIAS

An assessment is considered biased if it disadvantages a certain group of students, such as students of a certain gender, race, cultural background, or socioeconomic class. A **content bias** exists when the subject matter of a question or assessment is familiar to one group and not another—for example, a reading comprehension passage which discusses an event in American history would be biased against students new to the country. An **attitudinal bias** exists when a teacher has a pre-conceived idea about the likely success of an assessment of a particular individual or group. A **method bias** arises when the format of an assessment is unfamiliar to a given group of students. **Language bias** occurs when an assessment utilizes idioms, collocations, or cultural references unfamiliar to a group of students. Finally, **translation bias** may arise when educators attempt to translate content-area assessments into a student's native language—rough or hurried translations often result in a loss of nuance important for accurate assessment.

AUTHENTIC ASSESSMENTS

An authentic assessment is an assessment designed to closely resemble something that a student does, or will do, in the real world. Thus, for example, students will never encounter a multiple-choice test requiring them to choose the right tense of a verb, but they will encounter context in which they have to write a narration of an event that has antecedents and consequents spread out in time—for example, their version of what caused a traffic accident. The latter is an example of a potential **authentic assessment**.

Well-designed authentic assessments require a student to exercise **advanced cognitive skills** (e.g., solving problems, integrating information, performing deductions), integrate **background knowledge**, and confront **ambiguity**. Research has demonstrated that mere language proficiency is not predictive of future language success—learning how to utilize knowledge in a complex context is an essential additional skill.

The terms "authentic" and "performance-based" assessments are often used interchangeably. However, a performance-based assessment doesn't necessarily have to be grounded in a possible authentic experience.

PERFORMANCE-BASED ASSESSMENTS

A performance-based assessment is one in which students demonstrate their learning by performing a **task** rather than by answering questions in a traditional test format. Proponents of **performance-based assessments** argue that they lead students to use **high-level cognitive skills** as they focus on how to put their knowledge to use and plan a sequence of stages in an activity or presentation. They also allow students more opportunities to individualize their presentations or responses based on preferred learning styles. Research suggests that students welcome the chance to put their knowledge to use in real-world scenarios.

Advocates of performance-based assessments suggest that they avoid many of the problems of language or cultural bias present in traditional assessments, and thus they allow more accurate assessment of how well students learned the underlying concepts. In discussions regarding English as a second language, they argue that performance assessments come closer to replicating what should be the true goal of language learning—the effective use of language in real contexts—than do more traditional exams. Critics point out that performance assessments are difficult and time-consuming for teachers to construct and for students to perform. Finally, performative assessments are difficult to grade in the absence of a well-constructed and detailed rubric.

TECHNOLOGY-BASED ASSESSMENTS

Technology-based assessments provide teachers with multiple resources for evaluating student progress to guide instruction. They are applicable in most formal and informal instructional settings and can be utilized as formative and summative assessments. Technology-based assessments simplify and enhance the efficiency of determining comprehension and instructional effectiveness, as they quickly present the teacher with information regarding student progress. This data enables the teacher to make necessary adjustments to facilitate student learning and growth. Implementing this assessment format simplifies the process of aligning them to school and district academic standards. This establishes objectivity and uniformity for comparing results and progress among students, as well as ensures that all students are held to the same academic expectations. While technology-based assessments are beneficial, there are some shortcomings to consider. This format may not be entirely effective for all learning styles in demonstrating understanding, as individualization in technology-based assessment can be limited. These assessments may not illustrate individual students' growth over time, but rather their mastery of an academic standard, thus hindering the ability to evaluate overall achievement. As technology-based evaluation limits hands-on opportunities, the real-world application and relevancy of the assessment may be unapparent to students.

ADVANTAGES AND DISADVANTAGES OF TECHNOLOGY-BASED ASSESSMENTS

Technology-based assessments can have many advantages. They can be given to large numbers of students at once, limited only by the amounts of technological equipment schools possess. Many types of technology-based assessments are instantly scored, and feedback is quickly provided. Students are sometimes able to view their results and feedback at the conclusion of their testing sessions. Data can be quickly compiled and reported in easy-to-understand formats. Technology-based assessments can also often track student progress over time.

Technology-based assessments can have some disadvantages as well. Glitches and system errors can interfere with the assessment process or score reporting. Students must also have the necessary prerequisite technological skills to take the assessments, or the results may not measure the content they are designed to measure. For example, if students take timed computer-based writing tests, they should have proficient typing skills. Otherwise, they may perform poorly on the tests despite strong writing abilities. Other prerequisite skills include knowing how to use a keyboard and mouse and understanding how to locate necessary information on the screen.

PORTFOLIO ASSESSMENTS

A **portfolio** is a collection of student work in multiple forms and media gathered over time. Teachers may assess the portfolio both for evidence of progress over time or in its end state as a demonstration of the achievement of certain proficiency levels.

One advantage of **portfolio assessments** is their breadth—unlike traditional assessments which focus on one or two language skills, portfolios may contain work in multiple forms—writing samples, pictures, and graphs designed for content courses, video and audio clips, student reflections, teacher observations, and student exams. A second advantage is that they allow a student to develop work in authentic contexts, including in other classrooms and at home.

In order for portfolios to function as an objective assessment tool, teachers should negotiate with students in advance of what genres of work will be included and outline a grading rubric that makes clear what will be assessed, such as linguistic proficiency, use of English in academic contexts, and demonstrated use of target cognitive skills.

CURRICULUM-BASED ASSESSMENTS

Curriculum-based assessments, also known as **curriculum-based measurements (CBM)**, are short, frequent assessments designed to measure student progress toward meeting curriculum **benchmarks**.

Teachers implement CBM by designing **probes**, or short assessments that target specific skills. For example, a teacher might design a spelling probe, administered weekly, that requires students to spell 10 unfamiliar but level-appropriate words. Teachers then track the data over time to measure student progress toward defined grade-level goals.

CBM has several clear advantages. If structured well, the probes have high reliability and validity. Furthermore, they provide clear and objective evidence of student progress—a welcome outcome for students and parents who often grapple with less-clear and subjective evidence. Used correctly, CBMs also motivate students and provide them with evidence of their own progress. However, while CBMs are helpful in identifying *areas* of student weaknesses, they do not identify the *causes* of those weaknesses or provide teachers with strategies for improving instruction.

TEXTBOOK ASSESSMENTS

Textbook assessments are the assessments provided at the end of a chapter or unit in an approved textbook. **Textbook assessments** present several advantages for a teacher: they are already made; they are likely to be accurate representations of the chapter or unit materials; and, if the textbook has been prescribed or recommended by the state, it is likely to correspond closely to Common Core or other tested standards.

Textbook assessments can be limiting for students who lag in the comprehension of academic English, or whose preferred learning style is not verbal. While textbooks may come with DVDs or recommended audio links, ESOL teachers will likely need to supplement these assessment materials with some of their own findings. Finally, textbook assessments are unlikely to represent the range of assessment types used in the modern classroom, such as a portfolio or performance-based assessments.

PEER ASSESSMENT

A peer assessment is when students grade one another's work based on a teacher-provided framework. **Peer assessments** are promoted as a means of saving teacher time and building student metacognitive skills. They are typically used as **formative** rather than summative assessments, given concerns about the reliability of student scoring and the tensions that can result if student scores contribute to overall grades. Peer assessments are used most often to grade essay-type written work or presentations. Proponents point out that peer assessments require students to apply metacognition, builds cooperative work and interpersonal skills, and broadens the sense that the student is accountable to peers and not just the teacher. Even advocates of the practice agree that students need detailed rubrics in order to succeed. Critics often argue that low-performing students have little to offer high-performing students in terms of valuable feedback—and this disparity may be more pronounced in ESOL classrooms or special education environments than in mainstream ones. One way to overcome this weakness is for the teacher to lead the evaluation exercise, guiding the students through a point-by-point framework of evaluation.

Chapter Quiz

Ready to see how well you retained what you just read? Scan the QR code to go directly to the chapter quiz interface for this study guide. If you're using a computer, simply visit the bonus page at **mometrix.com/bonus948/pectprek4** and click the Chapter Quizzes link.

Collaboration and Professionalism

Transform passive reading into active learning! After immersing yourself in this chapter, put your comprehension to the test by taking a quiz. The insights you gained will stay with you longer this way. Scan the QR code to go directly to the chapter quiz interface for this study guide. If you're using a computer, simply visit the bonus page at **mometrix.com/bonus948/pectprek4** and click the Chapter Quizzes link.

Early Childhood Legal Responsibilities

LEGAL RESPONSIBILITIES OF EARLY CHILDHOOD PROFESSIONALS

Historically, special education was introduced with the purpose of separating special-needs children from their normally developing peers. However, since 1991, the IDEA legislation has established the necessity of inclusion in normal care and educational environments, including early childhood (EC) settings, for children with disabilities. EC professionals know excluding any child is illegal. Another example of legal responsibilities is the "mandated reporter" status of caregivers, teachers, and other adults working with children and families. They are legally required to report suspected child abuse and neglect; the law penalizes them for not reporting. For example, say an EC teacher sees injuries to a child. The child knows the mother has a new boyfriend, displays a fearful attitude, and responds evasively to teacher questions. Later, the child tells the teacher that he or she has been hurt by the boyfriend. The teacher pities the mother, realizing she needs the boyfriend financially and emotionally, and reporting suspected abuse could make the mother lose her children or their home. Regardless, the teacher must report suspicions by law, which was enacted to stop violence against children.

REGULATIONS REGARDING THE CONFIDENTIALITY OF RECORDS

In early childhood settings, records kept about children and their families must be treated with strict confidentiality. Early childhood centers/programs/preschools/agencies should limit access to student records to children's immediate family members, only those employees authorized, and agencies having legal authority to access records. Confidentiality of records and restricted access to them in all centers/programs/preschools/agencies that receive federal funding are mandated by the **Family Educational Rights and Privacy Act (FERPA)**. Moreover, with the ongoing trend toward educational inclusion, many EC settings serve children with disabilities, whose student records are additionally subject to regulations under the federal **Individuals with Disabilities Education Act (IDEA)** and also to the special education laws of their respective US states. An exception to the laws regarding records confidentiality is mandated reporting by EC personnel of suspected child abuse and neglect. Laws applying to child abuse and neglect supersede FERPA regulations. Legally, EC employees are required to report the suspected abuse and neglect of children, and they are immune from liability for releasing child records information relevant to their reporting.

QUALITY CARE AND ECONOMIC CONSIDERATIONS

To furnish and sustain quality care in early childhood settings is always challenging to care providers. It is even more so during difficult economic times. Many early childhood centers must face whether to downsize the services they offer or to go out of business. When administrators choose to remain in operation, they encounter equally difficult decisions regarding how to reduce services, but not at the expense of quality. A legal issue related to such economic considerations is that EC personnel are often placed at legal risk when service quality is compromised. While EC employers, employees, young children's parents, and educational researchers are all interested in and pursue a definition of quality care, no single operational definition has been attained. However, early childhood professionals with ample work experience in EC centers have contributed various definitions. The consensus of their contributions includes the following common elements:

91

a nurturing environment; employees trained in EC development and methods; age-appropriate curricula; sufficient space, equipment, and materials; safety and good maintenance of physical environments; and good parent-teacher communication.

MEDICAL CARE AND TREATMENT EMPHASIZED IN LEGAL REGULATIONS

The child care licensing regulations of each US state government mostly govern children's medical care and treatment in early childhood settings. Overall, state regulations emphasize four areas of medical care and treatment:

- Health requirements for all employees, such as having no communicable diseases, passing a TB test, having no health conditions preventing active child care, and maintaining accurate employee and child health records
- Administration by staff of medication to children being served in EC settings
- Management by EC staff of emergencies due to illness, injury, and accidents
- Treatment of nonemergency minor illnesses, injuries, and accidents occurring to children in EC settings

To protect children's health and safety, EC programs/schools/centers must maintain written policies and procedures for emergency and nonemergency care. To protect personnel from litigation, they must adhere scrupulously to written policies and procedures. Litigation for damages or injury is likely when not following procedures. Not reporting suspected or observed child abuse/neglect and not completing accident reports also invite lawsuits.

ADMINISTRATION OF MEDICATION GUIDELINES

The administration of medication to children in early childhood settings has been subject to much controversy due to obvious issues of dangers and liability. EC centers and programs must write their policies and procedures to include their state government's licensing requirements for medical care and treatment, which they must follow closely. Experts recommend that parent and doctor permission be required for administering any prescription and nonprescription medications to children. EC settings should keep on file written parental consent for each medication and review these records regularly for changes. They should also post separate charts, easily accessible to staff, with each child's name, medication, dosage, administration time, and teacher initials. These provide documentation of teachers following parent directions and can prevent mistakes. Staff should label all medications with the drug name, child's name, doctor's name and contact information, and administration instructions. EC centers seasonally and frequently contain many children simultaneously recovering from a variety of illnesses; labeling prevents giving children the wrong medication. Empty drug containers should be returned to parents.

TRANSPORTATION FROM EARLY CHILDHOOD LOCATIONS AND EMERGENCY MEDICAL TREATMENT

For a child's non-life-threatening medical emergencies, early childhood personnel should request transportation by the child's parents. However, if parents cannot transport the child, or in a more severe emergency, EC administrators should call an ambulance. In life-threatening emergencies that preclude waiting for an ambulance, EC administrators must designate the vehicle and responsible employee for transporting the child to the hospital; this information should be posted in the facility's emergency procedures. Administrators should keep the number of staff involved in emergency medical treatment to a minimum. Those employees they designate for involvement should be willing to take on the responsibility and should have current first aid training. The administrators can include a clause in these employees' job descriptions providing for their transporting children in the event of an emergency. The EC facility may also pay for additional or separate liability insurance coverage of the employees they designate as responsible for providing necessary emergency medical treatment.

CHILD CUSTODY ISSUES INVOLVING EARLY CHILDHOOD FACILITIES

EC facilities are affected by two types of issues involving child custody:

- Parents are pursuing legal and/or physical custody of the child, but they are not living together.
- State authorities have removed a child from the parents' legal and physical custody.

Parents frequently demand the right to visit with and/or take the child home on occasion. Two types of custody are legal custody, defined as an individual's or agency's right to make decisions on a child's behalf regarding the child's place of residence, medical treatment, and education; and physical custody, defined as an individual's or agency's right and responsibility to provide a child with immediate care, and a household or care facility for the present and immediate future. Physical custody does not include all of the rights of full legal custody. It is serious for a child to be in the middle of a custody battle between divorcing parents or between parents and foster parents; therefore, early childhood facilities need the most concise, clear-cut guidelines possible.

EMERGENCY MEDICAL TREATMENT AND FIRST AID RECOMMENDATIONS

EC programs and preschools must write specific, detailed procedures regarding emergency treatment and keep these on file. Children's parents as well as early childhood administrators and staff need to be informed regarding what will occur in the event of a child's serious illness or injury. EC settings must also keep written, signed parental consent forms on file, as well as parent contact information, parental physician and hospital preferences, and health insurance information. EC staff should have current, regularly updated first aid training. First aid equipment should be stored in locations accessible to personnel, who should be frequently reminded of these locations. Lists of each staff member's first aid responsibilities and training should be posted, also accessibly. Licensing regulations require early childhood facilities to notify parents of emergencies; not doing so is subject to legal action. In non-life-threatening emergencies, staff should ask parents to furnish transportation and medical treatment. For grave emergencies, parental consent forms should be filed and updated semiannually, including physician and hospital names, ambulance service, and other transportation procedures.

NON-EMERGENCY MEDICAL ILLNESSES

EC programs must keep procedures for, and reports on, nonemergency medical treatment of children on file just as they do for emergency procedures and reporting. Staff must contact and notify a sick child's parents, who decide if the child should leave the center/preschool. If so, parents should transport their child. Parental consent forms should authorize a doctor or nurse to provide routine medical treatment. early childhood centers/preschools should have sick children wait to be picked up in a location that is separate from other children and activities but closely supervised by staff. For children with allergies, diabetes, and other chronic medical conditions, early childhood centers/preschools should not only keep this information on file in records but also post it accessibly at all times for staff reference. Instructions for any special treatment should be included. For any health impairments a child has that could potentially involve emergency treatment, directions for staff should be visibly posted, including specific employees designated to administer treatment. This protects children from harm and caregivers and educators from legal liability.

CUSTODY STATUS

It is recommended that during a child's enrollment, early childhood programs procure a signed, dated document clarifying the child's custody status, including names, contact information, and relationships of all individuals authorized to pick up the child. Copies of any separation agreement or court decree should also be filed. Any time EC staff do not recognize an individual coming to pick up a child, they should ask the person to produce photo identification, which they should closely inspect. EC program administrators cannot make decisions regarding who has legal or physical custody of a child they serve. When a parent or other adult enrolls a child in an early childhood program, that adult is asked to list other persons to be contacted in the event of an emergency. EC administrators are advised to present all parents/guardians with a statement that the early childhood center will only release their child to someone the enrolling parent/adult listed on the emergency form as authorized to pick up the child.

PICKING UP CHILDREN

NON-CUSTODIAL OR NON-AUTHORIZED ADULTS ATTEMPTING TO PICK UP CHILDREN

EC centers should always have up-to-date documentation on file of a child's custodial arrangements, signed and dated by the enrolling adult. If an adult not authorized to pick up the child attempts to do so, an early childhood administrator should inform that adult of the center's policies and procedures regarding custody. They may even show the unauthorized adult their copy of the custodial court order if needed. If the unauthorized adult then departs, the administrator must notify the enrolling adult of the incident; file a written report of it; meet with the custodial adult to clarify custody arrangements anew; document this meeting, including its date and signatures; and file the document in the child's record. If the unauthorized adult refuses to leave and makes a scene or threatens/displays violence, the EC administrator should call the police if needed. The EC center's having a procedure in place for protecting children against emotionally upsetting scenes and/or violent adult behavior is crucial to the children's safety and well-being.

LEGAL RESPONSIBILITIES WHEN CHILDREN ARE NOT PICKED UP TIMELY

If a child is not picked up on time from an early childhood center at the end of its defined day, the EC center has the legal responsibility for the child's welfare as long as the child is on the premises. In the event that a child is left at the EC center for a long time and the parent/authorized adult has not notified the center why and/or when the child will be picked up, EC personnel are advised that keeping the child at the center is less likely to incur legal liability than for the child to stay at an EC staff member's home, for example. If the child has to be removed, it is important for EC staff to inform the police of this and where they are taking the child. If parents are chronically tardy picking up children, EC staff should review the child's information and/or inquire further of parents to ascertain reasons and possible solutions because they are legally responsible for reporting suspected child neglect.

ATTRIBUTES INDICATING EARLY CHILDHOOD EDUCATORS' PROFESSIONALISM AND PROFESSIONAL RESPONSIBILITY

While care and instruction of young children are delivered through a variety of program types, early childhood educators share common general goals. They appreciate early childhood as a unique period in life. They work to educate holistically, considering the mind, feelings, and body of the whole child. The educational goals they develop are designed to support each child's fulfilling his or her individual potential within relationship contexts. EC professionals realize children are inseparable from their social milieus of family, society, and culture; they work to relate to and understand children in these contexts while also appreciating and supporting family ties. They apply their knowledge of child development, teaching according to how children learn and what they need, and apply research in the field to differentiate common assumptions and myths from valid scientific findings. They have appropriate behavioral expectations for children at each developmental stage. EC professionals realize the significance of confidentiality; they never gossip or tell families personal information about other families. Lifelong learners, they set their own professional goals, pursuing ongoing professional development.

INTERACTIONS WITH ADULTS IN THE LEARNING ENVIRONMENT

Regarding teachers' roles, much of the focus is on observing children and their behaviors, helping children manage peer interactions, and giving children opportunities for developing peer-group social skills. Too often, a similar emphasis is not accorded to teachers' reflecting on their interactions and behaviors with other adults, learning to collaborate with other adults, and developing skills for conflict resolution and managing disagreements with other adults. Some experts say teachers should work diligently and deliberately to make adult interactions integral parts of daily classroom activity. For group early childhood education settings to attain their goals, adults must make and implement plans collaboratively. However, mandatory staff meetings are commonly occupied with curricular and administrative requirements; beyond these, little or no attention

94

or time is applied to nurturing adult-adult relationships. Adults interact during in-service trainings and professional development experiences but rarely outside of daily classroom settings. Nevertheless, these experiences can be used as foundations for better adult-adult communication within early childhood education contexts. Conscious efforts to develop adult-adult relationships benefiting children's growth, development, and learning are necessary.

POSITIVE INTERACTIONS AMONG ADULTS WITHIN THE EARLY CHILDHOOD EDUCATION SETTING

Adults engage in positive interactions with each other within early childhood education programs when they make time to share their anecdotal records and observations of their young students and collaboratively plan instruction based on their collective contributions. When adults share information and communicate with one another about the children and their families with whom they work, they interact positively together. When EC educators engage in problem-solving activities and dialogues, these help them identify which learning goals and experiences they can make more effective for the children and how they can do this. Adults within early childhood education settings should engage in reciprocal exchanging of ideas about the EC learning environment and about how to share responsibilities for performing instructional tasks, rearranging classrooms as needed, setting up class projects, taking care of class pets and plants, and other such daily duties.

ADULT-ADULT INTERACTIONS

Early childhood education research contains little work addressing adults' cooperation and collaborative expertise with each other and the influences of these on children. However, the HighScope curriculum model, The Creative Curriculum, and similar curriculum models and approaches do address adult-adult interactions by stressing how important teamwork is in planning lessons and sharing responsibilities and information. In addition, some educational experts have written about power struggles and other interactional dynamics in adult-adult relationships that can impede employee performance in a variety of settings. Professional development and training programs rarely include adult conflict-resolution techniques, instruction in working collaboratively, or adult learning principles. Hence, educators must consider how their adult-adult interactions can support children's development of competence, capability, and confidence. Sharing instructional goals, planning learning experiences that support goals, and sharing responsibilities as a team for implementing projects establishes climates of safety and trust for children.

APPLYING QUALITY TIME TO EARLY CHILDHOOD EDUCATORS' INTERACTIONS WITH ADULTS

Educators have noted that attitudes and things we commonly say to children, such as, "Your actions speak louder than your words," would equally benefit us in addressing our own behaviors as adults. Applying the same principles we teach children to interactions among adults in the learning community can positively influence those interactions, which in turn affects adult-child/teacher-student interactions and overall classroom atmospheres. Without such atmospheres conducive to trust and honesty in adult relationships, educators can fall prey to misunderstandings and internalizing negative attitudes, which influence not only coworker interactions but moreover classroom climates. One solution is for adults in early childhood education to establish occasions affording "quality adult time." Psychotherapist and psychological theorist Virginia Satir, pioneer of family therapy, found interpersonal dynamics influenced by positive adult-adult communication. Trust-building, mutual colleague support, and sharing experiences/feelings—related or unrelated to classrooms—promote adult relationships that benefit teacher-learner relationships and thus enhance young children's development and learning.

Early Childhood Programs and Approaches

MONTESSORI METHOD
SECTIONS OF THE MONTESSORI METHOD OF EARLY CHILDHOOD INSTRUCTION

- **The Practical Life Area**: These Montessori classes helps children develop care for self, others, and the environment. Children learn many daily skills, including buttoning, pouring liquids, preparing meals, and cleaning up after meals and activities.

- **The Sensorial Area**: This area gives young children experience with learning through all five senses. They participate in activities like ordering colors from lightest to darkest, sorting objects from roughest to smoothest texture, and sorting items from biggest to smallest/longest to shortest. They learn to match similar tastes, textures, and sounds.
- **The Language Arts Area**: This area encourages young children to express themselves in words, and they learn to identify letters, match them with corresponding phonemes (speech sounds), and manually trace their shapes as preparation for learning reading, spelling, grammar, and writing. In the
- **Mathematics and Geometry Area**: Children learn to recognize numbers, count, add, subtract, multiply, divide, and use the decimal system via hands-on learning with concrete materials. In the
- **Cultural Subjects Area**: Children learn science, art, music, movement, time, history, geography, and zoology.

ASPECTS OF THE PHILOSOPHY OF THE MONTESSORI METHOD AS A CURRICULUM APPROACH

Maria Montessori's method emphasizes children's engagement in self-directed activities, with teachers using clinical observations to act as children's guides. In introducing and teaching concepts, the Montessori Method also employs self-correcting ("autodidactic") equipment. This method focuses on the significance and interrelatedness of all life forms and the need for every individual to find his or her place in the world and to find meaningful work. Children in Montessori schools learn complex math skills and gain knowledge about diverse cultures and languages. Montessori philosophy puts emphasis on adapting learning environments to individual children's developmental levels. The Montessori Method also believes in teaching both practical skills and abstract concepts through the medium of physical activities. Montessori teachers observe and identify children's movements into sensitive periods when they are best prepared to receive individual lessons in subjects of interest to them that they can grasp readily. Children's senses of autonomy and self-esteem are encouraged in Montessori programs. Montessori instructors also strive to engage parents in their children's education.

GENERAL PRACTICES IN THE MONTESSORI METHOD

What Montessori calls "work" refers to developmentally appropriate learning materials. These are set out so each student can see the choices available. Children can select items from each of Montessori's five sections: Practical Life, Sensorial, Language Arts, Mathematics and Geometry, and Cultural Subjects. When a child is done with a work, he or she replaces it for another child to use and selects another work. Teachers work one-on-one with children and in groups; however, the majority of interactions are among children, as Montessori stresses self-directed activity. Not only teachers but also older children help younger ones in learning new skills, so Montessori classes usually incorporate 2- or 3-year age ranges. Depending on students' ages and the individual school, Montessori school days are generally half-days, 9 a.m.–noon or 12:30 p.m. Most Montessori schools also offer afternoon and/or early evening options. Children wanting to "do it myself" benefit from Montessori, as do special-needs children. Individualized attention, independence, and hands-on learning are emphasized. Montessori schools prefer culturally diverse students and teach about diverse cultures.

BANK STREET CURRICULUM APPROACH TO EARLY CHILDHOOD EDUCATION

Lucy Sprague Mitchell founded the **Bank Street** curriculum, applying theoretical concepts from Jean Piaget, Erik Erikson, John Dewey, and others. Bank Street is called a developmental-interaction approach. It emphasizes children's rich, direct interactions with a wide variety of ideas, materials, and people in their environments. The Bank Street method gives young children opportunities for physical, cognitive, emotional, and social development through engagement in various types of child care programs. Typically, multiple subjects are included and taught to groups. Children can learn through a variety of methods and at different developmental levels. By interacting directly with their geographical, social, and political environments, children are prepared for lifelong learning through this curriculum. Using blocks, solving puzzles, going on field trips, and doing practical lab work are among the numerous learning experiences Bank Street offers. Its philosophy is that school can simultaneously be stimulating, satisfying, and sensible. School is a significant part of children's lives, where they inquire about and experiment with the environment and share ideas with other children as they mature.

CLASSROOM CHARACTERISTICS FOR 5- TO 6-YEAR-OLDS

The Bank Street approach to teaching recommends that children 5–6 years old should have classrooms that are efficient, organized, conducive to working, and designed to afford them sensory and motor learning experiences. Classrooms should include rich varieties of appealing colors, which tend to energize children's imaginations and activity and encourage them to interact with the surroundings and participate in the environment. "Interest corners" in classrooms are advocated by the Bank Street approach. These are places where children can display their artworks, use language, and depict social life experiences. This approach also recommends having multipurpose tables in the classroom that children can use for writing, drawing, and other classroom activities. The Bank Street approach also points out the importance of libraries in schools, not just for supporting classroom content but for providing materials for children's extracurricular reading.

REQUIREMENTS AND ROLES OF CLASSROOMS AND TEACHERS

The Bank Street approach requires educators to create well-designed classrooms: this curriculum approach finds children are enabled to develop discipline by growing up in such controlled environments. Teachers are considered to be extremely significant figures in their young students' lives. The Bank Street approach requires that teachers always treat children with respect, to enable children to develop strong senses of self-respect. Teachers' having faith in their students and believing in their ability to succeed are found to have great impacts on young children's performance and their motivation to excel in school and in life. The Bank Street Curriculum emphasizes the importance of providing transitions from one type of activity to another. It also stresses changing the learning subjects at regular time intervals. This facilitates children's gaining a sense of direction and taking responsibility for what they do. Bank Street views these practices as helping children develop internal self-control, affording them discipline for dealing with the external world.

FROEBEL'S EDUCATIONAL THEORY REGARDING LEARNING AND TEACHING

Friedrich Froebel (1782–1852) originated the concept and practice of kindergarten (German for "child's garden"). He found that observation, discovery, play, and free, self-directed activity facilitated children's learning. He observed that drawing/art activities develop higher-level cognitive skills and that virtues are taught through children's games. He also found nature, songs, fables, stories, poems, and crafts to be effective learning media. He attributed reading and writing development to children's self-expression needs. Froebel recommended activities to develop children's motor skills and stimulate their imaginations. He believed in equal rather than authoritarian teacher-student relationships, and advocated family involvement/collaboration. He pointed out the critical nature of sensory experiences, and the value of life experiences for self-expression. He believed teachers should support students' discovery learning rather than prescribing what to learn. Like Piaget, Dewey, and Montessori, Froebel embraced constructivist learning, i.e. children construct meaning and reality through their interactions with the environment. He stressed the role of parents, particularly mothers, in children's educational processes.

FROEBEL'S FAMOUS ACHIEVEMENT

Froebel's theory of education had widespread influences, including using play-based instruction with young children. Froebel's educational theory emphasized the unity of humanity, nature, and God. Froebel believed the success of the individual dictates the success of the race, and that school's role is to direct students' will. He believed nature is the heart of all learning. He felt unity, individuality, and diversity were important values achieved through education. Froebel said education's goals include developing self-control and spirituality. He recommended curricula include math, language, design, art, health, hygiene, and physical education. He noted school's role in social development. According to Froebel, schools should impart meaning to life experiences; show students relationships among external, previously unrelated knowledge; and associate facts with principles. Froebel felt human potential is defined through individual accomplishments. He believed humans generally are productive and creative, attaining completeness and harmony via maturation.

SIEGFRIED ENGELMANN'S CONTRIBUTIONS TO EARLY CHILDHOOD EDUCATION

Siegfried Engelmann (b. 1931) cofounded the **Bereiter-Engelmann Program** with **Carl Bereiter** with funding from the US Office of Education. This project demonstrated the ability of intensive instruction to

97

enhance cognitive skills in disadvantaged preschool-aged children, establishing the **Bereiter-Engelmann Preschool Program**. Bereiter and Engelmann also conducted experiments reexamining Piaget's theory of cognitive development, specifically concerning the ability to conserve liquid volume. They showed it could be taught, contrary to Piaget's contention that this ability depended solely on a child's cognitive-developmental stage. Engelmann researched curriculum and instruction, including preschoolers with Down syndrome and children from impoverished backgrounds, establishing the philosophy and methodology of Direct Instruction. He designed numerous reading, math, spelling, language, and writing instruction programs, as well as achievement tests, videos, and games. Engelmann worked with Project Head Start and Project Follow Through. The former included his and Wesley Becker's comparison of their Engelmann-Becker model of early childhood instruction with other models in teaching disadvantaged children. The latter is often considered the biggest controlled study ever comparing teaching models and methods.

ENGELMANN'S METHODS AND FEATURES OF HIS CURRICULUM

In the 1960s, Engelmann noted a lack of research into how young children learn. Wanting to find out what kinds of teaching affected retention and what the extent was of individual differences among young learners, Engelmann conducted research, as Piaget had done, using his own children and those of colleagues and neighbors. With a previous advertising background, Engelmann formed focus groups of preschool children to test-market teaching methods. Main features of the curricula Engelmann developed included emphasizing phonics and computation early in young children's instruction; using a precise logical sequence to teach new skills; teaching new skills in small, separate, "child-sized" pieces; correcting learners' errors immediately; adhering strictly to designated teaching schedules; constantly reviewing to integrate new learning with previously attained knowledge; and scrupulous measurement techniques for assessing skills mastery. To demonstrate the results of his methods for teaching math, Engelmann sent movies he made of these to educational institutions. They showed that with his methods, toddlers could master upper-elementary-grade-level computations and even simple linear equations.

DIRECT INSTRUCTION METHOD OF TEACHING CHILDREN

Direct Instruction (DI) is a behavioral method of teaching. Therefore, learner errors receive immediate corrective feedback, and correct responses receive immediate, obvious positive reinforcement. DI has a fast pace—10–14 learner responses per minute overall—affording more attention and less boredom, reciprocal teacher-student feedback, immediate indications of learner problems to teachers, and natural reinforcement of teacher activities. DI thus promotes more mutual student and teacher learning than traditional "one-way" methods. Children are instructed in small groups according to ability levels. Their attention is teacher-focused. Teacher presentations follow scripts designed to give instruction the proper sequence, including prewritten prompts and questions developed through field-testing with real students. These optimized prepared lessons allow teachers to attend to extra instructional and motivational aspects of learning. Cued by teachers, who control the pace and give all learners with varying response rates chances for practice, children respond actively in groups and individually. Small groups are typically seated in semicircles close to teachers, who use visual aids like blackboards and overhead projectors.

PROJECT FOLLOW THROUGH

In 1967, President Lyndon B. Johnson declared his War on Poverty. This initiative included **Project Follow Through**, funded by the US Office of Education and Office of Economic Opportunity. Research had previously found that Project Head Start, which offered early educational interventions to disadvantaged preschoolers, had definite positive impacts, but these were often short-lived. Project Follow Through was intended to discover how to maintain Head Start's benefits. Siegfried Engelmann and Wesley Becker, who had developed the Engelmann-Becker instructional model, invited others to propose various other teaching models in communities selected to participate in Project Follow Through. The researchers asked parents in each community to choose from among the models provided. The proponents of each model were given funds to train teachers and furnish curriculum. Models found to enhance disadvantaged children's school achievement were to be promoted nationally. Engelmann's Direct Instruction model showed positive results surpassing all other models. However, the US Office of Education did not adopt this or other models found best.

APPROACHES TO REMEDIAL OR COMPENSATORY EDUCATION

A huge comparative study of curriculum and instruction methods, Project Follow Through incorporated three main approaches: Affective, Basic Skills, and Cognitive. Affective approaches used in Project Follow Through included the Bank Street, Responsive Education, and Open Education models. These teaching models aim to enhance school achievement by emphasizing experiences that raise children's self-esteem, which is believed to facilitate their acquisition of basic skills and higher-order problem-solving skills. Basic Skills approaches included the Southwest Labs, Behavior Analysis, and Direct Instruction models. These models find that mastering basic skills facilitates higher-order cognitive and problem-solving skills, and higher self-esteem. Cognitive approaches included the Parent Education, TEEM, and Cognitively Oriented Curriculum models. These models focus on teaching higher-order problem-solving and thinking skills as the optimal avenue to enhancing school achievement and to improving lower-order basic skills and self-esteem. Affective and Cognitive models have become popular in most schools of education. Basic Skills approaches are less popular but are congruent with other, very effective methods of specialized instruction.

CONTRIBUTIONS OF CONSTANCE KAMII TO EARLY CHILDHOOD EDUCATION

Professor of early childhood education **Constance Kamii**, of Japanese ancestry, was born in Geneva, Switzerland. She attended elementary school in both Switzerland and Japan, completing secondary school and higher education degrees in the United States. She studied extensively with Jean Piaget, also of Geneva. She worked with the **Perry Preschool Project** in the 1960s, fueling her subsequent interest in theoretically grounded instruction. Kamii believes in basing early childhood educational goals and objectives upon scientific theory of children's cognitive, social, and moral development, and moreover that Piaget's theory of cognitive development is the sole explanation for child development from birth to adolescence. She has done much curriculum research in the US and published a number of books on how to apply Piaget's theory practically in early childhood classrooms. Kamii agrees with Piaget that education's overall, long-term goal is developing children's intellectual, social, and moral autonomy. Kamii has said, "A classroom cannot foster the development of autonomy in the intellectual realm while suppressing it in the social and moral realms."

THEORETICAL ORIENTATION, PHILOSOPHY, AND APPROACH OF THE KAMII-DEVRIES APPROACH

Constance Kamii and Rheta DeVries formulated the **Kamii-DeVries Constructivist Perspective** model of preschool education. It is closely based upon Piaget's theory of child cognitive development and on the constructivist theory to which Piaget and others subscribed, which dictates that children construct their own realities through their interactions with the environment. Piaget's particular constructivism included the principle that through their interacting with the world within a logical-mathematical structure, children's intelligence, knowledge, personalities, and morality develop. The Kamii-DeVries approach finds that children learn via performing mental actions, which Piaget called operations, through the vehicle of physical activities. This model favors using teachers experienced in traditional preschool education, who employ a child-centered approach and establish active learning settings, are in touch with children's thoughts, respond to children from children's perspectives, and facilitate children's extension of their ideas. The Kamii-DeVries model has recently been applied to learning assessments using technology (2003) and to using constructivism in teaching physics to preschoolers (2011).

HIGHSCOPE CURRICULUM

David Weikart and colleagues developed the **HighScope Curriculum** in the 1960s and 1970s, testing it in the Perry Preschool and Head Start Projects, among others. The HighScope philosophy is based on Piaget's constructivist principles that active learning is optimal for young children; that they need to become involved actively with materials, ideas, people, and events; and that children and teachers learn together in the instructional environment. Weikart and colleagues' early research focused on economically disadvantaged children, but the HighScope approach has since been extended to all young children and all kinds of preschool settings. This model recommends dividing classrooms into well-furnished, separate "interest areas" and regular daily class routines, affording children time to plan, implement, and reflect upon what they learn and to participate in large and small group activities. Teachers establish socially supportive atmospheres; plan group learning activities; organize settings and set daily routines; encourage purposeful child activities, problem-

99

solving, and verbal reflection; and interpret child behaviors according to HighScope's key child development experiences.

HighScope Curriculum's Key Experiences for Preschoolers

The HighScope Curriculum model identified a total of **58 "key experiences"** it found critical for preschool child development and learning. These key experiences are subdivided into ten main categories:

- **Creative representation**, which includes recognizing symbolic use, imitating, and playing roles
- **Language and literacy**, which include speaking, describing, scribbling, and narrating/dictating stories
- **Initiative and social relations**, including solving problems, making decisions and choices, and building relationships
- **Movement**, including activities like running, bending, stretching, and dancing
- **Music**, which includes singing, listening to music, and playing musical instruments
- **Classification**, which includes sorting objects, matching objects or pictures, and describing object shapes
- **Seriation**, or arranging things in prescribed orders (e.g., by size or number)
- **Numbers**, which for preschoolers focuses on counting
- **Space**, which involves activities like filling and emptying containers
- **Time**, including concepts of starting, sequencing, and stopping actions.

Technology Use, School Day Durations and Settings, and Targets for Its Application

The HighScope Curriculum frequently incorporates computers as regular program components, including developmentally appropriate software, for children to access when they choose. School days may be full-day or part-day, determined by each individual program. Flexible hours accommodate individual family needs and situations. HighScope programs work in both child care and preschool settings. HighScope was originally designed to enhance educational outcomes for young children considered at-risk due to socioeconomically disadvantaged, urban backgrounds and was compatible with Project Head Start. This model of early childhood curriculum and instruction advocates individualizing teaching to each child's developmental level and pace of learning. As such, the HighScope approach is found to be effective for children who have learning disabilities and also for children with developmental delays. It works well with all children needing individual attention. HighScope is less amenable to highly structured settings that use more adult-directed instruction.

Head Start Program

Head Start was begun in 1964, extended by the Head Start Act of 1981, and revised in its 2007 reauthorization. It is a program of the US Department of Health and Human Services designed to give low-income families and their young children comprehensive services of health, nutrition, education, and parental involvement. While Head Start was initially intended to "catch up" low-income children over the summer to reach kindergarten readiness, it soon became obvious that a six-week preschool program was inadequate to compensate for having lived in poverty for one's first five years. Hence, the Head Start Program was expanded and modified over the years with the aim of remediating the effects of system-wide poverty upon child educational outcomes. Currently, Head Start gives local public, private, nonprofit, and for-profit agencies grants for delivering comprehensive child development services to promote disadvantaged children's school readiness by improving their cognitive and social development. It particularly emphasizes developing early reading and math abilities preschoolers will need for school success.

Genesis and Rationale of the Head Start Program

After research had accumulated considerable evidence of how important children's earliest years are to their ensuing growth and development, the US Department of Health and Human Services Administration for Children and Families' Office of Head Start established the Early Head Start Program in 1995. Early Head Start works to improve prenatal health, improve infant and toddler development, and enhance healthy family functioning. It serves children from 0–3 years. Like the original program, Early Head Start stresses parental engagement in children's growth, development, and learning.

PLAY-BASED CURRICULUM

To plan a curriculum based on children's natural play with building blocks (Hoisington, 2008), a teacher can first arrange the environment to stimulate further such play. Then he or she can furnish materials for children to make plans/blueprints for and records and models of buildings they construct. The teacher can make time during the day for children to reflect upon and discuss their individual and group-building efforts. Teachers can also utilize teaching strategies that encourage children to reflect on and consider in more depth the scientific principles related to their results. A teacher can provide building materials of varied sizes, shapes, textures, and weights, and can provide props to add realism, triggering more complex structures and creative, dramatic, emotional, and social development. Teachers can take photos of children's structures as documents for discussions, stimulating language and vocabulary development. Supplying additional materials to support and stick together blocks extends play-based learning. Active teacher participation by offering observations and asking open-ended questions promotes children's standards-based learning of scientific, mathematical, and linguistic concepts, processes, and patterns.

SUPPORTING AND INTEGRATING STANDARDS-BASED LEARNING IN SCIENTIFIC, MATHEMATICAL, AND LINGUISTIC DOMAINS

When children play at building with blocks, for example, they investigate material properties such as various block shapes, sizes, and weights and the stability of carpet vs. hard floor as bases. They explore cause-and-effect relationships, make conclusions regarding the results of their trial-and-error experiments, draw generalizations about observed patterns, and form theories about what does and does not work to build high towers. Ultimately, they construct their knowledge of how reality functions. Teachers support this by introducing relevant learning standards in the play context meaningful to children. For example, math standards, including spatial awareness, geometry, number, operations, patterns, and measurement, can be supported through planning play. By encouraging and guiding children's discussion and documentation of their play constructions, and supplying nonfictional and fictional books about building, a teacher also integrates learning goals and objectives for language and literacy development. Teachers can plan activities specifically to extend learning in these domains, like counting blocks, comparison/contrast, matching, sorting, sequencing, phonological awareness, alphabetic awareness, print awareness, book appreciation, listening, comprehension, speech, and communication.

USING THEMATIC TEACHING UNITS

To develop a thematic teaching unit, a teacher designs a collection of related activities around certain themes or topics that crosses several curriculum areas or domains. **Thematic units** create learning environments for young children that promote all children's active engagement, as well as their process learning. By studying topics children find relevant to their own lives, thematic units build upon children's preexisting knowledge and current interests and also help them relate information to their own life experiences. Varied curriculum content can be more easily integrated through thematic units in ways that young children can understand and apply meaningfully. Children's diverse individual learning styles are also accommodated through thematic units. Such units involve children physically in learning; teach them factual information in greater depth; teach them learning process-related skills, such as "learning how to learn"; holistically integrate learning; encourage cohesion in groups; meet children's individual needs; and provide motivation to both children and their teachers.

PROJECT APPROACH

The **Project Approach** (Katz and Chard, 1989) entails having young children choose a topic interesting to them, studying this topic, researching it, and solving problems and questions as they emerge. This gives children greater practice with creative thinking and problem-solving skills, which supports greater success in all academic and social areas. For example, if a class of preschoolers shows interest in the field of medicine, their teacher can plan a field trip to a local hospital to introduce a project studying medicine in depth. During the trip, the teacher can record children's considerations and questions, and then use these as guidelines to plan and conduct relevant activities that will further stimulate the children's curiosity and imagination. Throughout this or any other in-depth project, the teacher can integrate specific skills for reading, writing, math, science, social studies, and creative thinking. This affords dual benefits: enabling both children's skills advancement and their gaining knowledge they recognize is required and applies in their own lives. Children become life-long learners with this recognition.

INTEGRATED CURRICULUM AND EARLY CHILDHOOD EDUCATION

An **integrated curriculum** organizes early childhood education to transcend the boundaries between the various domains and subject content areas. It unites different curriculum elements through meaningful connections to allow study of wider areas of knowledge. It treats learning holistically and mirrors the interactive nature of reality. The principle that learning consists of series of interconnections is the foundation for teaching through use of an integrated curriculum. Benefits of integrated curricula include an organized planning mechanism, greater flexibility, and the ability to teach many skills and concepts effectively, include more varied content, and enable children to learn most naturally. By identifying themes children find most interesting, teachers can construct webs of assorted themes, which can provide the majority of their curriculum. Research has proven the effectiveness of integrated teaching units for both children and their teachers. Teachers can also integrate new content into existing teaching units they have identified as effective. Integrated units enable teachers to ensure children are learning pertinent knowledge and applying it to real-life situations.

SKILLS, TOPICS, STRATEGIES, AND BENEFITS RELATED TO CREATING THEMATICALLY-BASED TEACHING UNITS

EC teachers can incorporate many skills into units organized by theme. This includes state governments' educational standards/benchmarks for various skills. Teachers can base units on topics of interest to young children, such as building construction, space travel, movie-making, dinosaurs, vacations, nursery rhymes, fairy tales, pets, wildlife, camping, the ocean, and studies of particular authors and book themes. Beginning with a topic that motivates the children is best; related activities and skills will naturally follow. In planning units, teachers should establish connections among content areas like literacy, physical activity, dramatic play, art, music, math, science, and social studies. Making these connections permits children's learning through their strongest/favored modalities and supports learning through meaningful experiences, which is how they learn best. Theme-based approaches effectively address individual differences and modality-related strengths, as represented in Gardner's theory of multiple intelligences. Thematic approaches facilitate creating motivational learning centers and hands-on learning activities and are also compatible with creating portfolio assessments and performance-based assessments. Teachers can encompass skill and conceptual benchmarks for specific age/developmental levels within engaging themes.

Roles and Responsibilities within the Local Education System

DEPARTMENT CHAIRPERSONS

Department chairpersons are appointed to act as **leaders** within their subject area. These individuals are responsible for a variety of instructional and administrative duties to ensure the **efficacy** of their academic department in supporting the goals and mission of the school. This includes contributing to curriculum development, communicating instructional expectations from administration to their colleagues, and ensuring that daily instruction within the department aligns with campus and district academic standards. Department chairpersons also serve as **resources** for their team, including collaborating with them to design instructional activities and assessments, offering support, and facilitating positive communication with administration. When working with administration, department chairpersons discuss the progress of their department in meeting academic goals, collaborate to develop strategies for assisting faculty in supporting student learning, and ensure their colleagues have the support, materials, and resources necessary for effective instruction. In addition, department chairpersons are often responsible for coordinating department activities and programs that promote student achievement and contribute to creating a positive school community.

SCHOOL PRINCIPAL

The primary role of the **principal** is establishing and maintaining a **school culture** that supports students, teachers, staff, and families in the educational program. This role comprises a multifaceted array of responsibilities that extend to nearly every aspect of the school. The principal is responsible for supervising the **daily operations** of the school to ensure a safe, orderly environment in which teachers, staff, and students are working in alignment with the school's mission. To achieve this, the principal must communicate expectations for a positive, productive school community, ensure academic and behavioral policies are followed by staff and students, and assign staff members specific duties to facilitate an organized, efficient learning environment. In addition, it is important that the principal support staff, students, and families by engaging in frequent, open communication, addressing concerns, and providing resources necessary to promote growth and achievement. The principal is also responsible for ensuring that the school's educational program is effective in supporting teachers, staff, and students in the achievement of academic standards. This includes overseeing curriculum, monitoring instructional practices, measuring their school's performance in relation to district academic standards, as well as communicating the progress and needs of the school to the board of education.

BOARD OF TRUSTEES

Each school within a district is overseen by a **board of trustees** responsible for making decisions to ensure that the educational program supports students' learning needs for academic achievement. The board of trustees is comprised of a group of **elected individuals** that are typically members of the community in which they serve. As such, they have an understanding of the educational needs of the students within the community and can apply this knowledge to make effective decisions regarding the learning program. Members within a board of trustees are responsible for creating an educational program in alignment with students' needs, as well as setting goals and developing strategies that support students in achieving them. This includes determining a **budget plan, allocating resources**, and making **administrative decisions** that benefit the school. In addition, board members are responsible for analyzing assessment data to make informed decisions regarding strategies to best support individual schools within the district and ensuring that measures are being implemented to effectively meet students' learning needs.

CURRICULUM COORDINATORS

Curriculum coordinators are responsible for the **development** and **implementation** of curriculum that is aligned with campus and district academic goals. These individuals work closely with teachers and administrators to analyze student progress in relation to the educational program, primarily through **assessment scores**, to determine the overall effectiveness of the curriculum in supporting students' achievement. Analyzing student progress enables curriculum coordinators to identify strengths and areas for improvement within the curriculum to make adjustments that best meet students' learning needs as they work to achieve learning targets. Ensuring that curriculum aligns with academic standards and students' learning needs facilitates more effective teaching and learning. Doing so provides teachers with a clear understanding of how to adequately prepare students for success, thus allowing them to design focused instruction and implement necessary supports to promote the achievement of campus and district academic standards.

SCHOOL TECHNOLOGY COORDINATORS

Incorporating technology into the classroom is highly valuable in diversifying instructional strategies to promote student learning and engagement. School **technology coordinators** facilitate this integration to enhance teaching and learning, as they are responsible for the **organization, maintenance**, and **allocation** of available technology resources within the school building. This includes ensuring that all technology is functional, updated, properly stored, and accessible to teachers. These individuals are also responsible for **staying current** on developing digital resources that could be implemented to improve the learning experience, as well as communicating with the board of education regarding **acquiring** technology resources for their school. Doing so ensures that teachers have the materials necessary to best support students' learning. In addition, technology coordinators **educate** teachers and staff on the uses of technology resources, as well as strategies to implement them in the classroom for more effective instruction.

SPECIAL EDUCATION PROFESSIONALS

Special education professionals work with students of various disabilities, their teachers, and families to provide an equitable, inclusive environment that supports learning and development. These individuals are responsible for creating an educational plan that is tailored to support the unique needs of disabled students and ensuring that this plan is followed in all areas of the school. Special educators develop **individualized education programs** (IEPs) according to students' areas of need, develop academic and behavioral goals, as well as provide supports and modifications to accommodate students in achieving them. Special education professionals work with teachers to educate them on the proper implementation of individualized accommodations to ensure all students have the support necessary to successfully engage in learning. This includes collaborating with teachers to adapt and modify curriculum, instructional activities, and assessments to meet the individual needs of students with disabilities. In addition, special educators may work alongside classroom teachers in a team-teaching setting or provide individualized instruction as necessary. Students' academic and behavioral progress is monitored over time, and special educators communicate this information to families in order to collaborate in developing future goals and strategies to support achievement.

ROLES AND RESPONSIBILITIES OF PROFESSIONALS WITHIN THE EDUCATION PROGRAM

The roles and responsibilities of various professionals within the educational program are described as follows:

- **Principal**—The principal is responsible for ensuring that the daily operations of the school function in a safe, orderly manner that aligns with the goals of the educational program. This includes delegating tasks to staff, enforcing academic and behavioral policies, ensuring instructional practices support student achievement, and communicating with students, staff, and families to establish a positive learning environment.
- **Vice Principal**—The vice principal's role is to assist the principal in supervising the daily operations of the school to create a safe, orderly, and productive learning environment. They are responsible for working with teachers, staff, students, and families to support them in the educational program. This includes enforcing academic and behavioral policies, addressing concerns, facilitating communication, and ensuring instructional practices support student achievement of campus and district academic goals.
- **Board of Trustees**—The board of trustees is responsible for developing an educational program that reflects the learning needs of students within the community. This includes developing educational goals, strategies to support students in achieving them, and ensuring that schools within the district are in alignment with the educational program. The board of trustees is also responsible for such administrative decisions as developing a budget plan and allocating resources to schools within the district according to students' needs.
- **Curriculum Coordinator**—Curriculum coordinators are responsible for developing a curriculum that aligns with campus and district academic goals, and ensuring it is implemented properly to support student achievement. This includes working with teachers and administrators to measure student progress within the curriculum and adjusting instructional strategies as necessary to support student success.
- **Assessment Coordinator**—Assessment coordinators schedule, disperse, and collect standardized assessments and testing materials within the school building. They are responsible for educating teachers on proper assessment protocols to ensure that all practices align with district policies, collaborating with them to develop strategies that support student achievement, and ensuring all students are provided with necessary accommodations according to individual need.

- **Technology Coordinator**—Technology coordinators facilitate the integration of digital resources into the curriculum. They are responsible for acquiring, organizing, maintaining, and allocating technology within the school. These individuals also work with teachers and staff to educate them on ways to utilize technology resources to enhance instruction.
- **Department Chair**—Department chairpersons act as leaders among the teachers within their content area. Their responsibilities include contributing to curriculum development, facilitating communication between administration and their colleagues, and ensuring instructional practices align with the educational program. They also collaborate with members of their team to develop instructional practices that best support student achievement of campus and district academic goals.
- **Teacher Assistant**—The teacher assistant's role is to support the classroom teacher in both instructional and non-instructional duties. This includes assisting with the preparation, organization, and cleanup of lesson materials, working with small groups of students, managing student behavior, and ensuring the classroom functions in a safe, orderly manner.
- **Paraprofessional**—Paraprofessionals are licensed within the field of education and are responsible for assisting the teacher with daily classroom operations. This includes working with individual or small groups of students to provide instructional support, assisting with the preparation of lesson plans and materials, managing student behavior, and completing administrative duties.
- **Speech-Language Pathologist**—Speech-Language pathologists are special education professionals that work with students that have varying degrees of language and communication difficulties. They are responsible for evaluating and diagnosing disabilities related to speech and language, as well as developing individualized treatment programs. Speech-language pathologists then work with these students to remedy language and communication disabilities, as well as collaborate with teachers, staff, and families regarding ways to support their progress.
- **ESL Specialist**—ESL (English as a second language) specialists work with students for whom English is not their native language. They are responsible for evaluating students' levels of English language proficiency across the domains of reading, writing, speaking, and listening, determining necessary linguistic supports, and working with teachers to develop strategies that support English language acquisition. ESL specialists also work with individual or small groups of students to monitor progress and develop English language proficiency skills.
- **Guidance Counselor**—The role of guidance counselors is to support students' social, emotional, academic, and behavioral needs. This includes providing counseling services, mediation, and for upper grade level students, advice regarding course selection and career choices. These individuals communicate with teachers, staff, and families to develop and implement plans to support students' personal growth and academic achievement.
- **School Nurse**—The school nurse is responsible for providing a range of healthcare to students and staff in the school building. This includes evaluating the physical, mental, and emotional health of students and staff, as well as delivering general first-aid treatments. School nurses are also responsible for organizing and dispersing prescribed medications to students in accordance with their healthcare plan and educating teachers and staff regarding best practices for ensuring students' health and safety. School nurses may work with special education professionals to assess students' needs in the development of an individualized education program.
- **Building Service Worker**—Building service workers are responsible for the general maintenance of the school building and outside campus. This includes ensuring that all areas, equipment, and furniture are clean, functional, and safe for student and staff use. These individuals are also responsible for transporting heavy equipment and furniture throughout the school building.
- **Secretary**—The school secretary is responsible for assisting the principal, vice principal, and other office personnel in daily administrative duties. This individual assumes a variety of responsibilities to ensure the efficient function of daily operations within the school. Their responsibilities include communicating with students, families, and other office visitors, directing phone calls to the appropriate location, handling financial matters, and coordinating the school calendar.

- **Library/Media Specialist**—Library and media specialists coordinate the organization, maintenance, and allocation of all library and media resources within the school building. They are responsible for educating students regarding the proper use of library and media resources to locate information, including how to navigate the internet safely and appropriately for educational purposes. Library and media specialists also direct students toward reading material aligned with their literacy skills and provide teachers with learning materials to incorporate into instruction.
- **Instructional Leadership Team (ILT)**—An instructional leadership team is comprised of individuals responsible for educating teachers regarding current and relevant instructional philosophies and practices to enhance student learning. These individuals collaborate with teachers to educate them regarding how to implement instructional strategies, activities, and assessments to effectively meet students' learning needs and support their achievement of campus and district academic goals.
- **School Resource Officer**—The role of the school resource officer is to maintain a safe, orderly environment for teachers, staff, and students. They are responsible for ensuring the physical security of the school, handling legal infractions within the school, and addressing conflicts among students. The school resource officer also works with administration and staff to develop emergency drill procedures.
- **Pupil Personnel Worker (PPW)**—Pupil personnel workers are responsible for addressing issues that hinder the academic achievement of at-risk students. These individuals communicate with teachers, administration, staff, and families to ensure these students are supported both within and outside of the school building. This includes addressing issues related to behavior, crisis intervention, attendance, and home lives. Pupil personnel workers direct families toward school and community support resources and collaborate with teachers to implement supports that facilitate success in learning.

Professional Development

AVAILABLE RESOURCES AND SUPPORT SYSTEMS

Effective educators continuously seek professional development opportunities to refine their teaching practice. There are multiple resources and support systems that teachers can utilize to develop their professional knowledge and skills. Within the school building, mentors are available to offer ideas, advice, and support in developing teaching practices and strategies to implement in the classroom for effective teaching and learning. The school's **instructional leadership team** (ILT) is also a valuable resource for educating teachers regarding current instructional practices to enhance student engagement and learning. Teachers can continue their professional education by enrolling in university courses or participating in state-initiated programs to stay informed on relevant pedagogical theories and practices. Service centers are also available that offer workshops, training, and conferences on a variety of topics related to education to support teachers' professional development. In addition, numerous digital support resources are available that allow teachers to enroll in courses, participate in informational webinars, and collaborate with other educators in professional learning communities to build and enhance their teaching practice.

EXAMPLE OPPORTUNITIES THAT CAN ENHANCE TEACHING PRACTICE

Professional development opportunities are available to address a variety of needs for refining one's practice and developing pedagogical knowledge. Professional development trainings can serve to educate teachers on how to utilize and incorporate current technologies into the classroom, as well as teach strategies for implementing relevant and engaging instructional techniques, materials, and resources into the classroom. These opportunities can also be beneficial in teaching educators how to demonstrate cultural competency and skills for productive collaboration with colleagues to enhance student learning. Teachers can also seek professional development opportunities to learn best practices for addressing a variety of student needs, such as intellectual, physical, social, or emotional disabilities, or linguistic needs of ELLs. Actively seeking and participating in professional development trainings helps to ensure teachers stay current on pedagogical theories that can serve as a framework for their instructional practice.

EFFECTIVELY UTILIZING RESOURCES AND SUPPORT SYSTEMS

The field of education is multifaceted and continuously evolving. As such, it is important that teachers of all experience levels engage in the vast array of **available resources** and **support systems** to develop and refine their professional skills. Doing so enhances students' learning, as teachers that actively seek professional development are more current on pedagogical theories and practices, as well as instructional strategies, resources, and technologies to incorporate in the classroom. This allows teachers to design and implement more effective instruction, as it provides them with an increased range of knowledge and tools to enhance student engagement and understanding. In addition, as students' individual needs are diverse, participating in resources and support systems allows teachers to educate themselves on how to properly accommodate them to enhance the learning experience. Utilizing resources and support systems also enables teachers to learn from and collaborate with other educators in professional learning communities to continuously develop new skills, ideas, and instructional methods that enhance student learning.

TEACHER APPRAISALS
CHARACTERISTICS, GOALS, AND PROCEDURES

Teacher appraisals are a method of evaluation intended to provide the teacher with continuous feedback regarding their **performance** and areas in which they can improve their professional skills to enhance student learning. Feedback is provided periodically throughout the school year and derives from classroom **observations** typically conducted by the principal or grade-level administrator. Observations can either be **formally** scheduled and last the duration of a lesson, or can be in the form of shorter, informal **walk-through** evaluations. In both instances, the observer watches and collects information as the teacher delivers instruction, directs learning activities, and interacts with students. The teacher's performance is then measured against **criteria** across several domains pertaining to planning, preparing, and delivering instruction. This score is used to provide the teacher with detailed feedback in post-observation meetings regarding their strengths and specific areas in which they can improve their practice to more effectively meet students' learning needs. Feedback is used to support the teacher in developing specific **professional goals** and strategies for improving their teaching skills.

BENEFITS OF APPRAISAL RESULTS IN IMPROVING PROFESSIONAL SKILLS

The results of teacher appraisals are beneficial in providing educators with **specific feedback** regarding areas in which they can improve their professional skills. Effective teachers understand the value of continuously **refining their practice** to enhance student learning, and therefore, actively seek opportunities to do so. However, it may prove difficult for teachers to objectively assess their own efficacy in the classroom. Appraisal results communicate feedback from the outside perspective of the observer for a comprehensive evaluation of their performance, thus providing teachers with clarity regarding their strengths and areas for growth. This allows educators to effectively develop **professional goals** to improve their skills in targeted areas and **strategies** to achieve these goals successfully.

WORKING WITH SUPERVISORS, MENTORS, AND COLLEAGUES
ENHANCING PROFESSIONAL KNOWLEDGE AND SKILLS

When teachers collaborate with supervisors, mentors, and other colleagues, it facilitates a productive **professional learning community** that supports the continuous development of knowledge and skills related to education. Doing so provides teachers with the opportunity to work with educational professionals of varying backgrounds, experiences, and expertise. This exposes teachers to a wide range of **perspectives**, **approaches**, and **philosophies** that they can learn from to build and enhance their practice. In such a setting, teachers can interact with other professionals within the school community to share ideas, support one another, and collaborate productively in developing strategies to improve their efficacy in the classroom. Additionally, actively engaging with supervisors, mentors, and colleagues facilitates the open communication necessary for productive collaboration in effectively addressing issues to enhance the school community.

ADDRESSING ISSUES AND BUILDING PROFESSIONAL SKILLS

Productive collaboration with supervisors, mentors, and colleagues is essential to addressing issues related to the educational program and continuously developing professional practices. There are multiple opportunities for such collaboration within the school community that accommodate varying purposes. By participating in **professional learning communities**, members of the educational program can collaborate and support one another in addressing concerns and building professional skills. In subject-area **department** or **team meetings**, educators can work together to share ideas, strategies, and resources related to their content area for more effective instruction. Working with supervisors and mentors in **post-observation conferences** provides teachers with valuable feedback regarding their strengths and areas for improvement. Such collaboration is beneficial in creating specific goals and strategies for professional growth. Additionally, engaging in collaborative **professional development opportunities**, including workshops, conferences, programs, and courses, is beneficial in allowing educators to build upon one another's experiences, backgrounds, and expertise to enhance professional practices.

PROFESSIONAL DEVELOPMENT RESOURCES

The various professional development resources available to teachers and staff are discussed below:

- **Mentors/Support Systems**: Mentors and other dedicated support resources within the school system are intended to provide teachers with guidance to enhance their professional knowledge, skills, and expertise. These individuals are typically highly experienced and work with teachers to develop effective instructional strategies, classroom management techniques, and learning materials to improve their teaching skills.
- **Conferences**: Education conferences are multifaceted events in which teachers can learn about current developments in their field to improve their professional knowledge, pedagogical skills, and technical expertise. Conference events are comprised of numerous professional development opportunities, including presentations on current pedagogical theories and practices, collaborative workshops, and training sessions regarding the implementation of new instructional strategies and technology resources. At these events, teachers can also network with one another to connect and share resources, ideas, and strategies that enhance their teaching practice.
- **Professional Associations**: Education associations provide teachers with access to numerous professional development opportunities for improving knowledge, pedagogical skills, and technical expertise. These associations can be related to general education or content specific, and offer information regarding education conferences, workshops, training opportunities, and courses to enhance teaching practices. Professional education associations also allow teachers the opportunity to network with one another to build professional knowledge by sharing ideas, resources, and strategies to implement in the classroom.
- **Online Resources**: Numerous online resources, including websites, blogs, webinar trainings, and discussion forums are available to support teachers in enhancing their professional knowledge, skills, and technical expertise on a variety of topics. Teachers can utilize these resources to learn current pedagogical theories and practices, instructional and classroom management strategies, as well as relevant technology resources to implement in the classroom for enhanced student learning. Online resources are also valuable for collaborating with other teachers in building professional knowledge and sharing ideas, learning materials, and resources that improve instructional practices.
- **Workshops**: Workshop training sessions provide teachers the opportunity to build professional knowledge, skills, and expertise by educating them on current instructional strategies, classroom management techniques, and digital resources in a hands-on setting. Workshops are typically dedicated to a specific pedagogical topic and allow teachers to collaborate with one another in learning how to implement it in their classroom.

- **Journals**: Education journals publish newly researched information regarding pedagogical theories and practices teachers can utilize to enhance their professional knowledge. These journals include scholarly articles and case studies regarding topics such as instructional strategies and practices, classroom management techniques, and the implementation of digital resources. Education journals allow teachers to stay current on pedagogical developments in order to continuously improve their teaching skills.
- **Coursework**: Engaging in coursework is beneficial in continuing formal professional education to enhance knowledge, pedagogical skills, and technical expertise. Doing so allows teachers to learn from other experienced educators regarding current educational theories, practices, instructional strategies, and technology resources. By participating in formal coursework, teachers can continuously build upon their teaching skills and stay current regarding developments in their field.

REFLECTION AND SELF-ASSESSMENT
IMPROVING TEACHING PERFORMANCE AND ACHIEVING PROFESSIONAL GOALS

Just as students are encouraged to reflect upon their academic performance, it is important that teachers **reflect** on and **self-assess** their own efficacy in the classroom. Doing so is integral for improving professional knowledge and skills to enhance student learning. Effective teachers continuously self-evaluate their performance to ensure they are providing engaging, relevant instruction that effectively meets students' learning needs for success. Frequently reflecting upon and assessing the effectiveness of their lesson plans, instructional strategies, assessments, and approaches to classroom management is beneficial in providing teachers with insight regarding their **professional strengths** as well as specific **areas for growth**. With this insight, teachers can identify the knowledge, skills, and strategies they need to improve upon to deliver more effective instruction. This ultimately allows teachers to set relevant professional goals to enhance their teaching practice and determine the steps they need to take in achieving them.

METHODS

Continuous reflection and self-assessment through a variety of methods is beneficial in providing teachers with insight into the effectiveness of their teaching practice. **Reflecting on lessons** after they are finished allows teachers to self-assess their instruction by identifying specific elements that were successful, as well as components that can be improved in the future to enhance student learning. By eliciting **student feedback**, teachers can evaluate whether their instructional strategies, lesson activities, and assessments promote student engagement and understanding. Working with **mentors** and **colleagues** to discuss the effectiveness of lessons, instructional approaches, and classroom management techniques is also valuable in facilitating self-evaluation of teaching practices to seek areas for improvement. In addition, teachers are typically provided the opportunity to **respond to post-observation feedback** prior to attending an appraisal conference. This provides teachers with the opportunity to reflect on their overall performance and prepare to collaborate with the observer in developing professional goals.

Team Teaching and Professional Collaboration

TEAM TEACHING

Team teaching refers to the collaboration of two or more teachers, paraprofessionals, instructional aides, or special education workers in planning and delivering instruction and assessments. There are **several structures** to this approach to accommodate varying teaching styles and student needs. One teacher may provide direct instruction while another engages in lesson activities or monitors student progress. Similarly, one teacher may instruct while another observes and collects information to improve future planning. Students may be grouped with teachers according to their needs to provide differentiation, or teachers may participate simultaneously and equally in all aspects of the learning process. The intention of this approach is to create a **student-centered environment** focused on enhancing and deepening the learning experience. Team teaching is beneficial in allowing increased **individualized instruction** that more effectively meets students' learning needs. Additionally, when multiple teachers are present, students have access to varying ideas and **perspectives** that strengthen their understanding. Team teaching also benefits teachers, as it enables them to utilize one another's strengths for improved instruction. There are, however, limitations to this approach. Differences in **classroom management** styles, **teaching practices**, and **personalities**, when not addressed properly through respectful communication and flexibility, hinder the effectiveness of team teaching.

VERTICAL TEAMING

Communication and collaboration among teachers of varying grade levels is integral to effective instruction that supports students' learning and development. Through **vertical teaming**, content specific teachers **across grade levels** have the opportunity to work together in discussing and planning curriculum, instruction, assessments, and strategies that prepare students for achievement. Teachers of lower grade levels are often unsure of what students in upper grade levels are learning. As a result, these teachers may be uncertain of the skills and abilities their students need to be adequately prepared for success as they transition through grade levels. Likewise, teachers of upper grade levels are often unsure of what students have learned in previous grades, thus hindering their ability to adequately plan instruction and implement necessary learning supports. Vertical teaming facilitates the communication necessary for teachers across grade levels to collaborate in **establishing expectations for preparedness** at each grade level and developing a common curriculum path. This enhances teaching and learning, in that teachers are more effectively able to plan instruction that is aligned with learning targets and prepare students with the necessary knowledge, tools, and supports for continued academic success.

HORIZONTAL TEAMING

Horizontal teaming refers to the collaboration of **same-grade level** teachers and staff that work with a common group of students. These teams may comprise teachers within a **single subject area** or **across disciplines** and may also include special education workers, grade-level administrators, paraprofessionals, and guidance counselors. Horizontal teaming is beneficial in facilitating the **coordinated planning** of curriculum, instruction, and assessments, as well as discussion regarding students' progress in the educational program. In addition, this method of teaming provides teachers and staff the opportunity to work together in developing educational goals, addressing areas of need, and implementing strategies to support students' success in learning. Horizontal teaming is also beneficial in encouraging teachers and staff to cooperate with one another in alignment with the goals and mission of the school to create a positive learning community focused on promoting student achievement.

BENEFITS OF MENTORS IN ENHANCING PROFESSIONAL KNOWLEDGE AND SKILLS

Mentors within the school community are typically experienced teachers that are available to offer support, guidance, and expertise to new teachers. As these individuals typically have a great deal of experience as educators, they are highly valuable resources in increasing professional knowledge and improving teaching skills. Mentors can provide **strategies, tools**, and **advice** for planning and delivering instruction, classroom management, and meeting students' learning needs to promote achievement. This includes suggesting ideas and resources for lesson activities and assessments, as well as techniques for differentiating instruction, enhancing student engagement, and promoting positive behavior. In addition, mentors can offer insight on how to effectively **navigate the school community**, including how to interact appropriately with colleagues and superiors, complete administrative duties, and communicate effectively with students' families. Regularly working with mentors in the school building ensures that new teachers are supported in developing the knowledge and skills necessary to become effective educators.

INTERACTION WITH PROFESSIONALS IN THE SCHOOL COMMUNITY

In order for an educational community to function effectively, professionals in the building must work together cohesively on a daily basis to support the school's mission and student learning. The nature of these interactions significantly determines the climate and culture of the school environment. Appropriate, professional interactions are important in facilitating the productive collaboration necessary to create a positive school community that promotes student success in learning. All interactions must therefore be

110

respectful, constructive, and sensitive to the varying backgrounds, cultures, and beliefs among professionals in the school community. This includes using appropriate language, practicing active listening, and ensuring that discussions regarding colleagues, superiors, students, and other individuals in the building remain positive. When interacting in a team setting, it is important to maintain open dialogue and support one another's contributions to the educational program. All professionals in the school building must understand one another's roles and appreciate how these roles function together to support the educational program. Doing so ensures that collaboration is productive, purposeful, and aligned with enhancing students' learning experience.

SUPPORTIVE AND COOPERATIVE RELATIONSHIPS WITH PROFESSIONAL COLLEAGUES
SUPPORTS LEARNING AND ACHIEVEMENT OF CAMPUS AND DISTRICT GOALS

Effective collaboration among school staff and faculty members is reliant on establishing and maintaining supportive, cooperative professional relationships. Doing so facilitates a sense of mutual respect and open communication that allows colleagues to work together constructively in developing educational goals, plans to support students in achieving them, and strategies to address areas of need within the educational program. Mutual support and cooperation are also beneficial in fostering the coordinated planning of curriculum, learning activities, assessments, and accommodations to meet students' individual needs for academic achievement. Such professional relationships allow for more effective teaching and learning, as students are supported by a school community that works together cohesively to promote learning and the achievement of campus and district academic goals.

STRATEGIES FOR ESTABLISHING AND MAINTAINING RELATIONSHIPS

Building and maintaining professional relationships founded on mutual support and cooperation is integral in creating a positive, productive school community focused on student achievement. Frequent communication with colleagues in a variety of settings is an important factor in establishing and sustaining such professional relationships. Maintaining continuous and open communication allows professional colleagues in the school building to develop the respect for and understanding of one another necessary to establish a strong rapport. By participating together in school activities, events, and programs, teachers and staff members can build connections while contributing to enhancing the school community and climate. Community building strategies, such as participating in activities or games that require teamwork, are also valuable opportunities for developing supportive and cooperative professional relationships among colleagues. In addition, collaborating with one another in regard to curriculum, lesson planning, and promoting student achievement, contributes significantly to developing positive professional relationships. There are multiple avenues for such collaboration, including participating in professional learning communities (PLC's), department meetings, vertical or horizontal teaming, or engaging in team teaching. Doing so provides teachers and staff the opportunity to communicate and develop mutual goals that support the educational program and student learning.

Disability Education Laws

INDIVIDUALS WITH DISABILITIES EDUCATION ACT

The Individuals with Disabilities Education Act (IDEA) includes six major principles that focus on students' rights and the responsibilities public schools have for educating children with disabilities. One of the main principles of the IDEA law is to provide a free and appropriate public education (FAPE) suited to the individual needs of a child with a disability. This requires schools to provide special education and related services to students identified as having disabilities. Another purpose of IDEA is to require schools to provide an appropriate evaluation of a child with a suspected disability and an Individualized Education Program (IEP) for a child with a disability who qualifies under IDEA. Students with IEPs are guaranteed least restrictive environment (LRE), or a guarantee that they are educated in the general education classroom as much as possible. IDEA also ensures parent participation, providing a role for parents as equal participants and decision makers. Lastly, **procedural safeguards** also serve to protect parents' rights to advocate for their children with disabilities.

PEOPLE PROTECTED BY PARTS B AND C OF IDEA LAW

Early intervention services are provided to children with special needs from birth to age three under **IDEA Part C**. Children from birth to age 3 who are identified as having disabilities and qualify under IDEA receive **Individualized Family Service Plans (IFSPs)**.

Special education and related services are provided to children with disabilities from ages 3 to 21 under **IDEA Part B**. Children ages 3 to 21 who are identified as having disabilities and qualify under IDEA receive educational documents, called **Individualized Education Programs (IEPs)**.

INDIVIDUALIZED EDUCATION PROGRAMS VS. INDIVIDUALIZED FAMILY SERVICE PLANS

IFSPs and IEPs are both educational documents provided under IDEA to service the rights of children with disabilities and their families. The major differences between IEPs and IFSPs, aside from the ages they service, is that **IFSPs** cover **broader services** for children with disabilities and their families. IFSP services are often provided in the children's homes. **IEPs** focus on special education and related services within the children's **school settings**.

PURPOSE OF IEPS AND FUNCTION OF THE PLOPS

An IEP is a written statement for a child with a disability. Its primary purposes are to establish **measurable annual goals** and to list the **services** needed to help the child with a disability meet the annual goals.

The IDEA law mandates that a statement of the child's academic achievement and functional performance be included within the IEP. This statement is called **Present Levels of Performance (PLOPs)**. It provides a snapshot of the student's current performance in school. Present Levels of Performance should also report how a student's disability is affecting, or not affecting, progress in school.

The IDEA law mandates that an **Annual Goals section** be provided within the IEP. Annual goals outline what a student is expected to learn within a 12-month period. These goals are influenced by the student's PLOPs and are developed using objective, measurable data based on the student's previous academic performance.

> **Review Video: 504 Plans and IEPs**
> Visit mometrix.com/academy and enter code: 881103

CHILD FIND LAW

Child Find is part of the Individuals with Disabilities Education Act (IDEA) and states that schools are legally required to find children who have **disabilities** and need **special education** or other services. According to the **Child Find law**, all school districts must have processes for identifying students who need special education and related services. Children with disabilities from birth to age 21, children who are homeschooled, and children in private schools are all covered by the Child Find law. Infants and toddlers can be identified and provided with services so that parents have the right tools in place to meet their children's needs before they enter grade school. The Child Find law does not mean that public schools need to agree to evaluate students when evaluations are requested. Schools may still refuse evaluation if school professionals do not suspect the children of having disabilities.

STEPS TO IMPLEMENTING IEPS

The five most important steps in the **Individualized Education Program (IEP)** process are the identification via "Child Find" or the referral for special education services, evaluation, determination of eligibility, the first IEP meeting at which the IEP is written, and the ongoing provision of services during which progress is measured and reported. The referral can be initiated by a teacher, a special team in the school district, the student's parent, or another professional. The evaluation provides a snapshot of a student's background history, strengths, weaknesses, and academic, behavioral, or social needs. An IEP team of professionals as well as the student's parents/guardians use the evaluation and any other reports regarding a student's progress to determine if the student is eligible for special education services. Once a student has been found eligible for special education, the first IEP meeting is held during which an IEP is written by a special education teacher or other specialist familiar with the student. The IEP meeting, either initial or annual, is held before the new IEP is implemented. Once the IEP meeting has occurred, services will be provided as detailed in the written IEP, during which the student's progress will continually be measured and reported. The IEP team includes the student, parents/guardians, special education teacher, general education teacher, school psychologist, school administrator, appropriate related service professionals, and any other professionals or members that can comment on the student's strengths.

MANIFESTATION DETERMINATION

Manifestation determination is a process defined by the Individuals with Disabilities Education Act (IDEA). The **manifestation determination process** is put into effect when a student receiving special education needs to be removed from the educational setting due to a suspension, expulsion or alternative placement. Manifestation determination is the process that determines if the **disciplinary action** resulted from a **manifestation of the student's disability**. This is important because if the action was a manifestation of the disability, the outcome of the disciplinary action may change. During the initial part of this process, relevant data is collected about the student and the circumstances of the offending behavior. The student's Individualized Education Program team determines whether or not the student's behavior was related to the disability. If they determine that the behavior was not related to the disability, the disciplinary action is carried out. If the behavior is determined to be related to the disability, the student is placed back into the original educational setting.

PROVISION OF TITLE III OF THE AMERICANS WITH DISABILITIES ACT

Title III of ADA prohibits the discrimination of people with disabilities in **public accommodations**. Title III seeks to level the playing field of access for people with disabilities participating in public activities. Businesses open to the public, such as schools, restaurants, movie theaters, day care facilities, recreation facilities, doctor's offices, and restaurants, are required to comply with **ADA standards**. Additionally, commercial facilities, such as privately-owned businesses, factories, warehouses, and office buildings, are required to provide access per ADA standards. Title III of ADA outlines the general requirements of the **reasonable modifications** that businesses must provide. Title III also provides detailed, specific requirements for reasonable modifications within businesses and requires new construction and building alterations to abide by ADA regulations. Title III also outlines rules regarding **enforcement of ADA regulations**, such as the consequences for a person or persons participating in discrimination of a person with a disability. Title III provides for **certification of state laws or local building codes**. This means that a state's Assistant Attorney General may issue certification to a place of public accommodation or commercial facility that meets or exceeds the minimum requirements of Title III.

LARRY P. V. RILES

The *Larry P. v. Riles* (1977) court case examined possible **cultural discrimination** of African-American students. The court case questioned whether an intelligence quotient (IQ) test was an accurate measurement of a student's true intelligence. The case argued that there was a disproportionate number of African-American students identified as needing special education services (EMR program services). The court plaintiff Larry P. argued that IQ tests were **biased** against African-American students, which resulted in their placements in limiting educational settings. The defendant Riles argued that the prevalence of African-American students in the EMR classes was due to genetics and social and environmental factors. The court ultimately ruled that the IQ tests were discriminatory and resulted in the disproportionate placement of African-American students in the EMR setting. It was determined that these particular assessments were **culturally biased**, and the students' performances would be more accurately measured using adaptive behavior assessments, diagnostic tests, observations, and other assessments.

DIANA V. STATE BOARD OF EDUCATION

Diana v. State Board of Education (1970) is a court case that examined the case of a student who was placed in special education after results of the Stanford Binet Intelligence test indicated she had a mild case of "mental retardation." This class-action lawsuit was developed on behalf of nine **Mexican-American children**, arguing that IQ scores were not an adequate measurement to determine special education placement in the EMR setting. The case argued that Mexican-American children might be at a disadvantage because the IQ tests were written and administered in English. This might possibly constitute **discrimination**. The plaintiffs in the case argued that IQ scores were not a valid measurement because the children might have been unable to comprehend the test written in English. In the conclusive results of this case, the court ordered children to be tested in their primary language, if it was not English. As a result of this case, IQ tests were no longer used as the sole assessments for determining **special education placement**. There was also increased focus on **cultural and linguistic diversity** in students.

WINKELMAN V. PARMA CITY BOARD OF EDUCATION

This court case began as an argument against a **free and appropriate public education** as required by the Individuals with Disabilities Education Act (IDEA). The parents of Jacob Winkelman believed their son was not provided with a FAPE in his special education setting in Parma City Schools. The disagreement became about whether or not children can be **represented by their parents** per IDEA law in federal court. The U.S Court of Appeals for the Sixth Circuit argued that IDEA protected the rights of the children and not the parents. In the end, the District Court ruled that parents could represent their children within disputes over a free and appropriate public education as constituted by IDEA. Ultimately, this settled the question of whether or not **parents have rights under IDEA**, in addition to their children. The court case determined that parents play a significant role in the education of their children on Individualized Education Programs (IEPs) and are IEP team members. Therefore, parents are entitled to litigate *pro se* for their children.

HONIG V. DOE

Honig v. Doe (1998) was a Supreme Court case examining the violation of the **Education for All Handicapped Children Act** (EAHCA, an earlier version of the Individuals with Disabilities Education Act) against the California School Board. The offense occurred when a child was suspended for a violent behavior outburst that was related to his disability. The court case centered on two plaintiffs. Both were diagnosed with an Emotional Disturbance and qualified for special education under EAHCA. Following the violent incident, the school suspended the students and recommended them for expulsion. The plaintiff's case argued that the suspension/expulsion went against the **stay-put provision of EAHCA**, which states that children with disabilities must remain in their current educational placements during review proceedings unless otherwise agreed upon by both parents and educational representatives. The defendant argued that the violence of the situation marked an exception to the law. The court determined that schools are able to justify the placement removal of a student when maintaining a **safe learning environment** outweighs a student's right to a free and appropriate public education.

PENNSYLVANIA ASSOCIATION FOR RETARDED CHILDREN V. COMMONWEALTH OF PENNSYLVANIA

The Commonwealth of Pennsylvania was accused by the Pennsylvania Association for Retarded Children (PARC 1971), now known as the Arc of Pennsylvania, of denying a **free and appropriate public education** to students with disabilities. The Commonwealth of Pennsylvania was accused of refusing to educate students who had not met the "mental age of 5." The groups argued before the District Court of the Eastern District of Pennsylvania. This case was significant because PARC was one of the first institutions in the country to challenge the **placement of students with special needs**. The plaintiffs argued that all children should and would benefit from some sort of educational instruction and training. Ultimately, this was the beginning of instituting the state requirement of a free and appropriate public education (**FAPE**) for all children in public education from ages 6–21. The Commonwealth of Pennsylvania was tasked with providing a FAPE and sufficient education and training for all eligible children receiving special education. They could no longer deny students based on their mental ages. This triggered other state institutions to make similar decisions and led to the creation of similar federal policies in the **Education for All Handicapped Children Act** (1974).

1990 AMENDMENTS TO THE IDEA

The **Individuals with Disabilities Education Act (IDEA)** replaced the Education for All Handicapped Children Act in 1990. IDEA amendments changed the **age range** for children to receive special education services to ages 3–21. IDEA also changed the language of the law, changing the focus onto the **individuals with disabilities** rather than the **handicapped children**. Therefore, the focus shifted from the conditions or disabilities to the individual children and their needs. IDEA amendments also **categorized** different disabilities. IDEA 1997 increased the emphasis on the individualized education plans for students with disabilities and increased parents' roles in the educational decision-making processes for their children with disabilities. Part B of the 1997 amendment provided services to children ages 3–5, mandating that their learning needs be outlined in **Individualized Education Programs** or **Individualized Family Service Plans**. Part C of IDEA provided **financial assistance** to the families of infants and toddlers with disabilities. Part C states that educational agencies must provide **early intervention services** that focus on children's developmental and medical needs, as well as the needs of their families. Part C also gives states the option to provide services to children who are at risk for developmental disabilities.

EFFECT OF THE INDIVIDUALS WITH DISABILITIES EDUCATION IMPROVEMENT ACT OF 2004 ON IDEA

In 2004, the Individuals with Disabilities Education Act implemented the **Individuals with Disabilities Education Improvement Act**. IDEA was reauthorized to better meet the needs of children in special education programs and children with special needs. As a result of these changes:

- Special educators are required to achieve **Highly Qualified Teacher status** and be **certified in special education**.
- Individualized Education Programs must contain measurable **annual goals** and descriptions of how progress toward the goals will be **measured and reported**.
- Schools or agencies must provide science or research-based **interventions** as part of the evaluation process to determine if children have specific learning disabilities. This may be done in addition to assessments that measure achievement or intelligence.

The changes made to require science or research-based interventions resulted in many districts implementing **Response to Intervention procedures**. These procedures meet the IDEA 2004 requirement of providing interventions in addition to achievement reports or intelligence tests on the Individualized Education Programs for children with disabilities.

DEVELOPMENT OF EDUCATIONAL LAWS LIKE GOALS 2000 AND NO CHILD LEFT BEHIND

President Bill Clinton signed the **National Educational Goals Act**, also known as Goals 2000, into effect in the 1990s to trigger standardized educational reform. The act focused on **outcomes-based education** and was intended to be completed by the year 2000. The goals of this act included ensuring that children are ready to learn by the time they start school, increasing high school graduation rates, demonstration of competency by students in grades 4, 8, and 12 in core content areas, and positioning the United States as first in the world in mathematics and science achievement. Goals 2000 was withdrawn when President George W. Bush implemented the **No Child Left Behind Act (NCLB)** in 2001. NCLB also supported standards-based reform, and it mandated that states develop more **skills-based assessments**. The act emphasized state testing, annual academic progress, report cards, and increased teacher qualification standards. It also outlined changes in state funding. NCLB required schools to meet **Adequate Yearly Progress (AYP)**. AYP was measured by results of achievement tests taken by students in each school district, and consequences were implemented for school districts that missed AYP during consecutive years.

EVERY STUDENT SUCCEEDS ACT OF 2015

NCLB was replaced in 2015 by the Every Student Succeeds Act (**ESSA**). ESSA built upon the foundations of NCLB and emphasized **equal opportunity** for students. ESSA currently serves as the main K–12 educational law in the United States. ESSA affects students in public education, including students with disabilities. The purpose of ESSA is to provide a **quality education** for all students. It also aims to address the achievement of

disadvantaged students, including students living in poverty, minority groups, students receiving special education services, and students with limited English language skills. ESSA determined that states may decide educational plans as long as they follow the government's framework. ESSA also allows states to develop their own educational standards and mandates that the curriculum focus on preparing students for post-secondary educations or careers. The act requires students to be tested annually in math and reading during grades 3–8 and once in high school. Students must also be tested in science once in elementary school, middle school, and high school. **School accountability** was also mandated by ESSA. The act requires states to have plans in place for any schools that are underperforming.

ESL RIGHTS FOR STUDENTS AND PARENTS

As public schools experience an influx of English as a Second Language (ESL) students, knowledge of their **rights** becomes increasingly important. The **Every Student Succeeds Act (ESSA)** of 2015 addresses funding discrepancies for ESL students and families. ESSA allocates funds to schools and districts where low-income families comprise 40% or more of the enrollment. This is intended to assist with ESL students who are underperforming or at risk for underperforming. ESSA also provides funding for ESL students to become English proficient and find academic success. However, in order for schools and districts to receive this funding, they must avoid discrimination, track ESL student progress, assess ESL student English proficiency, and notify parents of their children's ESL status. Avoiding discrimination includes preventing the over-identification of ESL students for special education services. The referral and evaluation process must be carried out with caution to ensure that students' perceived disabilities are actual deficits and not related to their English language learning abilities.

REHABILITATION ACT OF 1973

The Rehabilitation Act of 1973 was the law that preceded IDEA 1975. The Rehab Act serves to protect the rights of people with disabilities in several ways.

- It protects people with disabilities against discrimination relating to **employment**.
- It provides students with disabilities equal access to the **general education curriculum** (Section 504).

AMERICANS WITH DISABILITIES ACT OF 1990 (ADA)

The Americans with Disabilities Act (1990) also protects the rights of people with disabilities.

- The ADA provides **equal employment** for people with disabilities. This means employers must provide reasonable accommodations for people with disabilities in their job and work environments.
- It provides **access** for people with disabilities to both public and private places open to the public (i.e. access ramps and automatic doors).
- It provides **telecommunications access** to people with disabilities. This ensures people with hearing and speech disabilities can communicate over the telephone and Internet.

ELEMENTARY AND SECONDARY EDUCATION ACT (ESEA)

The Elementary and Secondary Education Act (ESEA) also protects the rights of people with disabilities.

- Passed by President Johnson in 1965, ESEA was part of the president's "War on Poverty." The law sought to allow **equal access to a quality education**.
- ESEA extended more funding to secondary and primary schools and emphasized high **standards and accountability**.
- This law was authorized as **No Child Left Behind** (2001) under President Bush, then reauthorized as the **Every Student Succeeds Act** (ESSA) under President Obama.

SECTION 504

A Section 504 Plan comes from the civil rights law, Section 504 of the Rehabilitation Act of 1973, and protects the rights of individuals with disabilities. A 504 Plan is a formal plan or blueprint for how the school will provide services to a student with a disability. This essentially removes barriers for individuals with disabilities by ensuring that **appropriate services** are provided to meet their special needs. A 504 Plan includes:

- **Accommodations**: A 504 Plan includes accommodations a student with a disability may need to be successful in a regular education classroom. For example, a student with ADHD may need to sit near the front of the room to limit distractions.
- **Related Services**: A 504 Plan includes related services, such as speech therapy or occupational therapy, a student may need to be successful in the general education classroom.
- **Modifications**: Although it is rare for a 504 Plan to include modifications, sometimes they are included. Modifications change what the student is expected to do, such as being given fewer homework assignments.

504 Plans vs. Individualized Education Programs

- A 504 Plan and an Individualized Education Program are similar in that they serve as a blueprint for a student with a disability. However, a 504 Plan serves as a blueprint for how the student will have **access to school**, whereas the IEP serves as a blueprint for a student's **special education experience**.
- A 504 Plan helps level the playing field for a student with a disability by providing services and changes to the **learning environment**. An IEP provides individualized special education and related services to meet the **unique needs of a student with a disability**. Both IEPs and 504 Plans are provided at no cost to parents.
- The 504 Plan was established under the **Rehabilitation Act of 1973** as a civil rights law. The Individualized Education Program was established under the **Individuals with Disabilities Education Act** (1975 and amended in 2004).
- Unlike an IEP, a 504 Plan does **not** have to be a planned, written document. An IEP is a **planned, written document** that includes unique annual learning goals and describes related services for the student with a disability.

Informed Parental Consent

The Individuals with Disabilities Education Act (IDEA) requires that parents be **informed** before a student is evaluated for special education services. IDEA mandates that a school district receive **parental consent** to initiate an evaluation of a student for special education services. Consent means the school district has fully informed the parent of their intentions or potential reasons for evaluation of the student. Legally, the request must be written in the parent's native language. This consent does not mean the parent gives consent for a student's placement in special education. In order for a student to be initially placed in special education or receive special education services, parental consent must be given for this issue separately. At any time, parents can withdraw consent for special education placement or special education services. Schools are able to file **due process** if they disagree with the parental withdrawal of consent. Parents also have a right to consent to parts of a student's Individualized Education Program (IEP), but not necessarily all of the IEP. Once parental consent is granted for all parts of the IEP, it can be implemented.

Tiers of the Response to Intervention Model

- **Tier 1: High Quality Classroom Instruction, Screening, and Group Interventions**: In Tier 1, all students are screened using universal screening and/or the results of statewide assessments. Students identified as at risk receive supplemental instruction. Students who make adequate progress are returned to their regular instruction. Students who do not make adequate progress move to Tier 2.
- **Tier 2: Targeted Interventions**: These interventions are designed to improve the progress of the students who did not make adequate progress in Tier 1. Targeted instruction is usually in the areas of reading and math and does not last longer than one grading period.
- **Tier 3: Intensive Interventions and Comprehensive Evaluation**: Students who are not successful in Tier 2 move on to Tier 3. They receive intensive interventions that target their specific deficits. Students who do not meet progress goals during intensive interventions are referred to receive comprehensive evaluations and are considered to be eligible for special education under IDEA.

STAKEHOLDERS IN SPECIAL EDUCATION

Stakeholders that play roles in educating students with disabilities include the students, parents, general educators, administrators, and community members. Students should receive an educational **curriculum** based on strict standards, such as the Common Core Content Standards. This ensures that they receive good educational foundations from which to grow and expand upon during their school careers. Parents, legal guardians, and sometimes agencies act in the best interests of their children. If they do not think the Individualized Education Programs suit the needs of their children, they can request **due process hearings** in court. FAPE and LRE ensure that students are educated alongside peers in general education classrooms by general educators. General educators collaborate with special educators to create **successful inclusion classrooms**. When inclusion is done successfully, the students with disabilities meet their IEP goals.

INFORMATION TO BE EVALUATED DURING MULTI-FACTORED EVALUATIONS OR EVALUATION TEAM REPORTS

Multi-Factored Evaluations are processes required by the Individuals with Disabilities Education Act to determine if a student is eligible for special education. When a student is suspected of having a disability, the parent or school district can initiate the evaluation process. **Student information** that is evaluated in a Multi-Factored Evaluation includes background information, health information, vision testing, hearing testing, social and emotional development, general intelligence, past and current academic performance, communication needs, gross and fine motor abilities, results of aptitude or achievement tests, academic skills, and current progress toward Individualized Education Program (IEP) goals. Progress reporting on IEP goals is only appropriate during an annual MFE when a student has already qualified for special education services. The purpose of an MFE is to provide **comprehensive information** about a student for professionals working with the student. An MFE also helps determine what academic or behavioral **goals** or related services might be appropriate for a student with disabilities.

FREE AND APPROPRIATE PUBLIC EDUCATION COMPONENTS

The Individuals with Disabilities Education Act (IDEA) defines free and appropriate public education (FAPE) as an educational right for children with disabilities in the United States. FAPE stands for:

- **Free**: All students found eligible for special education services must receive free services, expensed to the public instead of the parents.
- **Appropriate**: Students are eligible for educations that are appropriate for their specific needs, as stated in their Individualized Education Programs (IEPs).
- **Public**: Students with disabilities have the right to be educated in public schools.
- **Education**: An education must be provided to any school-aged child with a disability. Education and services are defined in a student's IEP.

Ideally, FAPE components are put in place in order to guarantee the best education possible that also suits the individual needs of a student with a disability. FAPE should take place in the least restrictive environment, or the environment with the fewest barriers to learning for the individual student with a disability.

MULTI-FACTORED EVALUATION OR EVALUATION TEAM REPORT

A Multi-Factored Evaluation (**MFE**), sometimes referred to as an Evaluation Team Report (**ETR**), serves as a snapshot of a child's abilities, strengths, and weaknesses. An MFE is conducted to determine a student's eligibility for special education. Once a student with a disability qualifies for special education, an MFE is conducted at least every three years after the initial MFE date. MFEs are conducted for students ages 3 to 21 who are on IEPs. The purpose of the MFE is to influence a student's **Individualized Education Program**. An MFE reports on a student's **current abilities** and how the disability may affect **educational performance**. MFEs can also determine if a student qualifies for related services, such as occupational therapy or speech-language therapy. An MFE can be requested by a parent or school district when a child is suspected of having a disability. The school district typically has 30 days or less to respond to a parental request to evaluate a student, giving consent or refusal for an evaluation. While initial MFEs are conducted as a means to determine

118

special education qualification, annual MFEs are conducted to address any changes in the needs or services of a student already receiving special education services.

LEAST RESTRICTIVE ENVIRONMENTS TO DELIVER SPECIAL EDUCATION SERVICES

Special education services are delivered to students that qualify with a **disability** defined by the Individuals with Disabilities Education Act (IDEA). IDEA law also requires that students who qualify for special education must receive special education services in **least restrictive environments** that provide the fewest barriers to their learning. A student's most appropriate instructional setting is written out in the **Individualized Education Program (IEP)**. Some special education instructional settings include:

- no instructional setting
- mainstream setting
- resource room
- self-contained classroom
- homebound instruction

With **no instructional setting**, students participate in the general education curriculum but may receive related services, such as speech-language therapy or occupational therapy. In the **mainstream setting**, students are instructed in the general education classroom for most or part of the day and provided with special education supports, accommodations, modifications, and related services. A **resource room** is an environment where students receive remedial instruction when they cannot participate in the general curriculum for one or more subject areas. A **self-contained classroom** is a setting for students who need special education and related services for more than 50% of the day. **Homebound instruction** is for students who are homebound or hospital bound for more than four consecutive weeks.

DUE PROCESS RIGHTS AVAILABLE TO PARENTS AND LEGAL GUARDIANS

When parents or legal guardians and school districts cannot agree on components of a student with a disability's Individualized Education Program (IEP), parents and legal guardians have a right to **due process**. Due process is a legal right under the Individuals with Disabilities Education Act (IDEA) that usually involves the school district violating a legal rule. Examples of these violations include a school district not running an IEP meeting, failing to conduct a tri-annual evaluation, or failing to implement a student's IEP. Disputes often involve a student's instructional placement, appropriate accommodations or modifications, related services, or changes to IEPs. School districts' due process policies vary depending on the district. IDEA, however, mandates that a **due process legal form** be completed by the parent or legal guardian in order to move forward. This form must be completed within two years of a dispute. **Mediation**, or the process of coming to an agreement before filing due process, can be a solution to the dispute. IEP meetings, even when it is not time for an annual review, are also appropriate options for resolving a dispute before filing due process.

PURPOSE OF MEDIATION IN LIEU OF A PARENT OR LEGAL GUARDIAN FILING FOR DUE PROCESS

Mediation is a process used to address a dispute prior to a parent or legal guardian filing for due process. The purpose of mediation is to **resolve a dispute** between the parent or legal guardian of a student with a disability and the school district. Disputes occur when the parent or legal guardian does not agree with an IEP component, such as what related services are provided or the way a student's IEP is being implemented. Mediation is not a parent or legal guardian's legal right, but school districts often support mediation to offset a **due process filing**. Mediation involves the attempt to resolve a dispute and includes a meeting between the parent or legal guardian, school district member, and a neutral third party, such as a mediator provided by the state. States have lists of **mediators** available for these situations. Agreements that come out of the mediation process are put into writing and, if appropriate, put into a student's IEP. Disagreements can continue to be mediated, or the decision may be made to file due process. Prior to mediation, parents or legal guardians and school districts have the option of holding IEP meetings (outside of annual meetings) to resolve disputes.

MAINTAINING CONFIDENTIALITY AND PRIVACY OF STUDENT RECORDS

Similar to the Health Insurance Portability and Accountability Act of 1966 (HIPAA), **FERPA** is a law that protects privacy. However, FERPA is specific to the privacy of students. The FERPA law applies to any school or agency that receives funds from the US Department of Education. This ensures that schools or agencies cannot share any confidential information about a student without a parent or student's written consent. **Student educational records** can be defined as records, files, documents, or other materials which contain a student's personal information. **Individualized Education Programs (IEPs)** and **Evaluation Team Reports (ETRs)** are examples of private documents under the FERPA law. The responsibility of a school covered by FERPA is to maintain confidentiality and privacy. The members of an IEP team, such as special educators, related service professionals, general educators, or other professionals, cannot share any identifying, private information about a student. Information addressing the needs of individual students found on an IEP, Evaluation Team Report, or other identifying document must remain confidential unless express written consent is given by the parent or legal guardian.

PRE-REFERRAL/REFERRAL PROCESS FOR IDENTIFYING AND PLACING A STUDENT WITH A DISABILITY

The purpose of a pre-referral process for a child with a suspected disability is to attempt **reasonable modifications and accommodations** before the child is referred for special education services. Schools often have **pre-referral teams** whose purpose is to identify the strengths and needs of a child, put reasonable strategies into action, and evaluate the results of this pre-referral intervention. If the results do not show any change, another intervention can be attempted, or the student can be referred for a special education evaluation.

If a child is suspected of having a disability and did not succeed with pre-referral interventions, the school or parent can request an **evaluation**. During the evaluation process, the school compiles information to see if the student needs special education or related services. This information is used to determine if the student's disability is affecting school performance and if the student qualifies for special education. The evaluation lists and examines the student's strengths, weaknesses, and development and determines what supports the student needs in order to learn. An evaluation must be completed before special education services can be provided.

ROLE OF A SCHOOL PSYCHOLOGIST IN SPECIAL EDUCATION

School psychologists are certified members of school teams that **support the needs of students and teachers**. They help students with overall academic, social, behavioral, and emotional success. School psychologists are trained in data collection and analysis, assessments, progress monitoring, risk factors, consultation and collaboration, and special education services. In special education, school psychologists may work directly with students and collaborate with teachers, administrators, parents, and other professionals working with particular students. They may also be involved in counseling students' parents, the Response to Intervention process, and performing initial evaluations of students who are referred for special education services. School psychologists also work to improve academic achievement, promote positive behavior and health by implementing school-wide programs, support learning needs of diverse learners, maintain safe school environments, and strengthen and maintain good school-parent relationships.

OVERREPRESENTATION OF STUDENTS FROM DIVERSE BACKGROUNDS

Disproportionate representation occurs when there is not an equal representation of students from different **cultural and linguistic backgrounds** identified for special education services. Students from different cultural and linguistic groups should be identified for special education services in similar proportions. This ensures that no one group is **overrepresented** and **overidentified as having special needs** due to their cultural or linguistic differences. Disproportionality can occur based on a child's sex, language proficiency, receipt of free and reduced lunch, or race and ethnicity. Historically, most disproportionality has been a civil rights issue and due to a child's cultural or linguistic background. Recently, the focus has been on the disproportional number of students who spend time in special education classrooms instead of being educated alongside regularly educated peers.

The referral process, **Response to Intervention (RTI)**, provides safeguards against disproportionality. The RTI process requires instruction and intervention catered to the unique, specific needs of the individual student. The purpose of RTI is not the identification of a disability or entitlement to services. Instead, it focuses on data used to make educational decisions about individuals, classrooms, schools, or districts. Models like RTI address disproportionate representation, but they are not perfect.

Family Involvement and Collaboration

EFFECTIVELY WORKING AND COMMUNICATING WITH FAMILIES

Utilizing multiple means of communication when working with students' families ensures information is **accessible** to and **inclusive** of all involved family members. As students' home lives are dynamic, conveying information through several avenues allows families in various situations to participate in their child's education. This is invaluable in establishing and maintaining the positive relationships necessary between students' families and schools for effective teaching and learning. General classroom information, including concepts being taught, important dates, assignments, or suggestions for activities to do at home that reinforce learning in the classroom, can be communicated both digitally and in written form. Newsletters, calendars, or handouts can be both printed and included on a class website to ensure accessibility for all families. Updates regarding individual students can be communicated electronically, through writing, or in person. Email, digital communication apps, and the telephone allow for frequent communication to address students' progress, express concerns, or offer praise. Teachers and families can also communicate through handwritten notes, progress reports, or students' daily agendas. In-person communication, such as during a scheduled conference, is beneficial for discussing individual students' progress and goals related to the education program in depth, as well as ways to support their success in learning.

BUILDING POSITIVE RELATIONSHIPS THAT ENHANCE OVERALL LEARNING

Students are more supported and learn more effectively when the relationships between their teachers and families are founded on **mutual respect**, **understanding**, and **cooperation**. Establishing this positive rapport requires the teacher to work and communicate frequently with students' families. Doing so creates an inviting learning atmosphere in which family members feel welcomed and included as **equal contributors** to the educational program. This sentiment empowers and encourages family members to take an active role in their children's education, thus strengthening students' support system and enhancing the overall learning experience. In addition, family members that feel a strong connection to their children's school are more likely to model positive attitudes toward education and reinforce learning at home. When teachers and family members communicate frequently, they develop a mutual sense of trust for one another. This allows for **productive collaboration** and the exchange of valuable insight regarding how to best support students' learning needs both within and outside of the classroom.

APPROPRIATE COLLABORATION AND COMMUNICATION WITH FAMILIES

To effectively collaborate and communicate with students' families, the teacher must carefully consider appropriate methods for doing so. Communication and collaboration must always be **positive, respectful,** and **inclusive** to all families to ensure they feel welcomed as equal participants in their children's education. As such, the teacher must be mindful and responsive to the fact that students come from a variety of backgrounds, family dynamics and living situations. This includes demonstrating **cultural competency** when interacting with families from different backgrounds, providing multiple and varied opportunities for family involvement, and communicating through a variety of means. Doing so ensures that families of varying situations have access to pertinent information and feel equally included in the educational program. The teacher must also be mindful of the nature and purpose of communication in order to ensure that sensitive details about individual students are shared only with appropriate family members. General classroom information, such as important dates, events, or assignments, may be shared publicly among the classroom community, whereas such matters as individual student progress or behavior records must be reserved for private communication with the appropriate family members.

INVOLVEMENT OF FAMILIES, PARENTS, GUARDIANS, AND LEGAL CAREGIVERS
STRATEGIES TO ENCOURAGE ENGAGEMENT

As students' family dynamics are diverse, it is important that the teacher implement a variety of methods to engage parents, guardians, and legal caregivers into the educational program. Doing so creates an inviting atmosphere in which family members of all situations feel encouraged to participate in their children's education. Efforts to engage families must always be **positive, inclusive**, and **accommodating** to a variety of needs, schedules, and situations. This includes ensuring that all opportunities for involvement are culturally sensitive, meaningful, and accepting of all families. Utilizing a variety of **communication methods**, such as weekly newsletters, calendars, phone calls, and electronic communication, ensures that opportunities to engage in the educational program are accessible to all families. Providing **multiple** and **varied** opportunities for involvement, such as family nights, field trips, award ceremonies, or inviting families to participate in classroom activities, further encourages family engagement in the educational program. This enables families in various situations to become involved in their children's education in the way that best suits their needs and abilities.

FORMS OF ACTIVE INVOLVEMENT

Active involvement in the educational program can take a variety of forms both within and outside of the classroom to accommodate differences in families' schedules, dynamics, and abilities. Providing multiple avenues for involvement engages families of various situations to actively participate in their children's education. Within the classroom, family members can **volunteer** their time to assist as teacher's aides, tutors, or chaperones. In addition, if a family member is skilled in an area related to instruction, the teacher can ask them to come in to speak or teach a lesson. Inviting family members to **visit the classroom** or participate in special class activities allows them to actively engage in the learning process and gain insight into the educational program. Outside of daily classroom activities, family members can be encouraged to participate by attending **family nights, school social events, fundraisers**, or **parent-teacher association meetings**. Active involvement in the educational program can also occur at home. By frequently communicating with teachers, assisting with projects or homework, and emphasizing the importance of learning at home, family members can be informed and actively involved in their children's education.

IMPORTANCE IN CHILDREN'S EDUCATION

As students spend a great deal of time between school and home, the degree to which their family is involved in the educational program significantly influences the quality of the learning experience. When teachers take measures to engage families in their children's education, they establish a welcoming tone that facilitates relationships founded on mutual respect, understanding, and acceptance. These positive relationships are necessary for encouraging and empowering families to actively participate in the learning process. Such involvement contributes to establishing a **positive learning community** in which teachers and families can collaborate productively to enhance students' learning. When students' families are actively involved in their education, it strengthens the **support system** in both influential areas of their lives, thus establishing a sense of security that allows them to confidently engage in learning. Families that participate in the educational program are more likely to emphasize its value at home by extending and reinforcing learning outside of the classroom. This is highly beneficial in promoting positive attitudes toward learning, academic achievement, and social and emotional development.

INFLUENCE ON STUDENT LEARNING AND DEVELOPMENT

The degree of family involvement in the educational program significantly influences the quality of students' learning and development. Learning is more effective when parents, guardians, or legal caregivers are actively engaged in their child's education, as this promotes positive relationships between students' school and home lives that strengthen their **support system** and encourage the extension of learning beyond the classroom. Families that participate in the educational program are likely to emphasize and model its importance at home, thus influencing students to adopt the same positive attitudes toward learning. This facilitates **academic achievement, decreased absences** from school, and **positive learning habits**. In addition, when families are actively involved in the educational process, they are more effectively able to support students with resources at home that reinforce concepts learned in the classroom to strengthen connections and understanding. Students develop healthy **social and emotional skills** as well when their families are actively involved in the educational program. This facilitates positive self-esteem and interpersonal skills that contribute to academic success and fewer behavioral issues in the classroom.

BENEFITS FOR PARENTS, FAMILIES, GUARDIANS, AND LEGAL CAREGIVERS

Families, parents, guardians, and legal caregivers that are actively involved in the educational program gain greater **insight**, **understanding**, and **resources** that enable them to support their children's learning more effectively both within and outside of the classroom. Active engagement in the educational program fosters a positive rapport founded on mutual respect and support among family members, teachers, and school. This provides family members with a sense of **confidence** in the merits of the educational program while contributing to the sense that they are **equal participants** in the learning process. These family members are more informed regarding what is being taught in the classroom, as well as beneficial resources to reinforce learning at home. This leaves family members feeling more **empowered** and willing to reinforce their students' learning. In addition, participating in the learning process provides family members with a greater understanding of the characteristics and capabilities of their children's developmental level, thus equipping them with the knowledge to effectively support learning and growth.

BENEFITS FOR EFFECTIVE TEACHING

The involvement of families, parents, guardians, and legal caregivers in the educational program is highly beneficial for effective teaching. Family members that actively participate in the learning process are likely to develop a greater sense of **understanding** and **appreciation** of the teacher's role within it. Such involvement also facilitates positive and frequent communication with families that fosters relationships founded on mutual respect and increases the teacher's **morale**, and therefore effectiveness, in the classroom. Active engagement from family members also allows the teacher to gain a better understanding of how to support individual students' needs. Family members provide valuable insight regarding students' cultures, values, beliefs, educational goals, and learning needs to allow for more effective teaching. In addition, family members that are involved in their children's education are more likely to reinforce and extend learning at home, thus allowing for more effective teaching in the classroom.

POSITIVE RAPPORT

A positive rapport between teachers and families enhances the quality of the learning experience. Establishing these positive relationships requires that teachers frequently take measures to engage families in the educational program in ways that are **meaningful**, **relevant**, and **responsive** to varying situations, backgrounds, and needs. In doing so, teachers communicate the sentiment that all families are welcomed, valued, and considered equal participants in the learning process. This serves to create an open, inviting learning atmosphere in which family involvement is encouraged, thus fostering the **participation** and **communication** necessary for developing a mutual positive rapport. Working to build positive relationships strengthens the connection between schools and families that facilitates productive **collaboration** to best support and enhance students' learning.

INTERACTING WITH FAMILIES OF VARIOUS BACKGROUNDS
DIVERSITIES THAT MAY BE ENCOUNTERED

Appropriate interaction when working and communicating with students' families requires the teacher to recognize the wide range of diversities in characteristics, backgrounds, and needs that they will inevitably encounter. With **culturally diverse** families, the teacher will likely experience variances in language, values, traditions, and customs, including differences in beliefs regarding best practices for raising and educating children. **Socioeconomic** differences may influence the degree to which families have the ability and access to resources to support their children in learning. In some instances, socioeconomic differences may also impact the level of education that family members have attained and potentially the value they place on the importance of education. The teacher must also be mindful of the diversities that exist among **family**

123

dynamics. Some families may have a single caregiver, whereas others may have many. Students may be only children, have several siblings, or come from a blended family. Differences in dynamics also include varying work schedules, lifestyle demands, and living situations that the teacher must consider when working and communicating with families. By acknowledging the diverse characteristics, backgrounds, and needs of students' families, the teacher can take measures to ensure appropriate and inclusive interactions that enhance the learning experience.

APPROPRIATE AND PRODUCTIVE INTERACTIONS

Recognizing the diverse nature of students' cultures, backgrounds, and experiences provides teachers with insight regarding how to interact with their families appropriately and productively. By self-educating to become **culturally competent** and building relationships with students, teachers develop an understanding of the unique characteristics, values, beliefs, and needs of each family. This enables teachers to tailor their communication with individual families in a way that is respectful, **culturally sensitive**, and responsive to their concerns and needs. Doing so ensures that all families feel welcomed and supported in the school environment, thus establishing positive relationships that encourage families to actively engage in the educational program and collaborate productively with teachers to enhance students' learning.

POSSIBLE OBSTACLES

As teachers work and interact with families of diverse backgrounds and experiences, they likely will encounter obstacles that must be addressed to facilitate effective communication. **Cultural differences** in values, beliefs, language, and nonverbal communication may cause misinterpretations between teachers and families that make it difficult to understand one another. It is, therefore, important that the teacher educate themselves regarding students' backgrounds to learn how to communicate in a culturally sensitive manner. When language barriers are present, learning common words and phrases in the language or utilizing an interpreter is beneficial in facilitating communication. Family members may have experienced **negative interactions** with teachers in the past that affect their willingness to engage in communication. Taking measures to establish an inviting, accepting atmosphere that promotes open communication is beneficial in encouraging these families to become involved. **Lifestyle differences**, including varying work schedules, living situations, and family dynamics, may make it difficult to establish effective communication. In addition, **accessibility issues**, including lack of access to transportation, technology devices, or the internet, may hinder family members' abilities to maintain frequent communication. To address these issues, teachers must utilize several communication methods that accommodate families' varying needs and situations.

CONSIDERATIONS TO ENSURE BENEFICIAL INTERACTIONS

The ultimate goal when working and communicating with families is to benefit students' learning and development. When teachers and families develop a positive rapport between one another, it fosters productive collaboration to support the students' educational and developmental goals. Doing so requires that teachers ensure all interactions with students' families are appropriate, respectful, and considerate. This includes demonstrating awareness of varying **backgrounds, characteristics**, and **needs** of each family and interacting in a way that is responsive and accepting of differences. Teachers must practice **cultural competency** when communicating with families, including recognizing differences in perspectives, values, beliefs, and nonverbal communication. Teachers must also consider families' unique situations, including differing **work schedules**, **living arrangements**, and **family dynamics** to ensure that all interactions are considerate of their time, accommodating to their needs, and supportive of their role in the educational program. When interacting with families, it is important that teachers practice active listening and respond appropriately, meaningfully, and constructively. This communicates to families that their opinions, goals, and concerns related to the educational program are respected, thus encouraging them to actively participate in supporting their children's progress and development.

REGULAR COMMUNICATION WITH FAMILIES

STUDENTS' PROGRESS AND IMPORTANT CLASSROOM INFORMATION

Frequent communication regarding individual student progress and important classroom information is essential to actively engaging family members as equal contributors to the educational program. Doing so creates an inviting atmosphere focused on open and productive dialogue to enhance students' learning and development. Regular communication with families through a variety of methods establishes a strong connection between students' school and home lives that supports their achievement. When families are consistently updated and informed regarding their children's progress in the educational program, they can more effectively collaborate with the teacher to **proactively** address concerns and **implement necessary supports** for successful learning. Frequently communicating important classroom information, including curriculum, assignments, events, and opportunities for involvement, ensures that families are always informed regarding their children's educational program and ways in which they can actively participate. This equips family members with the knowledge and resources necessary to effectively support and reinforce learning both in the classroom and at home.

> **Review Video: Collaborating with Families**
> Visit mometrix.com/academy and enter code: 679996

POSITIVE RAPPORT THAT ENHANCES TEACHING AND LEARNING

Regularly interacting and working with students' families facilitates the **continuous** and **open** line of communication necessary to establishing and sustaining a positive rapport. Building such positive relationships is integral to quality teaching and learning, as frequent communication allows families and teachers to develop a sense of mutual respect, trust, and understanding over time. By frequently communicating with families, teachers create a welcoming, inclusive learning environment in which family members feel encouraged and empowered to contribute as **equal participants** in their child's educational program. This facilitates productive collaboration between teachers and families that supports and enhances students' learning. Developing a positive rapport with family members is also valuable in providing teachers with insight regarding strategies to best support and accommodate students' learning styles, needs, and individual differences. When teachers and families have a positive relationship with one another, students feel more supported in their learning both within and outside of the classroom, thus promoting positive attitudes toward learning and academic achievement.

LISTENING AND RESPONDING TO FAMILIES' CONCERNS

Actively **listening** and **responding** to students' families when interacting with them is an important part of building positive relationships that enhance teaching and learning. By listening attentively to families' concerns, ideas, and information regarding their child and the educational program, teachers gain a greater awareness of their unique backgrounds, characteristics, and experiences. With this understanding in mind, teachers can ensure that they respond to family members in a **sensitive**, **accepting**, and **empathetic** manner to promote the development of a mutual positive rapport. Doing so conveys the sentiment that family members are valued and respected as equal participants in the educational program, thus encouraging them to engage in positive communication to support their children's learning. Families can provide valuable insight regarding their children's learning styles, needs, and behaviors. When teachers listen and respond constructively to this information, they foster positive relationships with families by validating and including them in the learning process. In addition, listening and responding appropriately to students' families indicates acknowledgement and appreciation for their participation in the educational program that contributes to building positive relationships and encourages continued communication.

CONFERENCES

BUILDING POSITIVE RELATIONSHIPS BETWEEN SCHOOLS AND FAMILIES

Frequently conducting conferences with parents, guardians, and legal caregivers facilitates the consistent **in-person communication** necessary for building positive relationships founded on mutual understanding and respect. The conference setting provides a space in which teachers, school staff, and families can discuss the educational program and the student's individual progress, as well as address concerns and collaborate in developing goals. By conducting conferences regularly, teachers, school staff, and families can maintain a continuous, **open dialogue** that provides insight regarding one another's perspectives, intentions, and roles in the educational program. This allows for increased understanding and appreciation for one another that contributes to building positive relationships. Families that attend conferences regularly feel more included in the educational program as equal contributors to their children's learning, thus encouraging them to establish positive strong connections with the school.

SUPPORT OF STUDENTS' SUCCESS IN LEARNING

Effective conferences between teachers and families are focused on open communication, productive collaboration, and strengthening the connection between students' home and school lives. When families and teachers work together in conferences to benefit the student, it strengthens their **support system** in both influential areas of their lives. This is beneficial in enhancing students' **academic achievement**, promoting **healthy development**, and encouraging **positive attitudes toward learning**. Conducting conferences frequently ensures that family members are consistently **informed** and **involved** as equal participants in their child's progress and the educational program. This equips families with the information, understanding, and resources to more effectively support their child's learning both within and outside of the classroom. In addition, effective conferences provide teachers with insight from families regarding students' learning needs, behaviors, and individual situations. With this knowledge in mind, teachers can work with families to develop a plan and implement strategies that best support students' learning and development.

GUIDELINES FOR EFFECTIVENESS

Family conferences are a valuable opportunity to discuss students' individual progress, collaborate to develop educational goals, and address concerns. To ensure conferences are productive, teachers must take measures to make families feel welcomed, respected, and included in the process. Conferences must be scheduled at a **convenient time** for all attending family members in order to accommodate varying needs and situations. It is also important that conferences take place in a comfortable, **inviting atmosphere**, as this establishes a positive tone and facilitates discussion. Teachers must arrive **on time** and **prepared** with specific information to discuss regarding the student, including positive remarks that highlight their strengths. This demonstrates that teachers know the student well and want them to succeed, thus making family members feel comfortable in discussing their child. Asking **open-ended questions**, encouraging families to talk, and practicing active listening is important in facilitating productive discussion, as well as ensuring families feel heard and respected in their concerns. **Direct criticism** of the student must always be avoided; rather, teachers should focus on discussing ways that student can apply their strengths to improve in other areas.

FAMILY SUPPORT RESOURCES THAT ENHANCE FAMILY INVOLVEMENT

Families that are supported through school, community, and interagency resources are equipped to effectively support their child's learning and development. Often, families may be hesitant to become actively involved in their children's education because they lack the skills and understanding of how to do so. These support systems are beneficial in providing family members with the **tools, knowledge**, and **resources** that prepare them to effectively participate in the educational program and extend learning outside of the classroom. Such resources are valuable in educating families on the characteristics, needs, and abilities of their children's developmental level, as well as strategies for developing and engaging in age-appropriate activities that support learning at home. This instills a sense of confidence within families regarding their ability to successfully support their children's learning that empowers and encourages them to become actively involved.

When families are supported through **school**, **community**, and **interagency** resources, they are able to more effectively become involved in the educational program. Numerous resources dedicated to educating families on ways they can support their children's learning are available to accommodate varying situations, needs, and abilities. Within the school, **teachers**, **guidance counselors**, and other **staff members** can provide valuable information regarding students' developmental characteristics, needs, and abilities, as well as ways families can become involved to enhance learning within and outside of the classroom. **Support groups** hosted by the school enable families to share experiences and discuss ways to become involved in the learning process. Community support resources are often tailored to address the specific needs of families within the community. These resources offer **family education services** such as classes, meetings, or programs designed to provide families with the training, strategies, and knowledge necessary to become actively involved in their children's education. Several **national family support agencies** are also available to educate families on ways to become involved in their children's learning. Such agencies often have multiple locations, as well as an array of digitally printed information, discussion forums, and training opportunities to enhance family involvement in learning.

Chapter Quiz

Ready to see how well you retained what you just read? Scan the QR code to go directly to the chapter quiz interface for this study guide. If you're using a computer, simply visit the bonus page at **mometrix.com/bonus948/pectprek4** and click the Chapter Quizzes link.

Language and Literacy Development

Transform passive reading into active learning! After immersing yourself in this chapter, put your comprehension to the test by taking a quiz. The insights you gained will stay with you longer this way. Scan the QR code to go directly to the chapter quiz interface for this study guide. If you're using a computer, simply visit the bonus page at **mometrix.com/bonus948/pectprek4** and click the Chapter Quizzes link.

Literacy Instruction for Young Children

EMERGENT LITERACY THEORY
EMERGENT LITERACY VERSUS READING READINESS

Historically, early childhood educators viewed "reading readiness" as a time during young children's literacy development when they were ready to start learning to read and write, and taught literacy accordingly. However, in the late 20th and early 20th centuries, research has found that children have innate learning capacities and that skills emerge under the proper conditions. Educational researchers came to view language as developing gradually within a child rather than a child's being ready to read at a certain time. Thus, the term *emergent* came to replace *readiness*, while *literacy* replaced *reading* as referring to all of language's interrelated aspects of listening, speaking, writing, and viewing, as well as reading. Traditional views of literacy were based only on children's reading and writing in ways similar to those of adults. However, more recently, the theory of emergent literacy has evolved through the findings of research into the early preschool reading of young children and the associated characteristics of them and their families.

EMERGENT LITERACY THEORY'S PRINCIPLES ABOUT HOW YOUNG CHILDREN LEARN TO READ AND WRITE

Through extensive research, emergent literacy theorists have found the following:

- Young children develop literacy through being actively involved in reading and rereading their favorite storybooks. When preschoolers "reread" storybooks, they have not memorized them; rather, theorists find this activity to exemplify young children's reconstruction of a book's meaning. Similarly, young children's invented spellings are examples of their efforts to reconstruct what they know of written language; they can inform us about a child's familiarity with specific phonetic components.
- Adults' reading to children, no matter how young, is crucial to literacy development. It helps children gain a "feel" for the character, flow, and patterns of written/printed language, and an overall sense of what reading feels like and entails. It fosters positive attitudes toward reading in children, strongly motivating them to read when they begin school. Being read to also helps children develop print awareness and formulate concepts of books and reading.
- Influenced by Piaget and Vygotsky, emergent literacy theory views reading and writing as developmental processes having successive stages.

PERSPECTIVE REGARDING INSTRUCTIONAL MODELS

The emergent literacy theoretical perspective yields an instructional model for the learning and teaching of reading and writing in young children that is founded on building instruction from the child's knowledge. Emergent literacy theory's assumption is that young children already know a lot about language and literacy by the time they enter school. This theory furthermore regards even 2- and 3-year-olds as having information about how the reading and writing processes function, and as having already formed particular ideas about what written/printed language is. From this perspective, emergent literacy theory then dictates that teaching should build upon what a child already knows and should support the child's further literacy development.

Researchers conclude that teachers should furnish open-ended activities allowing children to show what they already know about literacy, to apply that knowledge, and to build upon it. From the emergent literacy perspective, teachers take the role of creating a learning environment with conditions that are conducive to children's learning in ways that are ideally self-motivated, self-generated, and self-regulated.

HOW BABIES AND YOUNG CHILDREN LEARN TO READ AND WRITE

According to the theory of emergent literacy, even infants encounter written language. Two- and three-year-olds commonly can identify logos, labels, and signs in their homes and communities. Also, young children's scribbles show features/appearances of their language's specific writing system even before they can write. For example, Egyptian children's scribbles look more like Egyptian writing; American children's scribbles look more like English writing. Young children learn to read and write concurrently, not sequentially; the two abilities are closely interrelated. Moreover, though with speech, receptive language comprehension seems to develop easier/sooner than expressive language production, this does not apply to reading and writing: first learning activities involving writing are found easier for preschoolers than those involving reading. Research finds that form follows function, not the opposite: young children's literacy learning is mostly through meaningful, functional, purposeful/goal-directed real-life activities. Literacy comprises not isolated, abstract skills learned for their own sake but rather authentic skills applied to accomplish real-life purposes, the way children observe adults using literacy.

DEVELOPMENTALLY INAPPROPRIATE KINDERGARTEN AND PRESCHOOL LITERACY PRACTICES

Research finds some preschools are like play centers but are not optimal for literacy because their curricula exclude natural reading and writing activities. Researchers have also identified a trend in many kindergartens to ensure children's "reading readiness" by providing highly academic programs, influencing preschool curricula to get children "ready" for such kindergartens. Influenced and even pressured by kindergarten programs' academic expectations, parents have also come to expect preschools to prepare their children for kindergarten. However, experts find applying elementary-school programs to kindergartens and preschools developmentally inappropriate. Formal instruction in reading and writing and worksheets are not suitable for younger children. Instead, research finds print-rich preschool environments both developmentally appropriate and more effective. For example, when researchers changed classrooms from having a "book corner" to having a centrally located table with books plus paper, pencils, envelopes, and stamps, children spent 3 to 10 times more time on direct reading and writing activities. Children are found to take naturally to these activities without prior formal reading and writing lessons.

Language and Literacy Development

COMMUNICATION DEVELOPMENT NORMALLY OCCURRING WITHIN A CHILD'S FIRST FIVE YEARS OF LIFE

Language and communication development depend strongly on the language a child develops within the first five years of life. During this time, three developmental periods are observed. At birth, the first period begins. This period is characterized by infant crying and gazing. Babies communicate their sensations and emotions through these behaviors, so they are expressive; however, they are not yet intentional. They indirectly indicate their needs through expressing how they feel, and when these needs are met, these communicative behaviors are reinforced. These expressions and reinforcement are the foundations for the later development of intentional communication. This becomes possible in the second developmental period, between 6 and 18 months. At this time, infants become able to coordinate their attention visually with other people relative to things and events, enabling purposeful communication with adults. During the third developmental period, from 18 months on, children come to use language as their main way of communicating and learning. Preschoolers can carry on conversations, exercise self-control through language use, and conduct verbal negotiations.

Milestones of Normal Language Development by the 2 Years Old

By the time most children reach the age of 2 years, they have acquired a vocabulary of about 150 to 300 words. They can name various familiar objects found in their environments. They are able to use at least two prepositions in their speech (e.g., *in, on*, and/or *under*). Two-year-olds typically combine the words they know into short sentences. These sentences tend to be mostly noun-verb or verb-noun combinations (e.g., "Daddy work," "Watch this"). They may also include verb-preposition combinations (e.g., "Go out," "Come in"). By the age of 2 years, children use pronouns, such as *I, me*, and *you*. They typically can use at least two such pronouns correctly. A normally developing 2-year-old will respond to some commands, directions, or questions, such as "Show me your eyes" or "Where are your ears?"

Salient General Aspects of Human Language Abilities from Before Birth to 5 Years of Age

Language and communication abilities are integral parts of human life that are central to learning, successful school performance, successful social interactions, and successful living. Human language ability begins before birth: the developing fetus can hear not only internal maternal sounds, but also the mother's voice, others' voices, and other sounds outside the womb. Humans have a natural sensitivity to human sounds and languages from before they are born until they are about 4½ years old. These years are critical for developing language and communication. Babies and young children are predisposed to greater sensitivity to human sounds than other sounds, orienting them toward the language spoken around them. Children absorb their environmental language completely, including vocal tones, syntax, usage, and emphasis. This linguistic absorption occurs very rapidly. Children's first 2½ years particularly involve amazing abilities to learn language, including grammatical expression.

6 Months, 12 Months, and 18 Months

Individual differences dictate a broad range of language development that is still normal. However, parents observing noticeably delayed language development in their children should consult professionals. Typically, babies respond to hearing their names by 6 months of age, turn their heads and eyes toward the sources of human voices they hear, and respond accordingly to friendly and angry tones of voice. By the age of 12 months, toddlers can usually understand and follow simple directions, especially when these are accompanied by physical and/or vocal cues. They can intentionally use one or more words with the correct meaning. By the age of 18 months, a normally developing child usually has acquired a vocabulary of roughly 5 to 20 words. Eighteen-month-old children use nouns in their speech most of the time. They are very likely to repeat certain words and/or phrases over and over. At this age, children typically are able to follow simple verbal commands without needing as many visual or auditory cues as at 12 months.

Three Years

By the time they are 3 years old, most normally developing children have acquired vocabularies of between 900 and 1,000 words. Typically they correctly use the pronouns *I, me*, and *you*. They use more verbs more frequently. They apply past tenses to some verbs and plurals to some nouns. 3-year-olds usually can use at least three prepositions; the most common are *in, on*, and *under*. The normally developing 3-year-old knows the major body parts and can name them. 3-year-olds typically use 3-word sentences with ease. Normally, parents should find approximately 75 to 100 percent of what a 3-year-old says to be intelligible, while strangers should find between 50 and 75 percent of a 3-year-old's speech intelligible. Children this age comprehend most simple questions about their activities and environments and can answer questions about what they should do when they are thirsty, hungry, sleepy, hot, or cold. They can tell about their experiences in ways that adults can generally follow. By the age of 3 years, children should also be able to tell others their name, age, and sex.

Four Years

When normally developing children are 4 years old, most know the names of animals familiar to them. They can use at least four prepositions in their speech (e.g., *in, on, under, to, from*, etc.). They can name familiar

130

objects in pictures, and they know and can identify one color or more. Usually, they are able to repeat four-syllable words they hear. They verbalize as they engage in their activities, which Vygotsky dubbed "private speech." Private speech helps young children think through what they are doing, solve problems, make decisions, and reinforce the correct sequences in multistep activities. When presented with contrasting items, 4-year-olds can understand comparative concepts like bigger and smaller. At this age, they are able to comply with simple commands without the target stimuli being in their sight (e.g., "Put those clothes in the hamper" [upstairs]). Four-year-old children will also frequently repeat speech sounds, syllables, words, and phrases, similar to 18-month-olds' repetitions but at higher linguistic and developmental levels.

FIVE YEARS

Once most children have reached the age of 5 years, their speech has expanded from the emphasis of younger children on nouns, verbs, and a few prepositions, and is now characterized by many more descriptive words, including adjectives and adverbs. Five-year-olds understand common antonyms, such as big/little, heavy/light, long/short, and hot/cold. They can now repeat longer sentences they hear, up to about 9 words. When given three consecutive, uninterrupted commands, the typical 5-year-old can follow these without forgetting one or two. At age 5, most children have learned simple concepts of time like today, yesterday, and tomorrow; day, morning, afternoon, and night; and before, after, and later. Five-year-olds typically speak in relatively long sentences and normally should be incorporating some compound sentences (with more than one independent clause) and complex sentences (with one or more independent and dependent clauses). Five-year-old children's speech is also grammatically correct most of the time.

PERSONAL NARRATIVES

Personal narratives are the way that young children relate their experiences to others by telling the stories of what happened. The narrative structure incorporates reporting components such as who was involved, where the events took place, and what happened. Understanding and using this structure is crucial to young children for their communication; however, many young children cannot follow or apply this sequence without scaffolding (temporary support as needed) from adults. Adults can ask young children guiding questions to facilitate and advance narratives. They can also provide learning tools that engage children's visual, tactile (touch), and kinesthetic (body position and movement) senses. This reinforces narrative use, increases the depth of scaffolding, and motivates children's participation. Children learn to play the main character, describe the setting, sequence plot actions, and use words and body language to express emotions. Topic-related action sequences or "social stories" are important for preschoolers to comprehend and express to promote daily transitions and self-regulation. Such conversational skills attainment achieves milestones in both linguistic and emotional-social development.

ACHIEVEMENTS OR PROCESSES ENABLED BY ORAL LANGUAGE SKILLS DEVELOPMENT

Crucial oral language development skills enable children to do the following:

- Communicate by listening and responding to others' speech
- Comprehend meanings of numerous words and concepts encountered in their listening and reading
- Acquire information on subjects they are interested in learning about
- Use specific language to express their own thoughts and ideas

Research finds young children's ability to listen to, understand, and use spoken and written language is associated with their later reading, spelling, and writing literacy achievement. Infants typically begin developing oral language skills, which continue developing through life. Babies develop awareness of and attend to adult speech and soon begin communicating their needs via gestures and speech sounds. Toddlers express emotions and ideas and solicit information via language. They start uttering simple sentences, asking questions, and giving opinions regarding their likes and dislikes. Young preschoolers expand their vocabularies from hearing others' speech and from books. They describe past and possible future events and unseen objects, tell fictional or "make-believe" stories, and use complete sentences and more complex language.

BENEFITS OF PLAY-BASED ACTIVITIES

When young children play, they often enact scenarios. Play scenarios tell stories that include who is involved, where they are, what happens, why it happens, and how the "actors" feel about it. Children engage in planning when they decide first what their playing will be about, which children are playing which roles, and who is doing what. This planning and the thought processes involved reflect narrative thinking and structure. Children who experience difficulties with planning play are more likely to avoid participating or to participate only marginally. Since playing actually requires these thought and planning processes, children who do not play spontaneously can be supported in playing by enabling them to talk about potential narratives/stories as foundations for play scenarios. When conflicts emerge during play, conversation is necessary to effect needed change. Narrative development constitutes gradual plot development; play conflicts are akin to fictional/personal narrative problems and result in changed feelings. Adults can help young children discuss problems, identify the changed feeling they cause, and discuss plans/actions for resolution.

CONVERSATION OF ADULTS WITH YOUNG CHILDREN

Adults should converse with young children so the children get practice with hearing and using rich and abstract vocabulary and increasingly complex sentences, using language to express ideas and ask questions for understanding, and using language to answer questions about past, future, and absent things rather than only about "here-and-now" things. To ensure they incorporate these elements in their conversations, adults can consider whose voices are heard most often and who does the most talking in the home, care setting, or classroom; the child, not the adult, should be talking at least half of the time. Adults should be using rich language with complex structures when conversing with young children. Adults should be talking with, not at children; the conversation should be shared equally rather than adults doing all the talking while children listen to them. Adults should also ask young children questions, rather than just telling them things. Additionally, adult questions should require that children use language to formulate and communicate abstract ideas.

NATURAL VS. INTENTIONAL

Children enjoy conversing with significant adults, including parents, caregivers, and teachers, and they require practice with doing so. Caregivers tend to talk with young children naturally, sometimes even automatically, throughout the day, which helps children develop significant language skills. However, caregivers can enhance young children's oral language development further through intentional conversations. One element of doing this is establishing an environment that gives the children many things to talk about and many reasons to talk. Another element of intentionally promoting oral language skills development is by engaging in shared conversations. When parents and caregivers share storybook reading with young children, this affords a particularly good springboard for shared conversations. Reading and conversing together are linguistic interactions supplying foundations for children's developing comprehension of numerous word meanings. Researchers find such abundant early word comprehension is a critical basis for later reading comprehension. Asking questions, explaining, requesting what they need, communicating feelings, and learning to listen to others talk are some important ways whereby children build listening, understanding, and speaking skills.

ONE-TO-ONE CONVERSATIONS WITH CHILDREN

When parents, caregivers, or teachers converse one-to-one with individual children, children reap benefits not as available in group conversations. Caregivers should therefore try to have such individual conversations with each child daily. In daycare and preschool settings, some good times for caregivers to do this include when children arrive and leave, during shared reading activities with one or two children, and during center time. Engaging in one-to-one talk allows the adult to repeat what the child says for reinforcement and allows the adult to extend what the child said by adding more information to it, like new vocabulary words, synonyms, meanings, or omitted details. It allows the adult to revise what the child said by restating or recasting it. It allows the child to hear his or her own ideas and thoughts reflected back to them when the adult restates them. Moreover, one-to-one conversation allows adults to contextualize the discussion accordingly with an individual child's understanding. It also allows adults to elicit children's comprehension of abstract concepts.

EXTENDED CONVERSATIONS AND TURN-TAKING

When adults engage young children in extended conversations, including taking many "back-and-forth" turns, these create the richest dialogues for building oral language skills. Adults make connections with and build upon children's declarations and questions. Adults model richer descriptive language by modifying/adding to children's original words with new vocabulary, adjectives, adverbs, and varying sentences with questions and statements. For example, a child shows an adult his or her new drawing, saying, "This is me and Gran in the garden," and the adult can build on this/invite the child to continue by saying, "What is your gran holding?" The child identifies what they planted: "Carrot seeds. Gran said to put them in the dirt so they don't touch." The adult can then encourage the child's use of language to express abstract thoughts: "What could happen if the seeds were touching?" The adult can then extend the conversation through discussion with the child about how plants grow or tending gardens. This introduces new concepts, builds children's linguistic knowledge, and helps them learn to verbalize their ideas.

> **Review Video: What is Sensory Language?**
> Visit mometrix.com/academy and enter code: 177314

IN-DEPTH COMPREHENSION OF WORD MEANINGS

To support deeper word-meaning comprehension, teachers can give multiple definitions and examples for the same word and connect new vocabulary with children's existing knowledge. For example, a teacher conducting a preschool classroom science experiment incorporates new scientific concepts with new vocabulary words and conversational practice: Pouring water on a paper towel, the teacher asks children what is happening to the water. A child answers, "It's going into the paper." The teacher asks how. Another child says, "The paper's soaking it up." The teacher confirms this, teaches the word *absorb*, compares the paper to a sponge, and asks how much more water will be absorbed. A child responds probably no more since water is already dripping out. The teacher pours water on a plastic lid, asking if it absorbs. Children respond, "No, it slides off." Confirming, the teacher teaches the word *repel*. This teacher has introduced new science concepts and new vocabulary words, engaged the children in conversation, related new concepts and words to existing knowledge, and added information to deepen comprehension.

ADULTS' NARRATION OF CHILD ACTIVITIES AND ACTIONS

One oral language development technique adults can use is to narrate, or describe what a child is doing as he or she does it. For example, a caregiver can say, "I see you're spreading paste on the back of your paper flower—not too much so it's lumpy, but not too little so it doesn't stick. Now you're pressing the flower onto your poster board. It sticks—good work!" Hence, narration can be incorporated as prelude and segue to verbal positive reinforcement. This promotes oral language development by introducing and illustrating syntaxes. Communicating locations and directionality employs verbs and prepositions. Describing intensity and manner employs adverbs. Labeling objects/actions that are currently present/taking place with new vocabulary words serves immediately to place those words into natural contexts, facilitating more authentic comprehension of word meanings and better memory retention. Caregivers/teachers can narrate children's activities during formal instructional activities and informal situations like outdoor playtime, snack time, and cleanup time, and subsequently converse with them about what they did.

TOPICS THAT YOUNG CHILDREN ENJOY TALKING ABOUT

Personal content is important with young children, who enjoy talking about themselves, such as what their favorite color is or where they got their new shirt; about their activities, like what they are constructing with Legos or shaping with Play-Doh; or about familiar events and things that access their knowledge, like their family activities and experiences with neighbors and friends. Here is an example of how a teacher can make use of children's conversation to reinforce it, expand it, and teach new vocabulary and grammar. The teacher asks a child what he or she is building, and the child answers, "A place for sick animals." The teacher asks, "You mean an animal hospital [or vet clinic]?" and the child confirms. When a child says someone was taken to a hospital "in the siren," the teacher corrects the usage by saying, "They took him to the hospital in the

133

ambulance with the siren was sounding?" This recasts *siren* with the correct word choice, *ambulance*. It incorporates *siren* correctly and extends the statement to a complete sentence.

STORYTELLING

Young children like to communicate about their personal life experiences. When they can do this through narrative structure, it helps them use new words they are learning, organize their thoughts to express them coherently, and engage their imaginative powers. Teachers/caregivers can supply new words they need, model correct syntax for sentences by elaborating on or extending child utterances and asking them questions, and build further upon children's ideas. For example, a teacher asks a child what they did at her sister's birthday party. When the child describes the cake and makes gestures for a word she doesn't know, the teacher supplies "candles," which the child confirms and repeats. When the child then offers, "Mom says be careful with candles," the teacher asks what could happen if you're not careful. The child replies that candles can start a fire. In this way, teachers give young children models of sentence structure, teach vocabulary, and guide children in expressing their thoughts in organized sequences that listeners can follow.

SHARED BOOK READING

When teachers share books with preschoolers, they can ask questions and discuss the content, giving great opportunities for building oral language through conversation. Books with simple text and numerous, engaging illustrations best invite preschoolers to talk about the characters and events in the pictures and the plotlines they hear. Children's listening and speaking skills develop, they learn new information and concepts, their vocabularies increase, and their ability to define words and explain their meanings is enhanced through shared reading. Many children's books include rich varieties of words that may not occur in daily conversation, used in complete-sentence contexts. Teachers should provide preschoolers with fictional and nonfictional books, poetry and storybooks, children's reference books like picture dictionaries/encyclopedias, and "information books" covering single topics like weather, birds, reptiles, butterflies, or transportation whereby children can get answers to questions or learn topical information. Detailed illustrations, engaging content, and rich vocabulary are strong elements motivating children to develop oral language and understand how to form sentences, how to use punctuation, and how language works.

Abstract thought is stimulated by asking young children to think about things not observed and/or current. During/after sharing books, teachers can ask children what else might happen in the story; what they imagine the story's characters could be feeling or thinking—which also engages their imaginations; and ask them the meaning of the story's events using questions necessitating children's use of language to analyze this meaning. Teachers can ask younger children vocabulary words ("What did we call this animal?") and encourage them to use language by asking them to describe story details, like "How do the firemen reach people up high in the building?" Once younger children are familiar with a story, teachers can activate and monitor their retention and recall by saying, "Do you remember what happened to Arthur the day before that?" Teachers can ask older children to predict what they think will happen next in a story, to imagine extensions beyond the story ("What would you do if...?"), and make conclusions regarding why characters feel/behave as they do.

ENHANCING THE EFFECTS OF SHARED READING

According to researchers' findings, the effectiveness of shared reading experiences is related to the ways that adults read with young children. Rather than merely labeling objects or events with vocabulary words, teachers should ask young children to recall the shared reading, which monitors their listening comprehension and retention abilities. They should ask children to predict what will happen next based on what already happened in a book; speculate about what could possibly happen; describe characters, actions, events, and information from the shared reading; and ask their own questions about it. Shared reading with small groups of 1–3 children permits teachers to involve each child in the book by questioning and conversing with them about the pictures and plots. To teach vocabulary, teachers can tell children word meanings; point to illustrations featuring new words; relate new words to words the children already know; give multiple, varied examples of new words; and encourage children to use new words they learn in their conversations.

REPEATING SHARED READING

Young children develop preferences for favorite books. Once they know a story's plot, they enjoy discussing their knowledge. Teachers can use this for extended conversations. They can ask children who the characters are, where the story takes place, and why characters do things and events occur. They can ask specific questions requiring children to answer how much, how many, how far a distance, and how long a time. Teachers can also help children via prompting to relate stories to their own real-life experiences. In a thematic approach, teachers can select several books on the same theme, like rain forests or undersea life. This affords richer extended conversations about the theme. It also allows teachers to "recycle" vocabulary by modeling and encouraging use of thematically related words, which enhances memory and in-depth comprehension of meanings. Teachers can plan activities based on book themes, like painting pictures/murals, sculpting, making collages, or constructing models, which gives children additional motivation to use the new language they learn from shared readings of books.

READING ALOUD

Just before reading a story aloud to young students, the teacher should identify vocabulary words in the story that he or she will need to go over with the children. The teacher can write these words on the board or on strips of paper. Discussing these words before the reading will give the children definitions for new/unfamiliar words and help them understand word meanings within the story's context. Teachers can also give young children some open-ended questions to consider when listening to the story. They will then repeat these questions during and after the reading. Questions should NOT be ones children can answer with yes/no. When discussing vocabulary words, the teacher can also ask the children to relate words to personal life experiences. For example, with the word *fish*, some children may want to talk about going fishing with parents. Teachers can encourage children to tell brief personal stories, which will help them relate the story they are about to hear to their own real-life experience, making the story more meaningful.

Before reading a story aloud, adults should tell young children its title and the author's name. Then they can ask the children what an author does (children should respond "write stories" or something similar). Giving the illustrator's name, the adult also can then ask the children what illustrators do (children should respond "draw pictures" or something similar). Holding up the book, an adult can identify the front, spine, and back and ask the children if we start reading at the front or back (children should respond "at the front"). Adults can show young children the illustration on the front cover of the book and ask them, "From this picture, what do you think is going to happen in this story?" and remind them to answer this question in complete sentences. These exchanges before reading a story aloud activate children's fundamental knowledge regarding print and books, as well as the last example's exercising their imagination and language use.

When a teacher is reading a story aloud to young children, after reading each page aloud, he or she should have the children briefly discuss the picture illustrations on each page and how they relate to what was just read aloud. After reading aloud each plot point, action, event, or page, the teacher should ask the children open-ended (non yes/no) questions about what they just heard. This monitors and supports listening comprehension and memory retention/recall and stimulates expressive language use. When children associate something in the story with their own life experiences, teachers should have them explain the connection. As they read, teachers should stop periodically and ask the children to predict or guess what will happen next before continuing. This promotes abstract thinking and understanding of logical sequences and also exercises the imagination. After reading the story, teachers should ask children whether they liked it and why/why not, prompting them to answer using complete sentences. This helps children to organize their thoughts and opinions and to develop clear, grammatical, complete verbal expression.

ENVIRONMENTAL PRINT

Street signs, traffic signs, store and restaurant names, candy wrappers, food labels, and product logos—all the print we see in everyday life—are environmental print. Just as parents often play alphabetic games with children in the car ("Find something starting with A...with B..." etc.), adults can use environmental print to enhance print awareness and develop reading skills. They can ask children to find letters from their names on

135

colorful cereal boxes. They can select one sign type, such as stop, one-way, or pedestrian crossing, and ask children to count how many they see during a car trip. They can have children practice reading each sign and talk about the phonemes (speech sounds) each letter represents. Adults can take photos of different signs and compile them into a little book for children to "read." By cutting familiar words from food labels, they can teach capitalized and lowercase letters, associate letters with phonemes, have children read the words, and sort words by their initial letters and by categories (signs, foods, etc.).

ALPHABETIC PRINCIPLE

The alphabetic principle is the concept that letters and letter combinations represent speech sounds. Children's eventual reading fluency requires knowing these predictable relationships of letters to sounds, which they can then apply to both familiar and unfamiliar words. Young children's knowing the shapes and names of letters predicts their later reading success: knowing letter names is highly correlated with the ability to view words as letter sequences and to remember written/printed words' forms. Children must first be able to recognize and name letters to understand and apply the alphabetic principle. Young children learn letter names first, via singing the alphabet song and reciting rhymes and alphabetical jump-rope chants ("A my name is Alice, I come from Alabama, and I sell Apples; B my name is Betty…" etc.). They learn letter shapes after names, through playing with lettered blocks, plastic/wood/cardboard letters, and alphabet books. Once they can recognize and name letters, children learn letter sounds after names and shapes and spellings after sounds.

To help young children understand that written or printed letters represent corresponding speech sounds, teachers should teach relationships between letters and sounds separately and in isolation and should teach these directly and explicitly. They should give young children daily opportunities during lessons to practice with letter-sound relationships. These opportunities for practice should include cumulative reviews of sound-letter relationships they have already learned and new letter-sound relationships as well. Adults should begin early in providing frequent opportunities to young children for applying their increasing knowledge and understanding of sound-letter relationships to early experiences with reading. They can do this by providing English words that are spelled phonetically (i.e., spelled the same way that they sound) and have meanings that are already familiar to the young learners.

PRINT AWARENESS

Even before they have learned how to read, young children develop print awareness, which constitutes children's first preparation for literacy. Children with print awareness realize that spoken language is represented by the markings on paper (or computer screens). They understand that the information in printed books adults read comes from the words, not the pictures. Children who have print awareness furthermore realize that print serves different functions within different contexts. They know that restaurant menus give information about the foods available; books tell stories or provide information; some signs show the names of stores, hotels, or restaurants; and other signs give traffic directions or danger warnings. Moreover, print awareness includes knowledge of how print is organized (words are combinations of letters and have spaces in between them). Children with print awareness also know that English print is read from left to right and top to bottom, book pages are numbered, words convey ideas and meaning, and reading's purpose is to understand those ideas and acquire that meaning.

One way in which a teacher can get an idea of whether or to what extent a young child has developed print awareness is to provide the child with a storybook. Then the teacher can ask the child the following: "Show me the front of the book. Show me the back of the book. Show me the spine of the book. Where is the book's title? Where in the book are you supposed to start reading it? Show me a letter in the book. Now show me a word. Show me the first word of a sentence. Can you show me the last word of a sentence? Now will you show me the first word on a page? Please show me the last word on a page. Can you show me a punctuation mark? Can you show me a capital letter? Can you find a small letter/lowercase letter?" The teacher should also praise each correct response, supply the correct answers for incorrect responses, and review corrected answers.

Teachers should show young children the organization of books and the purpose of reading. When they read to them, they should use books with large print, which are more accessible for young children to view and begin to learn reading. Storybook text should use words familiar/predictable to young children. While reading together, teachers should point out high-frequency words like *the*, *a*, *is*, *was*, and *you*, as well as specific letters, words, and punctuation marks in a story. Teachers can use index cards to label objects, areas, and centers in the classroom, pairing pictorial labels with word labels, and direct children's attention to them. They can invite preschoolers to play with printed words by making greeting cards, signs, or "writing" shopping lists and personal letters. They should point out print in calendars, posters, and signs. Also, teachers can have children narrate a story using a wordless picture book, write down their narrative on a poster, and reinforce the activity with a reward related to the story (e.g., eating pancakes after narrating the book *Pancakes*).

SELF-CONCEPT

Self-concept development begins during early childhood. Children come to identify characteristics, abilities, values, and attitudes that they feel define them. From 18–36 months, children develop the categorical self. This is a concrete view of oneself, usually related to observably opposite characteristics such as child versus adult, girl versus boy, short versus tall, and good versus bad. A 4-year-old might say, "I'm shorter than Daddy. I have blue eyes. I can help Mommy clean house!" Young children can also describe emotional and attitudinal aspects of self-concept ("I like playing with Joshua. I'm happy today."). Preschoolers do not usually integrate these aspects into a unified self-portrait, however. Also, many preschoolers do not yet realize one person can incorporate opposite qualities; a person is either good or bad to them, rather than having both good and bad qualities. The remembered self develops with long-term memory, including autobiographical memories and things adults have told them, to comprise one's life story. The inner self is the child's private feelings, desires, and thoughts.

PHONICS INSTRUCTION

Because children display individual differences in their speeds of learning sound-to-letter relationships, instruction should consider this; there is no set rate. Generally, a reasonable pace ranges from two to four sound-letter relationships per week. Relationships vary in utility: many words contain the letters *m*, *a*, *t*, *s*, *p*, and *h*, which are high-utility, but *x* in *box*, *gh* in *through*, *ey* in *they*, and *a* in *want* are lower-utility. High-utility sound-letter relationships should be taught first. Teachers should first introduce consonant relationships using *f*, *m*, *n*, *r*, and *s*, which are continuous sounds children can produce in isolation with less distortion than word-initial or word-medial stops like *p*, *b*, *t*, *d*, *k*, and *g*. Teachers should also introduce similar-sounding letters like *b* and *v* or *i* and *e*, and similar-looking letters like *b* and *d* or *p* and *g*, separately to prevent confusion. Single consonants versus clusters/blends should be introduced in separate lessons. Blends should incorporate sound-letter relationships children already know.

LANGUAGE EXPERIENCE APPROACH (LEA)

The **LEA** teaches beginning reading by connecting students' personal life experiences with written/printed words. A unique benefit is students using their own language and words, enabling them to interact with texts on multiple levels simultaneously. They thus realize they acquire knowledge and understanding through not just instruction but also their own experiences. The four steps for implementing the LEA with EC groups are as follows:

1. Children and the teacher choose a topic, like an exciting trip, game, or recent TV show, to discuss with teacher guidance
2. Each child takes a turn saying a sentence using his or her own words that advances the discussion/story. The teacher writes the children's words verbatim without corrections, visibly and clearly
3. Every few sentences or several words, the teacher stops and reads the record aloud for children to confirm accuracy

4. The teacher points to each word, they read aloud together, or children repeat after the teacher. The teacher gives children copies of the record for independent review and possible compilation into books of LEA stories

WHOLE LANGUAGE APPROACH

The **whole language approach concentrates** on children's seeking, finding, and constructing meaning in language. As such, young children's early technical correctness is not the priority. Whole language teachers do not ignore children's errors. However, they do not make correction more important than overall engagement, understanding, and appreciation of reading, writing, and literature. Instead, teachers make formative assessments taking into account the errors each child makes. Then they design learning experiences for children that give them opportunities and assistance in acquiring mechanically correct linguistic forms and structures. While this holistic approach finds analytical techniques that break language down into components like phonemes and alphabet letters less useful, children with language processing/reading problems need to learn phonemic awareness, phonics, and other decoding skills to develop reading fluency. The National Reading Panel conducted a study (1997–2000) to resolve controversy over phonics vs. whole language as the best teaching method, finding that any effective reading instruction program must teach phonemic awareness, phonics, reading fluency, vocabulary development, and reading comprehension.

The whole language approach is based on constructivist philosophy and psychology: children construct their own knowledge through their interactions with their environments. In contrast to analytical approaches like phonics and alphabetic learning, constructivism views learning as an individual's unique cognitive experience of acquiring new knowledge, shaped by the individual's existing knowledge and personal perspective. Whole language instruction emphasizes helping children create meaning from their reading and express meaning in their writing. The whole language philosophy emphasizes cultural diversity, integrating literacy instruction across subject domains, reading high-quality literature, and giving children many opportunities for independent reading, small-group guided reading, and being read to aloud by teachers. Whole language believes children learn to read by writing and vice versa. Realistically purposeful reading and writing are encouraged, as is using texts that motivate children to develop a love for literature. Early grammatical/spelling/technical correctness is not stressed, which can be problematic for children with reading/language processing disorders, who need explicit instruction in decoding skills and strategies.

ADDRESSING EARLY MECHANICAL ERRORS IN LEARNING READING AND WRITING

The basal reader is America's commonest approach, used in an estimated 75–85 percent of K–8th-grade classrooms. The number of publishers offering basal reading series has decreased to about one-fourth of that in the 20th century, decreasing teacher responsibility for investigating/piloting readers for district approval. Using basal readers is a skills-based/bottom-up approach. Teaching smaller-to-larger reading subskills in systematic, rigid sequence assists students' transition from part to whole. Texts graded by reading level contain narration and exposition organized thematically by unit, including children's literature and diverse other genres. Phonics and other specific instructional strands with practice assignments develop skills, which are assessed with end-of-unit tests. For young children, text decoding is enabled through exact control of vocabulary items and word analysis skills, "big [enlarged] books," and word and picture cards. Twentieth-century and older series sacrificed comprehension and enjoyment for vocabulary control and skill acquisition, but 21st-century series vary methods more (like multiple story versions or book excerpts enabling selection sharing), affording children more motivation to read.

DIRECTED READING ACTIVITY (DRA) AND THE DIRECTED READING-THINKING ACTIVITY (DR-TA)

Using basal readers, the DRA comprises the following:

1. The teacher prepares children for reading by stimulating their motivation and introducing new concepts and/or vocabulary
2. Students read silently, guided by teacher questions and statements

138

3. The teacher develops student comprehension, and students discuss characters, plots, or concepts to further comprehension
4. After silent reading, students read aloud and read answers to teacher questions, known as "purposeful rereading"
5. Students' follow-up workbook activities/practice review comprehension and vocabulary.

Some selections may include enrichment activities relating them to writing, art, drama, or music. The DR-TA approach is designed to develop critical readers through instruction in group comprehension. It requires children's active engagement in reading by processing information, asking questions, and receiving feedback as they read. The first phase of DR-TA is the teacher's direction of student thought processes throughout reading. The second phase involves developing student skills according to their needs as identified in phase 1 and additional extension or follow-up activities.

DIFFERENCES BETWEEN DRA AND DR-TA APPROACHES

- One main difference is that the DR-TA approach gives teachers all the responsibility and greater flexibility for developing lessons. As such, it contains fewer directions than the DRA approach, which contains specific materials and questions to use, specific guidelines, and is more teacher-manual-oriented and materials-oriented. Therefore, DR-TA can be used for not only basal readers but also planning lessons in other curriculum areas involving reading; the DRA approach applies more directly to basal reader programs.
- DRA manuals use mostly literal, factual questions, requiring only convergent thinking for student responses. However, in DR-TA, questions also demand divergent (creative) thinking of students, stimulating higher-level reading comprehension and interpretation.
- New vocabulary is pretaught in the DRA approach before children read. The DR-TA approach excludes preteaching, realistically requiring student decoding of new vocabulary words during reading.
- DRA manuals specify when to teach which skills for reading comprehension. DR-TA approaches do not, requiring more questioning expertise and acceptance of some alternative student responses by teachers.

Teaching English Language Learners

ENGLISH LANGUAGE LEARNERS
CHARACTERISTICS AND NEEDS OF LANGUAGE PROFICIENCY LEVELS

The term **English language learner** (ELL) refers to students acquiring English as a second language, and consists of beginner, intermediate, and advanced levels of English language proficiency. Each proficiency level is determined by specific characteristics and requires differing linguistic supports across listening, speaking, reading, and writing domains. **Beginning** ELLs have little or no ability to understand the English language across domains and rely heavily on linguistic aids such as visual representations, gestures, verbal cues, and environmental print. These students communicate through memorized high-frequency words or phrases and often require individualized instruction. **Intermediate** ELLs have acquired some foundational knowledge on the English language and can communicate with increasing complexity. They are generally able to understand, speak, read, and write in short, simple sentences and follow clear, routine directions. These students are able to seek clarification for misunderstandings but continue to require linguistic supports such as repetition, slowed speech, visual representations, and body language. **Advanced** ELL students are generally able to understand and utilize the English language with minimal error and often do not require extensive linguistic support outside of occasional repetition or clarification. Their proficiency is comparable to that of their native English-speaking peers.

ACQUIRING LISTENING AND SPEAKING SKILLS

The acquisition of **listening** and **speaking** skills are interrelated and often are the first two domains in which English language proficiency is developed. As the ELL hears and observes the teacher modeling proper speech and active listening, they begin acquiring listening skills. Additionally, listening to and observing classmates is integral for the development of listening and speaking skills. By watching and imitating their peers, ELLs build understanding of the nuances of the English language in different settings. When words and phrases heard are linked to a particular action or event, the ELL derives meaning and can utilize the newly acquired vocabulary, thus developing listening and speaking skills simultaneously. The development of listening and speaking skills is enhanced in a **language-rich environment** in which students are provided multiple opportunities to practice and develop their skills in a natural setting. Therefore, the teacher must include opportunities for ELLs to speak, actively listen, and work collaboratively. Incorporating materials such as songs, games, stories, and digital media further immerse the ELL in a language-rich environment and allow them to attach meaning to new vocabulary to build proficiency.

ACQUIRING READING AND WRITING SKILLS

The acquisition of listening and speaking skills in English provides the foundation for developing **reading** and **writing** skills. Reading and writing abilities develop in relation to one another, as when students begin acquiring reading skills, they learn to attach meaning to vocabulary and texts that enable them to express themselves in writing. The development of reading skills begins with understanding simple, high-frequency vocabulary and simple sentence structures as a foundation, building upon this knowledge with increasingly complex vocabulary and sentence structures. Similarly, writing ability increases in complexity from basic labels, lists, and copying and develops into expression though simple sentences on familiar topics, and ultimately, complex writing abilities that employ higher-order thinking on abstract concepts. Reading and writing skill development is enhanced through consistent practice in a **print** and **literacy-rich** environment. Students should be provided with multiple opportunities for reading and expressing themselves through writing throughout instruction. Reading materials with varying levels of complexity should be readily available for students, and literacy development must be incorporated into all subject areas to build vocabulary and comprehension.

> **Review Video: Stages of Reading Development**
> Visit mometrix.com/academy and enter code: 121184
>
> **Review Video: The Link Between Grammar Skills and Reading Comprehension**
> Visit mometrix.com/academy and enter code: 411287

PRINT AND LITERACY-RICH LEARNING ENVIRONMENT

A print and literacy-rich learning environment is beneficial for providing an **immersive** experience that promotes the development of students' reading, writing, speaking, and listening skills. Such an environment typically incorporates a variety of learning resources and strategies to encourage literacy. The walls are often decorated with a variety of print materials, such as posters, captions, word walls with high-frequency or thematic vocabulary words, signs, labels, bulletin boards, and anchor charts. Students are provided with authentic printed and digital literacy materials, such as newspapers, magazines, shopping advertisements, video clips, songs, and documentaries to increase relevancy and personal connections. A print and literacy-rich classroom also includes a class library that offers texts of varying genres, formats, and levels of complexity. Learning activities provide multiple opportunities to develop literacy skills in a natural setting, such as opportunities for collaborative learning, self-selected reading, and free-write sessions.

> **Review Video: Print Awareness and Alphabet Knowledge**
> Visit mometrix.com/academy and enter code: 541069

COMPONENTS OF LANGUAGE

All languages are comprised of syntax, semantics, morphology, phonology, and pragmatics.

- **Syntax** refers to the structure and arrangement of words within a sentence, which controls the functions of grammar.
- **Semantics** refers to how language conveys meaning.
- **Morphology** refers to how words are constructed of smaller parts, such as root words, prefixes, and suffixes.
- **Phonology** refers to how words are pronounced.
- **Pragmatics** refers to the practical, social applications of language and its use in the real world, including non-verbal communication.

These components heavily overlap with one another. For instance, morphology is heavily involved in constructing the meaning of a word, which largely falls under the category of semantics and without a logical ordering of the words in a sentence (syntax), the sentence could mean something completely different, or be altogether incoherent. Each of these systems needs to be well-established for communication in English or any other language. Some of these components, such as morphology, can be particularly targeted to support content-based instruction. For instance, a teacher might work on prefixes and root words that commonly occur in science, such as bio-, geo-, tele-, -logy, -scope, and -graphy.

ENGLISH LANGUAGE PROFICIENCY FOR LISTENING AND SPEAKING
DESCRIPTORS FOR ENGLISH LANGUAGE PROFICIENCY FOR EACH ABILITY LEVEL

Development of English language proficiency is marked by descriptors for each ability level in listening and speaking. **Beginner** ELLs are highly limited or unable to understand or speak English in any setting. They have difficulty understanding and using simple vocabulary even with the help of linguistic aids and rely on single words for basic communication. Grammatically, they are unable to construct full sentences. **Intermediate** ELLs understand and speak using high-frequency English vocabulary on familiar topics and settings. They speak and understand short sentences and demonstrate a basic understanding of English grammatical patterns for constructing simple sentences but need linguistic aids for unfamiliar vocabulary. Additionally, they make several errors when communicating, but can ask in English for clarification, and are usually understood by those familiar with working with ELLs. **Advanced** ELLs can speak and understand grade-appropriate English with linguistic supports. They understand and participate in longer conversations about familiar and unfamiliar topics, but may rely on linguistic aids, repetition, or clarification. These students still make some errors in communication but are often understood by people unfamiliar with working with ELLs. **Advanced high** ELLs require minimal linguistic support and can understand and speak English at a similar level to native English-speaking peers.

TEACHING STUDENTS AT DIFFERENT PROFICIENCY LEVELS

Teaching students with different proficiency levels for listening and speaking English implies that students will require varying degrees of linguistic support to develop their skills and provide them with an equitable learning environment. Specifically, students with lower proficiency levels in these areas will rely more on linguistic accommodations than students with more developed abilities. Teachers must be knowledgeable of the descriptors for each proficiency level to implement the proper supports and instructional strategies to address individual learning needs for developing listening and speaking skills in English. Instructional strategies should aim to promote the acquisition of skills through building background knowledge and providing context in multiple ways. This includes modeling proper speaking and listening skills, accompanying instruction with verbal cues, slower speech, repetition, gestures, and visual aids to improve student comprehension and build vocabulary. Additionally, incorporating several cooperative learning opportunities provides scaffolding and opportunities to practice and build upon listening and speaking abilities. Content instruction can be supported with the implementation of digital resources that promote the acquisition and development of listening and speaking skills and can be tailored to students' individual abilities.

> **Review Video: ESL/ESOL/Second Language Learning**
> Visit mometrix.com/academy and enter code: 795047

ENGLISH LANGUAGE PROFICIENCY FOR READING AND WRITING

DESCRIPTORS FOR ENGLISH LANGUAGE PROFICIENCY AT EACH ABILITY LEVEL

English language proficiency for ELLs is determined by descriptors for each ability level in reading and writing. **Beginning** ELLs possess little or no ability to read, understand, or write in English. Comprehension is restricted to single, familiar vocabulary words, and writing is limited to lists, labels, and vocabulary accompanied by pictures. These students rely heavily on linguistic supports for understanding, and their writing is unclear to those unfamiliar with working with ELLs. **Intermediate** ELLs can read, understand, and write short sentences and simple language structures on familiar material with the help of linguistic aids. They engage in writing assignments, but their writing contains errors and is unclear to those unfamiliar with working with ELLs. **Advanced** ELLs read, understand, and write using more expansive vocabulary and sentence structures with the help of linguistic accommodations. They may have difficulty with unfamiliar vocabulary but can read and write at a faster pace with increased accuracy. These students demonstrate more complex writing abilities, and their writing is usually understood by those unfamiliar with working with ELLs. **Advanced high** ELLs can read, understand, and write using grade-appropriate English with minimal linguistic support at a level similar to native English-speaking peers.

TEACHING STUDENTS AT DIFFERENT PROFICIENCY LEVELS

Teaching students with different proficiency levels for reading and writing English means linguistic accommodations in the classroom will need to be scaffolded to address the needs and abilities of individual students and promote the development of skills in these areas. Students with lower proficiency levels in reading and writing will require more linguistic aids than students with more developed abilities. Thus, the teacher must have a deep understanding both of individual student needs and of descriptors for proficiency at each level to effectively support students in their acquisition of reading and writing skills. Instructional strategies should foster the acquisition of these skills through providing several ways to allow students to build background knowledge and context to increase understanding. This includes creating a language-rich classroom environment that emphasizes the development of literacy skills in the form of environmental print, word walls and charts for new vocabulary and high-frequency words, labels, and visual aids. Reading materials on subject content should be available at each reading level. Additionally, the use of graphic organizers and outlines increases comprehension and writing ability through breaking information into smaller portions to provide scaffolding.

CREATING EQUITABLE LEARNING ENVIRONMENT FOR ELLS USING LINGUISTIC SUPPORTS

To create an equitable learning environment, ELL students must be provided with linguistic supports that are applicable across content areas in order to ensure they are provided with an equal opportunity for success in learning. Teachers can implement varying supports appropriate to students' levels of English language proficiency that are beneficial in facilitating both English language and content-specific learning. Such supports include incorporating verbal cues, gestures, and visual representations into instruction to provide context and build background knowledge. The use of environmental print, word walls, and labels are also effective in supporting English language skills while simultaneously providing context for facilitating learning in the content area. Teachers should model speaking and listening skills, and practice slow speech or repetition when necessary to ensure understanding. Scaffolding instruction and activities across content areas through such supports as graphic organizers, outlines, and cooperative learning opportunities serve to assist ELL students in building English language proficiency skills across content areas at a pace appropriate for their ability level. By implementing the proper supports, teachers can effectively foster English language learning in all subject areas while ensuring that students simultaneously learn content-specific material.

INSTRUCTIONAL STRATEGIES FOR ENGLISH LANGUAGE LEARNING IN ALL SUBJECT AREAS

Language acquisition occurs across content areas for ELL students, as each subject is comprised of different vocabulary, grammatical patterns, and methods of expressing ideas. Thus, it is important that teachers provide these students with learning strategies that are applicable in all subject areas in order to effectively support English language acquisition and content-specific learning. Through a metacognitive approach, teachers can facilitate ELL students in thinking about how they learn, reflecting on their strengths and weaknesses, and applying useful learning strategies from one content area to another to develop their English language skills in all subjects. This strategy enhances learning through teaching students how to apply learning strategies from one instructional context to another when developing language skills. By activating students' prior knowledge when introducing new material in a given subject area, teachers promote English language learning through providing context and encouraging students to consider what they may already know about a new concept. Such methods as pre-teaching, anticipatory guides, graphic organizers, and brainstorming allow ELL students to make connections that build their language abilities across content areas.

ADAPTING INSTRUCTION FOR VARYING LEVELS OF ENGLISH LANGUAGE PROFICIENCY

When encountering ELL students with varying English language skills, it is imperative to adapt instruction to accommodate these differences and ensure that all students receive appropriate linguistic support. Instruction must be communicated, sequenced, and scaffolded to support learners with different English proficiency abilities. The teacher must communicate instruction clearly while allowing time for repetition or slowed speech as necessary. In addition, teachers must supplement instruction with linguistic supports such as verbal cues, gestures, and visual representations as needed to provide assistance and context appropriate to individual ability levels. Instruction must also be sequenced logically and clearly communicate the expectations and steps of learning experiences. This is achieved by indicating an explicit beginning, middle, and end to activities through transition words and actions appropriate to students' levels of English proficiency. Teachers must scaffold instruction, activities, and assessments to meet individual students' language learning needs. Supports such as word walls, graphic organizers, charts, labels, and pairing students with others who can provide assistance are effective means of scaffolding learning to accommodate varying ability. By communicating, sequencing, and scaffolding instruction in a way that is tailored to ELL students' individual language needs, teachers effectively foster an equitable environment that promotes success in learning.

Print-Rich Environments for Early Childhood

PRINT-RICH CLASSROOMS

In early childhood classrooms, print-rich environments contain books and texts of different genres and topics, including both audio and digital texts. Walls and shelves have signs and labels to help with classroom procedures and organization. Posters display information related to content students have been studying. Reading, writing, and listening centers are available for students to explore during center time. Puppet theaters and flannel boards are present to encourage oral language and storytelling. There are also many literacy-related materials, such as letter tiles and sight word cards. Word walls are posted.

In **print-rich environments**, students are encouraged to share and display texts they have created. They may add their own stories to the classroom libraries or hang up signs they have made. Materials created during shared and interactive reading and writing experiences may also be displayed.

In classrooms for older students, signs and posters are displayed containing academic vocabulary, content students have been studying, and classroom procedures. Written and digital texts from a range of genres are present. There are also ample resources available for students to use to locate and share information, such as computers, tablets, dictionaries, and thesauri.

PROMOTING LITERACY DEVELOPMENT WITH DRAMATIC PLAY CENTERS

Dramatic play centers are common in early childhood classrooms. These centers allow children to act out realistic situations through play. Examples include pretend restaurants, homes, veterinary clinics, and grocery stores. While engaging in dramatic play, children read, write, listen, and speak for authentic purposes.

As children role-play and interact with other children in dramatic play centers, they develop oral language skills. They engage in conversations and practice using language to accomplish tasks, such as ordering in restaurants. They also listen to peers and follow directions, such as when they are pretending to be restaurant servers.

Children also engage in reading activities in dramatic play centers. Labels and realistic print materials can be included. For example, pretend restaurants may include labeled cabinets and menus. Children can practice writing through dramatic play. For example, children who are pretending to be servers may write down orders on notepads.

BUILDING LITERACY ACTIVITIES INTO DAILY ROUTINES AND ACTIVITIES

Teachers can plan reading, writing, listening, and speaking activities across all subject areas. This can include a mixture of independent literacy activities and shared and interactive reading and writing experiences. Texts focusing on topics that are being studied in all content areas can be accessible in the classroom. Students can also write in all subject areas. For example, they can write the processes used to solve problems in math and create travel brochures in social studies.

Teachers of early childhood and elementary students can plan morning meetings in which daily written messages are read and discussed. Students can share current events and topics of interest with their classmates during these meetings, while other students listen and ask questions.

Early childhood and elementary teachers can also incorporate oral language and listening into daily routines. For example, they may recite specific chants or songs during transitions.

Chapter Quiz

Ready to see how well you retained what you just read? Scan the QR code to go directly to the chapter quiz interface for this study guide. If you're using a computer, simply visit the bonus page at **mometrix.com/bonus948/pectprek4** and click the Chapter Quizzes link.

Social Studies, Arts, and Humanities

Transform passive reading into active learning! After immersing yourself in this chapter, put your comprehension to the test by taking a quiz. The insights you gained will stay with you longer this way. Scan the QR code to go directly to the chapter quiz interface for this study guide. If you're using a computer, simply visit the bonus page at **mometrix.com/bonus948/pectprek4** and click the Chapter Quizzes link.

Social Studies Foundations

HUMAN SOCIALIZATION AND MAJOR SOCIALIZING AGENCIES

Socialization is the process by which individuals learn their society's norms, values, beliefs, and attitudes and what behaviors society expects of them relative to those parameters. This learning is imparted by agencies of socialization. The family, peer groups, and leaders of opinion are considered primary socializing agencies. The family is probably the most important because it has the most significant influence on individual development. Families influence the self-concept, feelings, attitudes, and behaviors of each individual member. As children grow, they encounter peer groups throughout life, which also establish norms and values to which individual group members conform. Schools, workplaces, religions, and mass media are considered secondary socializing agencies. Schools dictate additional academic and behavioral norms, values, beliefs, and behaviors. Workplaces have their own cultures that continue, modify, and/or add to the values and behaviors expected of their members. Religions also regulate members' behavior through beliefs, values, goals, and norms that reflect moral principles within a society. Mass media communicate societal conventions (e.g., fashion/style), which enables individuals to learn and adopt new behaviors and/or lifestyles.

INFLUENCE OF INSTITUTIONS ON THE DEVELOPMENT OF INDIVIDUAL IDENTITY, RELATIONSHIPS, BELIEFS, AND BEHAVIORS

Family is the first and most important socializing agent. Infants learn behavioral patterns from mothers. Their primary socialization is enabled through such early behaviors as nursing, smiling, and toddling. Babies soon interact with other family members. All the infant's physiological and psychological needs are met within the family. Babies learn their sleeping, eating, and toileting habits within the family environment. Babies' personalities also develop based on their early experiences, especially the amounts and types of parental love and affection they receive. School is also a critical socializing agent. Children extend family relationships to society when they go to school. Cognitive and social school experiences develop children's knowledge, skills, beliefs, interests, attitudes, and customs and help determine the roles children will play when they become adults. In addition to family relationships, receiving reinforcements at school and observing and imitating teachers influence personality development. Peer groups that are based on friendships, shared ideas, and common interests in music and sports teach children/teens about conforming to rules and being rejected for not complying with these rules. Mass media like TV profoundly influence children, both negatively and positively.

CULTURE

While no single definition of culture is universally embraced, one from the cultural anthropology perspective is "...a system of shared beliefs, values, customs, behaviors and artifacts that members of society use to cope with their worlds and with one another, and that are transmitted from generation to generation through learning." (Bates and Fratkin, 2002) Cultural groups are based on a wide range of factors, including geographic location, occupation, religion, sexual orientation, and income. Individuals may follow the beliefs and values of more than one culture concurrently. For instance, recent immigrants often espouse values and beliefs from both their original and adopted countries. Traditionally, social systems like education and healthcare have approached cultural diversity by focusing on race/ethnicity and common beliefs about various racial/ethnic group customs. These are frequently generalizations (e.g., lumping Mexican, Cuban, and Puerto Rican cultures together and describing them as "Latino" culture). This type of practice can lead to oversimplified stereotypes and, therefore, to unrealistic behavioral expectations. Service professionals need more detailed knowledge of cultural complexities and subtleties to effectively engage and interact with families.

COLLECTIVISM AND INDIVIDUALISM

Certain world cultures are oriented more toward **collectivism**, while others are oriented more toward individualism. Native American, Latin American, Asian, and African cultures are more often collectivistic, focusing on interdependence, social interactions, relationships, and connections among individuals. North American, Canadian, European, and Australian cultures are more commonly individualistic, focusing on independence, uniqueness, self-determination, and self-actualization (realizing one's full potential). Individualism favors competition and distinguishing oneself as an individual, while collectivism favors cooperation that promotes and contributes to the harmony and well-being of the group. **Individualist** cultures value teaching young children object manipulation and scientific thinking, while collectivist cultures value social and relational behaviors. For example, adults in collectivist cultures may interpret a child's first steps as walking toward the adult, while adults in individualist cultures interpret them as developing motor skills and autonomy. These interpretations signify what each culture values most, forming the child's cultural orientation early in life. The planning and design of educational and other programs should be informed by a knowledge of these and other cultural differences.

CULTURAL COMPETENCE

CULTURALLY COMPETENT PROFESSIONALS

A **culturally competent professional** demonstrates the ability to enable "...mutually rewarding interactions and meaningful relationships in the delivery of effective services for children and family whose cultural heritage differs from his or her own." (Shonkoff, National Research Council and Institute of Medicine, 2000) Providing interpreters and/or translators does not on its own constitute cultural competence. Hiring racially diverse educational staff in schools is also not enough. Culturally competent educators demonstrate highly developed self-awareness of their own cultural values and beliefs. They must also have and/or develop communication skills that allow them to elicit information from students and families regarding their own cultural beliefs. Further, they must be able to understand how diverse cultural views may affect a child's education, as well as how parents/families receive, comprehend, interpret, and respond to educators' communications. Therefore, educators must develop communication skills to meet educational goals.

ASPECTS OF CULTURAL COMPETENCE

It is important for educational professionals to acquire and demonstrate cultural competence at the individual level to effectively interact with individual children and their families. Moreover, cultural competence is also important at the program level, the school level, and the system level. According to the **National Center for Cultural Competence** (NCCC), system-level cultural competence is a continuing process that includes "...valuing diversity, conducting self-assessments (including organizational assessments), managing the dynamics of differences, acquiring and institutionalizing cultural knowledge, and adapting to the diversity and cultural contexts of the individuals and communities served." (Goode, 2001) Individual educational interactions are informed by a knowledge of cultural diversity and of the importance of such diversity in educational settings, an ability to adapt to the population's cultural needs, and a willingness to engage in ongoing self-reflection. This same set of knowledge and skills is also applied at the system level. Family engagement is important in early childhood care and education. This includes understanding the developmental needs of families as well as their children, especially when families and/or children speak different languages.

ACCULTURATION VERSUS ASSIMILATION

Acculturation describes the process whereby people adapt or change their cultural traditions, values, and beliefs as a result of coming into contact with and being influenced by other cultures over time. Some cultures adopt certain characteristics from other cultures they are exposed to, and two or more separate cultures may sometimes virtually fuse. However, **assimilation**, wherein various ethnic groups unite to form a new culture, is different from acculturation. One dominant culture may assimilate others. A historical example is the Roman Empire, which forced many members of ancient Greek, Hebrew, and other cultures to abandon their own cultures and adopt Roman law, military allegiance, traditions, language, religion, practices, and customs (including dress). The extent of a diverse cultural group's acculturation influences how it interacts with social systems like education and healthcare. Groups that are strongly motivated to maintain their cultural identity may interact less with mainstream systems that significantly conflict with or vary from their own cultural beliefs.

MEASURING THE ACCULTURATION OF IMMIGRANTS AND DIVERSE CULTURAL GROUPS IN AMERICA

Social scientists currently use indices such as people's country of birth, how long they have lived in America, their knowledge of the English language, and their level of English language use to study acculturation. However, these factors are measured not because they are the core elements of acculturation but because they are easier to validly and reliably measure than the underlying cultural beliefs, attitudes, and behaviors they reflect, which are harder to quantify. The interactions between American educators and culturally diverse families can be problematic on both sides. Educators have difficulty interacting, communicating, and collaborating with families that come from a variety of other countries, speak various other languages, and differ in their degree of acculturation to American culture. On the other hand, immigrant and culturally diverse families encounter a foreign language, different cultural customs and practices, and an unfamiliar educational system with different methods of assessment, placement, curriculum planning and design, instruction, and evaluation—not to mention different special education laws and procedures. Thus, the acculturation challenges related to interactions between American educators and culturally diverse families are bilateral.

CULTURAL DIFFERENCES IN PARENTS' GOALS FOR RAISING THEIR CHILDREN

Depending on their cultural group, parents have varying goals for their children and use different practices to achieve those goals. For example, research on four different cultural groups in Hawaii found the following differences related to what parents visualized when they pictured their children as successful adults:

- **Native Hawaiians** most wanted their children to have social connections, be happy in their social networks, and demonstrate self-reliance as adults.
- **Caucasian American** parents most valued self-reliance, happiness, spontaneity, and creativity as developmental outcomes for their children.
- **Filipino American** parents most valued the development of traits related to obedience, citizenship, respect for authority, and good conduct and manners in their children.
- **Japanese American** parents placed priority on their children's achievement, as well as their ability to live well-organized lives, stay in contact with family, and master the demands of life.

Such distinct, significant differences imply that these parent groups would vary in how they would respond to young children's assertive behaviors, in their disciplinary styles (e.g., permissive, authoritative, authoritarian), and in the emphasis they would place on activities focusing on physical and cognitive skill mastery vs. social competence and connection.

EDUCATIONAL SERVICES ACCESSED BY DIFFERENT CULTURES

Parents in America have been found to show distinct preferences for the kinds of care and educational services they access for their children. For example, Caucasian parents in America are more likely to turn to preschool centers for help with their young children's care and instruction. This preference is influenced not only by custom but also by scientific evidence that center-based preschool experience improves children's skills and prepares them for school. Hispanic parents in America are more likely to use home-based and/or family-based care settings. This preference probably reflects the more collectivist Hispanic perspective, which places more importance on social relationships than on structured learning in early childhood. Educators can take a culturally competent approach to such cultural diversity by looking for ways in which young children's school readiness skills can be promoted in family and home-based child care settings.

DIFFERENT VIEWS ON CARE, EDUCATION, AND THE NATURE OF THEIR COGNITIVE ABILITIES

Depending on their native culture, parents vary in terms of the early experiences they select for their young children. For example, Latino parents tend to prefer family-based/home-based care. White parents tend to prefer center-based daycare and education designed to promote school readiness. Another cultural difference is parental beliefs about children's learning capacities. For example, research in California found that the majority of Latino parents believed their children's learning capacity is set at birth; only a small minority of white parents held this belief. Parents subscribing to a transactional child development model view the complex interaction between child and environment as creating a dynamic developmental process. These parents are more likely to value the stimulation of early childhood development, seek/implement activities that will provide such stimulation, and access early intervention services for children with developmental delays/difficulties. Parents subscribing to a view of fixed, innate cognitive capacity are less likely to believe their children's cognitive abilities can be influenced by educational experiences, and may not see the benefits of or seek out early learning stimulation and intervention.

CULTURAL AND OTHER INFLUENCES AND HOW MUCH PARENTS IN AMERICA READ TO THEIR CHILDREN

Researchers analyzing national early childhood surveys have identified significant variations in how often white, Asian, and Hispanic parents read to their young children. This variation is not solely due to varying cultural values. Additional factors include parents' financial limitations; time limitations; familiarity and comfort with accessing libraries and other government resources, websites, etc.; and literacy levels in both English and their native languages. Educators must realize that trying to encourage or even teach parents to read to their children earlier and/or more often is unlikely to be successful if parents do not place value or priority on the benefits of being read to, or do not view the outcomes of reading aloud to children as benefits. Reading to children is known to promote school readiness and academic success. Educators should also understand that some children, despite not being read to in early childhood, become successful adults. Additionally, some cultures, including African Americans, emphasize oral learning traditions more than written ones, developing different skills, such as the basic understanding of story flow.

FACTORS AFFECTING PARENTS WHO ARE IMMIGRANTS TO AMERICA

Parents educated in other countries may not know a great deal about the American educational system and may not be aware of the educational demands made on their children, even in early childhood. Educators need to work with these parents to find common ground by identifying shared goals for children. While culturally diverse parents may disagree with some educators' goals, they can collaborate with educators to promote those on which they do agree. Immigrant parents may also be unaware of additional services available in America for children with developmental and/or learning problems. Educators can help parents by providing this information. Another consideration is that some other cultures have more paternalistic educational systems. Parents from such cultures, rather than vocally advocating for their children who need services, tend to wait for teachers/specialists to voice concerns before communicating any problems they have observed. Thus, they could miss out on the chance to obtain helpful services. Even worse, educators could misconstrue their behavior as a lack of interest in children's progress, or as resistance to confronting problems.

DEVELOPMENTAL MILESTONES VARYING BY CULTURE

Research has found that different cultures have different age expectations for many early childhood developmental milestones. For example, Filipinos expect children to eat using utensils at 32.4 months. Anglo families expect children to do this at 17.7 months, and Puerto Ricans expect children to reach this milestone at 26.5 months. Filipino cultures expect children to sleep all night by 32.4 months; Puerto Rican and Anglo cultures expect this at 14.5 and 14.4 months, respectively. Similarly, while Anglos expect children to sleep by themselves at around 13.8 months and Puerto Ricans at around 14.6 months, Filipinos do not expect this until 38.8 months. Filipinos expect children to eat solid food by 6.7 months, Anglos by 8.2 months, and Puerto Ricans by 10.1 months. In Anglo families, an 18-month-old not drinking from a cup could indicate developmental delay if parents introduced the cup when the child was one year old and regularly continued encouraging cup use. But, Filipino parents of an 18-month-old have likely not even introduced the child to a cup yet, so the fact that the child is not using a cup would not be cause for concern from a development standpoint.

When early childhood researchers investigated the average expectations of different cultural groups of when children would reach various developmental milestones, some of the milestones they examined included eating solid food, weaning from nursing, drinking from a cup, eating with the fingers, eating with utensils, sleeping alone, sleeping through the night, choosing one's own clothes, dressing oneself, and playing alone. They also looked at daytime and nighttime toilet training. Educators must become aware of different cultures' different socialization goals before assuming culturally diverse children have developmental delays. On the other hand, they must also avoid automatically attributing variations in milestone achievement to cultural child-rearing differences when full developmental assessments might be indicated. Family expectations and values influence the complex process of developmental assessment. When families and assessors share common cultures, it is more likely that valid data will be collected and interpreted. When their cultures differ, however, it is more likely that the assessment information will be misinterpreted. Employing early childhood teachers/care providers who are familiar with the child, family, and assessment setting as mediators can make developmental assessments more culturally competent.

ESSENTIAL GEOGRAPHICAL CONCEPTS

Ten concepts considered essential to the study of geography are as follows:

- **Location** identifies "where" a place is and examines the positive and negative properties of any place on the surface of the Earth. Absolute location is based upon latitude and longitude. Relative location is based upon changing characteristics of a region and is influenced by surrounding areas. For example, urban areas have higher land prices than rural ones.
- **Distance** identifies "how far" a place is, and is often described in terms of location. It is also related to the effort required to meet basic life needs. For example, the distance of raw materials from factories affects transportation costs and hence product prices. In another example, land costs less the farther it is from highways.
- **Achievability** identifies how accessible a geographical area is based on the conditions on the Earth's surface. For example, villages on beaches are easier to reach. Villages surrounded by forests or swamps are harder to reach. As its economy, science, technology, and transportation develop, a region's level of dependency on other areas changes.
- **Patterns** are found in geographical forms and in how geographical phenomena spread, which affects dependency on those phenomena. For example, in fold regions (areas where the folding of rocks forms mountains), the rivers typically form trellis patterns. Patterns are also seen in human activity that is based on geography. For example, in mountainous regions, settlements predominantly form spreading patterns.
- **Morphology** is the shape of our planet's surface resulting from inner and outer forces. For example, along the northern coast of Java, sugarcane plantations predominate in the lowlands.
- **Agglomeration** is defined as collecting into a mass and refers to a geographic concentration of people, activities, and/or settlements within areas that are most profitable and relatively narrow in size.
- **Utility value** refers to the existence and relative usefulness of natural resources. For example, fishermen find more utility value in the ocean than farmers do, and naturalists perceive more utility value in forests than academics would.

- **Interaction** is the reciprocal and interdependent relationship between two or more geographical areas, which can generate new geographical phenomena, configurations, and problems. For example, a rural village produces raw materials through activities like mining ores or growing and harvesting plant crops, while a city produces industrial goods. The village needs the city as a market for its raw materials and may also need the city's industrial products. The city needs the village for its raw materials to use in industrial production. This interdependence causes interaction.
- **Area differentiation** informs the study of variations among regional geographical phenomena. For example, different plants are cultivated in highlands vs. lowlands due to their different altitudes and climates. Area differentiation also informs the study of regional variations in occupation (farming vs. fishing, etc.).
- **Spatial interrelatedness** shows the relationship between/among geographic and non-physical phenomena, like rural and urban areas. The example above of village-city interaction also applies here.

GEOGRAPHICAL MAPS
GENERAL FEATURES AND PURPOSES

Maps can be drawn to show natural or man-made features. For example, some maps depict mountains, elevations (altitudes), average rainfall, average temperatures, and other natural features of an area. Other maps are made to depict countries, states, cities, roads, empires, wars, and other man-made features. Different types of maps are described according to their purposes. For example, political maps are made to depict countries, areas within a country, and/or cities. Physical maps are drawn to display natural features of the terrain in an area, such as rivers, lakes, and mountains. Thematic maps are drawn to focus on a more specific theme or topic, such as the locations and names of battles during a war or the average amounts of rainfall a country, state, or region receives in a given year or month. Some maps are made for more than one purpose and indicate more than one of the types of information described above.

BASIC TOOLS SUPPLIED ON MAPS

On maps depicting local, national, and world geography, cartographers supply tools for navigating these maps. For example, the compass rose indicates the directions of north, south, east, and west. By looking at the compass, people can identify the locational relationships of places (e.g., in South America, Chile is west of Argentina). The scale of miles indicates how distances on a map correspond to actual geographical distances, enabling us to estimate real distances. For example, the scale might show that one inch is equal to 500 miles. By placing a piece of paper on the map, we can mark it to measure the distance between two cities (e.g., Washington, DC, in the USA and Ottawa in Canada) on the map, and then line the paper up with the scale of miles to estimate an actual distance of approximately 650 miles between the two cities. Map keys/legends identify what a map's symbols and colors represent.

GRIDS

Maps show absolute geographic location (i.e., the precise "address" of any place on the planet) using a grid of lines. The lines running from east to west are called parallels or latitudes, and they correspond to how many degrees away from the equator a place is located. The lines running from north to south are called meridians or longitudes, and they correspond to how many degrees away from the prime meridian a place is located. To determine the absolute location of a place, we find the spot on the map where its latitude and longitude intersect. This intersection is the place's absolute location. For example, if we look at Mexico City on a map, we will find that its latitude is 19° north and its longitude is 99° west, which is expressed in cartography as 19° N, 99° W. Numbers of latitudes and longitudes like these are also referred to as coordinates.

READING AND ANALYZING A SPECIAL PURPOSE MAP

First, read a map's title and look at the overall map. This provides a general idea of what the map shows. For example, a map entitled "Battles of the Punic Wars" would not be a good choice if someone was looking for the political boundaries of modern-day Greece, Italy, and Spain.

150

Next, read the map's legend/key to see what symbols and colors the map uses and what each represents. For example, some lines represent divisions between countries/states; some, roads; some, rivers; etc. Different colors can indicate different countries/states, elevations, amounts of rainfall, population densities, etc. These are not uniform across all maps, so legends/keys are necessary references.

Use the legend/key to interpret what the map shows. For example, by looking at colors representing elevations, one can determine which area of a country has the highest/lowest altitude.

Draw conclusions about what the map displays. For example, if a country map mainly has one color that indicates a certain elevation range, it can be concluded that this is the country's most common elevation.

GRAPHS

Graphs display numerical information in pictorial forms, making it easier to view statistics quickly and draw conclusions about them. For example, it is easier to see patterns and trends like increases and decreases in quantities using visual graphs than columns of numbers. Line graphs, bar graphs, and pie charts are the most common types of graphs. Line graphs depict changes over time by plotting points for a quantity measured each day, week, month, year, decade, or century and connecting the points to make a line. For example, showing the population of a city each decade in a line graph reveals how the population has changed over time. Bar graphs compare quantities related to different times, places, people, and things. Each quantity is depicted by a separate bar, and its length corresponds to a number. Bar graphs make it easy to see which amounts are largest and smallest within a group (e.g., which of several countries has the largest population). Circle graphs (also called pie charts) divide a circle into segments (like slices of a pie) showing percentages or parts of a whole, which facilitates making comparisons between a few categories. For example, the department with the largest budget is the largest segment on a pie chart of company expenses.

> **Review Video: Data Interpretation of Graphs**
> Visit mometrix.com/academy and enter code: 200439

IMPORTANCE OF CHRONOLOGICAL THINKING TO UNDERSTANDING HISTORY

To see cause-and-effect relationships in historical events and explore and understand relationships among those events, students must have a solid grasp of when things happened and in what time sequence (chronology). Teachers can help students develop **chronological thinking** by using and assigning well-constructed/well-written narratives. These include histories written in the same style as stories, works of historical literature, and biographies. These hold students' attention, allowing them to focus on authors' depictions of temporal relationships among antecedents, actions, and consequences; of historical motivations and deeds of individuals and groups; and of the time structure of sequential occurrences. By middle school, students should have the skills needed to measure time mathematically (e.g., in years, decades, centuries, or millennia), interpret data displayed in timelines, and calculate time in BC and AD. High school students should be able to analyze patterns of historical duration (e.g., how long the US Constitutional government has lasted) and patterns of historical succession (e.g., the development of expanding trade and communication systems, from Neolithic times through ancient empires and from early modern times to modern global interaction).

REASONS/PURPOSES FOR OUR COUNTRY'S LAWS AND TEACHING CITIZENSHIP

Young children must understand the purposes of rules/laws: They identify acceptable/unacceptable citizen behaviors; make society and life predictable, secure, and orderly; designate responsibilities to citizens; and prevent persons in authority positions from abusing their roles by limiting their power. Understanding these functions of laws/rules enables children to realize that our government consists of individuals and groups authorized to create, implement, and enforce laws and manage legal disputes. Some creative early childhood teachers have used children's literature to illustrate these concepts. Children can relate personally to stories' characters, and story situations make the concepts real and concrete to children. Stories can be springboards for discussing rules and when they do or do not apply. One activity involves children in small groups making class rules (e.g., "No talking" and "Stay in your seat"), and then rewriting these to be more realistic (e.g., "Talk softly in class; listen when others talk" and "Sit down and get right to work"). When children consider issues of safety or fairness, they begin to develop an understanding of judicial and legislative roles.

Historiography

COMMON TERMINOLOGY USED WHEN STUDYING HISTORY

When studying history, it is important to have a clear understanding of various terms that can be used interchangeably. The term **time** refers to the continuous passing of events in the past, present, and future. Time is a scientific measure that conventionally uses minutes, hours, days, and years as its **standard measures**. Time passes with or without significant events taking place. **History** is distinct from time as it is the record of **significant events** throughout the past. The term **chronology** refers to the arrangement of events in their correct order. As history contains uncertainty, the chronology of particular events is up for debate. Terms used to describe the ebb and flow of history are change and continuity. **Continuity** refers to periods of time that are relatively stable in history with no major changes, whereas times of **change** refer to rich periods in history with significant events that alter the common practices of that time, often leading into a new era. When describing what has changed for a civilization over time, it is common to focus on political, economic, social, and technological aspects. For instance, the United States government was established in 1776 and continues today. This demonstrates a change at the beginning of the timeline related the United States, but since then, there has been political continuity as it has existed for roughly 250 years. Other aspects of life in this period may have experienced other changes, such as the innovation of electricity, steam engines, and automobiles. When a portion of time has relatively stable conditions such that it can be summed up by a common characterization, it is called a **period of time**; this process of summing up time into periods is called **periodization**.

CIVILIZATION, CITY-STATES, AND EMPIRES

Since history is the study of recorded events throughout time, it is naturally tied to organized society with a developed language to record the events. The development necessary to record history generally coincides with early civilization. A **civilization** is a human society that has established complex means of surviving as a group. These **functions** are developing a food supply, a social structure, a shared language, a culture, and technology. The first known complex civilization is Mesopotamia, which was more easily developed due to its fertile farmlands, access to water through an available river. Mesopotamia is a good example of a **city-state**, which is essentially an independently sovereign city that does not depend on another government. Mesopotamia, as an early civilization, was the central hub and government in its region. The model of city-states still exists today, though they are often comparatively less significant in size and economy compared to other nation-states. Examples of modern city-states include Monaco, Vatican City, and Singapore. As the early civilizations continued to develop, they would eventually grow into **empires**, which are larger sovereign states with multiple territories, though they are usually governed centrally by a monarch or emperor.

INTERPRETING TIMELINES

Timelines are a useful tool for visualizing the chronology of events as well as a great method to map out periods and view changes or continuity throughout history. Timelines can focus on either small or large ranges and can be multifaceted so that one period or type of event can be compared with another. A key element of a timeline is having a consistent interval mapped out. For instance, if we wanted to construct a timeline to map the events that happened for a single day, we would likely use hours to plot out the continuum. One might start the timeline at 12am and end the timeline at 12am the next night to show the picture of the entire day. Each event or period, such as sleeping, waking up, eating, going to work, and special occurrences can be marked on the timeline to plot out the day. If someone wanted to compare multiple days, these timelines could be lined up and compared and contrasted to find what is common to all days and what is unique. These same concepts can be applied to historical timelines as well. Instead of mapping just one day, one might consider mapping the events leading up to and throughout a particular war. The significance of events should change with the focus of the timeline. Seeing events plotted on a steady continuum of time can be very helpful in understanding the pacing of events throughout history.

RELATIONSHIPS BETWEEN HISTORICAL EVENTS AND THEIR IMPLICATIONS

As one aspect of society changes, it frequently proves to have significant effects on other parts of society. One of the easiest ways to see this effect is the innovation of new technologies. An example of a highly impactful technology is the printing press. Prior to this invention, all written documents had to be written by hand, which was time-consuming and costly. Books were very expensive and rare, which put the burden of education on mainly religious authorities and very wealthy classes of people. This new innovation allowed for more written works to be spread, which caused a need for literacy and education, ultimately evoking huge cultural and political changes. Technology tends to be a much quicker influencer of change in civilization, as it is sudden and can have dramatic impacts on how things are done. Cultural, political, and economic effects tend to move more gradually but likewise have strong effects that can change civilization forever.

PRIMARY AND SECONDARY SOURCES OF HISTORICAL INFORMATION

When studying history, it is important to consider the reliability, validity, and availability of sources of information. **Primary sources** are first-hand accounts of an event, such as a transcript of a speech, a recording, statistics, or a work of art. **Secondary sources** are indirect records, such as text books, newspapers, and other forms of reviews of the primary sources. Secondary sources of information can still be valid and useful, but are more open to **interpretation** and **bias**. Information from recent history, such as the election of a president in the 2010s is very reliable, as there are many sources of information that are in consensus about the objective event. Furthermore, many people still alive are primary sources since they were alive and witnessed the election. This is not true of less modern history, such as the election of Abraham Lincoln in 1860. There are still plentiful records of the information, but all witnesses to the election have passed away at this point. This event took place in an era where newspapers and legitimate documentation was widespread and available. The clarity and objectivity of sources are indisputable because they are so abundant. If, however, we only had political cartoons and election campaign brochures to go by, the reliability and accuracy of the information may be up for debate because the source materials are only secondary sources of information and are likely to contain biases. Generally, the further back in history one researches, the fewer sources are available due to lack of documentation, technological limitations, and language barriers. With fewer sources, and possibly conflicting information, historians must put together the most reasonable explanation of what took place during the period in question, given the amount of information available to them.

TYPES OF SOURCES OF INFORMATION USED IN HISTORICAL RESEARCH

- **Almanacs**—books that are published each year to express current information for consideration in the coming year. These often act as time capsules for that particular year and can give historians insight into economic and technological details of the time.
- **Encyclopedias**—resources that cover a variety of topics broadly for the purpose of giving the reader an overview. Wikipedia is an internet-based version of an encyclopedia that is useful for finding leads or obtaining general information about a topic.
- **Bibliographies**—a list of resources used in composing a scholarly work. These are usually primary and secondary sources that can be used to check an author's sources or to give leads on similar research. Similar concepts include works-cited pages and literature reviews.
- **Periodical Guides**—a series of publications over time, usually in the form of magazines or journals. These usually broach a more specific category of information, such as on research methods, psychology, or medical procedures, and are intended to help members of a particular field stay up-to-date with current research in their field.
- **Biographical Dictionaries**—a resource that contains a list of important names to know about the given subject and a description of how they contributed to the field. For instance, if one were interested in the Revolutionary War, a biographical dictionary would include information on each of the founding fathers and other significant individuals of the time.

- **Maps**—representations of land and territories that can display a variety of factors, including geographical features, political features, economics, demographics, and many more aspects. Digital maps can generally be manipulated to show multiple features at once.

USES AND LIMITATIONS OF VARIOUS HISTORICAL SOURCE MATERIALS

Historical source materials are a type of primary source material that offer historians the opportunity to study people, places, and events that occurred in the past. Unfortunately, there are limitations to what these materials can tell us. A limitation of **historical source materials** is that they may be biased by those who created them. For example, those who create historical documents such as letters may leave out details or exaggerate parts in order to make their points more convincing. Another limitation might be that some historical sources only provide evidence for certain points of view, as they were recorded by those with specific interests and perspectives.

- An **oral history** provides an account of an event that happened in the past, which is told by the person who was there when it happened. Oral histories are important because they allow us to learn about things that may not be written in books or recorded in documents.
- **Newspapers** are important source materials for scholars because they provide a detailed account of the past, which cannot be found in books or other sources. Newspapers are not always reliable as they may not be based on fact, while others might omit certain information or give undue weight towards one side of an issue at the expense of another.
- **Diaries** and personal **journals** can provide valuable information for historians because they are detailed histories of people's lives. However, the reliability of these accounts is always in question because they were created by just one person and aren't always written with the intention of sharing.
- **Artifacts** can be defined as objects created by humans, which can give hints at the peoples' material culture and intangible culture. Material culture includes things like buildings or furniture while intangible culture includes things like music or dance. The benefits of artifacts are that they can offer insights into how people lived in the past. They can also be used to shed light on the thoughts, feelings, fears, tensions, customs, rituals, and other social practices at that time.
- **Tax lists** and **census data** are useful sources of insight into how people lived during a certain time. They provide us with reliable information about the income, demographics, and beliefs of the people living in a particular time.
- **Personal correspondence** has been an important form of historical information for historians. It gives an insight into the lives and interactions of ordinary people. The main benefits of using personal correspondence as a source for history is that it provides an authentic portrayal of the author's thoughts and feelings during a time period or in response to significant events.

HISTORICAL INTERPRETATION AND BIASES

History is a discipline that relies on the interpretation of **facts** to create **narratives**. Due to the types and availability of sources, history tends to leave itself open to **subjectivity**. Often, this means that **biases** are introduced at either the source of information, the interpretation of the information, or at the explanation of the information. For instance, if the only **sources of information** about an event are newspapers, the author of these historical sources may have been biased, causing the **interpretation** of the actual events to be skewed from the start. Similarly, the person interpreting the source may have their own biases that they introduce or even **teach** to others in the process of communicating the historical narrative. Commonly described biases in modern interpretation of history generally revolve around sociopolitical issues such as Eurocentrism, popular political parties, economic biases, and cultural favoritism.

Fine Arts Foundations and Creativity

LEARNING OUTCOMES ACHIEVED THROUGH VISUAL ARTS

The arts are just as important to include in curricula as language, math, science, social studies, health, and physical education. Early learning standards in many states now reflect the goal to integrate the arts into the overall curriculum. Teachers need to provide young children with activities that promote development of fine motor skills, exploration of art materials and processes, and symbolic representation of concepts through artworks. Early childhood educators should not merely assign isolated art activities. They can clarify many concepts and improve learning by providing art projects that fit into the overall curriculum and are relevant to individual learning units. Teachers should develop detailed, well-organized step lists for each activity. Clear directions not only maintain classroom order but also provide children with a structure within which to experiment with art and enhance their sequencing skills. Teachers should use process-oriented activities, both on their own and within lessons that require products. For example, painting pictures of animals combines product (representing an animal) with process (exploring paint use). Teachers should supply and explain rules/steps for process activities that explore the use of art materials and processes.

VIKTOR LOWENFELD

Viktor Lowenfeld (1903–1960) taught art to elementary school students and sculpture to blind students. Lowenfeld's acquaintance with Sigmund Freud, who was interested in his work with people with visual impairments, motivated Lowenfeld to pursue scientific research. He published several books on using creative arts activities therapeutically. Lowenfeld was familiar with six stages previously identified in the growth of art. He combined these with principles of human development drawn from the school of psychoanalytic psychology founded by Freud. In his adaptation, he named the six stages reflecting the development of children's art as scribble, preschematic, schematic, dawning realism, pseudorealistic, and period of decision. Lowenfeld identified adolescent learning styles as haptic, focused on physical sensations and subjective emotional experiences, and as visual, focused on appearances, each demanding corresponding instructional approaches. Lowenfeld's book *Creative and Mental Growth* (1947) was the most influential text in art education during the later 20th century. Lowenfeld's psychological emphasis in this text gave scientific foundations to creative and artistic expression and identified developmentally age-appropriate art media and activities.

STAGES OF GROWTH AND DEVELOPMENT IN ART

Austrian and German art scholars established six stages in art.

1. **Scribble stage:** from 2–4 years, children first make uncontrolled scribbles, then controlled scribbling, then progress to naming their scribbles to indicate what they represent.
2. **Preschematic stage:** From ages 4–6, children begin to develop a visual schema. Schema, meaning mental representation, comes from Piaget's cognitive-developmental theory. Without complete comprehension of dimensions and sizes, children may draw people and houses the same height; they use color more emotionally than logically. They may omit or exaggerate facial features, or they might draw sizes by importance (e.g., drawing themselves as largest among people or drawing the most important feature, such as the head, as the largest or only body part).
3. **Schematic stage:** from 7–9 years, drawings more reflect actual physical proportions and colors.
4. **Dawning realism:** from ages 9–11, drawings become increasingly representational.
5. **Pseudorealistic stage:** from ages 11–13, children reflect their ability to reason.
6. **Period of decision stage:** children ages 14+ reflect the adolescent identity crisis.

CHARACTERISTICS IN ART REFLECTING PERCEPTUAL, COGNITIVE, AND MOTOR DEVELOPMENT

Observations of young children find that while a 2½-year-old can grasp a crayon and scribble with it, by the age of 4 years, he or she can draw a picture we recognize as human. The typical 4-year-old drawing of a human being is called the "tadpole person" because it has no body, a large head, and stick limbs. Between the ages of 3 and 4 years, children typically make a transition from scribbling to producing tadpole person drawings. This development is enabled by greater development in motor control and eye-hand coordination, among other variables. Between the ages of 4 and 5 years, children make another transition by progressing from drawing tadpole persons to drawing complete figures with heads and bodies. Howard Gardner, psychologist and author of the theory of multiple intelligences, stated that children achieve a "summit of artistry" by the end of their preschool years. He describes their drawings as "characteristically colorful, balanced, rhythmic, and expressive, conveying something of the range and...vitality associated with artistic mastery." (1980)

PLANNING ART ACTIVITIES OR PROJECTS

Early childhood teachers should first establish the concept they want to teach, the objectives they want to meet through planning and teaching the lesson/activity, and the learning objectives they want the children to meet through participating. Then, a teacher can construct a simple prototype for the project. This enables the teacher to estimate how long it will take the children to complete the activity and to explore and discover the optimal sequencing of steps for the activity. The teacher should then write down the plan, step-by-step. Steps should include those that need to be completed before the activity. These might include preliminary discussion, book reading/sharing related to the project, viewing related artworks and/or photos, etc. Steps should also include those that need to be completed while setting up the activity, such as dispensing paints and clay, assembling paintbrushes/other instruments, and passing out paper and other materials. Teachers do not need to be artistically proficient. Young children are not art critics, and teachers can find a great deal of information about art materials and processes by reading books and searching online. Available professional development courses focusing on art can also give teachers more ideas for lesson plans.

> **Review Video: Learning Objectives**
> Visit mometrix.com/academy and enter code: 528458

FUNCTIONS OF ART
SOCIAL FUNCTIONS

Artworks can be created for physical, social, and personal purposes. When art focuses on the social lives of groups rather than on one individual's experiences or viewpoint, it serves social functions. Art carrying political stances/messages always performs social functions. Dadaist Oppenheim's hair-covered tea set did not perform any physical function but served social functions by politically protesting World War I and many other social/political issues. During the Great Depression, photographers like Dorothea Lange, Gordon Parks, Walker Evans, and Arthur Rothstein, commissioned by the Farm Security Administration, produced stark records of people's suffering. These depictions of social conditions also served social functions. Fine artists like Francisco Goya and William Hogarth, as well as cartoonists like Thomas Nast and Charles Bragg, created satirical works of art lampooning various social and political customs and situations. Satire is intended not only to provide comic relief, insight, and perspective but also to stimulate social change. Therefore, it serves social functions. Another social function is improving community status and pride through art treasures.

PHYSICAL FUNCTIONS

Ascertaining the function of a work of art requires considering its context. Half of the context involves the artist. Knowing the artist's country, the historical time period during which the artist lived, and the social and political culture of the time informs artwork and our ability to infer what the artist was thinking and intending when he or she was creating it. The other half of the context involves the viewer. Knowing what the artwork means to you in your own place and time informs your perception of and response to it. Taken within context, art serves physical, personal, and social functions. For example, architecture, industrial design, and crafts have physical functions. A raku pottery bowl made in Japan serves a physical function during a tea ceremony. However, a teacup covered with hair (paired with a hair-covered saucer and spoon) by Dada artist Meret Oppenheim (1936) makes an artistic statement but serves no physical function. When we view a tribal war club in a museum, regardless of the exquisite craftsmanship it may demonstrate, we realize it was made primarily for bludgeoning enemies.

PERSONAL FUNCTIONS

Works of art can have physical, social, and personal functions. Of these three, the personal functions of art are the most variable. Artists' motivations to create works include the desire to express their feelings and ideas, to obtain gratification through producing art, to communicate messages to viewers, to enable both themselves and their viewers to have an aesthetic experience, and to simply entertain viewers. Some artists also claim that they sometimes create art for no particular reason and that the art produced has no meaning. Art can perform a personal function of control. For example, some artists use their work to give order to the world's apparent chaos. Others use art to create chaos in an overly orderly, boring environment. Art can be therapeutic for both artists and viewers. Much art has served the personal function of religion. Artworks with biological purposes, like cultural fertility symbols or bodily decorations designed to attract mates for procreation, are also examples of the personal functions of art.

LEARNING OBJECTIVES

When children participate in teacher-designed art activities, they can fulfill learning objectives such as exploring various art materials and processes; developing awareness of visual art and its basic elements (e.g., line, shape, color, and texture); using art forms to represent feelings, thoughts, and/or stories; developing the skills of color recognition and discrimination; and even building their vocabularies and language skills, depending on the activities. Teachers can integrate such objectives with an overall theme for each art activity/project that they integrate with the current theme for their lesson or curriculum unit. For example, if space travel is the class theme one week, constructing model rocket ships is more appropriate than painting self-portraits. Even open-ended activities to explore art materials and processes can be integrated with thematic units. For example, teachers can apply activities exploring cutting and gluing processes to a theme of one specific color by providing various materials and textures that are all the same color. In this way, teachers can connect a learning concept to experimentation with artistic processes.

CREATING, PERFORMING, AND RESPONDING

Three processes common to all branches of the arts—visual, musical, dance, dramatic, and performance art—are **creating**, **performing**, and **responding**. The first of these, creating, involves the genesis of the artistic product.

There are several steps in creating:

- **Imagining** is the step during which the artist develops his or her ideas and considers the concepts and feelings which he or she wants to communicate and express through the work.
- **Planning** is the step during which the artist researches, experiments with, and designs the means by which he or she will present ideas and emotions (e.g., the materials that will be used and how they will be manipulated to produce the desired effects).
- **Making, evaluating, and refining** is the step during which the artist applies his or her skills and various techniques to create an artistic product that will bring his or her ideas and feelings to life.
- **Presenting** is the step during which the artist exhibits visual art in a gallery, private exhibit, or another type of showing. The artist might also perform music, dance, theater, or performance art for an audience so that others can participate in and respond to the artwork.

PROCESSES INVOLVED IN THE PRODUCTION AND RECEPTION OF WORKS OF ART

In all branches of the arts, artists and their audiences (who may also be participants in the case of performance art) complete three basic artistic processes that are closely related: creation, performance, and response.

The performance process includes five steps:

- **Selecting** is the step during which the artist makes a choice about what to present. For example, musicians choose pieces to play. Dancers choose choreographic pieces to perform. Visual artists select which of their paintings, drawings, sculptures, and mobiles/stabiles to display. Theater producers, directors, and actors choose a play to perform.
- **Analyzing** is the step during which the performer researches the background of the chosen work and analyzes its structure to understand it and its import.
- **Interpreting** is the step during which the performer develops a personal idea about what the work should express or accomplish.
- **Rehearsing, evaluating, and refining** is the step during which the performer applies his or her skills and techniques to develop a personal interpretation that will enable his or her performance to make the work come alive. The artist then evaluates the performance and makes further refinements to subsequent presentations.
- **Presenting** is the final step, during which the artist performs the work for others.

FUNDAMENTAL ARTISTIC PROCESSES COMMON TO ALL BRANCHES OF THE ARTS

The artistic process of responding to artwork includes four steps:

- **Selection** is the step during which the person(s) who will receive the artwork choose what they want to experience (possible choices include attending a gallery exhibit of paintings, drawings, or sculptures; going to see a theatrical play or a movie; attending a dance performance; attending/participating in a performance art show; or reading a book of poetry or prose).
- **Analysis** is the step during which the viewers, audience, participants, or readers see/hear and understand the components of the work and mentally bring these components together to perceive the work as a whole.
- **Interpretation** is the step during which those experiencing the work and/or its performance construct meaning from what they have witnessed, developing a personal response to the creator(s)' and performer(s)' expressions of concepts and emotions.
- **Evaluation** is the final step, during which the respondent(s) assess the quality of the artwork and of its performance.

FACILITATING STUDENT LEARNING WITH CREATING, PERFORMING, AND RESPONDING

The artistic processes have many steps in common. This interrelatedness among the processes informs students' development of educated responses to artworks. For instance, when students learn the step of evaluating their own artworks, they learn to apply better critical approaches when interpreting the artworks created by others. They also use their experiences to direct their selection of works they want to witness and respond to in the future. When students learn how to evaluate and refine their own work, this facilitates their subsequent evaluation and selection of others' works to watch, to perform themselves, and/or to purchase. Teachers can promote this by encouraging students to transfer their learning from one artistic process to another. For example, teachers can introduce students to others' work while they are creating their own so they can transfer what they learn about the creation process to the responding process. When students are solving specific creative/artistic problems, teachers can expose them to other artists' solutions and encourage students to consider these solutions.

LINES

In visual media, a line is the path of a moving point, the edge of a flat or two-dimensional shape, or the outline of a solid, three-dimensional object. Lines are longer than they are wide. The term *measure* refers to the width of a line. Lines can be straight, curved, wavy, angular, or zigzag. Lines can be horizontal (side to side), vertical (up and down), or diagonal (at an angle between vertical and horizontal). Lines can also be implied. In this case, they are not physically present, but the artist's arrangement of other elements suggests lines, which organize the picture and/or guide viewers' eyes. The movement a line follows/appears to show is called direction. Where and how a line is placed in a picture/design is called location. Lines define areas and imply or create open or closed shapes like circles, rectangles, etc. Lines combined with shapes create implied volume in paintings/drawings and actual volume in sculptures. Lines express various qualities by being jagged, loopy, bold, repetitive, etc., and evoke different emotional and mental viewer responses.

SHAPE, FORM, AND VALUE

Shape refers to two-dimensional areas created by connecting lines to outline the contours of objects depicted in art. Shapes can be positive or negative (i.e., defined not by their own outlines but by the edges of surrounding shapes). Shapes may be biomorphic (i.e., shapes found in nature) or geometric. Variations in value, texture, or color can make shapes stand out in a piece. Form is the three-dimensional projection of shape. Form has dimension and volume. In paintings and drawings, form appears to have mass, while in sculptures, it actually does have mass. The term *form* can also be used to describe an artwork's overall structure. Value refers to the appearance and range of lights and darks seen in a visual work of art. Regardless of color, value varies between black and white, with an indefinite range of various shades of gray between these two absolutes.

TEXTURE AND SPACE

Texture refers to how rough or smooth a surface appears or feels. Everyday materials have texture, as do works of art. An object or a work of art can look and/or feel spongy or glassy, wet or dry, soft or hard, etc. Texture can be real, as with sandpaper and other rough-textured materials used to create works of art, or it can be illusory, as when materials appear hard or soft but are really not. Space is defined as the measurable distance between predetermined points. It can be shallow or limited, with a foreground and a background, or it can be deep or extended, with a middle ground as well as a foreground and a background. Two-dimensional space has height and width; three-dimensional space has height and width, plus volume and time. Like negative shape (shape that is not defined by its own outlines but by the surrounding shapes and their outlines), negative space appears in art. It is the space around and between the positive objects or shapes depicted. This negative space forms its own shapes around positive subjects.

RHYTHM

In visual art, rhythm is achieved through repeating visual movement. Visual movement is created by arranging lines, shapes, and/or colors to give the viewer's eye a sense of motion and direction. Just as we hear rhythm in music through aural beats and varying note durations, we see rhythm in paintings through visual movement of lines, angles, shapes, and other elements. Just as Beethoven used repetition of musical phrases and themes to create mood, drama, and movement, artists use movement and repetition to create visual rhythm. For example, in "Nude Descending a Staircase, No. 2" (1912) by Marcel Duchamp, the artist depicts an abstracted human figure, repeating the figure using overlapping placements in a diagonal, downward pattern. The series of repeated shapes and angles gives the impression of viewing action in strobe lighting or via stop-action photography. The figures are physically still but visually convey the effect of moving down a staircase. By directionally repeating the figure, Duchamp shows movement and rhythm within the static medium of a painting.

COLOR

Color refers to the wavelengths of light reflected by a surface. Some wavelengths are absorbed by paints and other visual art media/materials; we do not see these. Other wavelengths are reflected; these are the ones we see as colors. Primary colors are pure, individual colors that cannot be separated into other colors or produced by mixing colors. The three primary colors are red, blue, and yellow. Secondary colors are combinations of two primary colors (e.g., orange = red + yellow, green = blue + yellow, and violet = red + blue). Intermediate colors are produced by mixing a primary and a secondary color (e.g., red-orange, yellow-orange, blue-green, yellow-green, blue-violet, or red-violet). Colors are arranged on the color wheel. Analogous colors are adjacent to each other on the wheel. Examples of analogous colors include yellow and orange, orange and red, blue and green, and green and yellow. Complementary colors are opposite each other on the color wheel. Examples of complementary colors include blue and orange, yellow and purple, and red and green. Mixing equal parts of two complementary colors produces brown. Blue and predominantly blue colors are cool. Red, yellow, and predominantly red/yellow colors are warm. Colors identify objects, evoke moods, and influence emotions.

BALANCE

Balance refers to how visual weight is distributed in a work of visual art. In two-dimensional art like paintings, balance is the visual equilibrium among the painting's elements, which makes the entire picture look balanced. Balance can be symmetrical (both sides are equal) or asymmetrical, with shapes and spaces that are unequal and/or unevenly distributed. This produces psychological rather than physical balance, creating tension and suggesting movement. Radial balance/symmetry uses images radiating from a center, such as wheel spokes or ripples around a pebble thrown into water. An example of balance is seen in the painting "Dressing for the Carnival" (1877) by Winslow Homer. The central figure of a carnival performer putting on his costume is the focal point. The performer is surrounded by two adult assistants and a group of fascinated children who are watching him. The shapes, values, and colors are balanced to produce overall visual equilibrium and unity (another organizing principle of art).

VISUAL MOVEMENT

Artists create a visual sense of movement in paintings to direct the viewer's eyes. Direction is frequently toward a focal point or area within the painting. Artists can direct movement along lines, edges, shapes, and colors, but especially along parts with equal value (dark/light), which best facilitates the eyes' movement. For example, in "Liberation of the Peon" (1931), Diego Rivera depicts soldiers liberating a slave by cutting the ropes binding him while clothing his nakedness with a blanket or garment. Paths of movement in the painting all lead to the focal point of the knife cutting the ropes. (Emphasis, another art/design principle, is also seen in how the action of freeing the peon is made more important than the soldiers performing that action.) By painting all humans in the scene with their eyes focused on the slave, Rivera creates movement directing our view toward him. At the same time, he painted all horses with their eyes focused out at the viewer, drawing the viewer into the scene.

USING EMPHASIS

Artists use the design principle of emphasis to call attention to particular elements in their works. Emphasis directs the viewer's focus to certain parts of a painting and makes certain components of a work dominant. Emphasis can be achieved in art by emphasizing various design elements like value (light/dark), color, shape, line, etc. Artists also use contrast (e.g., contrasting values, colors, shapes, etc.) to create emphasis. To emphasize a focal area, a center of interest that focuses on the most important part of a painting, an artist can create visual emphasis through extreme contrasts of light and dark values. Strongly contrasting shapes and/or marked contrasts in other design elements also create visual emphasis. As an example of visual emphasis, in the painting "At the Moulin Rouge" (1892/1895), Henri de Toulouse-Lautrec emphasizes the focal area of a group of friends conversing in a cabaret through contrasting colors and values, as well as through movement directing the eye toward the group. His use of color, light, and shape also help create the scene's atmosphere.

UNITY

One of the most important characteristics of a well-developed work of visual art is its visual unity. When we view a painting without unity, we may see a collection of disconnected parts that do not come together to form a whole. We may perceive it as fragmentary, disorganized, and incomplete. When an artist achieves visual unity, all of the elements in a painting appear to belong together. Unity affords paintings the quality of cohesion that makes them look and feel finished and complete. For example, in the painting "Starry Night" (1889), Vincent van Gogh used his characteristic large, visible brush strokes in a swirly pattern throughout the landscape, providing visual unity through the texture, rhythm, pattern, and movement of the lines and shapes. He used predominantly cool colors (blues and bluish browns), providing unity through color. (He also provided emphasis by adding contrasting yellow stars.) The result is a unified painting whose elements work together, strongly conveying the atmosphere, mood, emotion, and story that the artist wanted to express.

CONTRAST

Contrast refers to significant differences in the values (lights and darks), colors, textures, shapes, lines, and other elements of visual artworks. Visual contrast creates interest and excitement and avoids monotony in art. For example, in the painting "Still Life with Apples and Peaches" (1905), Paul Cézanne combined all seven elements and all seven principles of design to create a unified composition. Among these, he used at least eight kinds of contrast:

- Unpatterned vs. intricately patterned surfaces (pattern contrast)
- Soft vs. hard/found edges (edge contrast)
- Dark vs. light vs. middle values (value contrast)
- Pure vs. muted/blended colors (intensity contrast)
- Cool vs. warm colors (temperature contrast)
- Textured vs. smooth surfaces (texture contrast)
- Organic vs. geometric shapes (shape contrast)
- Large vs. small objects/shapes (size contrast)

PATTERN

Pattern is the organized or random repetition of elements. Music is made up of sound patterns. Visual patterns often appear in nature. Artists frequently create works featuring repeated designs that produce patterns inspired by those seen in the natural world. Visual art is enhanced by pattern, which enriches surface interest to augment visual excitement. For example, in "Numbers in Color" (1958-59), the artist Jasper Johns created a regular pattern by assembling 11 rows of 11 stacked rectangles each. He painted various numerical digits from 0 to 9 within most of the rectangles. He made these numbers look irregular by irregularly distributing, varying, and applying the colors he used. Many patterned paintings do not include a focal point or area. This often makes them look more like designs—even when they include recognizable images—than portraits, landscapes, still-lifes, or other types of paintings that do not have such repetitive patterning.

INVOLVEMENT OF MUSIC IN THE DEVELOPMENT OF INFANTS AND YOUNG CHILDREN

Long before they can speak, and before they even comprehend much speech, infants respond to the sounds of voices and to music. These responses are not only to auditory stimulation but moreover to the emotional content in what they hear. Parents sing lullabies to babies; not only are these sounds pleasant and soothing but they also help children develop trust in their environment as secure. Parents communicate their love to children through singing and introduce them to experiences of pleasure and excitement through music. As children grow, music progresses to be not only a medium of communication but also one of self-expression as they learn to sing and play musical sounds. Music facilitates memory, as we see through commercial jingles and mnemonic devices. Experiments find music improves spatial reasoning. Children's learning of perceptual and logical concepts like beginning and ending, sequences, cause-and-effect, balance, harmony and dissonance, and mathematical number and timing concepts is reinforced by music. Music also promotes language development. Children learn about colors, counting, conceptual relationships, nature, and social skills through music.

ENHANCING THE EMOTIONAL, SOCIAL, AESTHETIC, AND SCHOOL READINESS SKILLS WITH MUSIC

Young children who are just learning to use spoken language often cannot express their emotions very well verbally. Music is a great aid to emotional development in that younger children can express happiness, sadness, anger, and more through singing and/or playing music more easily than they can with words. Children of preschool ages not only listen to music and respond to what they hear, but they also learn to create music through singing and playing instruments together with other children. These activities help them learn crucial social skills for their lives, like cooperating with others, collaborating, and making group or team efforts to accomplish something. When children are given guided musical experiences, they learn to make their own

161

judgments of what is good or bad music; this provides them with the foundations for developing an aesthetic sense. Music promotes preliteracy skills by enhancing phonemic awareness. As growing children develop musical appreciation and skills, these develop fundamental motor, cognitive, and social skills they need for language, school readiness, literacy, and life.

PITCH, TEMPO, AND RHYTHM IN THE MUSICAL ARTS

Pitch is the frequency of a sound, such as a musical note. We hear high-, middle-, and low-frequency sound waves as high-, middle-, and low-pitched sounds, respectively. Various pitches are combined in musical compositions to create variety. A series of connected notes of different pitches creates a melody. Sounding (playing/singing) several pitches simultaneously and combining them produces harmonies and chords. Connected series of harmonies/chords, in turn, create harmonic/chord progressions. **Tempo** is the speed of music. Fast tempo can evoke happiness, excitement, fear, anger, or urgency. Slow tempo can evoke serenity, grandeur, solemnity, sadness, or ominousness. Musical compositions commonly direct the tempo using terms like andante (walking speed), adagio (slow), allegro (happy/quick), lento (slow), and largo (expansively slow). **Rhythm** includes the overall beat/time signature (number of beats per measure) and the variations among note lengths that produce patterns (e.g., legato describes smoothly connected series of notes, while staccato describes sharply disconnected notes that are cut short and sounded separately). Composers combine pitch, tempo, and rhythm in music to create atmosphere and mood, and to evoke emotion in listeners. They also arrange these elements to construct/recall musical themes/motifs within compositions.

Chapter Quiz

Ready to see how well you retained what you just read? Scan the QR code to go directly to the chapter quiz interface for this study guide. If you're using a computer, simply visit the bonus page at **mometrix.com/bonus948/pectprek4** and click the Chapter Quizzes link.

Mathematics, Science, and Health

Transform passive reading into active learning! After immersing yourself in this chapter, put your comprehension to the test by taking a quiz. The insights you gained will stay with you longer this way. Scan the QR code to go directly to the chapter quiz interface for this study guide. If you're using a computer, simply visit the bonus page at **mometrix.com/bonus948/pectprek4** and click the Chapter Quizzes link.

Mathematics

MATH FOUNDATIONS
PREMATHEMATICAL LEARNING EXPERIENCES

Preschool children do not think in the same ways as older children and adults do, as Piaget observed. Their thinking is strongly based upon and connected to their sensory perceptions. This means that in solving problems, they depend mainly on how things look, sound, feel, smell, and taste. Therefore, preschool children should always be given concrete objects that they can touch, explore, and experiment with in any learning experience. They are not yet capable of understanding abstract concepts or manipulating information mentally, so they must have real things to work with to understand **premath** concepts. For example, they will learn to count solid objects like blocks, beads, or pennies before they can count numbers in their heads. They cannot benefit from rote math memorization or "sit still and listen" lessons. Since young children "centrate" on one characteristic, object, person, or event at a time, adults can offer activities encouraging decentration/incorporating multiple aspects (e.g., not only grouping all triangles but grouping all red triangles separately from blue triangles).

PROBLEM SOLVING SKILLS

Being able to solve problems is fundamental to all other components of mathematics. Children learn the concept that a question can have more than one answer and a problem can have more than one solution by participating in problem-solving activities. To solve problems, a child must be able to explore a problem, a situation, or a subject; think through the problem, situation, or subject; and use logical reasoning. These abilities are needed to not only solve routine, everyday problems but also novel or unusual ones. Using problem-solving skills not only helps children think mathematically but also promotes their language development and their social skills when they work together. Children are naturally curious about how to solve everyday problems. Adults can take advantage of this inherent curiosity by discussing everyday challenges, asking children to propose ways to solve them, and asking them to explain how they arrived at their solutions. Adults can also invite children to propose problems and ask questions about them. This helps them learn to analyze different types of problems and realize that many problems have multiple possible solutions.

COMMON STEPS THAT PREPARE CHILDREN TO LEARN MATH

The process of solving problems often involves the following steps:

1. Understanding the problem
2. Coming up with a plan to solve the problem
3. Putting that plan into action, and, finally, observing the outcome
4. Reflecting on whether the solution was effective and whether the answer arrived at makes sense

Solving problems not only involves learning this series of steps but also requires children to develop the qualities needed to solve problems. Children who are able to solve problems have a number of characteristics.

For example, children who are effective problem solvers are able to focus their attention on the problem and its individual component parts. They can formulate hypotheses about the problem/situation and then test them for veracity. They are willing to take risks within reason. They are persistent if they do not solve a problem right away and do not give up if their first attempt at solving a problem is unsuccessful. They maintain flexibility and experiment with alternate methods. They also demonstrate self-regulation skills.

USING PROBLEM SOLVING SKILLS IN DAILY LIFE

Young children continually explore their environments to unravel mysteries about how things work. For example, preschoolers use math concepts to understand that they have three toys, to comprehend that three fingers equals three toys, or to understand that two cookies plus one more equals three cookies. To do abstract mathematics in the future, young children will need two major skills that are also used to solve problems: being able to visualize a scenario and being able to apply common sense thinking. Thinking and planning to achieve goals within the constraints of the properties of the surrounding environment is a natural behavior for young children. They will persist in their efforts to get an older sibling to stop another activity to play with them, to repair broken toys with tape or chewing gum, to manipulate a puzzle or plastic building blocks to get one uncooperative piece to fit, etc. The great 20th-century mathematician and teacher George Polya stated that problem-solving is "the most characteristically human activity." He pointed out that problem-solving is a skill learned by doing, and that developing this skill requires a great deal of practice.

GAMES/ACTIVITIES THAT ENCOURAGE THE USE OF PROBLEM-SOLVING SKILLS

One method that has been found to enhance children's reasoning skills is using adult-child conversations to play mental mathematics games. For example, once children are able to count beyond five, adults can give them basic oral story problems to solve (e.g., "If you have two plums and I give you two more, how many will you have?"). Using children's favorite foods in story problems, which takes advantage of their ready ability to envision these foods, is a good place to start. Thereafter, adults can add story problems involving pets, toys, cars, shopping, and other familiar objects, animals, or activities. Experts advise adults not to restrict the types of problems presented to a child based solely on the child's grade level. Children can work with any situation if they can form mental imagery. Adults can sometimes insert harder tasks (e.g., problems involving larger numbers, problems involving division with remainders, or problems with negative number answers). Even toddlers can solve problems such as how to divide three cookies between two people. The division may not be fair, but it will likely be efficient. Adults should use the Socratic method, asking guiding questions to allow children to arrive at a solution to a problem themselves, rather than telling them a "right" answer.

BENEFICIAL PRACTICES OF PLAYING MENTAL MATH GAMES

Adults can use children's favorite foods and toys to pose story problems to children that involve addition and subtraction. For example, they can ask them questions like "If I give you [this many] more, how many will you have?" or "If we take away [this many], how many are left?" It is better to ask children questions than to give them answers. It is important to use turn-taking. In this method, the adult poses a story problem to the child, and then the child gets to pose one to the adult. Adults must try to solve the problem, even if the child makes up numbers like "bazillion" or "eleventy." Games should be fun, not strictly factual like math tests. Adults can introduce age-appropriate story topics as children grow older. At the end of early childhood/around school age, children can handle the abstract algebraic concept of variables or unknown numbers (which some experts call "mystery numbers") and use this concept in games. Adults can pose riddles where x or n is the unknown number, and children must use an operation (e.g., $x + 4 = 7$) to solve the riddle.

> **Review Video: Mathematical Operations**
> Visit mometrix.com/academy and enter code: 208095

REASONING SKILLS
COMMUNICATING WITH CHILDREN TO PROMOTE MATHEMATICAL REASONING SKILLS

Adults should reciprocally talk to and listen to children during communication that is focused on using mathematical skills like problem-solving, reasoning, making connections, etc. To promote young children's understanding, adults can express mathematical concepts using pictures, words, diagrams, and symbols. Encouraging children to talk with their peers and adults helps them clarify their own thoughts and think about what they are doing. Communicating with children about mathematical thinking problems also develops their vocabularies and promotes early literacy and reading skills. Adults should listen to what children want to say and should have conversations with them. Communicating about math can also be accomplished through reading children's books that incorporate numbers and/or repetition or rhyme. In addition to talking, adults can communicate math concepts to children by drawing pictures or diagrams and using concrete objects (e.g., blocks, crayons, pieces of paper, fingers, etc.) to represent numbers and/or solve problems. Children also share their learning of math concepts through words, charts, drawings, tallies, etc. Even toddlers hold up fingers to tell others how old they are.

USING REASONING SKILLS TO UNDERSTAND AND APPLY EARLY MATHEMATICAL AND SCIENTIFIC CONCEPTS

A major component of problem-solving is **reasoning**. Children reason when they think through questions and find usable answers. They use reasoning skills to make sense of mathematical and scientific subject matter. Children use several abilities during the reasoning process. For example, they use logic to classify objects or concepts into groups. They follow logical sequences to arrive at conclusions that make sense. They use their analytical abilities to explain their own thought processes. They apply what they have learned about relationships and patterns to help them find solutions to problems. They also use reasoning to justify their mental processes and problem solutions. To support children's reasoning, adults can ask children questions, give them time to think about their answers, and listen to their answers. This simple tactic helps children learn how to reason. Adults can also ask children why something is as it is—letting them think for themselves rather than looking for a particular answer—and listen to the ideas they produce.

ROLE OF REPRESENTATION SKILLS IN CHILDREN'S LEARNING

Young children develop an understanding of **symbolic representation**—the idea that objects, written letters, words, and other symbols are used to represent other objects or concepts—at an early age. This is evident in their make-believe/pretend play and in their ability to learn written language and connect it to spoken language. As children develop early math skills, representing their ideas and the information they acquire helps them organize, document, and share these ideas and facts with others. Children may count on their fingers; create tallies using checkmarks, tick marks, and/or words; draw pictures or maps; and, as they grow older, make graphs. Teachers must help children apply mathematical process skills as they use learning center materials. For example, when a child enjoys sorting rocks by color, the teacher can state that the child is classifying them, bridging informal math activities with math vocabulary. Asking the child how he or she is categorizing the rocks emphasizes math vocabulary. Asking the child after he or she finishes what other ways the rocks could be classified encourages problem-solving.

MAKING CONNECTIONS AND HELPING CHILDREN TRANSITION FROM INTUITIVE TO FORMAL MATH THINKING

Children informally learn intuitive mathematical thinking through their everyday life experiences. They naturally apply mathematical concepts and reasoning to solve problems they face in their environment. However, one frequent problem among children when they begin formal education is that they can come to see academic mathematics as a collection of procedures and rules, instead of viewing it as a means of finding solutions to everyday, real-life problems. This view will interfere with children's ability to apply the formal mathematics they learn to their lives in a practical and useful way. Teachers can help prevent this outcome by establishing the connection between children's natural intuitive math and formal mathematics. They can do this by teaching math through the use of manipulative materials familiar to children. They can use mathematics vocabulary words when describing children's activities, which enables children to develop an awareness of the natural mathematical operations they use in their daily lives. When a teacher introduces a new mathematical concept to children, he or she can give illustrative examples that draw upon the children's actual life experiences.

RELATIONSHIP OF MATHEMATICS TO EVERYDAY LIFE AND OTHER ACADEMIC SUBJECTS

We use math throughout our lives during everyday activities. There are countless examples and combinations of various mathematical concepts in the real world. Additionally, math concepts inform other academic content areas, including music, art, and the sciences. Therefore, it is important for children not to view math as an isolated set of procedures and skills. Children comprehend math more easily when they can make connections, which involves applying common mathematical rules to multiple, varied functions, processes, and real-life activities. For example, adults can ask children to consider problems they encounter daily and solve them. When a parent asks a child to help put away groceries, the child practices sorting categories of foods and packages, and experiments with comparative package sizes and shapes. Parents need not be concerned with what specific mathematical processes are involved but should simply look for examples of math in everyday life and expose children to these examples on a regular basis. For example, pouring liquid into containers of various sizes and speculating which one will hold the most is an easy, fun activity that incorporates a number of skills and concepts, including estimation, measurement, spatial sense, and conservation of liquid volume.

PATTERNS AND RELATIONSHIPS

Patterns are generally defined as things that recur or are repeated regularly. Patterns can be found in images, sounds, numbers, events, actions, movements, etc. Relationships are generally defined as connections or associations between things that are identified and/or described using logic or reasoning. Being aware of patterns and relationships among aspects of the environment helps us comprehend the fundamental structure of these aspects. This awareness enables us to predict what will occur next in a series of events, even before it actually happens. This gives us more confidence in our environment and in our ability to interact with it. We find patterns and relationships in such areas of life as art, music, and clothing. Math-specific activities like counting numbers and working with geometrical shapes, lines, arcs, and curves also involve patterns and relationships. When children understand patterns and relationships, they can understand repetition, rhythm, categorization, and how to order things from smallest to biggest, from shortest to longest, etc.

Adults can help young children develop their understanding of patterns and relationships in life by looking at pictures and designs with them, encouraging and guiding them to identify patterns within drawings, paintings, and abstract designs such as prints on fabrics and other decorative designs. When children participate in movement activities, including dancing to music, running, skipping, hopping, playing simple musical instruments, etc., adults can help them identify patterns in their own and others' movements. Adults can encourage young children to participate in hands-on activities, such as stringing wood, plastic beads, or penne and other hollow dry pasta tubes onto pieces of string to make necklaces with simple patterns (e.g., blue-yellow-blue-yellow). As children grow older, adults can encourage them to create more complicated patterns. They can alternate a larger number of colors, and they can vary the numbers of each color in more complex ways (e.g., three blue, two yellow, one red, etc.).

CONTRIBUTION OF NUMBER SENSE AND NUMBER OPERATIONS TO MATH COMPREHENSION

Counting is one of the earliest numeracy skills that young children develop. Even before they have learned the names of all the numbers, young children learn to count to three, then to five, etc. However, **number sense** involves a great deal more than just counting. Number sense includes understanding the various applications of numbers. For instance, we use numbers as tools for conveying and manipulating information, as tools for describing quantities, and as tools for characterizing relationships between or among things. Children who have developed number sense are able to count with accuracy and competence. Given a specific number, they can count upward from that number. They can also count backward. They are able to break down a number and then reassemble it. They are able to recognize relationships between or among different numbers. When children can count, are familiar with numbers, and have good number sense, they can also add and subtract numbers. Being familiar with numbers and being able to count easily helps young children understand all other areas of mathematics.

ACTIVITIES TO HELP DEVELOP NUMBER SENSE AND NUMERACY SKILLS

As children complete their daily activities, it is beneficial for adults to count real things with children and encourage them to count as well. This helps children understand numbers by using their own experiences with objects in the environment and gives them practice counting and using numbers. To help children understand that we use numbers to describe quantities and relationships, adults can ask children to sort objects by size, shape, or color similarity. They can also ask children to sort objects according to their differences (e.g., which object is bigger/smaller). Adults can also discuss with children how numbers are used to find street addresses and apartment numbers and to keep score during games. To help children count upward and downward with efficiency and accuracy, adults can point out that counting allows us to determine how many items are in a group. Adults should point to each object as they count it. They can count on their fingers and encourage young children to do the same. Adults should also help children count without repeating or skipping any numbers.

COUNTING

Counting is considered a math skill milestone for young children. Typical four-year-olds enjoy counting aloud. Experts identify three levels of counting. The first is counting from 1 to 12, which requires memorization. The second level is counting from 13 to 19, which requires not only memorization but also an understanding of the more unusual rules for "teen" numbers. The third level is counting from 20 on. This process is very consistent, and the numbers are ordered according to regular rules. Experts in math education believe that at this level of counting, children are discovering a regular mathematical pattern for the first time, which is base ten (i.e., 20, 30, 40, 50, etc. are 2 tens, 3 tens, 4 tens, 5 tens, etc., and after the base, a number between 1 and 9 is added). Researchers and educators in early childhood mathematics programs recommend encouraging children as young as four years old to learn to count up to 100. They find that doing this helps young children learn about and explore patterns in depth.

PERCEIVING AND IDENTIFYING SHAPES

The three levels of perceiving shapes that children typically move through sequentially are seeing, naming, and analyzing. Very young children recognize simple shapes like circles, squares, and triangles. As their cognitive and language skills develop, they learn the names for these shapes and use these names to identify single shapes. The third level is analyzing each shape to understand its properties. Whereas identifying shapes visually is intuitive and based on association, analyzing their properties is more abstract, since a shape can have a number of different appearances. For example, three-year-olds can differentiate a triangle from other shapes. However, if you show them a very tall and skinny, short and wide, lopsided, or crooked triangle, they will have trouble identifying it as a triangle. At the analysis level, children realize that a triangle has three sides, which are not necessarily equal in length. An activity that young children enjoy is closing their eyes, reaching into a bag of assorted shapes, finding a triangle by touch, and explaining why it is a triangle. This involves both the second and third levels of naming and analysis.

SPATIAL SENSE AND GEOMETRY

Spatial sense is an individual's awareness of one's own body in space and in relation to the objects and other people around the individual. Spatial sense allows young children to navigate environmental spaces without colliding with objects and other people; to see and hear adequately and to be aware of whether others can see and hear them; and to develop and observe a socially and culturally appropriate sense of their own and others' personal space. Geometry is the area of mathematics involving space, sizes, shapes, positions, movements, and directions. Geometry gives descriptions and classifications of our physical environment. By observing commonplace objects and spaces in their physical world, young children can learn about solid objects and substances, shapes, and angles. Adults can help young children learn geometry by identifying various shapes, angles, and three-dimensional figures for them; asking them to name these shapes, angles, and figures when they encounter them in the future; and asking them to describe different shapes, draw them in the air with their fingers, trace drawings of the shapes with their fingers, and then draw the shapes themselves.

ACTIVITIES TO HELP DEVELOP SPATIAL SENSE AND GEOMETRY

Because it involves many physical properties like shape, line, and angle, as well as abstract concepts, young children learn geometry most effectively via hands-on activities. Learning experiences that allow them to touch and manipulate concrete objects, such as boxes, containers, puzzles, blocks, and shape sorters, usually work best. Everyday activities can also help children learn geometry concepts. For example, adults can cut children's sandwiches into various geometrical shapes and let children fit them together and/or rearrange them into new patterns. Children become better able to follow directions and navigate through space when they develop geometric knowledge and spatial sense. Adults can provide activities that promote the development of geometric knowledge and spatial sense. For example, they can let children get into and out of big appliance boxes, climb over furniture, and go into, on top of, out of, under, around, over, and through different objects and structures to allow children to experience the relationship between their bodies and space and solids. As they mature, children can play games in which they search for "hidden" shapes. Such shapes may be irregular, may lack flat bases, or may be turned in various directions.

MEASUREMENT

Measurement is the process of determining how long, wide, and tall something is physically and how much it weighs by using measuring units such as inches, feet, yards, square feet, ounces, and pounds. Measurement is also used to quantify time using units like seconds, minutes, hours, days, weeks, months, years, centuries, and millennia. Measurement is not just a formal means of quantifying size, area, and time. It is also an important method for young children to seek and identify relationships between and among things they encounter outside of school in everyday life. When young children practice measuring things, they are able to understand not only the sizes of objects and beings but also their comparative sizes (i.e., how large or small something is compared to another object used as a reference). Furthermore, they are able to figure out how big or little something is on their own.

While it is obviously important for children to eventually learn standardized measurement units like inches, feet, and yards, adults can facilitate early development of measurement skills by letting children choose their own measurement units. For example, they might use their favorite toy to describe a playmate or sibling as "three teddy bears tall," or they might describe a room as "seven toy cars long." Similarly, when children are too young to know formal time measurements like minutes and hours, adults can support children's ability to quantify time using favorite TV shows. For example, four-year-olds can often relate to the idea of one episode of a show (whether it is 30 minutes or 60 minutes long) as a time measurement. Adults can apply this with statements like, "Daddy will be home in one episode." Numerous everyday activities, including grocery shopping, cooking, sewing, gardening, woodworking, and many others, involve measurement. Adults can ask children to help with these tasks and then discuss measuring with children as they participate.

MEASUREMENT OF TIME

Younger children typically do not have an understanding of the abstract concept of time. However, adults can still help children understand that time elapses and that we count/measure this process. For example, adults can ask younger children simple questions, such as "Who can stand on one foot longer?" This comparison strategy helps children figure out which of two or more actions/activities takes a longer/the longest period of time. Even when children do not yet understand what "five minutes" means, adults should still make such references (e.g., "You can play for five minutes longer, and then we must leave."). Repeating such references will eventually help children understand that time passes. Adults can time various everyday activities/events and tell children how long they took. They can also count the second hand's ticks on a watch/clock (e.g., "one second...two seconds...three seconds..."). This familiarizes children with counting, and with using counting to track the passage of time. Until children are old enough to understand abstractions like today/yesterday/tomorrow, adults can use concrete references like "after lunch" or "before bedtime."

FRACTIONS

Fractions are parts or pieces of a whole. While adults understand this and likely do not remember ever not understanding it, very young children think differently in this regard. As Piaget showed, children in the preoperational stage of cognitive development cannot perform logical or mathematical mental operations. They focus on one property of an object rather than all of its properties, a practice he called centration. Hence, if you cut an apple into pieces, very young children see that there are more pieces than there were before, and they believe that several apple pieces are more than one apple. They cannot yet comprehend the logical sequence of dividing an apple into fractions. To comprehend fractions, children must know what a whole unit consists of, how many pieces the unit is divided into, and whether the pieces are of equal size. Adults can help children understand fractions through informal sharing activities, such as slicing up a pizza or a pan of brownies, and/or equally dividing household/preschool chores and play materials.

ESTIMATION

Estimation is making an educated or informed guess about a measurement when no actual measurement is available. Adults often make estimates about the sizes of objects when their exact measurements are unknown, about the amounts of substances that have not actually been measured, and about the numbers of small objects in large collections when the objects have not actually been counted. However, young children are in the process of learning the concepts of sizes and numbers. Children must comprehend concepts of comparison and relativity (e.g., larger, smaller, more, less, etc.) before they will be able to make accurate estimates. When children start to develop the ability to estimate amounts or sizes, this process helps them learn related math vocabulary words, such as *about* or *around*, and *more than* and *less than* [something else]. Through estimating, they also learn how to make appropriate predictions and arrive at realistic answers. It is important for young children to learn how to make estimates, to recognize when it is appropriate to apply the estimation method, and to recognize when their estimates are reasonable.

ACTIVITIES TO HELP DEVELOP ESTIMATION

During everyday activities like shopping or eating, adults can ask children to estimate amounts of foods, numbers of items, or lengths of time. Later, adults can help children compare the actual outcome with their original estimate. This process helps children learn to make realistic/reasonable estimates. Activities promoting estimation skills can be very simple. Adults can ask children, for example, to guess which of their friends is tallest and then test the accuracy of the guess using real measurements. When children grow older, adults can write down estimates and real measurements and can then repeat the exercise described above or present a similar one. With repetition, children will eventually begin making more accurate estimates. The goal is not for children to come up with exact measurements but ones that are close to actual amounts/numbers. Giving children opportunities to practice improves their estimating skills.

PROBABILITIES AND STATISTICS

In general, when people work with statistics, they present them in graphs or charts to organize them, interpret them, and make it easier to see relationships among individual statistics. Graphs are visual alternatives that depict mathematical information and show relationships among individual statistics, especially changes over time. Graphs also allow for the comparison of different groups. Probabilities indicate the likelihood that something will happen. Adults use probabilities to predict things, such as people's risks of developing or dying from various diseases or medical conditions; the chances of accidents; children's risks of experiencing academic difficulties, dropping out, or developing emotional and behavioral disorders; and the chances that a certain area will receive rain or snow. Scientists use probabilities to predict the likelihood of various behaviors or outcomes they are studying. They use statistics to show the numbers and proportions of responses or results obtained in research studies. Calendars are one type of chart. Adults can help children use them to organize daily and weekly activities and to understand how we organize information.

CHARTS AND GRAPHS

According to experts, almost every daily activity can be charted in some way. For example, adults can help children peel the little stickers off of plums, bananas, etc. and stick them to a piece of paper/poster board divided into columns. After a week, they can count each column to determine how many pieces of each kind of fruit they ate. Similarly, adults can show children how to use removable stickers or color forms to document the number of times they performed any daily activity. For example, children could place a color form near the front door every time somebody comes in, goes out, and/or rings the doorbell or knocks. This enables children to count the number of times given events occur by recording them. Some children are better able to understand math by viewing and making graphs. This is because creating graphs involves representing quantities visually instead of just listing numbers.

RATIONAL NUMBERS AND IRRATIONAL NUMBERS

In mathematics, **rational numbers** are numbers that can be written as ratios or fractions. In other words, a rational number can be expressed as a fraction that has a whole number as the numerator (the number on top) and the denominator (the number on the bottom). Therefore, all whole numbers are automatically rational numbers, because all whole numbers can be written as fractions with a denominator of 1 (e.g., $5 = 5/1$, $68 = 68/1$, $237 = 237/1$, etc.). Even very large, unwieldy fractions (e.g., $9,731,245/42,754,021$) are rational numbers, because they can be written as fractions. **Irrational numbers** can be written as decimal numbers, but not as fractions, because the numbers to the right of the decimal point that are less than 1 continue indefinitely without repeating. For example, the value of pi (π) begins as 3.141592... and continues without end or the square root of 2, $\sqrt{2} = 1.414213\ldots$, and so on. There are an infinite number of irrational numbers between 0 and 1. However, irrational numbers are not used as commonly in everyday life as rational numbers.

> **Review Video: Rational and Irrational Numbers**
> Visit mometrix.com/academy and enter code: 280645

CARDINAL, ORDINAL, NOMINAL, AND REAL NUMBERS

- **Cardinal numbers** are numbers that indicate quantity. For example, when we say "seven buttons" or "three kittens," we are using cardinal numbers.
- **Ordinal numbers** are numbers that indicate the order of items within a group or a set. For example, when we say "first," "second," "third," etc., we are using ordinal numbers.
- **Nominal numbers** are numbers that name things. For example, we use area code numbers along with telephone numbers to identify geographical calling areas, and we use zip code numbers to identify geographical mailing areas. Nominal numbers, therefore, identify categories or serve as labels for things. However, they are not related to the actual mathematical values of numbers, and do not indicate numerical quantities or operations.
- **Real numbers** include all rational and irrational numbers. Rational numbers can always be written as fractions that have both numerators and denominators that are whole numbers. Irrational numbers cannot, as they contain non-repeating decimal digits. Real numbers may or may not be cardinal numbers.

INTEGRATING MATH INTO EVERYDAY ACTIVITIES AND USING EARLY CHILDHOOD MATH CURRICULA

Integrating math into the context of everyday activities has been the philosophy of early childhood math education until recently. For example, when teachers have children line up, they ask them who is first, second, third, etc. to practice counting. When children play with blocks, teachers ask them to identify their shapes and whether one block is larger/smaller than another. During snack times, teachers help children learn 1:1 correspondence by having them place one snack on each plate. These activities are quite valuable. However, some educators maintain that they are insufficient when used on their own, because in larger classes, it is not always possible to take advantage of "teachable moments" with every child. Therefore, this educational approach cannot be applied systematically. These educators recommend that in addition to integration strategies, early childhood teachers should use a curriculum. The HighScope curriculum, the Creative Curriculum, and Big Math for Little Kids are just a few examples. Many teachers combine several curricula, selecting parts of different programs. Using a curriculum allows teachers to use a more planned approach to integrate math into all activities.

CLINICAL INTERVIEW
BACKGROUND, METHOD, AND ADVANTAGES

Clinical interviews have long been used by individual and family therapists, as well as by researchers. Piaget used them along with observations and case histories to understand young children's thinking as he formulated his cognitive developmental theory. Interviewers ask structured, semi-structured, and open-ended questions and listen to the responses, often recording them for accuracy. This method gives the interviewer a way to find out what the respondent is thinking and feeling inside, which cannot be determined by observing outward behaviors alone. In educational settings, a teacher might ask a child questions like, "How did you do this?" "What is happening now?" "Can you tell me more about this?" "Why are you doing this?" and "What are you thinking about now?". Flexible questioning helps uncover the child's thought process, which is what is leading him or her to engage in specific behaviors. Just observing the behaviors alone does not allow the child to express his or her knowledge. While fully interviewing each child in a classroom is not practical, teachers can adapt this method by asking clinical interview-type questions as part of their instruction.

USING QUESTIONING

Teachers can gain a lot of information and insight about how children are learning math concepts by observing their behaviors. For children to actually express their knowledge and thinking processes, however, teachers must ask them questions. For example, when a teacher introduces new shapes to young children, he or she can ask them the shapes' names, how they differ from one another, and why they think the shapes differ. Teachers can then use children's various responses to elicit further responses from them. This technique requires children to use language in significant ways during math activities. Therefore, these activities not only teach math skills but also promote literacy development. Asking clinical interview-type questions promotes children's development of math communication skills, one of the essential components of math education. Additionally, being able to put one's knowledge and thoughts into words is a skill that is very important in all areas of education, not just math education. Using clinical interview-type questions helps children learn to use language to explain their thinking, share ideas, and express themselves, promoting and strengthening children's awareness of the functions of mathematical language.

CHARACTERISTICS OF YOUNG CHILDREN'S THINKING AND LEARNING THAT INFORM EARLY CHILDHOOD MATH CURRICULA

Young children think in concrete ways and cannot understand abstract concepts, so effective early childhood math curricula typically use many concrete objects that children can see, feel, and manipulate to help them understand math concepts. Young children also naturally learn through exploring their environments, so good EC math curricula have many exploration and discovery activities that allow and encourage hands-on learning. In everyday life, young children start to observe relationships as they explore their surroundings. They match like objects, sort unlike objects, categorize objects, and arrange objects in simple patterns based on shared or contrasting properties. They start to understand words and phrases like *a little*, *a lot*, *more*, *less*, and *the same* [as...]. Preschoolers use available materials such as sticks, pieces of string, their feet, their hands, and their fingers as tools to measure objects. They also use rulers, measuring cups, and other conventional tools. They use their measurements to develop descriptions, sequences, and arrangements, and to compare various objects.

ACTIVITIES THAT HELP CHILDREN DEVELOP SPATIAL AWARENESS

When preschool children build structures with blocks and put together pieces of puzzles during play, they are not only having fun but are also developing spatial awareness. The relationships of objects to each other and within space are important concepts for children to learn, and serve as a foundation for the principles of geometry and physics that children will learn later. When they are moving around, preschoolers begin to notice how other people and objects are positioned in space and how their own bodies move through space in relationship to objects and other people. This type of spatial awareness supports children's developing gross motor skills, coordination, and social skills. Young children can and should learn a number of math concepts and skills, such as the ones recommended by preschool math curricula like the HighScope program's "Numbers Plus" preschool mathematics curriculum. These concepts and skills include number symbols and names, counting, shapes, spatial awareness, relationships of parts to the whole, measurement, units, patterns, and analyzing data.

ACTIVITIES AND GAMES THAT MAKE LEARNING FUN

BUTTON BOARD

By gluing buttons of various sizes and colors to a piece of cardboard, teachers can initiate a number of activities that help preschoolers learn math concepts while having fun. Preschoolers are commonly learning shapes and how to draw them. Teachers can give children lengths of string, twine, or yarn or long shoelaces and show them how to wrap them around different buttons to form shapes like rectangles, triangles, and squares. To practice counting and 1:1 correspondence, teachers can ask children to wrap their string around a given number of buttons. Preschoolers need to learn the concept that spoken number words like *five* can equate to a group of five concrete objects (such as buttons), and this activity promotes that learning. The button board is also useful for giving preschool children practice with sorting or classifying objects into groups based on a common characteristic. For example, the teacher can ask children to wrap their pieces of string around all the big buttons, all the little buttons, only the red buttons, only the blue buttons, etc.

BEANBAGS AND HOPSCOTCH

Teachers can encourage preschool children's counting and number development by creating a grid on the floor with the numbers 1 to 10 using masking tape, construction paper, and markers. Teachers could also draw the grid outdoors by drawing on pavement with chalk. The teacher arranges the numbers in ascending order within the grid of 10 squares and asks the children if they can name these numbers. The teacher provides beanbags. Each child gets a chance to throw a beanbag into any one of the numbered squares, which allows them to see how far they can throw and/or practice their aim. Each child names the number inside the square where his or her beanbag lands. The children then play a version of hopscotch by hopping from numbered square to square, collecting their beanbags, and then hopping back. If desired, the teacher can write the number each child's beanbag lands on onto a "scoreboard" graph. Teachers can review learning after the game to assess whether children can count using number words, name selected numbers, and throw accurately with consistency.

REUSING SECTIONED PLASTIC TRAYS

A teacher can wash and reuse the compartmentalized plastic trays from the grocery store that are used for vegetables and fruit to create a preschool counting activity. The teacher supplies beads, pennies, erasers, or other small objects, as well as about a dozen sticky notes, writing a number on each note. For older preschoolers, the teacher can write the numeral and the word (e.g., "7" and "seven"). For younger children, the teacher can write the numeric symbol ("7," for example) plus seven dots or other marks as a clue to that number symbol. The teacher puts one numbered note in each compartment and the supply of small objects in the central dip compartment. Then, he or she guides each child to transfer the correct number of each small object to the correct compartment. The child should count aloud while transferring each small object and should repeat this process until all compartments with a numbered sticky note have the correct number of objects. Children can then repeat the process to practice and perfect their counting, or the teacher can place notes with different numbers in the tray's compartments.

FISHING FOR NUMBERS

Teachers can help preschoolers practice identifying numbers and counting by creating a fun "fishing for numbers" game. Teachers cut 10 fish shapes that are about 6 inches long from pieces of construction paper that are different colors. Teachers then write a single number between 1 and 10 on each "fish." Near each fish "mouth," the teacher punches a hole and inserts a paper clip through it. The teacher makes "fishing rods" by tying strings to dowels and gluing a magnet to each string. After spreading out the fish so the children can easily see the numbers, the teacher assigns each child a number, and they "fish" for it, picking up the fish by bringing the magnet close to the paper clip. The children then "reel in" their catches. This gives children practice correctly identifying number names. The game can be adapted for more advanced math concepts as well. For example, the teacher can cut out fish shapes of various sizes and have children "fish" for larger or smaller fish. The activity can also be adapted to promote literacy development. The teacher can write letters instead of numbers on the fish to give students practice with alphabet recognition, or teacher can write a Dolch word/sight word on each fish to give students practice recognizing and identifying important vocabulary words.

COLLAGES

Fundamental math skills that prepare preschoolers for kindergarten include shape recognition. To introduce children to an activity they will view as fun rather than as work, teachers can show children how to make a collage of a familiar figure. This will also give children the opportunity to experiment with an artistic process. For example, they can create a Santa Claus or an Easter Bunny as a holiday art project. They can make **collages** of other imaginary or real people for various events, seasons, or topics. Teachers cut out paper templates, including circles for heads, triangles for hats, squares for bodies, and narrow rectangular strips for limbs. First, they help children name each shape. They have each child trace the template shapes onto paper and cut them out with child-safe scissors. The teacher then instructs the children to arrange their cutout shapes on a piece of cardboard or construction paper. Once they are in the correct positions, the children glue the shapes in place. Teachers can subsequently teach additional shapes (octagons, ovals, etc.), challenging children to make new, different collages.

GRAB BAG

Young children learn to name numbers in a way that is similar to how they learn to recite alphabet letters. However, learning to associate number symbols with concrete objects in the real world environment is a major advance in their cognitive development. The concept of 1:1 correspondence entails matching number symbols to the quantities they represent, an essential early math skill. Teachers can support the development of this math skill with a simple "grab bag" game youngsters enjoy. The teacher writes a number from 1 to 10 on each of the 10 cards, folding each card in half and putting them into a paper lunch bag. The teacher provides each child with a handful of pennies, play coins, buttons, or little blocks to use as counting tokens. Each child takes a turn closing his or her eyes and pulling a card out of the bag. The child reads the number on the card, counts out the corresponding number of pennies/tokens, and puts them with the card. As children learn, teachers can place additional and/or different numbers (e.g., 11 to 20) in the grab bag. To promote the development of early literacy skills, teachers can also include the name of the number on each card.

PATTERN RESIST ART

A significant mark of progress in early math skills development is the ability to not only identify various shapes but also to draw them. Once young children develop this ability, they typically want to practice it all the time. Teachers can encourage this by helping children make pattern resist paintings. The teacher tapes white paper to children's tables/trays, gives them crayons, and invites them to fill the paper with drawings of different shapes of various sizes and colors. Teachers can introduce young children to new shapes (e.g., ovals, stars, crescent moons, etc.) by drawing them on separate pieces of paper for children to look at and copy. Then, the teacher replaces the crayons with water, watercolor paints, and brushes; shows the children how to dip brushes into paint and water to dilute the colors; and allows them to paint over their crayoned shapes, covering all the white paper with color. The children see the shapes show through the paint, creating the pattern resist. Dipping brushes and diluting various colors also develop children's color recognition skills and their hand-eye coordination.

ICE CUBE NECKLACES

In hot weather, making ice cube necklaces is a fun activity that helps young children cool off while learning to sequence objects. The activity also helps children develop their manual motor skills and learn about liquid and solid states of matter. Regular ice cube trays are fine; those with "fun-shaped" compartments are even better. The teacher cuts plastic drinking straws so that they will fit into each ice cube compartment. The children participate, watching and/or helping pour water into trays and adding various food colorings/fruit juices. The teacher places one straw clipping into each compartment. While putting the trays into the freezer, the teacher tells the children that 32° Fahrenheit/0° Celsius is the temperature at which water freezes. Children practice making scientific observations by noting how long the water takes to freeze. They empty the cubes into a big bowl. The children put on bathing suits or other clothing that can get wet, and the class goes outdoors. The teacher provides strings that are knotted at one end, and calls out a color pattern (e.g., one blue cube, then a yellow cube, etc.). Children follow the teacher's instructions to create color-patterned necklaces they can tie, wear, and watch melt.

RED ROVER

Red Rover is a good game for groups of children who are attending parties or playing outdoors at parks or playgrounds. Two teams take turns calling and roving. The child called runs to the other team and tries to fit into its line. If successful, he or she gets to call another player to bring back to his or her home team. If not, the child joins the opposite team. The game continues until one team has no more members. Teachers can adapt this game to teach shape recognition by cutting out various shapes from construction paper of different colors and pinning a shape to each child's shirt. In large groups, more than one child can have the same shape or color. Instead of children's names, the teacher instructs players to use shapes and colors when calling (e.g., "Red Rover, Red Rover, blue circles come over!"). This supports the development of shape and color recognition skills. Teachers can vary action verbs (e.g., "...hop over/jump over/skip over") to support vocabulary development and comprehensive skills. When children perform such movements, they are also practicing and developing gross motor skills.

COUNTING ON FINGERS

A common practice among preschool children is counting on their fingers. Young children learn concretely before they develop abstract thought, so they must have concrete objects to work with to understand abstract mathematical concepts. They use their fingers to count because fingers are concrete. A simple activity that allows children to continue finger counting while removing additional visual support is "blind finger counting." Using eyesight to count objects we can see is relatively easy. However, when children cannot see objects, they must learn to count mentally instead. This allows them to take another step in their progress from concrete to abstract thinking. To count mentally without visual reinforcement takes practice. Teachers can tape a shoebox lid to the box and cut a small hole in it. Children can fit a hand through the hole, but cannot see inside. Children close their eyes; the teacher drops several small objects into the box; and each child reaches in, counting the objects using only touch. Varying objects and quantities maintains the fun of this activity.

SORTING AND CATEGORIZATION

One of the major learning accomplishments of young children is being able to identify similarities and differences among objects. Developing this ability enables children to sort like objects into groups and to place objects into categories based on their differences. When preschoolers compare and contrast objects, they demonstrate an important early step in the development of critical thinking, analytical, and problem-solving skills. For an easy, entertaining guessing game, adults can select assorted household items familiar to children and put them into a bag/pillowcase. They then give children various clues (e.g., "I stir lemonade with this...," "It's made of wood," "We keep it in the kitchen drawer...," etc.) and ask them to guess which items are in the bag. It is important to give young children one to two minutes to consider each clue before they make a guess. Adults repeat clues when children guess incorrectly. If children guess correctly, they are allowed to look inside the bag. Children greatly enjoy seeing that the object they guessed is actually inside the bag. Adults can gradually make the game more challenging by beginning with very common objects and then eventually progressing to more unusual ones.

BAKING COOKIES

Young children are typically curious about adult activities like baking. They usually want to know more about the process and often ask many questions. They also love to be included and to participate, frequently offering/asking to help. Letting them help builds their self-esteem and self-efficacy (i.e., their confidence in their competence to accomplish a task). Adults can allow children to help while also providing instruction and practice with shape recognition, measurement, sorting, and categorization. The adult prepares a favorite cookie recipe. Some children can help measure ingredients, which helps develop the math skill of measurement. With the dough rolled out, children use cookie cutters of various shapes. Recognizing, naming, and selecting the shapes promote the development of shape recognition skills. Adults "shuffle"/mix the baked cookie shapes and have children separate cookies with like shapes into groups, which promotes sorting skills. Having children identify similar/different shapes, sizes, and colors promotes categorization skills. Arranging cookie shapes into patterns for children to identify promotes pattern recognition skills, which are necessary for the development of math skills and many other skills. Giving each child a cookie to eat afterward is naturally reinforcing.

CREATIVE CRAFTS

Prerequisite abilities that young children need in order to develop early math skills include the ability to identify, copy, expand, and create patterns, as well as the ability to count. Adults can promote the development of these skills by giving children a craft project and introducing them to an interactive game they can play using their crafts. First, the children paint six ping pong balls red on one side to make red-and-white balls. Then, the children paint six ping pong balls blue on one side to make blue-and-white balls. Once the paint dries, the adult puts several balls into an egg carton so that one color is face up. The adult starts making a simple pattern (e.g., two white, then two red, then two blue) and asks each child to continue the pattern. Then, the adult allows each child to create his or her own original color patterns. Once a child masters creating patterns using solid colors, he or she can then use both the white and colored sides of the balls to create more complex patterns. Children can design an infinite number of patterns, which are often quite artistic.

SHAPE MATCHING GAMES

In one type of shape matching game, early childhood teachers help children make a game board out of construction paper that is shaped like a tree. Teachers first help the children cut a treetop and leaf shapes from green paper. They discuss children's preferences for tall/short and thick/thin trunks, giving them practice using descriptive vocabulary words, particularly ones related to size. This step builds both general and math concept vocabulary. Children cut trunks from brown paper and glue them on the treetops. While out of the children's sight, the teacher cuts 5 to 10 (or more) pairs of shapes per child/tree from different colors of construction paper. Pairs should not match exactly (e.g., a blue square can be paired with a red square). The teacher glues one of each pair of shapes to each child's tree while the child is not looking. The teacher then gives each child the rest of the shapes and invites children to see how quickly they can match each shape to its "partner" on the tree. The teacher can provide "warmer/cooler" distance clues and should provide reinforcement each time a child correctly matches a pair of shapes. Teachers can make this activity more challenging by using more shapes and/or getting students to match shapes that are different sizes (e.g., children can be asked to match smaller diamonds to larger diamonds).

HOMEMADE BEANBAG GAME

Young children enjoy tossing objects and practicing their aim. Adults can make a beanbag game that helps children learn numbers and identify sets, while also allowing them to construct their own game rules. First, the adult should cover five big, equally-sized coffee (or similar) cans with paper that is adhesive on one side. The adult should then use markers to write a number from 1 to 5 and draw the corresponding number of dots on each can. The next step is to fill 15 tube socks with beans and knot/tie/sew them shut. The following numerals and the corresponding number of dots should be written on each homemade beanbag using markers: the number 1 on five beanbags, the number 2 on four beanbags, the number 3 on three beanbags, the number 4 on two beanbags, and the number 5 on one beanbag. Next, the adult should attach the cans to the floor with tape or Velcro. Then, the adult should mark a line on the floor that children must stand behind, and should direct children ONLY to toss the beanbags into the cans. Children will devise various games/rules. First, they may simply toss the beanbags into the cans; then, some may try to toss beanbags into a can that has the same number as the one marked on the beanbag. Eventually, some may throw three beanbags into the "3" can. They may or may not keep score. Allowing children to determine the details and rules gives them an opportunity to develop their imagination and decision-making skills, and to create their own games while learning number and set identification.

GUESSING GAME

Adults can adapt the format of "20 Questions," "I Spy," and other similar guessing games to focus on numbers and help children learn number concepts. For example, adults could say, "I'm thinking of a number from 1 to 10...." and then give children 10 guesses. Adults give children cues as they guess, such as "higher" and "lower," to help them narrow down the number of possible correct answers. As children improve, adults can increase the number range (e.g., from 0 to 50) or use larger numbers (e.g., from 20 to 40). As children's skills and self-confidence develop, adults can reverse roles, having children think of numbers and give clues while adults guess. Young children enjoy the fun of guessing, getting closer using clues, deducing correct answers, and fooling adults with their own clues. Concurrently, they learn to describe numbers, compare them, and sequence them. Adults can make the game more difficult by limiting the number of guesses allowed and/or setting time limits. They can make it easier by providing a written number line for children to reference. This game requires no materials (or just a basic number line), is a great way to pass time, and entertains children while helping to develop numeracy skills.

ARTS AND CRAFTS

According to the US Department of Agriculture, preschoolers need three ½-cup servings of fruit and three ½-cup servings of vegetables daily. However, many young children are picky/resistant. Adults can motivate them to eat produce with a "food rainbow" project. Adults show children a picture of a rainbow and discuss its colors and their sequence (teaching some earth science, optics, and color theory). A fun art project is allowing students to color their own rainbows, which improves fine motor skills. Then, adults can have children cut out pictures from grocery circulars and name each food. The adult can help children find one healthy fruit/vegetable for each color, gluing each food to its corresponding stripe on the rainbow. Adults can then help children pull apart cotton balls and glue them to their rainbow pictures to represent clouds. Children can then post their food rainbows on refrigerators as artwork and as healthy eating reminders. At the bottom, children can draw and color one box (bottom-up) for each food they eat (e.g., blue for blueberries, orange for carrots, red for apples, etc.) to create a bar graph. Children should try to "eat" the entire rainbow every week. This activity gives children the opportunity to produce colorful art, eat better, track and document their diets, and develop graphing skills.

> **Review Video: Data Interpretation of Graphs**
> Visit mometrix.com/academy and enter code: 200439

TREASURE HUNT

A treasure hunt is an ideal outdoor activity for young children and can also be adapted for indoor fun. The treasure can be anything such as a small toy, play money, chocolate "coins," or rocks spray painted gold or silver. The adult should put the treasure in a paper bag marked with a large X. The adult should hide it somewhere where it is not visible but will not be overly difficult for children to find. Then, the adult should make a treasure map, using few words and many pictures, sketching landmark objects in the area (e.g., trees and houses if the activity will be done outdoors, and furniture and walls if the activity will be done indoors). The adult should ensure the map is developmentally appropriate for young children and that they will be able to read it independently. Adults with time and motivation can make the map look authentic by soaking it in tea/coffee, drying it in a 200° F oven, or even charring its edges. Adults should include a dotted line on the map that reinforces the simple directions and indicates the path to the treasure, which is indicated on the map by a large X. Children have fun, use their imaginations, make connections between symbols and images to corresponding real-world physical objects, and begin learning to read maps.

PASTA NECKLACE

Stringing beads/noodles is an activity that helps young children develop hand-eye coordination, which they will need for writing and other everyday activities that require fine motor coordination. Noodles are typically the perfect size for young children's hands. They are inexpensive, usually costing less than comparably-sized beads. Moreover, pasta is non-toxic, an advantage when working with children who put things in their mouths. Hollow, tubular noodles like penne, ziti, and wagon wheels are ideal. Fishing line, craft beading string, and other stiff string is best; soft, limp string/yarn is harder for young children to manipulate. Using multicolored vegetable pasta removes the need to use markers or dye to add color. If using white pasta, children can color the noodles with markers, but adults should keep in mind that the ink can bleed onto skin/clothes even when it is dry. Adults should cut pieces of string that are long enough to allow children to easily slip the necklaces on and off after they are tied. Adults should also use a knot to secure a noodle to one end of the string. By providing more than one noodle shape, adults can invite children to string the noodles to create patterns, which develops pattern recognition and pattern creation abilities. These abilities also inform repetition, rhythm, categorization, and sequencing skills, which are important in math, music, art, literature, and clothing design.

NUMBER DASH

A game for young children that some educators call "Number Dash" (Miller, ed. Charner, 2009) builds foundational math concepts and skills while providing physical activity. It can involve small or large groups (the referenced authors say "the more the merrier"). Help children write large numbers on a paved area with sidewalk chalk. Make sure numbers are spread far enough apart so children will not collide while running. There should be one of each number for each child (e.g., six 1s, 2s, 3s, etc. if there are six children). Use chalk colors that contrast with the pavement color to ensure the numbers will be highly visible. Tell children to run ("dash") to whichever number you call out and stand on it until you call another number. Call out numbers randomly. Encourage children who have located the number to help their classmates/playmates. This game develops gross motor skills, number writing skills, and number recognition skills. It also provides experience with playing organized games, following rules, following directions, and cooperating with and helping others. This game can also be played with letters, colors, and/or shapes.

INTRODUCING STANDARD MEASUREMENT USING A RULER

A teacher is introducing standard measures to her class as part of a unit on measurement, one of the early math skills. She shows the children a ruler, explaining that it is one foot long and that we can use it to measure inches and parts of inches. She demonstrates placing the ruler on paper to measure a given length, explaining that the ruler can also be used as a straight edge for drawing lines. One child asks, "How come you started with zero? Why don't you start with one like when we count?" The teacher responds, "That's a very good question! Zero means none/nothing. When we count, we start with one because we already have at least one of something. When you were born, you were not one year old; your age began at zero. After a year, on your first birthday, you were one year old. We also begin measuring distances at zero/none/nothing. The first unit of measurement is one, not two. The distance from zero to one is equal to one. To get to one inch, for example, we need to start at zero."

LEARNING ABOUT GEOMETRIC SHAPES AND THEIR PROPERTIES

A teacher has been working with students to help them develop their shape identification skills. They can recognize shapes by sight and have also learned the defining properties of different shapes (number of sides, etc.). The teacher shows the class this figure:

She asks how many rectangles they can find in the figure. One student answers, "There is one rectangle," which is incorrect because a square is a rectangle; this figure has four rectangles that are squares. Moreover, the entire figure is itself a rectangle. Another student therefore says, "There are five rectangles." This response is also incorrect. Two adjacent squares also form a rectangle; this means there are three additional rectangles. Three adjacent squares also form a rectangle; this means there are two additional rectangles. Thus, the figure has a total of 10 rectangles. Solving this puzzle requires the use of many skills, including analyzing visual information, synthesizing visual information, recognizing patterns, recognizing shapes, and identifying the properties of shapes.

COLLECTING, ORGANIZING, AND DISPLAYING DATA USING STICKY NOTES AND A TEACHER-MADE CHART

A preschool teacher is teaching her group of ten children about basic data collection, data arrangement, and data display. She shows children yellow, blue, and green sticky notes, and has each child select his or her favorite color. Five children choose yellow notes, three select blue, and two choose green. By choosing one of three colors, each child has participated in data collection. The teacher draws lines to divide a sheet of paper into three columns, and labels each column with one of the colors. She helps the children place their chosen sticky notes in the correct columns. By arranging the colored sticky notes into columns, the teacher and children have organized the data they gathered. Once all notes are in their proper color columns, the completed chart is an example of how collected, organized data can be displayed.

	Yellow sticky note	
	Yellow sticky note	
Blue sticky note	Yellow sticky note	
Blue sticky note	Yellow sticky note	Green sticky note
Blue sticky note	Yellow sticky note	Green sticky note
BLUE	**YELLOW**	**GREEN**

The teacher asks the children which color was chosen the most. Seeing five yellow notes, they answer, "yellow." She asks which color was chosen the least, and they say, "green." She asks them to use numbers to arrange the color choices from most popular to least popular. They arrive at, "five yellow, three blue, and two green." Together, the teacher and the children point to and count 10 children. She tells them 5 equals half of 10, and asks which color half of the children chose. Together, they figure out it was yellow. These are examples of analyzing and interpreting data.

Science

SCIENCE FOUNDATIONS

SCIENCE CONCEPTS YOUNG CHILDREN LEARN DURING EVERYDAY ACTIVITIES

Science entails asking questions, conducting investigations, collecting data, and seeking answers to the questions asked by analyzing the data collected. Natural events that can be examined over time and student-centered inquiry through hands-on activities that require the application of problem-solving skills are most appropriate for helping young children learn basic science. In their everyday lives, young children develop concepts of 1:1 correspondence through activities like fitting pegs into matching holes or distributing one item to each child in a class. They also develop counting concepts by counting enough items for each child in the group or counting pennies in a piggy bank. They develop classification concepts when they sort objects into separate piles according to their shapes or some other type of category (e.g., toy cars vs. toy trucks). When children transfer water, sand, rice, or other substances from one container to another, they develop measurement concepts. As they progress, children will apply these early concepts to more abstract scientific ideas during grade school.

SCIENCE CONCEPTS INFANTS AND TODDLERS LEARN IN NORMAL DEVELOPMENTAL PROCESSES

Infants use their senses to explore the environment and are motivated by innate curiosity. As they develop mobility, children gain more freedom, allowing them to make independent discoveries and think for themselves. Children learn size concepts by comparing the sizes of objects/persons in the environment to their own size and by observing that some objects are too large to hold, while others are small enough to hold. They learn about weight when trying to lift various objects. They learn about shape when they see that some objects roll away while others do not. Babies learn temporal sequences when they wake up wet and hungry, cry, and have parents change and feed them. They also learn this concept by playing, getting tired, and going to sleep. As soon as they look and move around, infants learn about space, including large and small spaces. Eventually, they develop spatial sense through experiences like being put in a playpen or crib in the middle of a large room. Toddlers naturally sort objects into groups according to their sizes, shapes, colors, and/or uses. They experiment with transferring water/sand among containers of various sizes. They learn part-to-whole relationships by building block structures and then dismantling them.

Naturalistic, Informal, and Structured Learning Experiences

Children actively construct their knowledge of the environment through exploring it.

- During **naturalistic learning**, young children's learning experiences are spontaneously initiated by the child during everyday activities and the child controls his or her choices and actions.
- **Informal learning experiences** also allow the child to choose his or her actions and activities, but they include adult intervention at some point during the child's engagement in naturalistic pursuits.
- In **structured learning experiences**, the adult chooses the activities and supplies some direction as to how the child should perform the associated actions.

One consideration related to early childhood learning that teachers should keep in mind is that within any class or group of children, there are individual differences in learning styles. Additionally, children from different cultural groups have varying learning styles and approaches. Early childhood teachers can introduce science content in developmentally appropriate ways by keeping these variations in mind.

Naturalistic Learning Experiences

Motivated by novelty and curiosity, young children spontaneously initiate naturalistic experiences during their everyday activities. Infants and toddlers in Piaget's sensorimotor stage learn by exploring the environment through their senses, so adults should provide them with many objects and substances they can see, hear, touch, smell, and taste. Through manipulating and observing concrete objects/substances, preschoolers in Piaget's preoperational stage begin learning concepts that will enable them to perform mental operations later on. Adults should observe children's actions and progress and should give positive reinforcement in the form of looks, facial expressions, gestures, and/or words encouraging and praising the child's actions. Young children need adult feedback to learn when they are performing the appropriate actions. For example, a toddler/preschooler selects a tool from the toolbox, saying, "This is big!" and the mother responds, "Yes!" A four-year-old sorting toys of various colors into separate containers is another example of a naturalistic experience. A five-year-old who observes while painting that mixing two colors yields a third color is yet another example.

Informal Learning Experience

Informal learning experiences involve two main components. First, the child spontaneously initiates naturalistic learning experiences during everyday activities to explore and learn about the environment. Second, the adult takes advantage of opportunities during naturalistic experiences to insert informal learning experiences. Adults do not plan these in advance but take advantage of opportunities that occur naturally. One way this happens is when a child is on the right track to solve a problem but needs some encouragement or a hint from the adult. Another way is when the adult spots a "teachable moment" during the child's naturalistic activity and uses it to reinforce a basic concept. For example, a three-year-old might hold up three fingers, declaring, "I'm six years old." The parent says, "Let's count fingers: one, two, three. You're three years old." Or, a teacher asks a child who has a box of treats if he or she has enough for the whole class, and the child answers, "I don't know." The teacher then responds, "Let's count them together," and helps the child count.

Structured Learning Experiences

Naturalistic learning experiences are spontaneously initiated and controlled by children. Informal learning experiences involve unplanned interventions by adults during children's naturalistic experiences, which is when adults offer suitable correction, assistance, and support. Structured learning experiences differ in that the adult pre-plans and initiates the activity/lesson and provides the child with some direction. For example, a teacher who observes a four-year-old's need to practice counting can give the child a pile of toys and then ask him or her how many there are. To develop size concepts, a teacher can give a small group of children several toys of different sizes and then ask the children to inspect them and talk about their characteristics. The teacher holds up one toy, instructing children to find one that is bigger or smaller. If a child needs to learn shape concepts, the teacher might introduce a game involving shapes, giving the child instructions on how to play the game. Or, a first-grade teacher, recognizing the importance of the concept of classification to the ability to organize scientific information, might ask students to bring in bones to classify during a unit on skeletons.

KINDERGARTEN ACTIVITY FOR COLLECTING AND ORGANIZING DATA

Preschoolers and kindergarteners continue their earlier practices of exploration to learn new things, and they apply fundamental science concepts to collect and organize data in order to answer questions. To collect data, children must have observation, counting, recording, and organization skills. One activity kindergarteners and teachers enjoy is growing bean sprouts. For example, the teacher can show children two methods: one using glass jars and paper towels saturated with water, the other using cups of dirt. The children add water daily as needed, observe developments, and report to the teacher, who records their observations on a chart. The teacher gives each child a chart that they add information to each day. The children count how many days their beans took to sprout in the glass jars and in the cups of dirt. They then compare their own results for the two methods, and they compare their results to those of their classmates. The children apply concepts of counting, numbers, time, 1:1 correspondence, and comparison of numbers. They also witness the planting and growing process.

SCIENCE PROCESS SKILLS

Science process skills include observation (using the senses to identify properties of objects/situations), classification (grouping objects/situations according to their common properties), measurement (quantifying physical properties), communication (using observations, classifications, and measurements to report experimental results to others), inference (finding patterns and meaning in experiment results), and prediction (using experimental experience to formulate new hypotheses). Inferences and predictions must be differentiated from objective observations. Classification, measurement, and comparison are basic math concepts that, when applied to science problems, are called process skills. The other science process skills named, as well as defining and controlling variables, are equally necessary to solve both science and math problems. For example, using ramps can help young children learn basic physics concepts. Teachers ask children what would happen if two balls were rolled down a ramp at the same time, if two balls were rolled down a ramp of a different height/length, if two ramps of different heights/lengths were used, etc. In this activity, children apply the scientific concepts of observation, communication, inference, and prediction, as well as the concepts of height, length, counting, speed, distance, and comparison.

SCIENTIFIC METHOD

Children are born curious and naturally engage in problem-solving to learn. Problem-solving and inquiry are natural child behaviors. Early childhood teachers can use these behaviors to promote children's scientific inquiry. Scientific inquiry employs the **scientific method**. The first step in the method is to ask a question, which is another natural child behavior. Just as adult scientists formulate research questions, the first step of the scientific method for children is asking questions they want to answer. Next, to address a question, both adults and children must form a hypothesis (an educated guess about what the answer will be). The hypothesis informs and directs the next steps: designing and conducting an experiment to test whether the hypothesis is true or false. With teacher instruction/help, children experiment. For example, they might drop objects of different weights from a height to see when each lands, as Galileo did. Teachers help record outcomes. The next steps are deciding whether the results support or disprove the hypothesis and reporting the results and conclusions to others.

PHYSICAL SCIENCE AND MATTER

Physical science is the science of the physical universe surrounding us. Everything in the universe consists of matter (i.e., anything that has mass and takes up space) or energy (i.e., anything that does not have mass or occupy space, but affects matter and space). The three primary states of matter are solid, liquid, and gas. Solids preserve their shape even when they are not in a container. Solids have specific, three-dimensional/crystalline atomic structures and specific melting points. Liquids have no independent shape outside of containers but have specific volumes. Liquid molecules are less cohesive than solid molecules but more cohesive than gas molecules. Liquids have flow, viscosity (flow resistance), and buoyancy. Liquids can undergo diffusion, osmosis, evaporation, condensation, solution, freezing, and heat conduction and convection. Liquids and gases are both fluids, and they share some of the same properties. Gases have no shape, expanding and spreading indefinitely outside of containers. Gases can become liquid and solid through cooling, compression, or both. Liquids and solids can become gaseous through heating. Vapor is the gaseous form of a substance that is solid/liquid at lower temperatures. For example, when water is heated, it becomes steam, a vapor.

LIQUIDS

Of the three states of matter—solid, liquid, and gas—liquids have properties that fall somewhere in between those of solids and gases. The molecules of solids are the most cohesive (i.e., they have the greatest mutual attraction). Gas molecules are the least cohesive, and liquid molecules are in between. Liquids have no definite shape, while solids do. Liquids have a definite volume, whereas gases do not. The cohesion of liquid molecules draws them together, and the molecules below the surface pull surface molecules down, creating surface tension. This property can be observed in containers of water. Liquid molecules are also attracted to other substances' molecules (i.e., adhesion). Surface tension and adhesion combined cause liquids to rise in narrow containers, a property known as capillarity. Liquids are buoyant (i.e., they exert upward force, so objects which have more buoyancy than weight float in liquids, while objects which have more weight than buoyancy sink in liquids). Liquids can be made solid by freezing and can be made gaseous by heating/evaporation. Liquids can diffuse, which means they can mix with other molecules. Liquid diffusion across semi-permeable membranes is known as osmosis.

SOLIDS

Solids maintain their shape when they are not inside of containers, whereas liquids and gases acquire the shapes of containers holding them. Containers also prevent liquids and gases from dispersing. Of the three forms of matter, solids have the most cohesive molecules. Solid molecules are most attracted to each other, and solid molecules are held together most strongly. Solid atoms are organized into defined, three-dimensional, lattice-shaped patterns (i.e., they are crystalline in structure). Solids also have specific temperatures at which they melt. Some substances that seem solid, such as plastic, gel, tar, and glass, are actually not true solids. They are amorphous solids because their atoms do not have a crystalline structure but are amorphous (i.e., the positions of their atoms have no long-range organization). They also have a range of melting temperatures rather than specific melting points.

GASES

Gases have the least cohesive (i.e., mutually attracted) molecules of the three states of matter, while solids have the most cohesive molecules. Gases do not maintain a defined shape, while solids do. If not contained within a receptacle, gases spread and expand indefinitely. Gases can be elementary or compound. An elementary gas is composed of only one kind of chemical element. At normal temperatures and pressures, 12 elementary gases are known: argon, chlorine, fluorine, helium, hydrogen, krypton, neon, nitrogen, oxygen, ozone, radon, and xenon. Elementary gases can be either monatomic or diatomic, meaning they are either made of single atoms like argon (Ar), or bound pairs of atoms like oxygen (O_2). Compound gases have molecules containing atoms of more than one kind of chemical element. Carbon monoxide (which contains one carbon and one oxygen atom) and ammonia (which contains nitrogen and hydrogen atoms) are common compound gases.

LIGHT

REFLECTION AND SCATTERING

When a beam of light hits a smooth surface like a mirror, it bounces back off that surface. This rebounding is **reflection**. In physics, the law of reflection states that "the angle of incidence equals the angle of reflection." This means that when light is reflected, it always bounces off the surface at the same angle at which it hit that surface. When a beam of light hits a rough rather than a smooth surface, though, it is reflected back at many different angles, not just the angle at which it struck the surface. This reflection at multiple and various angles is scattering. Many objects we commonly use every day have rough surfaces. For example, paper may look smooth to the naked eye but actually has a rough surface. This property can be observed by viewing paper through a microscope. Because light waves striking paper are reflected in every direction by its rough surface, scattering enables us to read words printed on paper from any viewing angle.

ABSORPTION

When light strikes a medium, the light wave's frequency is equal or close to the frequency at which the electrons in the medium's atoms can vibrate. These electrons receive the light's energy, making them vibrate. When a medium's atoms hang on tightly to their electrons, the electrons transmit their vibrations to the nucleus of each atom. This makes the atoms move faster and collide with the medium's other atoms. The energy the atoms got from the vibrations is then released as heat. This process is known as **absorption** of light. Materials that absorb light, such as wood and metal, are opaque. Some materials absorb certain light frequencies but transmit others. For example, glass transmits visible light (and therefore appears transparent to the naked eye), but absorbs ultraviolet frequencies. The sky looks blue because the atmosphere absorbs all colors in the spectrum except blue, which it reflects. Only blue wavelengths/frequencies bounce back to our eyes. This is an example of subtractive color, which we see in paints/dyes and all colored objects/materials. Pigments absorb some frequencies and reflect others.

REFRACTION

When light moves from one transparent medium to another (e.g., between water and air/vice versa), the light's speed changes, bending the light wave. It bends either away from or toward the normal line, an imaginary straight line running at right angles to the medium's surface. We easily observe this bending when looking at a straw in a glass of water. The straw appears to break/bend at the waterline. The angle of refraction is the amount that the light wave bends. It is determined by how much the medium slows down the light's speed, which is the medium's refraction index. For example, diamonds are much denser and harder than water and thus have a higher refraction index. They slow down and trap light more than water does. Consequently, diamonds sparkle more than water. Lenses, such as those in eyeglasses and telescopes, rely on the principle of refraction. Curved lenses disperse or concentrate light waves, refracting light as it both enters and exits, thus changing the light's direction. This is how lenses correct (eyeglasses) and enhance (telescopes) our vision.

MAGNETISM

Magnetism is the property some objects/substances have of attracting other materials. The form of magnetism most familiar to us is certain materials attracting iron. Magnets also attract steel, cobalt, and other materials. Generators supplying power include magnets, as do all electric motors. Loudspeakers and telephones contain magnets. Tape recorders use magnets. The tape they play is magnetized. Magnets are used in compasses to determine the location of north and various corresponding directions. In fact, the planet Earth is itself a giant magnet (which is why compasses point north). Hence, like the Earth, all magnets have two poles: a north/north-seeking pole and a south/south-seeking pole. Opposite poles attract and like poles repel each other. Magnets do not need to touch to attract or repel each other. A magnet's effective area/range is its magnetic field. All materials have some response to magnetic fields. Magnets can turn nearby magnetic materials into magnets, by a process known as magnetic induction. Materials that line up parallel to magnetic force field lines are paramagnetic, while materials that line up perpendicular to magnetic force field lines are diamagnetic.

MODERN THEORY OF MAGNETISM AND WHAT SCIENTISTS DO AND DO NOT KNOW

Scientists have known about the effects of magnetism for hundreds of years. However, they do not know exactly what magnetism is or what causes it. French physicist Pierre Weiss proposed a theory of magnetism in the early 20th century that is widely accepted. This theory posits that every magnetic material has groups of molecules—domains—that function as magnets. Until a material is magnetized, its domains have a random arrangement, so one domain's magnetism is canceled out by another's. When the material comes into a magnetic field—the range/area wherein a magnet is effective—its domains align themselves parallel to the magnetic field's lines of force. As a result, all of their north-seeking/north poles point in the same direction. Removing the magnetic field causes like poles to repel one another as they normally do. In easily magnetized materials, domains revert to random order. In materials that are harder to magnetize, domains lack sufficient force to disassemble, leaving the material magnetized. Later versions of Weiss's theory attribute domain magnetism to spinning electrons.

> **Review Video: Magnets**
> Visit mometrix.com/academy and enter code: 570803

INSULATION, CONDUCTION, AND THE FLOW OF ELECTRICITY

The smallest units of all matter are atoms. The nuclei of atoms are orbited by negatively charged electrons. Some materials have electrons that are strongly bound to their atoms. These include air, glass, wood, cotton, plastic, and ceramic. Since their atoms rarely release electrons, these materials have little or no ability to conduct electricity and are known as electrical insulators. Insulators resist/block conduction. Metals and other conductive materials have free electrons that can detach from the atoms and move around. Without the tight binding of insulators, materials with loose electrons enable electric current to flow easily through them. Such materials are called electrical conductors. The movements of their electrons transmit electrical energy. Electricity requires something to make it flow (i.e., a generator). A generator creates a steady flow of electrons by moving a magnet close to a wire, creating a magnetic field to propel electrons. Electricity also requires a conductor (i.e., a medium through which it can move from one place to another).

MOVEMENT OF ELECTRICAL CURRENTS BY A GENERATOR

Magnetism and electricity are related, and they interact with each other. Generators work by using magnets near conductive wires to produce moving streams of electrons. The agent of movement can range from a hand crank, to a steam engine, to the nuclear fission process. However, all agents of movements operate according to the same principle. A simple analogy is that a generator magnetically pushes electrical current the way a pump pushes water. Just as water pumps apply specific amounts of pressure to specific numbers of water molecules, generator magnets apply specific amounts of "pressure" to specific numbers of electrons. The number of moving electrons in an electrical circuit equals the current, or amperage. The unit of measurement for amperage is the ampere, or amp. The amount of force moving the electrons is the voltage. Its unit of measurement is the volt. One amp equals 6.24×10^{18} electrons passing through a wire each second. For example, a generator could produce 1 amp using 6 volts when rotating 1,000 times per minute. Today's power stations rely on generators.

POSITIONS AND MOTIONS OF OBJECTS AND NEWTON'S LAWS OF PHYSICS

Moving physical objects changes their positions. According **to Newton's first law of motion**, an object at rest tends to stay at rest, and an object in motion tends to stay in motion until a force changes the object's state of motion. For example, an object at rest could be a small rock sitting on the ground. If you kick the rock into the air, it moves through the air. The rock will continue to move, but when a force like gravity acts on it, it falls/stops moving. The resulting motion from kicking the rock illustrates Newton's third law of motion: for every action, there is an equal and opposite reaction. The acceleration or change in velocity (a) of an object depends on its mass (m) and the amount of force (F) that is applied to the object. Newton's second law of motion states that $F = ma$ (force equals mass times acceleration). Thus, moving objects maintain their speeds unless acted on by a force, like friction.

HEAT

Heat is transmitted through conduction, radiation, and convection. Heat is transmitted within solids by conduction. When two objects at different temperatures touch each other, the hotter object's molecules are moving faster. They collide with the colder object's molecules, which are moving slower. As a result of the collision, the molecules that are moving more rapidly supply energy to the molecules that are moving more slowly. This speeds up the movement of the (previously) slower-moving molecules, which heats up the colder object. This process of transferring heat through contact is called thermal conductivity. An example of thermal conductivity is the heat sink. Heat sinks are used in many devices. Today, they are commonly used in computers. A heat sink transfers the heat building up in the computer processor, moving it away before it can damage the processor. Computers contain fans, which blow air across their heat sinks and expel the heated air out of the computers.

ACOUSTICAL PRINCIPLES AND THE HUMAN HEARING PROCESS

When any physical object moves back and forth rapidly, this is known as **vibration**. The movements that occur during vibration disturb the surrounding medium, which may be solid, liquid, or gaseous. The most common sound conducting medium in our environment is gaseous: our atmosphere (i.e., the air). An object's vibratory movements represent a form of energy. As this acoustic energy moves through the air, it takes the form of waves, sound waves specifically. The outer ear receives and amplifies the sound and transmits it to the middle ear, where tiny bones vibrate in response to the sound energy and transmit it to the inner ear. The inner ear converts the acoustic energy into electrical energy. The electrical impulses are then carried by nerves to the brain. Structures in the brain associated with hearing receive these electrical signals and interpret them as sounds. The ears' reception of sound waves is auditory sensation, and the brain's interpretation of them is auditory perception.

SOLAR SYSTEM
SOLAR SYSTEM'S LOCATION AND COMPONENTS

The universe is composed of an unknown (possibly infinite) number of galaxies or star systems, such as the Spiral Nebula, the Crab Nebula, and the Milky Way. Our sun, Sol, is one of billions of stars in the Milky Way. The solar system's planets are held in position at varying distances (according to their size and mass) from the Sun by its gravitational force. These planets orbit or revolve around the Sun. From the closest to the Sun to the farthest away, the solar system's planets are Mercury, Venus, Earth, Mars, Jupiter, Saturn, Uranus, and Neptune. Pluto was historically included as the ninth planet but was demoted to a "dwarf planet" by the International Astronomical Union in 2006. Due to angular momentum, planets rotate on their axes, which are imaginary central lines between their north and south poles. One complete Earth rotation equals what we perceive as one 24-hour day. As the Earth turns, different portions face the Sun. These receive daylight, while the portions turned away from the Sun are in darkness. One complete revolution of the Earth around the Sun represents one calendar year.

PLUTO

Since more powerful observatories have enabled greater detection and measurement of celestial objects, the International Astronomical Union has defined three criteria for defining a planet. First, it must orbit the Sun. Pluto meets this criterion. Second, it must have enough gravitational force to shape itself into a sphere. Pluto also meets this criterion. Third, a planet must have "cleared the neighborhood" in its orbit. This expression refers to the fact that as planets form, they become the strongest gravitational bodies within their orbits. Therefore, when close to smaller bodies, planets either consume these smaller bodies or repel them because of their greater gravity, clearing their orbital area or "neighborhood." To do this, a planet's mass must sufficiently exceed the mass of other bodies in its orbit. Pluto does not meet this criterion, having only 0.07 times the mass of other objects within its orbit. Thus, astronomers reclassified Pluto as a "dwarf planet" in 2006 based on its lesser mass and the many other objects in its orbit with comparable masses and sizes.

EARTH

Earth is roughly spherical in shape. Its North and South Poles at the top and bottom are farthest away from and least exposed to the Sun, so they are always coldest. This accounts for the existence of the polar ice caps. The Equator, an imaginary line running around Earth at its middle exactly halfway between the North and South Poles, is at 0° latitude. Sunrises and sunsets at the Equator are the world's fastest. Days and nights are of virtually equal length at the Equator, and there is less seasonal variation than in other parts of the world. The equatorial climate is a tropical rainforest. Locations close to the North Pole, like Norway, are at such high latitudes that their nights are not dark in summertime, hence the expression "Land of the Midnight Sun." They also have very little light in wintertime. As Earth revolves around the Sun over the course of a year, the distance and angle of various locations relative to the Sun change, so different areas receive varying amounts of heat and light. This is what accounts for the changing seasons.

ROCKS FOUND ON THE EARTH'S SURFACE
SEDIMENTARY ROCKS

Earth's rock types are sedimentary, igneous, and metamorphic. These categories are based on the respective processes that form each type of rock. Igneous rocks are formed from volcanoes. Metamorphic rocks are formed when igneous and sedimentary rocks deep inside the Earth's crust are subjected to intense heat and/or pressure. **Sedimentary rocks** are formed on Earth's surface and characteristically accumulate in layers. Erosion and other natural processes deposit these layers. Some sedimentary rocks are held together by electrical attraction. Others are cemented together by chemicals and minerals that existed during their formation. Still others are not held together at all but are loose and crumbly. There are three subcategories of sedimentary rock. Clastic sedimentary rocks are made of little rock bits—clasts—that are compacted and cemented together. Chemical sedimentary rocks are frequently formed through repeated flooding and subsequent evaporation. The evaporation of water leaves a layer of minerals that were dissolved in the water. Limestone and deposits of salt and gypsum are examples. Organic sedimentary rocks are formed from organic matter, such as the calcium left behind from animal bones and shells.

METAMORPHIC ROCKS

Sedimentary rocks are formed on the Earth's surface by layers of eroded material from mountains that were deposited by water, minerals like lime, salt and gypsum deposited by evaporated floodwater, and organic material like calcium from animal bones and shells. Igneous rocks are formed from liquid volcanic rock—either magma underground or lava on the surface—that cools and hardens. **Metamorphic rocks** are formed from sedimentary and igneous rocks. This happens when sedimentary and/or igneous rocks are deep inside the Earth's crust, where they are subjected to great pressure or heat. The process of metamorphism does not melt these rocks into liquid, which would happen inside a volcano. Rather, the pressure and/or heat change the rocks' molecular structure. Metamorphic rocks are thus more compact and denser than the sedimentary or igneous rocks from which they were formed. They also contain new minerals produced either by the reconfiguration of existing minerals' structures or by chemical reactions with liquids infiltrating the rock. Two examples of metamorphic rocks are marble and gneiss.

IGNEOUS ROCKS

Igneous or volcanic rocks are formed from the magma emitted when a volcano erupts. Magma under the Earth's surface is subject to heat and pressure, keeping it in liquid form. During a volcanic eruption, some magma reaches the surface, emerging as lava. Lava cools rapidly in the outside air, becoming a solid with small crystals. Some magma does not reach Earth's surface, but is trapped underground within pockets in other rocks. Magma cools more slowly underground than lava does on the surface. This slower cooling forms rocks with larger crystals and coarser grains. The chemical composition and individual cooling temperatures of magma produce different kinds of igneous rocks. Lava that cools rapidly on the Earth's surface can become obsidian, a smooth, shiny black glass without crystals. It can also become another type of extrusive rock, such as andesite, basalt, pumice, rhyolite, scoria, or tuff (formed from volcanic ash and cinders). Magma that cools slowly in underground pockets can become granite, which has a coarse texture and large, visible mineral grains. It can also become another type of intrusive rock, such as diorite, gabbro, pegmatite, or peridotite.

EROSION

Erosion is a natural process whereby Earth's landforms are broken down through weathering. Rain and wind wear away solid matter. Over time, rain reduces mountains to hills. Rocks break off from mountains and, in turn, disintegrate into sand. Weathering and the resulting erosion always occur in downhill directions. Rain washes rocks off mountains and down streams. Rains, rivers, and streams wash soils away, and ocean waves break down adjacent cliffs. Rocks, dirt, and sand change their form and location through erosion. They do not simply vanish. These transformations and movements are called mass wasting, which occurs chemically (as when rock is dissolved by chemicals in water) or mechanically (as when rock is broken into pieces). Because materials travel as a result of mass wasting, erosion can both break down some areas and build up others. For example, a river runs through and erodes a mountain, carrying the resulting sediment downstream. This sediment gradually builds up, creating wetlands at the river's mouth. A good example of this process is Louisiana's swamps, which were created by sediment transported by the Mississippi River.

WEATHER, CLIMATE, AND METEOROLOGY

Meteorology is the study of the atmosphere, particularly as it pertains to forecasting the weather and understanding its processes. **Weather** is the condition of the atmosphere at any given moment. Most weather occurs in the troposphere and includes changing events such as clouds, storms, and temperature, as well as more extreme events such as tornadoes, hurricanes, and blizzards. **Climate** refers to the average weather for a particular area over time, typically at least 30 years. Latitude is an indicator of climate. Changes in climate occur over long time periods.

WINDS AND GLOBAL WIND BELTS

Winds are the result of air moving by convection. Masses of warm air rise, and cold air sweeps into their place. The warm air also moves, cools, and sinks. The term "prevailing wind" refers to the wind that usually blows in an area in a single direction. Dominant winds are the winds with the highest speeds. Belts or bands that run latitudinally and blow in a specific direction are associated with convection cells. Hadley cells are formed directly north and south of the equator. The Farrell cells occur at about 30° to 60°. The jet stream runs between the Farrell cells and the polar cells. At the higher and lower latitudes, the direction is easterly. At mid-latitudes, the direction is westerly. From the North Pole to the south, the surface winds are Polar High Easterlies, Subpolar Low Westerlies, Subtropical High or Horse Latitudes, North-East Trade winds, Equatorial Low or Doldrums, South-East Trades, Subtropical High or Horse Latitudes, Subpolar Low Easterlies, and Polar High.

RELATIVE HUMIDITY, ABSOLUTE HUMIDITY, AND DEW POINT TEMPERATURE

Humidity refers to water vapor contained in the air. The amount of moisture contained in air depends upon its temperature. The higher the air temperature, the more moisture it can hold. These higher levels of moisture are associated with higher humidity. **Absolute humidity** refers to the total amount of moisture air is capable of holding at a certain temperature. **Relative humidity** is the ratio of water vapor in the air compared to the amount the air is capable of holding at its current temperature. As temperature decreases, absolute humidity stays the same and relative humidity increases. A hygrometer is a device used to measure humidity. The **dew point** is the temperature at which water vapor condenses into water at a particular humidity.

PRECIPITATION

After clouds reach the dew point, **precipitation** occurs. Precipitation can take the form of a liquid or a solid. It is known by many names, including rain, snow, ice, dew, and frost. **Liquid** forms of precipitation include rain and drizzle. Rain or drizzle that freezes on contact is known as freezing rain or freezing drizzle. **Solid or**

frozen forms of precipitation include snow, ice needles or diamond dust, sleet or ice pellets, hail, and graupel or snow pellets. Virga is a form of precipitation that evaporates before reaching the ground. It usually looks like sheets or shafts falling from a cloud. The amount of rainfall is measured with a rain gauge. Intensity can be measured according to how fast precipitation is falling or by how severely it limits visibility. Precipitation plays a major role in the water cycle since it is responsible for depositing much of the Earth's fresh water.

CLOUDS

Clouds form when air cools and warm air is forced to give up some of its water vapor because it can no longer hold it. This vapor condenses and forms tiny droplets of water or ice crystals called clouds. Particles, or aerosols, are needed for water vapor to form water droplets. These are called **condensation nuclei**. Clouds are created by surface heating, mountains and terrain, rising air masses, and weather fronts. Clouds precipitate, returning the water they contain to Earth. Clouds can also create atmospheric optics. They can scatter light, creating colorful phenomena such as rainbows, colorful sunsets, and the green flash phenomenon.

LIVING ORGANISMS

All **living organisms** have fundamental needs that must be met. For example, plants that grow on land need light, air, water, and nutrients in amounts that vary according to the individual plant. Undersea plants may need less/no light. They need gases present in the water but not in the air above the water. Like land plants, they require nutrients. Like plants, animals (including humans) need air, water, and nutrients. They do not depend on light for photosynthesis like most plants, but some animals require more light than others, while others need less than others or none at all. Organisms cannot survive in environments that do not meet their basic needs. However, many organisms have evolved to adapt to various environments. For example, cacti are desert plants that thrive with only tiny amounts of water, and camels are desert animals that can also go for long periods of time with little water. Penguins and polar bears have adapted to very cold climates. Internal cues (e.g., hunger) and external cues (e.g., environmental change) motivate and shape the behaviors of individual organisms.

TYPES OF ANIMAL LIFE CYCLES

Most animals, including mammals, birds, fish, reptiles, and spiders, have simple life cycles. They are born live or hatch from eggs, and then grow to adulthood. Animals with simple life cycles include humans. Amphibians like frogs and newts have an additional stage involving a metamorphosis, or transformation. After birth, they breathe through gills and live underwater during youth (e.g., tadpoles). By adulthood, they breathe through lungs and move to land. Butterflies are examples of animals (insects) that undergo complete metamorphosis, meaning they change their overall form. After hatching from an embryo/egg, the juvenile form, or larva, resembles a worm and completes the majority of feeding required. In the next stage, the pupa does not feed, and is typically camouflaged in what is called an inactive stage. Mosquito pupae are called tumblers. The butterfly pupa is called a chrysalis and is protected by a cocoon. In the final stage, the adult (imago) grows wings (typically) and breeds. Some insects like dragonflies, cockroaches, and grasshoppers undergo an incomplete metamorphosis. There are egg, larva, and adult stages, but no pupa stage.

ECOLOGY

Ecology is defined as the study of interactions between organisms and their environments. **Abiotic factors** are the parts of any ecosystem that are not alive but which affect that ecosystem's living members. Abiotic factors also determine the locations of particular ecosystems that have certain characteristics. Abiotic factors include the sunlight; the atmosphere, including oxygen, hydrogen, and nitrogen; the water; the soil; the temperatures within a system; and the nutrient cycles of chemical elements and compounds that pass among living organisms and their physical environments. **Biotic factors** are the living organisms within any ecosystem, which include not only humans and animals but also plants and microorganisms. The definition of biotic factors also includes the interactions that occur between and among various organisms within an ecosystem. Sunlight determines plant growth and, hence, biome locations. Sunlight, in turn, is affected by water depth.

Ocean depths where sunlight penetrates, called photic zones, are where the majority of the photosynthesis on Earth occurs.

> **Review Video: <u>Photosynthesis</u>**
> Visit mometrix.com/academy and enter code: 227035

ORGANISM REPRODUCTION

A few examples of the many ways in which organisms reproduce include binary fission, whereby the cells of prokaryotic bacteria reproduce; budding, which is how yeast cells reproduce; and asexual reproduction. The latter occurs in plants when they are grafted, when cuttings are taken from them and then rooted, or when they put out runners. Plants also reproduce sexually, as do humans and most other animals. Animals, including humans, produce gametes (i.e., sperm or eggs) in their gonads through the process of meiosis. Gametes are haploid, containing half the number of chromosomes found in the body's cells. During fertilization, the gametes combine to form a zygote, which is diploid. It has the full number of chromosomes (half from each gamete), which are arranged in a genetically unique combination. Zygotes undergo mitosis, reproducing their gene combination with identical DNA sequences in all new cells, which then migrate and differentiate into organizations of specialized organs and tissues. These specialized organs in biologically mature organisms, alerted by signals such as hormonal cues, undergo meiosis to create new haploid gametes, beginning the cycle again.

PLANT REPRODUCTION

Most plants can reproduce asexually. For example, cuttings can be rooted in water and planted. Some plants put out runners that root new growths. Many plants can be grafted to produce new ones. Plants also reproduce sexually. Plants' sexual life cycles are more complex than animals', since plants alternate between haploid form (i.e., having a single set of chromosomes) and diploid form (i.e., having two sets of chromosomes) during their life cycles. Plants produce haploid cells called gametes (equivalent to sperm and egg in animals) that combine during fertilization, producing zygotes (diploid cells with chromosomes from both gametes). Cells reproduce exact copies through mitosis (asexual reproduction), becoming differentiated/specialized to form organs. Mature diploid plants called sporophytes—the plant form we usually see—produce spores. In sporophytes' specialized organs, cells undergo meiosis. This is part of the process of sexual reproduction, during which cells with half the normal number of chromosomes are produced before fertilization occurs. The spores produced by the sporophyte generation undergo mitosis, growing into a haploid plant of the gametophyte generation that produces gametes. The cycle then repeats.

ECOLOGICAL RELATIONSHIPS

Organisms interact, both with other organisms and their environments. Relationships wherein two differing organisms regularly interact so that one or both of them benefit are known as **ecological relationships**. In **mutualistic** relationships, both organisms benefit. For example, bacteria live in termites' digestive systems. Termites eat wood. However, they cannot digest the cellulose (the main part of plant cell walls) in wood. The bacteria in termites' guts break down the cellulose for them, releasing the wood's nutrients. Reciprocally, the termites as hosts give the bacteria a home and food. In **commensalistic** relationships, one organism benefits and the other one is unaffected. One example is barnacles attaching to whales. Barnacles, which are filter feeders, benefit from the whales' swimming, which creates currents in the water that bring the barnacles food. The whales are not disturbed by the barnacles. In **parasitic** relationships, the parasite benefits, but the host suffers. For example, tapeworms inside animals' digestive tracts get nutrients. The hosts lose the nutrients stolen by the worms and can sustain tissue damage because of the presence of the tapeworms.

Health

HEALTH AND PHYSICAL EDUCATION FOUNDATIONS
HUMAN HEALTH AND WELLNESS AND DISEASE PREVENTION

Healthy development and disease prevention both begin before birth. Expecting mothers need to be informed about good nutrition and the supplemental nutrition required for prenatal support of developing embryos and fetuses. Mothers should also get sufficient but not overly strenuous exercise, avoid undue stress, find effective coping skills to deal with unavoidable life stressors, and avoid exposure to environmental toxins, such as radiation, pollution, and chemicals. They should avoid alcohol, tobacco, and exposure to secondhand smoke, as well as most drugs—street, over-the-counter, herbal, and prescription—unless they are prescribed by obstetricians/other physicians who are aware of the pregnancy. Babies initially need their mother's colostrum to provide immunity, and subsequently require breast milk or approved infant formula. Babies must also be held, cuddled, and given attention and affection to ensure survival, growth, and health. Young children need smaller amounts of food than adults that is equally as nutritious; sufficient exercise; adequate sleep; and cognitive, emotional, and social stimulation and interaction. Appropriate nutrition and exercise, avoidance of alcohol/tobacco/other drugs, and positive relationships and interactions are essential for wellness and disease prevention at all ages.

2009 AMERICAN RECOVERY AND REINVESTMENT ACT

The 2009 American Recovery and Reinvestment Act has allotted $650 million for preventing chronic disease. To apply these funds, the US Department of Health and Human Services (HHS) has designed a comprehensive initiative entitled Communities Putting Prevention to Work. This initiative aims to create sustainable positive health changes in American communities, prevent or delay chronic disease, reduce disease risk factors, and promote child and adult wellness. Obesity and tobacco use, considered the foremost preventable sources of disability and death, are targeted by this initiative's evidence-based research programs and strategies, which are intended to reinforce state abilities and mobilize community resources. The initiative's central, $373-million community program includes support from the Centers for Disease Control and Prevention in selected communities for attaining the prevention outcomes of increasing physical activity levels, improving nutrition, reducing the incidence of obesity and higher than optimal body weights, decreasing tobacco use, and decreasing secondhand smoke exposure. Through this initiative, HHS hopes to produce effective models that can be reproduced in states and communities nationwide.

ENVIRONMENTAL HEALTH RISKS

Children's body systems, unlike those of mature adults, are still developing. They eat, drink, and breathe more in proportion to their body sizes than adults do. Typical child behaviors expose children to more potentially toxic chemicals and organisms. Therefore, children can be more vulnerable to environmental health risks. To protect children, adults can prohibit smoking in homes and cars; keep homes free of dust, mold, pet dander, and pests that can trigger allergies; avoid outdoor activities on high-pollution/"ozone alert" days; and carpool and/or use public transportation. Adults can prevent lead poisoning by only giving children cold water to drink and using cold water to prepare infant formula and cook food; washing bottles, pacifiers, and toys frequently; and protecting children from lead-based paints in older buildings. Adults must ensure children do not have access to toxic chemicals. Maintaining furnaces, chimneys, and appliances; using outdoor gas appliances and tools properly; refraining from using gas appliances and tools indoors; and installing approved CO alarms can all help prevent carbon monoxide poisoning. Choosing fish carefully can help prevent mercury toxicity. Keeping infants out of direct sunlight, using sun-protective clothing, and applying sunscreen on young children are also important.

FEDERAL EXECUTIVE ORDER 13045: PROTECTION OF CHILDREN FROM ENVIRONMENTAL HEALTH RISKS AND SAFETY RISKS (1997)

Passed by President Clinton, **Executive Order 13045** declares a policy for identifying and assessing environmental health and safety risks that affect children disproportionately, and for addressing these risks through the policies, standards, programs, and activities of every independent federal regulatory agency. This order defines environmental health and safety risks as those that can be attributed to substances children ingest or contact (e.g., air they breathe; food they eat; water they drink, bathe in, and swim in; soil they live upon; and products they are exposed to or use). The order established a task force reporting to the president and consulting with the Domestic Policy Council, the National Science and Technology Council, the Council on Environmental Quality, and the Office of Management and Budget. The task force is co-chaired by the HHS secretary and the EPA administrator. The task force oversees a coordinated, integrated federal research agenda and reports relevant research/data biennially; issues principle, policy, and priority statements; recommends appropriate federal/state/local/tribal government, nonprofit, and private sector partnerships; makes public outreach/communication proposals; identifies related high-priority initiatives; and evaluates new legislation to determine whether it will meet the goals of Executive Order 13045.

CIRCULATORY SYSTEM

The **circulatory system** continuously supplies blood containing oxygen and nutrients to all body tissue cells, exchanges oxygenated blood for the waste products produced during the metabolism process, and transports waste for elimination. Central to the vascular (vessel) system is the heart, which is located in the mediastinum within the thoracic cavity. The heart is encased and protected by the pericardium, a double-walled, tough fibrous sac. The heart has four chambers: two atria and two ventricles. A system of valves regulates opening and closing among the chambers, the aorta, the pulmonary artery, and the great vessels. The aorta, originating at the heart, is the body's largest artery. The pulmonary artery branches to the left and to the right and transports venous blood from the heart's lower right chamber to the lung for oxygenation. The pulmonary veins return oxygenated blood from the lung to the left atrium of the heart. The superior and inferior venae cavae are vessels that empty into the heart's right atrium.

INTEGUMENTARY AND MUSCULOSKELETAL SYSTEMS

In the human body, the **integumentary system** consists of skin, hair, nails, and oil and sweat glands. The skin has three layers: the epidermis, the dermis, and subcutaneous tissues. Skin protects tissues underneath it from bacterial infections, blocks most chemicals from entering, prevents fluid loss, and reduces the probability of mechanical injury to underlying body structures. Skin regulates body temperature and synthesizes needed chemicals. It is also a sense organ, as it has sensory receptors for touch, pressure, heat, and pain. It also contains motor fibers that enable necessary reactions to these sensations and stimuli. The **musculoskeletal system** includes bones, joints, and three types of connective tissues: tendons, ligaments, and cartilage. It is responsible for our body shape and provides stability and support. It also protects our internal organs and enables locomotion. Bones store calcium and other minerals, and bone marrow produces required blood cells. Muscle fibers contract to enable movement. Depending on their innervation, muscles can have voluntary or involuntary (like the heart) movements. Muscles need blood supply and oxygen to work. Thus, the musculoskeletal system depends on other systems, including the circulatory, nervous, and respiratory systems.

> **Review Video: Integumentary System**
> Visit mometrix.com/academy and enter code: 655980
>
> **Review Video: Skeletal System**
> Visit mometrix.com/academy and enter code: 256447

LYMPHATIC SYSTEM

The **lymphatic system** includes lymph (a fluid), collection ducts, and tissues. Lymphatic tissues comprise the lymph nodes, the thymus gland, the tonsils, and the Peyer's patches of the intestinal tract. Lymphoid components are also present in the lungs, the mucosa in the stomach and the appendix, and the bone marrow. Microscopic capillaries merge to form lymph-collecting ducts. These ducts drain to specific centers of lymphatic tissue. The lymph system's functioning is supported by the spleen and thymus glands. While not all characteristics and functions of the lymphatic system are established, known functions include: return transportation of lymph, protein, and microorganisms to the cardiovascular system; production of lymphocytes by the lymph nodes; filtering of the blood by the lymph nodes; production of antibodies to enable immune response against infection; absorption of fats and fat-soluble substances from the intestine; formation of blood cells in response to some illnesses/conditions; and phagocytosis (i.e., the surrounding/swallowing/"eating" of infectious particles by cells lining the sinuses of the lymph nodes, spleen, and liver). The lymph system defends the body against infection and supports the veins by helping to return fluids to the bloodstream.

RESPIRATORY SYSTEM

The **respiratory system** provides oxygen to the body and removes carbon dioxide, the waste product of respiration (breathing). In doing so, the respiratory system and many other body systems work together through complex interactions. Twelve thoracic vertebrae, twelve pairs of ribs, the sternum, the diaphragm, and the intercostal muscles comprise the thoracic cage containing the lungs. As one breathes in and out, the thoracic cage is always moving. The diaphragm, a muscular wall dividing the chest cavity and abdominal cavity, functions as a bellows for breathing and also plays a role in expelling feces and delivering babies. There are air pathways between the nose/mouth, pharynx, trachea, bronchi, bronchioles, and lungs. Alveoli, tiny air sacs in the lungs, exchange oxygen and carbon dioxide. During inspiration/inhalation, the ribs and sternum rise, the diaphragm contracts and lowers, the intercostal muscles contract, air pressure in the lungs decreases, and air enters the lungs. During exhalation, the intercostal muscles and diaphragm relax, the ribs and sternum return to a resting position, air pressure in the lungs increases, and air exits the lungs.

Review Video: Respiratory System
Visit mometrix.com/academy and enter code: 783075

THE BRAIN

The brain is divided into five major parts: the cerebrum, the midbrain, the cerebellum, the pons, and the medulla oblongata. The cranial nerves are:

ID	Name	Function
I	Olfactory	Controls the sense of smell
II	Optic	Controls vision
III	Oculomotor	Controls the movements of the eye muscles, the movements of the upper eyelids, and the pupillary reflexes (expanding and contracting to admit more/less light)
IV	Trochlear	Controls the movements of the superior oblique eye muscles
V	Trigeminal	Controls facial sensation, the eye's corneal reflex, and chewing
VI	Abducens	Controls the movements of the lateral rectus eye muscle
VII	Facial	Controls movement of the facial muscles and the taste sensation in the front two-thirds of the tongue
VIII	Vestibulocochlear	Controls equilibrium (balance) via the vestibular system in the inner ear, and hearing (the cochlea is in the inner ear)
IX	Glossopharyngeal	Controls the taste sensation in the rear one-third of the tongue
X	Vagus	Controls pharyngeal contraction (gag reflex), vocal cord movements, and soft palate movements
XI	Spinal accessory	Controls movement of the sternocleidomastoid and trapezius muscles
XII	Hypoglossal	Controls tongue movements

Review Video: Brain Anatomy
Visit mometrix.com/academy and enter code: 222476

Central Nervous System

Some main functions of the **central nervous system** (i.e., the brain and spinal cord) include controlling consciousness and all mental processes, regulating the functions and movements of the body, and sending and receiving nerve impulses to and from all parts of the body. For example, when we touch something hot, sensory nerve endings in our fingers send impulses to the brain, which interprets them as heat and sends a signal along motor nerves to pull our fingers away. The autonomic nervous system is automatic and involuntary. For example, it makes our heart beat. We cannot voluntarily start or stop our heartbeat. The voluntary nervous system is under our conscious control. For example, our brains use it to send impulses to our skeletal muscles when we want to sit, stand, or walk, and those muscles contract in response. The autonomic nervous system is divided into parasympathetic and sympathetic components. The parasympathetic portion stimulates muscular activity in the organs and gland secretion. The sympathetic portion stimulates heartbeat, vasoconstriction, and sweating. These two portions of the autonomic nervous system oppose/balance each other to regulate the system.

Digestive System

The chief functions of the **digestive system** are to provide nutrition to the body's cells and eliminate waste products left after nourishment is extracted from foods. The process consists of three phases: ingestion (taking in foods and liquids), digestion (converting ingested nutrients through physical and chemical means into forms that the cells of the body tissues can absorb and distribute), and elimination (removing the byproducts of digestion—also known as waste—that cannot be utilized). Other body systems work with the digestive system to process nutrients. For example, the nervous system plays a role in appetite, which is a signal for us to eat. The central nervous system also stimulates the release and flow of digestive juices. The endocrine system supplies chemicals (e.g., juices from the pancreas) that aid in digestion. The circulatory system delivers digested and absorbed nutrients to the tissue cells and also picks up waste products produced as a result of the metabolism process.

During chewing, the teeth and tongue physically break down food. Glands secrete saliva to provide lubrication during chewing and swallowing, and provide digestive enzymes to begin the process of chemically breaking down the foods we eat. The pharynx delivers food to the esophagus, where muscular contractions (peristalsis) move food downward. The epiglottis closes the trachea (windpipe) during swallowing to prevent food from being aspirated into the lungs. Glands in the stomach lining secrete gastric fluid comprised of hydrochloric acid and other chemicals, which dissolve food into semiliquid chyme. Chyme gradually passes into the small intestine, where most digestion and absorption occur. The small intestine is made up of the duodenum, the jejunum, and the ileum. The pancreas secretes digestive juices, the gallbladder secretes bile, and the intestinal mucosa secretes other juices into the duodenum to digest chyme. Digested nutrients are absorbed through the intestinal walls into capillaries and lymphatic vessels to be distributed to body cells. The large intestine consists of the cecum, the colon (ascending, transverse, descending, and sigmoid), the rectum, and the anus. The colon completes digestion and absorption and delivers wastes to the rectum, which eliminates them through the anus.

> **Review Video: Gastrointestinal System**
> Visit mometrix.com/academy and enter code: 378740

Urinary System

The function of the **urinary system** is to eliminate the liquid wastes produced through nutrient metabolism by excreting them from the body. The urinary system is made up of two kidneys, two ureters, the bladder, and the urethra. Behind the abdominal cavity at the thoracolumbar level are the kidneys, a pair of large bean-shaped glands. They continually remove water, salts, toxins, and nitrogenous wastes from the bloodstream and convert these substances into urine. Urine droplets flow from the kidneys into the ureters. The ureters are long, narrow tubes carrying urine to the bladder, which is a hollow, muscular, elastic organ. When enough urine collects in the bladder, nerves stimulate the body to empty it via urination. In human females, the urethra is about an inch and a half long and is located in the upper vaginal wall. In males, the urethra is about eight inches long and extends from the bladder through the prostate gland and the penis. Both urine and sperm pass through the male urethra, while the female urethra and vaginal canal are separate.

> **Review Video: Urinary System**
> Visit mometrix.com/academy and enter code: 601053

ENDOCRINE SYSTEM

The human **endocrine system** is one of the most complex body systems. Scientists understand many of its functions but not all of them. It is a system of ductless, internally secreting glands (some necessary to life) that extract various substances from tissue fluids and the bloodstream to create completely new substances (i.e., hormones). Operating without ducts, endocrine glands secrete hormones directly into the blood and lymph circulatory systems for distribution to the organs. The endocrine system's main glands include the pituitary, thyroid, parathyroid, and adrenal glands; the Islets of Langerhans in the pancreas; and the gonads (male testes and female ovaries). Additionally, the pancreas is both an endocrine and an exocrine gland. Its endocrine (internal secretion) function is to secrete insulin to regulate sugar metabolism; its exocrine (external secretion) function is to secrete pancreatic juice into the duodenum to aid in digestion. If the pancreas produces insufficient insulin, type 1 diabetes results. If the body responds insufficiently to insulin, type 2 diabetes results.

> **Review Video: Endocrine System**
> Visit mometrix.com/academy and enter code: 678939

PITUITARY, THYROID, AND PARATHYROID GLANDS

The **pituitary and thyroid glands** are both components of the endocrine system. The pituitary gland functions directly by regulating physical growth, development, and sexual maturation in children and adolescents; regulating the retention and excretion of fluid; regulating the balance of electrolytes (sodium, potassium, and chloride) in blood and tissues; and regulating new mothers' lactation (milk production). The pituitary is termed the hypophyseal "master" gland because it also regulates all other glands in the endocrine system. Therefore, it is involved in regulating food assimilation and metabolism through hydrating the thyroid gland; regulating body composition, adaptation, and resistance to stress through acting on the adrenal and parathyroid glands; regulating breathing, circulation, digestion, urine excretion, and muscular action through the collective activity of multiple hormones; and regulating sexual development, activity, and reproduction through acting on the gonads. The thyroid gland manufactures and secretes hormones that regulate child growth and development, as well as certain metabolic processes and their rates. It also stores iodine. The **parathyroid glands** secrete hormones that regulate blood calcium levels, phosphorus metabolism, and muscle and nervous system excitation.

REPRODUCTIVE SYSTEM

MALE

The scrotum and the penis are the external reproductive organs of the human male. The internal organs of the male reproductive system include two testes, two epididymides, two seminal ducts, two seminal vesicles, two ejaculatory ducts, two spermatic cords, the urethra, the prostate gland, and several other glands. The testes, which are glandular organs, hang on either side of the scrotum from spermatic cords. These cords contain the vas deferens, blood vessels, and supportive tissues. Male sperm cells and hormones are produced by the testes. Each testis has an epididymis connecting it to the vas deferens, an excretory seminal duct. The vas deferens travels upward inside the spermatic cords to the prostate gland, which is in front of the neck of the urinary bladder. There, the vas deferens joins with the pouch-like glands called seminal vesicles to form ejaculatory ducts. The prostate gland and seminal vesicles secrete substances into the semen that promote sperm motility. The ejaculatory ducts release semen into the urethra, and from here, the semen is ejected through the penis during sexual intercourse.

FEMALE

The external female reproductive organs include the mons pubis, the labia majora, the labia minora, the clitoris, the vestibule, the hymen, the Bartholin's glands, and several other glands. The breasts/mammary glands can also be considered parts of the reproductive system, as they produce milk for infants following reproduction. Internal organs include the vagina, the two fallopian tubes, the uterus, and the two ovaries. Hormones stimulate either ovary to produce an ovum/egg roughly once a month. A follicle containing an egg cell forms. When the egg matures, the follicle ruptures, releasing the egg. This is known as ovulation. The ovum passes into a fallopian tube and travels toward the uterus. Hormones have meanwhile also stimulated the endometrium (uterine lining) to thicken and increase its blood supply. When the egg reaches the womb, it is implanted in the endometrium if it was fertilized in the fallopian tube by a male sperm. This is known as conception. If the egg was not fertilized, hormone signals subside, causing the endometrium to detach from the uterine wall. The sloughed-off endometrial tissue, the resulting blood, and the unfertilized egg exit the body. This process is known as menstruation.

> **Review Video: Reproductive Systems**
> Visit mometrix.com/academy and enter code: 505450

INFLUENCE OF PHYSICAL, EMOTIONAL, AND SOCIAL FACTORS ON PERSONAL PHYSICAL HEALTH

The parts of the body, including the brain, are connected, related, interactive, and interdependent. As humans also interact and are interdependent with their environment, both internal and external factors influence their health. For example, physical factors like exposure to air pollution or radiation can cause illnesses like asthma, other lung diseases, and various cancers. Too much or too little nutrition can cause obesity and diabetes or malnutrition. Too much or too little exercise can cause exhaustion and injuries or weakness, diabetes, and cardiovascular and pulmonary problems. Not exercising enough may also be a factor in being overweight or obese. Diabetes itself causes many related health problems, including blindness, circulatory deficiencies, amputation, and cardiovascular disease. Water and/or sleep deprivation ultimately cause death. Emotional factors like depression, anxiety, and irritability can cause a host of health problems, including insomnia, overeating, anorexia, high blood pressure, and heart disease. Social factors include family influences. According to the family systems theory, dysfunctional family dynamics can cause a child to develop a physical illness. Whether the source is family, society outside the home, or both, stress is a social influence with multiple negative health impacts.

EFFECT OF NUTRITION ON DEVELOPMENT

Children must consume a full range of nutrients for their brains to work normally. They need protein for its amino acids, which enable the brain's neurotransmitters (chemical messengers) to fire and communicate with each other. They need fruit and vegetable sugars and other complex carbohydrates to supply fuel to power the brain's functioning. Children's nutrition begins before birth. Pregnant women who do not eat adequate nutrients, vitamins, and minerals have higher risks of delivering infants with low birth weights. Research has found that babies with low birth weights are more likely to experience hearing and vision problems and to need special education services in school at some point. Children in school who consume insufficient amounts of protein have been found to score lower on achievement tests than their peers who are getting enough protein. Children with iron deficiencies display fatigue and ADHD-like symptoms, including impaired concentration, shortened attention spans, and irritability. Children who miss breakfast consistently perform slower on problem-solving tests than those who do not. Their responses are also less accurate. Children who regularly miss meals have compromised immunity against illnesses and infections, and they miss more school.

MOTOR SKILLS

Motor skills are the large and small movements of the body. These movements include such things as pushing, pulling, lifting, and carrying larger objects using the legs, arms, and back, as well as picking up, grasping, and manipulating smaller objects using the hands and fingers. The former are gross motor skills, and the latter are fine motor skills. To develop these, children must make effective use of their mind-body connection (i.e., getting the muscles and bones to perform the movements the mind intends). They must also have developed spatial awareness (i.e., an accurate sense of the relationship between their bodies and the surrounding space and other bodies/objects). Teaching children to move large and small muscles in time to rhythmic songs helps develop motor skills. Teaching directions like up, down, clockwise, and counterclockwise helps with motor planning development. When children find motor skills challenging to master, educators must provide them with frequent instruction, adequate re-teaching, and ample modeling that allows them to observe and imitate problematic movements.

FINE MOTOR MOVEMENTS

Fine motor movements use small muscles in the eyes, lips, tongue, wrists, fingers, and toes. Fine/small motor movements work together with gross muscle movements to develop movement skills and patterns. Fine motor skills are often used for purposes of functional and expressive communication, like using tools, creating artworks, and writing and typing language. Eye-hand coordination, eye-foot coordination, and manual and finger dexterity are required for the fine motor movements used in drawing, writing, and typing. Fine motor practice also develops children's tactile (touch) awareness and spatial awareness. Rolling dough/putty/clay into balls and/or hiding things inside them promote fine motor skills. Tearing and cutting paper along dotted lines and creating patterns teach accurate size and shape perception and formation. Stringing, lacing, and creating structures using plastic building blocks develop hand-eye coordination and skills needed to create color patterns. Flip cards, pegs, and stickers promote object placement skills. Writing skills are developed by writing letters/numbers in shaving cream, sand, pudding, and/or on chalkboards using wet makeup sponges/cotton swabs; using toothbrushes on dry erase boards; and practicing placement on cardboard using rice, beans, pasta or glitter.

GROSS MOTOR SKILLS

Sitting, standing, crawling, walking, running, galloping, jumping, catching, throwing, and kicking use **gross motor skills**. Activities that help young children develop their gross motor skills include standing on dots/marks on the floor; crawling under and climbing over things, including objects that are part of obstacle courses; and balancing on balance beams. These develop body control, coordination, laterality (using the left/right sides of the body separately), and synchronization of the body's left and right sides. Children develop body control and balance through hopping around objects. They develop coordination and overall gross motor skills through jumping over things like boxes, beanbags, lines, and strings and by kicking objects like balls and balloons of various sizes. Walking and running around, through, and/or over obstacles like tires and hoops and/or participating in relays develop gross motor skills. Organized games involving skipping around things to music with various rhythms, and activities requiring twisting, turning, and bending all develop gross motor skills, preparing children for lifelong engagement in sports activities.

NEWBORN/INFANT MOTOR REFLEXES AND SKILLS

Newborns exhibit the tonic reflex, adopting the "fencing position." In this position, the head is turned to one side, the arm on that side is in front of the eyes, and the other arm is flexed. This normally disappears by the time an infant is around four months old. It may serve as preparation for reaching voluntarily for things/people. The stepping reflex disappears at around two months of age, and prepares babies for walking voluntarily. The palmar grasping reflex on an adult finger disappears by the time an infant is around three to four months old, and prepares babies for grasping voluntarily. When held upright, a baby can typically hold his/her head steady and erect by about six weeks of age on average. About 90 percent of infants will develop this skill between the ages of three weeks and four months. Babies lift up from the prone position using their arms by the time they are about two months old. About 90 percent of infants will develop this skill between the ages of three weeks and four months. Babies can also roll from side to back by the time they are about two months old. About 90 percent of infants will develop this skill between the ages of three weeks and five months. An infant can grasp a cube by the age of three months and three weeks on average. About 90 percent of infants will develop this skill between the ages of two and seven months.

INFANT MOTOR SKILLS MILESTONES

By four and a half months on average, babies can roll from back to side. The range within which 90 percent of infants will be able to do this is two to seven months. Most babies can sit unsupported by seven months on average. The range within which 90 percent of infants will be able to do this is five to nine months. Most infants also crawl by seven months on average. The range within which 90 percent of infants will be able to do this is five to eleven months. Babies pull themselves up to a standing position by around eight months on average. The range within which 90 percent of infants will be able to do this is five to twelve months. Babies play "patty-cake" by nine months, three weeks on average. The range within which 90 percent of infants will be able to do this is seven to fifteen months. Babies/toddlers can stand alone by 11 months on average. The range within which 90 percent of infants will be able to do this is 9 to 16 months. Toddlers can walk unassisted by the age of 11 months, 3 weeks on average. The range within which 90 percent of infants will be able to do this is 9 to 17 months. Children can stack two cubes by the age of 13 months, 3 weeks on average. The range within which 90 percent of infants will be able to do this is 10 to 19 months. They scribble energetically by the age of 14 months on average. The range within which 90 percent of infants will be able to do this is 10 to 21 months. They can climb stairs with assistance by the age of 16 months on average. The range within which 90 percent of infants will be able to do this is 12 to 23 months. Normally developing children can typically can jump in place by the age of 23 months, 2 weeks on average. The range within which 90 percent of infants will be able to do this is 17 to 30 months.

SALIENT ASPECTS OF TYPICAL EARLY CHILDHOOD PHYSICAL DEVELOPMENT

Early childhood physical growth, while significant, is slower than infant growth. From birth to 2 years, children generally grow to four times their newborn weight and 2/3 their newborn length and height. From 2–3 years, however, children usually gain only about 4 lb. and 3.5 inches. From 4–6 years, growth slows more; gains of 5–7 lb. and 2.5 inches are typical. Due to slowing growth rates, 3- and 4-year-olds appear to eat less food but do not; they actually just eat fewer calories per pound of body weight. Brain growth is still rapid in preschoolers: brains attain 55 percent of adult size by 2 years, and 90 percent by 6 years. The majority of brain growth is usually by 4–4.5 years, with a growth spurt around 2 years and growth rates slowing significantly between 5 and 6 years. Larger brain size indicates not more neurons but larger sizes, differences in their organization, more glial cells nourishing and supporting neurons, and greater myelination (development of the sheath protecting nerve fibers and facilitating their efficient intercommunication).

NATURE-NURTURE INTERACTION IN EARLY CHILDHOOD PHYSICAL DEVELOPMENT

The physical development of babies and young children is a product of the interactions between genetic and environmental factors. Also, a child's physical progress is equally influenced by environmental and psychological variables. For the body, brain, and nervous system to grow and develop normally, children must live in healthy environments. When the interaction of hereditary and environmental influences is not healthful, this is frequently reflected in abnormal patterns of growth. Failure to thrive syndrome is a dramatic example. When children are abused or neglected for long periods of time, they actually stop growing. The social environments of such children create psychological stress. This stress makes the child's pituitary gland stop releasing growth hormones, and growth ceases. When such environmental stress is relieved and these children are given proper care, stimulation, and affection, they begin growing again. They often grow rapidly enough to catch up on the growth they missed earlier. Normal body and brain growth—as well as psychological development—depend upon the collaboration of nature and nurture.

SIGNS OF PROGRESS IN TYPICAL MOTOR DEVELOPMENT

Genetics, physiological maturation, nutrition, and experience through practice combine to further preschoolers' motor skills development. Newborns' reflexive behaviors progress to preschoolers' voluntary activities. Also, children's perception of the size, shape, and position of the body and body parts becomes more accurate by preschool ages. In addition, increases in bilateral coordination of the body's two sides enhance preschoolers' motor skills. Motor skills development entails both learning new movements and gradually integrating previously learned movements into smooth, continuous patterns, as in learning to throw a ball with skill. Both large muscles (for gross-motor skills like climbing, running, and jumping) and small muscles (for fine-motor skills like drawing and tying knots) develop. Eye-hand coordination involves fine-motor control. Preschoolers use visual feedback, seeing whether they are making things go where and do what they want them to, in learning to manipulate small objects with their hands and fingers.

GENDER DIFFERENCES IN MOTOR DEVELOPMENT

On average, preschool boys have larger muscles than preschool girls, so they can run faster, climb higher, and jump farther. Boys at these ages tend to be more muscular physically. Preschool girls, while less muscular, are on the average more mature physically for their ages than boys. While boys usually exceed girls in their large-muscle, gross-motor abilities like running, jumping, and climbing, girls tend to surpass boys in small-muscle, fine-motor abilities like buttoning buttons, using scissors, and similar activities involving the manipulation of small tools, utensils, and objects. While preschool boys exhibit more strength in large-muscle, gross-motor actions, preschool girls are more advanced than preschool boys in large-muscle, gross-motor skills that do not demand strength so much as coordination, like hopping, balancing on one foot, and skipping. While these specific gender differences in preschoolers' physical and motor development have been observed consistently in research, it is also found that preschool girls' and boys' physical and motor development patterns are generally more similar than different overall.

CEPHALOCAUDAL AND PROXIMODISTAL DEVELOPMENT

Infant and child motor development follows the same developmental sequences as prenatal embryonic and fetal physical development. **Cephalocaudal** means head to tail. Just as the body develops from the head down before birth, babies and young children develop motor control of their heads before they develop control of their legs. **Proximodistal** means near to far (i.e., central to distant). Head, torso, and arm control develop prior to hand and finger control. Babies learn a lot about how things look, sound, and feel once they master gross motor skills for reaching and grasping. These then evolve toward fine motor skills. For example, at around three months of age, an infant's voluntary reaching gradually becomes more accurate. The infant will not need arm guidance, because he or she has spatial awareness of location and motion. Babies reach less by five months when they can move things within reach. By nine months, babies can redirect reaching to grasp objects moving in different directions. By six to twelve months, development of the pincer grasp enhances babies' capacities for object manipulation.

MOTOR SKILLS DEVELOPING BETWEEN AGES 2 AND 6

Children develop motor skills most quickly between the ages of two and six years. They demonstrate basic locomotion skills, first walking and then running, skipping, hopping, galloping, and jumping. They also develop ball-handling skills, fine motor eye-hand coordination, and—as an extension of previously developed creeping skills—climbing skills. By two years of age, children develop balance for basic kicking, which evolves into the ability to execute full kicks (including backswings) by six years of age. They try throwing by two to three years of age. They develop related skills—including taking a forward step—by the age of six. They develop the ability to shuffle by three years of age, which develops into the ability to skip by six years of age. By the age of three, children walk automatically. They try running, but they are clumsy and lack adequate control. This ability improves by between four and five years of age. By this time, children are also more skilled at executing starts, stops, and turns. By the age of five or six, children can run like adults. They develop climbing skills (ladders, etc.) between the ages of three and six. The ability to jump longer distances and hopping and galloping skills develop by age six. Children can catch a large ball while holding their arm straight by the age of three. They can catch a ball while holding their elbows out to the front by age four, and they can do this while holding their elbows at their sides by age six.

HOW COOKING AND SELF-CARE ACTIVITIES HELP DEVELOP FINE MOTOR SKILLS

Young children are often fascinated by adults' cooking activities, want to participate, and offer to help. Involving them is not only beneficial to their self-esteem but also develops various skills. Measuring amounts of liquids and solids in different forms develops children's math skills. Mixing, stirring, and blending ingredients using different parts of their hands develop children's fine motor skills. Life skills include self-care skills, such as combing one's hair, brushing one's teeth, fastening and unfastening buttons and snaps on clothing, and lacing and unlacing shoes. Life skills also require being able to open and close drawers, doors, and jars; to clean a house; and to wash things. It is necessary to children's normal development that they learn to combine multiple fine motor skills. Children's development of fine motor skills also needs to be integrated with the development of various self-care and other life skills (such as those described above) that are required for normal activities of daily living.

BENEFITS OF PHYSICAL ACTIVITY

When young children engage in physical activity, they learn new motor skills and reinforce, advance, and refine existing ones. They also learn important early math skills like spatial awareness. Whenever they attempt new activities, they encounter challenges, such as having to develop higher levels of coordination, control, precision, strength, speed, flexibility, and agility. They are also challenged to coordinate their mental and physical processes more closely and in a manner that is more complex. They learn to exert effort and to persevere in the face of difficulty. When they succeed at meeting these challenges, their self-esteem and self-efficacy (sense of competence to perform tasks) are enhanced. Since motor skills generally develop ahead of language skills, physical activity is a valuable means of direct self-expression. Young children learn many social skills through interacting with peers and adults during physical games, sports activities, etc. In addition to all these benefits, young children normally seek out physical activity, deriving a great deal of fun and enjoyment through moving, playing games/sports, and interacting physically with others.

NATIONAL PHYSICAL EDUCATION STANDARDS

The National Association for Sport and Physical Education (NASPE) has developed six national physical education standards. These standards state that someone who is physically educated:

1. Shows the motor skills and patterns of movement competencies s/he needs to conduct various physical activities
2. Shows comprehension of the basic concepts, main principles, methods, and techniques of movement as they relate to learning and executing physical activities
3. Regularly engages in physical activity
4. Reaches and sustains a level of physical fitness that enhances health
5. Demonstrates behaviors, personally and socially, that reflect self-respect and respect for others within contexts of physical activity
6. Places value upon the benefits of physical activities and of being fit and active, such as the pleasure; the improvement and maintenance of health; the physical, personal, and social challenges; and the opportunities to interact socially and express oneself

PHYSICAL, EMOTIONAL, AND SOCIAL FACTORS

Young children who have already become overweight/obese because of an improper diet and lack of exercise are more likely than children who are within a healthy weight range to find physical activity uncomfortable and avoid it. Even those who enjoy activity are more at risk of injury if they are overweight or lack physical conditioning. Exercise is more challenging for children with illnesses. For example, asthma interferes with breathing. Therefore, asthmatic children must be supervised and monitored when exercising. So must diabetic children, whose blood sugar can fluctuate excessively due to exercising. Their food intake must be monitored and coordinated with exercise. Children with physical disabilities may require adaptive equipment and/or alternative methods of physical instruction and exercising. Emotionally, children experiencing depression are likely to be apathetic and uninterested in movement. Hyperactive children (e.g., those with ADHD) are often overactive physically to the point of exhaustion. Children lacking adequate social skills, friends, and/or peer groups have fewer opportunities and are less likely to engage in physical games and sports with others, so their motor skills and physical fitness may suffer.

AMOUNTS AND PROPORTIONS OF ENGAGEMENT IN PHYSICAL ACTIVITY

The **World Health Organization** (WHO) advises that children between the ages of 5 and 17 should engage in a minimum of 1 hour (continuously or incrementally) of moderate to vigorous physical activity per day.

According to the WHO, exercising for more than one hour daily (within reason) will confer additional health benefits. The majority of children's physical activity should be aerobic in nature. Aerobic exercise uses large muscle groups, is rhythmic and continuous, and works the heart and lungs so that the pulmonary and cardiovascular systems become more efficient at absorbing and transporting oxygen. Children should take part in exercises and/or activities that strengthen the muscles and bones through weight-bearing and other methods at least three times per week. Children's play activities that can fulfill bone-strengthening requirements include running, jumping, turning, and playing various games. Engaging in general play, playing games, playing sports, doing chores, using exercise as a means of transportation (e.g., walking, biking, etc.), participating in planned exercise sessions, and attending physical education classes are all activities available in family, community, and school settings that can allow children to meet physical activity and fitness requirements.

Chapter Quiz

Ready to see how well you retained what you just read? Scan the QR code to go directly to the chapter quiz interface for this study guide. If you're using a computer, simply visit the bonus page at **mometrix.com/bonus948/pectprek4** and click the Chapter Quizzes link.

PECT Practice Test #1

Child Development, Learning, and Assessment

1. In a third-grade classroom, students receive tickets for on-task behavior that can be redeemed for special prizes at the end of each week. Students that do not follow classroom expectations lose recess time. This strategy is most aligned with which of the following learning theories?

    a. Constructivism
    b. Behaviorism
    c. Assertive discipline
    d. Social learning

2. In a kindergarten classroom, the teacher has included several learning stations, such as a dramatic play area, sensory bin, science center, music area, and art center. In doing so, the teacher supports students' learning and development by providing multiple opportunities for:

    a. Direct instruction
    b. Formative assessment
    c. Hands-on learning experiences
    d. Individualized instruction

3. According to Jean Piaget's theory of cognitive development in children, prekindergarten students are most likely to engage in:

    a. Circular reactions
    b. Logical problem-solving
    c. Symbolic play
    d. Abstract reasoning

4. A new fourth-grade teacher in a culturally diverse school is unfamiliar with the backgrounds, experiences, and needs of his students. Which of the following strategies would best help this teacher provide learning experiences that are responsive to all of his students' needs?

    a. Self-educating regarding the needs and priorities of the community
    b. Working with a mentor teacher to develop effective instructional strategies
    c. Integrating students' diversities into the curriculum
    d. Recognizing and eliminating personal biases

5. A first-grade teacher works with a group of students that have varying skills, abilities, and learning needs. During English language arts lessons, she groups students based upon literacy abilities and English language proficiency levels, and she adapts texts to vary in complexity. This is an example of which of the following instructional strategies?

   a. Inquiry-based learning
   b. Total participation techniques
   c. Scaffolding
   d. Student-led learning

6. Which of the following strategies would likely be most effective in developing and implementing culturally competent learning experiences that meet the needs of all students?

   a. Incorporating opportunities for student choice in learning
   b. Attending back-to-school night to meet students' families
   c. Supplementing instruction with appropriate accommodations and modifications
   d. Diversifying instruction to accurately and respectfully reflect differences within the classroom

7. Meeting the developmental learning needs of kindergarten students requires that the classroom environment includes multiple opportunities for:

   a. Individualized instruction
   b. Self-reflection
   c. Structured and unstructured play
   d. Logical reasoning and problem-solving

8. A group of prekindergarten students is learning about patterns by arranging beads on a string after watching a demonstration from the teacher. Which of the following teacher questions would best promote inquiry and logical reasoning skills as students work?

   a. "What color beads are you using?"
   b. "Why did you choose this bead to go next in your pattern?"
   c. "What kind of pattern are you making with your beads?"
   d. "Which bead comes next in your pattern?"

9. A kindergarten class activity involves building shapes using a variety of materials. As students work, the teacher conducts observations using a checklist to determine their mastery of the concept. This strategy is an example of which of the following?

   a. Diagnostic assessment
   b. Summative assessment
   c. Formative assessment
   d. Authentic assessment

10. Which of the following best describes the primary purpose of using student portfolios as a method of assessment?

   a. To evaluate students' individual progress and development over time
   b. To avoid personal bias when assessing student progress
   c. To assess students' mastery of a particular skill in a natural setting
   d. To determine students' level of background knowledge

11. **Throughout instruction, a second-grade teacher uses a variety of strategies to determine students' level of understanding and engagement, such as total participation activities, checks for understanding, and exit tickets at the end of each lesson. In doing so, the teacher uses formative assessments to:**

    a. Determine students' mastery of a particular skill or concept
    b. Holistically evaluate student progress and development
    c. Align assessments to state and district academic standards
    d. Evaluate instructional effectiveness and make adjustments as necessary

12. **In preparation for the upcoming standardized assessment in English language arts, a third-grade teacher uses formative assessments, short quizzes, and reflection activities to determine students' understanding of the content. Which of the following best describes the intended purpose for implementing these strategies?**

    a. Creating an inclusive and engaging learning atmosphere
    b. Identifying areas of whole-class and individual student need
    c. Determining the need for testing accommodations prior to the standardized assessment
    d. Updating students' families on overall progress and development

13. **A fourth-grade teacher is preparing to administer an end-of-unit test to a linguistically diverse group of students. To ensure ethical assessment practices, which of the following is the teacher responsible to provide to the English language learners in her class?**

    a. The option to take the test in their preferred language
    b. The opportunity to retake the test if necessary to improve students' grades
    c. A qualified interpreter to translate the test
    d. Linguistic aids aligned with students' English language proficiency levels

14. **A third-grade student has been medically diagnosed with dyslexia, which often impacts her decoding and processing skills when reading. Which of the following would be considered a reasonable accommodation to support this student's learning needs when taking assessments?**

    a. Preferential seating near the front of the classroom
    b. An alternative testing location
    c. Verbal test directions and questions
    d. Reduced or simplified test questions

15. **Each week, a second-grade teacher inputs students' performance data into an online gradebook. Which of the following best describes how this is beneficial?**

    a. Identifying areas of individual and whole-class need to inform future instruction
    b. Providing families with documentation of student progress
    c. Providing students with multiple opportunities to achieve success
    d. Formatively assessing students' progress toward achieving academic benchmarks

16. **A kindergarten teacher uses a digital app to provide families with daily updates on students' progress, the curriculum, and important classroom information. Students' families can also use the app to message the teacher individually with questions and concerns regarding their children's performance. Which of the following best describes the benefit of using this resource for communication?**

    a. Establishing and maintaining partnerships with families to enhance student learning and development
    b. Documenting interactions with students' families
    c. Improving students' behavior in the classroom
    d. Encouraging students' families to become active participants in the education program

17. Which of the following strategies would best incorporate students' cultural and linguistic diversities into instruction?

a. Establishing and maintaining frequent communication with students' families
b. Collaborating with grade-level colleagues to host a culture day for students
c. Selecting instructional materials and resources that reflect students' backgrounds
d. Teaching about the customs, traditions, and values of different cultures around the world

18. A third-grade English language learner communicates fluently with her classmates in English. However, the teacher has noticed that this student continues to have difficulty in class, particularly with reading comprehension and writing assignments. Which of the following is the most likely reason this student struggles academically despite being socially fluent in English?

a. The student gets distracted by her peers and struggles to focus.
b. Academic English language is typically more difficult to acquire.
c. The students' parents do not encourage her to learn English.
d. Instruction lacks adequate linguistic supports.

19. A first-grade teacher works with a beginner-level ELL student who has minimal previous experience with the English language. After reading an illustrated book aloud to the class, the teacher asks the student to sort events from the story using pictures and a graphic organizer. The student is then asked to describe his favorite character to his table partner. These activities demonstrate the teacher's understanding of which of the following in regard to implications for teaching ELL students?

a. Beginner-level ELLs can understand general language related to the content area and can produce short, simple sentences.
b. It is important to incorporate linguistic aids to help beginner-level ELLs.
c. Social language is developed in collaborative settings for beginner-level ELLs
d. Academic language is typically more difficult for ELLs to acquire

20. A second-grade teacher has noticed that one student consistently struggles to focus in class. The student often fidgets, speaks out of turn, and has difficulty staying in her seat. The student also has difficulty with reading comprehension, and is not developing at a grade-level-appropriate pace. This may be indicative of which of the following?

a. The student's family does not reinforce learning at home
b. A potential behavioral disorder that impedes effective learning
c. A learning disability that impacts literacy skills
d. Inadequate classroom management procedures

21. A third-grade student has a physical health impairment that makes lengthy writing assignments time-consuming and painful. Which of the following accommodations would best support this student's ability to participate in writing activities?

a. Reducing the length requirement of writing assignments
b. Preferential seating in the front of the classroom
c. The option to complete an alternative assignment
d. Speech-to-text technology

22. A fourth-grade general education teacher has been asked to contribute to the development of an Individualized Education Program (IEP) for one of her students. Which of the following best describes the teacher's responsibilities as a contributor in this process?

a. To become aware of the student's accommodations for future instructional planning
b. To provide information and input regarding curriculum, accommodations and supports, as well as the student's individual progress
c. To learn strategies for supporting the student's learning needs during instruction
d. To establish a sense of partnership with the student's family

Collaboration and Professionalism

23. A prekindergarten teacher maintains an online blog to document and share teaching experiences, instructional strategies, and classroom activities. The teacher wants to post photos of a recent activity her students completed in class. Before posting the photos, which of the following measures must the teacher take in order to protect students' right to privacy?

   a. Request permission from the school administration to create the post
   b. Remove students' faces from the photos
   c. Inform students' families that pictures of a classroom activity will be posted online
   d. Ensure that the photos do not include students' personally identifiable information

24. A second-grade student has been exhibiting disruptive behavior in class. According to the family systems theory, which of the following should the teacher examine first to determine the cause of such behavior?

   a. The dynamics of and interactions within the student's family
   b. The student's relationships with other classmates
   c. The cognitive developmental level of the student
   d. The effectiveness of current classroom management procedures

25. A kindergarten teacher strives to create positive, collaborative relationships with students' families. To achieve this, the teacher utilizes multiple methods of communication, including a class website, a paper-based newsletter, phone calls, emails, and in-person conferences. Which of the following best describes how this helps establish and maintain such relationships?

   a. Using cross-culturally competent communication practices
   b. Meeting the communication needs of all students' families
   c. Documenting interactions for use in family conferences
   d. Gaining insight into students' backgrounds, experiences, and individual learning needs

26. To develop culturally competent teaching practices, teachers must first:

   a. Address the various communication needs of students' families
   b. Recognize and eliminate their own biases and assumptions toward other cultures
   c. Work with colleagues in developing instructional strategies to accommodate diverse learning needs
   d. Incorporate elements of students' culture into instruction

27. A fourth-grade teacher notices that one of her students is often tired in class and has been coming to school without lunch. Upon contacting the student's family, the teacher has learned that they have been struggling financially and often cannot afford to buy food. Which of the following actions should the teacher take in response to this situation?

   a. Provide the family with information regarding community food-assistance programs.
   b. Refer the student's family to the school guidance counselor for assistance.
   c. Offer to provide lunch for the student.
   d. Ask the administration to add the student to the school's free and reduced lunch program.

28. A first-grade teacher is new to the profession and is working to develop best practices for promoting student learning and development. Which of the following would best help this teacher learn about effective strategies, resources, and approaches from more experienced colleagues in the building?

   a. Consulting the school website for information regarding the school mission and the roles of various professionals in the school building
   b. Participating in an online discussion board related to early childhood education
   c. Becoming involved in professional learning communities (PLCs) within the school
   d. Asking colleagues to borrow their lesson plans to get ideas on effective instructional strategies

29. A third-grade teacher works with a group of students that have a diverse range of backgrounds, experiences, and needs. At the beginning of the school year, the teacher included students in the creation of classroom norms and expectations. In addition, the teacher begins each school day with a brief meeting in which students are invited to share thoughts and ideas and ask questions. Implementing these strategies will likely contribute to which of the following?

   a. A flexible and student-directed learning environment
   b. Positive feedback on the teacher's end-of-year evaluation
   c. Increased family involvement in the education program
   d. Establishing a positive social context for learning

30. Which of the following best represents the ultimate goal of the federally funded program, Head Start?

   a. Improve student achievement on standardized assessments
   b. Provide low-income families with child care
   c. Promote the learning and development of prekindergarten students from socioeconomically disadvantaged backgrounds
   d. Provide universal access to preschool

31. According to the National Association for the Education of Young Children (NAEYC) Code of Ethical Conduct, which of the following should be the focus of assessments?

   a. Measuring students' progress in relation to same-age peers
   b. Using a variety of information sources to assess students' overall learning and development
   c. Providing all students with uniform assessments to ensure objectivity
   d. Creating a learning environment focused on inclusivity and appreciation for differences

32. A third-grade teacher has noticed that one of her students seems particularly agitated and hostile in class lately. This student is typically outgoing and friendly, but has recently been refusing to complete classwork and lashing out in anger toward the teacher and classmates. Yesterday, the student came to class with a bruise on his arm. Which of the following represents the teacher's legal and professional responsibility in this situation?

   a. Contact the student's family to discuss her concerns
   b. Provide the student's family with information regarding community support resources
   c. Ask colleagues if they have also noticed any changes in the student's behavior
   d. Report her suspicions to the appropriate agency

33. A second-grade teacher has noticed that one of her students is struggling with literacy skill development and is beginning to fall behind academically as a result. The teacher has tried implementing multiple teaching strategies and learning supports, but suspects the student may have an undiagnosed learning disability. Which of the following best describes how the teacher could advocate for this student to meet his learning needs?

   a. Refer the student for an initial evaluation to determine the need for special education services.
   b. Contact the student's family to discuss her concerns.
   c. Continue to observe and document the student's progress.
   d. Suggest to the administration that the student repeat second grade.

34. A veteran teacher wants to learn more about available educational technology resources to improve her instruction and create a more engaging learning experience. Which of the following professional development opportunities would be most beneficial?

   a. Keep a daily self-reflection journal.
   b. Research the benefits of using technology in the classroom.
   c. Collaborate with a mentor teacher within the school building.
   d. Participate in a professional development workshop focused on educational technology.

35. A kindergarten teacher is new to the profession and is working to develop effective strategies for meeting students' learning and developmental needs. Which of the following professionals in the school building would be most beneficial in helping this teacher develop his pedagogical practice?

   a. The school vice principal
   b. A mentor teacher
   c. The school special education teacher
   d. The grade-level department chair

36. After each lesson, a first-grade teacher records notes in a journal regarding the effectiveness of instructional strategies, activities, and assessments, as well as overall student engagement. Which of the following best describes the benefit of such self-reflection?

   a. Collecting artifacts that the teacher can include in her Domain 4 portfolio
   b. Documenting students' progress for use in family conferences
   c. Informing future instructional planning to enhance student learning and development
   d. Ensuring that lesson activities prepare students for the summative assessment

Language and Literacy Development

37. A kindergarten teacher is planning a lesson on identifying key details and literary elements within a fictional text. The teacher will use a grade-level-appropriate work of children's literature, and will include a read-aloud followed by several corresponding activities. According to Pennsylvania's PreK-4 standards in language arts, the teacher can reasonably expect students to do which of the following by the end of the lesson?

   a. Make inferences based upon literary techniques found in the text.
   b. Cite evidence from the text to support what it says explicitly.
   c. Determine the moral of the story and explain how it is conveyed in the text.
   d. Identify characters, setting, and major events of the story with prompting and support.

38. A prekindergarten teacher uses daily circle time for reading aloud to students. When introducing new vocabulary words from a text, the teacher pauses to explain their meaning, and adds them to the class word wall with corresponding pictures. After each read-aloud, the teacher also asks students to discuss their favorite parts of the story. By implementing these strategies, the teacher demonstrates understanding of which of the following?

   a. Individual differences in developmental levels among young children
   b. The role of receptive and expressive language in literacy development
   c. Interventions for supporting literacy development in struggling students
   d. The importance of differentiating instruction to align with individual students' needs

39. A first-grade teacher works with students of varying levels of literacy skill development. Which of the following strategies would likely best address these students' individual learning needs to build fluency and promote reading comprehension skills?

   a. Homogenous flexible grouping with leveled texts
   b. Scheduling daily class read-aloud time
   c. Creating a print-rich environment
   d. Providing struggling students with individualized instruction

40. A third-grade teacher strives to incorporate opportunities for students to engage in reading, writing, speaking, and listening throughout the school day. For example, students keep an observation journal for science lessons, read grade-level-appropriate current-event articles in social studies, and frequently solve word problems during math lessons. Which of the following best describes how implementing these strategies is beneficial in creating a literate environment for students?

a. Promoting the development of expressive and receptive language skills
b. Differentiating instructional activities to meet students' learning preferences
c. Making overt connections between the curriculum and students' lives
d. Infusing literacy throughout the curriculum

41. Which of the following instructional strategies likely best promotes development of phonemic awareness in early childhood students?

a. Providing multiple opportunities for students to engage in writing activities
b. Asking students to sequence the events of a story using pictures
c. Incorporating activities such as rhymes, songs, and alphabet games
d. Creating a print-rich environment using labels, word walls, posters, and bulletin boards

42. A kindergarten teacher reads a series of vocabulary words aloud and asks students to identify which sound they hear at the beginning of each one. In doing so, this teacher is assessing which of the following skills?

a. Expressive language
b. Students' ability to identify high-frequency words
c. Phonemic isolation
d. Reading comprehension

43. A second-grade teacher is planning a lesson focused on identifying the main idea of an informational text. After carefully researching, the teacher chooses a developmentally appropriate multi-paragraph online article about the impacts of environmental changes. For new vocabulary words, the teacher plans to scaffold definitions and provide several examples for additional clarification. In doing so, this teacher demonstrates knowledge of which of the following?

a. Evidence-based strategies for selecting instructional materials that are aligned with state learning standards and appropriate for meeting students' needs in language and literacy
b. Differentiating instruction to accommodate a variety of skills and ability levels in literacy
c. Methods for developing phonological awareness in young children
d. Strategies for emphasizing the connection between spoken and written language

44. A first-grade teacher has noticed that one student struggles to recall stories in the correct sequence. The student often mixes up events from the beginning, middle, and end of the story, and confuses important connecting details. Which of the following strategies would likely best support this student's language skill development in this area?

a. Fostering personal connections between the student's life and events from stories
b. Providing the student aids such as graphic organizers, story maps, and pictures that correspond with events from stories
c. Exposing the student to a variety of texts relevant to her personal interests
d. Reading aloud to the student individually and asking open-ended questions about the story

45. A fourth-grade teacher has just completed a unit focused on writing narratives, and wants to determine whether students mastered the concept of using transitional phrases to organize events in a story. Which of the following assessment approaches would be most appropriate?

    a. Administering a self-selected response exam
    b. Assigning an oral presentation about an informational topic
    c. Instructing students to write an original story
    d. Assigning a research project on a topic of students' choosing

46. Which of the following strategies would best demonstrate to prekindergarten students the purpose and use of a printed book?

    a. Taking a class trip to the school library
    b. Asking students to bring in their favorite book from home
    c. Modeling how to hold a book, turn pages, read from left to right, and pointing out key characteristics
    d. Incorporating time for reading aloud into the school day

47. A first-grade student is having difficulty blending sounds of multisyllabic words. When asked to read such words aloud, he pronounces each letter sound independently. Which of the following intervention strategies would likely best promote the development of this skill?

    a. Scaffolding definitions of new vocabulary words
    b. Providing corresponding pictures for vocabulary words to clarify meaning
    c. Having the student practice spelling words with letter tiles, reading the words aloud, and clapping out syllables
    d. Pointing out examples of rhyming words and alliteration in poems and stories

48. A kindergarten teacher uses color-coded letter cards to spell a word and asks students to read it aloud. The teacher then replaces one letter card with a different one, and asks students to identify the new word. For example, after spelling the word "cat," the teacher replaces the letter "c" with "b" and asks students to read the new word. This strategy is likely intended to teach which of the following skills?

    a. Phoneme substitution
    b. Alliteration
    c. Identification of rhyming words
    d. The alphabetic principle

49. Which of the following strategies would likely be most effective in developing awareness of the alphabetic principle among prekindergarten students?

    a. Teaching the concepts of consonants and vowels separately
    b. Introducing and focusing lessons on new letters and sounds individually, or a few at a time
    c. Using rhyming games and songs to emphasize individual sounds within words
    d. Using manipulatives to teach segmenting and blending of multisyllabic words

50. The suffixes "-able," "-ful," and "-er" are examples of which of the following?

    a. Syllables
    b. Diphthongs
    c. Blends
    d. Morphemes

51. A fourth-grade student has difficulty distinguishing between homophones, particularly during writing activities. For example, when writing, she often mixes up such words as "they're," "there," and "their"; "here" and "hear"; and "eight" and "ate." Which of the following interventions would likely best address this issue?

 a. Assigning vocabulary lists that include frequently confused homophones and administering weekly spelling tests
 b. Implementing sentence dictation exercises, providing visual aids, and reviewing the morphology of frequently confused homophones
 c. Having the student practice reading aloud from a variety of texts that incorporate homophones
 d. Asking the student to practice segmenting complex multisyllabic words

52. A first-grade teacher has included some non-decodable words on students' weekly vocabulary list. Each day, the teacher reviews these words using flashcards as a whole-class activity. During class circle time, the teacher reads aloud a story that incorporates these vocabulary words. Students also practice tracing and writing the new words, as well as using them in sentences. These strategies are likely intended to promote the development of which of the following skills?

 a. Recognizing consonant-vowel-consonant (CVC) words as individual units
 b. Morpheme division in multisyllabic words
 c. Irregular sight word recognition
 d. Distinguishing between digraphs and blends

53. A second-grade teacher wants to measure students' progress toward reaching academic benchmarks related to expressing opinions through writing. Which of the following assessment practices would be most effective in informally evaluating this skill?

 a. Reviewing students' responses to journal prompts focused on opinion writing
 b. Measuring students' accuracy as they complete sentence dictation exercises
 c. Observing students as they peer-edit one another's writing
 d. Administering a brief constructed-response exam on a variety of writing topics

54. When reading grade-level texts, a third-grade student struggles to recognize both new and familiar vocabulary words. The student reads slowly, and often has trouble deriving meaning from what he has read. Based upon this information, this student appears to have difficulty with which of the following skills?

 a. Irregular sight word recognition
 b. Prosody
 c. Phonemic awareness
 d. Automaticity

55. A second-grade teacher is planning a reader's theater in which students will act out the story of a familiar text. Students will practice in small groups throughout the week, and will be encouraged to focus on expression, inflection, and intonation as they read the story's dialogue. This activity is most likely intended to promote the development of which of the following skills?

 a. Prosody
 b. Automaticity
 c. Sight word recognition
 d. Phonological awareness

56. A fourth-grade teacher schedules class time every day for self-selected reading. Students can bring in a book from home, or choose one from either the classroom or school library. Which of the following best describes how this strategy contributes to students' vocabulary and reading comprehension skill development?

   a. Ensuring students spend as much time as possible engaging in reading
   b. Immersing students in a print-rich environment
   c. Allowing students to read books aligned with their level of literacy development
   d. Encouraging students to read independently

57. A first-grade teacher is planning instruction focused on the structural analysis of words to promote vocabulary acquisition and decoding skills. Which of the following strategies would be most effective in achieving this?

   a. Using rhymes and songs to promote phonemic awareness
   b. Having the class participate in a choral reading of a familiar text
   c. Creating a word-building game in which students construct vocabulary from a set of root words and affixes
   d. Holding a reader's theater in which students act out dialogue from a story

58. A third-grade teacher is planning a unit in which students will independently read a work of fictional literature. Which of the following prereading strategies would likely be most effective in enhancing students' overall comprehension of the text?

   a. Administering a diagnostic exam to determine students' level of literacy development
   b. Providing students with a word bank of unfamiliar vocabulary from the text
   c. Scaffolding the text by chunking it into smaller parts
   d. Having students complete an anticipation guide prior to reading the text

59. A second-grade teacher would like to promote students' ability to read independently and retell stories by recalling major details, such as the characters, plot, setting, and central message. Which of the following instructional resources would be most beneficial in achieving this?

   a. Story maps that students can complete as they read
   b. Comprehension questions that correspond with each story
   c. Anticipation guides for students to complete prior to engaging in reading
   d. Pretests to activate students' prior knowledge

60. A fourth-grade class is reading an informational text about the role of local, state, and national government in daily life. As they read, the teacher instructs students to highlight unfamiliar vocabulary words, circle important information, and write down questions about parts they do not understand. Which of the following skills does this promote?

   a. Phonological processing
   b. Structural analysis
   c. Critical analysis
   d. Contextual analysis

61. A second-grade teacher is planning a unit on English grammatical conventions to ultimately develop students' writing skills. Before beginning the unit, the teacher administers a pretest that includes questions about capitalization, punctuation, and spelling. Which of the following best describes how the data from this pretest will improve instructional effectiveness?

   a. Providing students with context regarding what they will be learning
   b. Determining students' areas of strengths and needs to inform instructional planning
   c. Exposing students to material that will appear on the summative assessment
   d. Promoting students' curiosity and interest in the upcoming unit

62. A third-grade teacher is planning a lesson in which students will independently read an informational text. Prior to beginning the lesson, the teacher will review new vocabulary words and add them to the class word wall. As students read the text, they will fill out a guided summary frame. Afterward, students will discuss their summaries with a table partner. These strategies are likely intended to promote students' skills in which of the following areas?

a. Irregular sight word recognition
b. Using text features to locate information
c. Comprehension of academic language
d. Understanding the relationship between written and spoken language

63. When reading aloud to students, a kindergarten teacher makes sure to speak expressively by pausing at the end of each sentence, changing intonation, and correlating inflection with differences in punctuation within the text. In doing so, the teacher models which of the following?

a. The correct usage of academic language
b. Differences in writing styles of literary and informational texts
c. Interest and enthusiasm for reading
d. The relationship between English grammatical conventions in written and spoken language

64. Which of the following strategies would likely be most effective in teaching prekindergarten students to listen responsively to directions?

a. Implementing listening games with simple multi-step directions
b. Choral reading poems, rhymes, and familiar stories
c. Changing intonation when giving verbal directions
d. Using gestures, body language, and visual cues

65. A kindergarten student has difficulty enunciating words, which is impacting her ability to communicate clearly and intelligibly. For example, she often mumbles words and pronounces both the letters "r" and "l" as "w". Which of the following interventions would be most effective in developing this student's speaking skills?

a. Pairing the student with another who can provide scaffolding during speaking activities
b. Reviewing the pronunciation of regular and irregular sight words
c. Providing the student with individualized instruction focused on letter and word sounds
d. Implementing assistive technology to alleviate the student's speech difficulties

66. A third-grade teacher is planning a unit in which students will be assigned to write fictional narratives. Prior to engaging in writing, the teacher wants to develop students' ability to gather and coherently organize ideas. Which of the following strategies would likely be most effective in achieving this?

a. Demonstrating and having students practice the steps of the research process
b. Providing students with a graphic organizer as a pre-writing activity
c. Incorporating peer-editing opportunities throughout the writing process
d. Conferencing individually with students to provide feedback on their narratives

Social Studies

67. Which of the following strategies would best introduce the concept that organizations have leaders with specific roles to kindergarten students?

    a. Assigning each student a weekly classroom job
    b. Identifying and discussing the roles of the principal, guidance counselor, school nurse, and other professionals in the school building
    c. Explaining the purpose of rules in maintaining safety and order
    d. Providing examples of the role of local, state, and national government in daily life

68. A second-grade teacher is planning a unit focused on markets and economic systems. After a field trip to the grocery store, students will participate in a classroom market with a limited number of available items. Each student will be given pretend money to spend, and will plan a budget, as well as a list of items they intend to purchase. By implementing these strategies, the teacher demonstrates knowledge of which of the following?

    a. Techniques for selecting appropriate activities to support children's development and fostering connections between social studies and other content areas
    b. Criteria for designing and adapting tools and technologies to differentiate instruction
    c. Understanding of how to use formative assessment throughout instruction to evaluate student understanding and engagement
    d. Strategies for supporting children's learning of major concepts related to government

69. A third-grade teacher is planning a lesson on identifying and describing natural physical characteristics. It will include four learning stations. In the first station, students will read a passage on the topic and answer some corresponding comprehension questions. The second station will include a short video describing various landforms. Students will work together in the third station to label a map, and will draw several landforms in the fourth station. By implementing this strategy, the teacher does which of the following?

    a. Modifies instruction to accommodate students' varying abilities
    b. Provides active-learning experiences to foster student engagement
    c. Recognizes the importance of incorporating play into instruction for young children
    d. Differentiates instruction to align with students' learning styles, needs, and preferences

70. After completing a unit focused on the human characteristics of places and regions, a fourth-grade class will create an original settlement in a real or imagined region. Students will be asked to determine the population of the area, choose economic activities based on the natural physical characteristics of the region, decide on a political system, and establish a culture. This instructional activity is an example of which of the following assessment approaches?

    a. Total participation activity
    b. Formative assessment
    c. Project-based summative assessment
    d. Benchmark assessment

71. A first-grade teacher has organized a food drive in which students are encouraged to bring in cans of nonperishable food for donation. Which of the following best describes the benefit of such a project?

    a. Achieving academic benchmarks related to civic rights and responsibilities
    b. Developing students' civic values through public service
    c. Providing hands-on learning experiences that incorporate student choice
    d. Instilling a sense of personal responsibility among students

72. **A fourth-grade teacher is planning a lesson on locating and describing the physical features of various regions throughout the United States. In a virtual activity, students will use an online satellite map to locate and explore several physical landmarks, and will complete an observation log of their findings. By implementing this activity, the teacher applies knowledge of which of the following?**

 a. Methods for differentiating instruction to appeal to multiple learning styles
 b. Strategies for creating student-led learning opportunities
 c. Knowledge of appropriate assessment tools in social studies and how to utilize them for specific purposes
 d. Selecting technologies to support children's learning in using and interpreting maps for geographic inquiry

73. **Which of the following strategies would best support first-grade students' understanding of slogans, symbols, and mottos that represent the state of Pennsylvania?**

 a. Providing opportunities to research the state's cultural diversity
 b. Discussing how events from Pennsylvania's history impact the present-day community
 c. Identifying state slogans, symbols, and mottos in photographs, artifacts, documents, and items from events in the state
 d. Having students draw and color images of symbols, slogans, and mottos that represent the state

74. **A second-grade teacher is planning an economics lesson, and wants to develop students' understanding of opportunity cost. Which of the following instructional activities would likely best achieve this goal?**

 a. A collaborative think-aloud activity in which students are given pretend money and discuss whether to save it or spend it on a desired item
 b. A project in which students create a budget and plan an imaginary trip
 c. A class discussion regarding the differences between wants and needs in a community
 d. A brainstorming activity in which students devise creative ways to earn extra money

Arts and Humanities

75. **A prekindergarten teacher leads the class in singing a song that incorporates movement and dance. Throughout the song, students can run in place, jump, wave their arms, and kick their legs. The teacher likely selected this song to promote students' development of which of the following?**

 a. Phonological awareness
 b. Fine motor skills
 c. Gross motor skills
 d. Auditory discrimination

76. **During an unstructured art activity, a kindergarten teacher walks around the room and asks individual students about their projects. One student is creating a collage using colored paper, glitter, and beads. Which of the following prompts best fosters this student's creative development?**

 a. "What materials are you using for this project?"
 b. "Why don't you try adding a bit more color here?"
 c. "That's a very interesting landscape you're making."
 d. "Tell me about your project. What made you think of it?"

77. A prekindergarten teacher has brought in several costumes for students to use for dressing up, as well as props to represent a restaurant, bank, doctor's office, and kitchen. This teacher demonstrates understanding of which of the following?

a. Strategies for developing gross and fine motor skills in early childhood students
b. The importance of dramatic play for early childhood development
c. Activities for supporting cross-curricular learning
d. Effective assessment approaches in arts and humanities

78. To best promote creative expression and development among young children, it is important to ensure that art materials in the classroom are:

a. Used to supplement regular instruction
b. Varied, readily accessible, and plentiful
c. Provided sparingly to sustain student engagement
d. Limited to one medium at a time to prevent conflict among students

79. A first-grade teacher wants to monitor individual students' progress in developing several artistic skills throughout the school year. Which of the following assessment approaches would best achieve this goal?

a. Collecting samples of students' artwork to create individual portfolios
b. Periodically observing students using a checklist to assess skill development
c. Grading students based on participation in art projects
d. A multiple-choice quiz to determine students' knowledge of key vocabulary related to various forms of art

80. Some basic elements of music that an early childhood educator should know include:

a. Bass, treble, alto, and soprano
b. Common instruments and how to read music
c. Rhythm, melody, harmony, timbre, texture, and form
d. Strings, percussion, woodwinds, and bass

81. A second-grade teacher is planning a lesson on the life cycle of plants. Which of the following strategies would best incorporate arts and humanities into this lesson?

a. Having students participate in a class nature walk to observe and record various types of plants
b. Allowing students to observe the details of various plants using a microscope
c. Leading a class discussion on the similarities and differences between the life cycles of plants and animals
d. Having students create paintings or drawings to depict each stage of the plant life cycle, and incorporating a song focused on the topic

Mathematics

82. A first-grade teacher is planning a lesson on telling time to the nearest half hour. Before acquiring this skill, students must first have mastered which of the following concepts?

a. Pattern recognition properties of operations
b. The difference between a digital and analog clock
c. Estimation and counting upward by fives
d. Number recognition and counting

83. A prekindergarten teacher places two groups of eight one-unit cubes on a table. In one group, the cubes are arranged neatly into two small rows of four. In the other group, the cubes are spread far apart. When asked which group has more cubes, students chose the pile in which the cubes were spread apart. Which of the following best explains the reason for the students' answer?

    a. The teacher did not ask students to count the unit cubes individually.
    b. Students have not yet learned one-to-one correspondence.
    c. Prekindergarten students have not yet developed an understanding of conservation.
    d. Students did not have the opportunity to physically manipulate the unit cubes.

84. To prepare for an art activity, a kindergarten teacher selects three students to pass out materials. These students are instructed to make sure everyone in the class receives one cup of crayons, one pair of scissors, and one glue stick. In asking students to pass out an equal number of materials to each classmate, the teacher promotes the development of which of the following skills?

    a. Number sequence
    b. Pattern recognition
    c. Problem-solving
    d. Gathering, organizing, and displaying data

85. A second-grade teacher is planning a lesson on using place-value concepts to represent numbers of tens and ones. Which of the following learning materials would be most developmentally appropriate in promoting students' understanding of this concept?

    a. Base-ten blocks
    b. Pretend money
    c. A geoboard and rubber bands
    d. Number strips

86. In a first-grade art class, students are working on a project in which they draw and cut out squares, rectangles, trapezoids, and triangles to create an original mosaic piece. This teacher fosters students' ability to:

    a. Use logical reasoning skills to engage in problem-solving
    b. Make connections between mathematics and other content areas
    c. Distinguish between two- and three-dimensional shapes
    d. Use knowledge of fractions to divide shapes into halves and quarters

87. A third-grade teacher is planning a unit to introduce the concept of equivalent fractions. Prior to instruction, the teacher administers a pretest containing material from the upcoming unit. The teacher plans to use the data from the pretest to group students based on ability for learning activities. The teacher is likely using the assessment results to:

    a. Determine students' progress toward achieving academic standards.
    b. Differentiate instruction and implement appropriate accommodations.
    c. Align instructional activities with students' learning styles.
    d. Familiarize students with the new material prior to beginning the unit.

88. At the end of the first semester, a second-grade teacher administers a formal exam that consists of all curriculum covered in the first half of the year. Which of the following best explains the purpose of using this assessment approach?

    a. To determine students' level of understanding throughout instruction
    b. To assess students' background knowledge and level of understanding
    c. To provide the teacher with immediate feedback regarding instructional effectiveness
    d. To measure students' progress in relation to achieving district and state academic standards

89. During a lesson on two- and three-dimensional shapes, a second-grade teacher leads students around the school and asks them to identify triangles, quadrilaterals, pentagons, cubes, and hexagons within the architecture of the building. In doing so, this teacher demonstrates to students which of the following concepts?

    a. How to develop mathematical communication skills
    b. Connections between mathematics and other content areas
    c. Applications of mathematics in real-world contexts
    d. Problem-solving strategies

90. During a lesson on representing and interpreting data using charts, a first-grade teacher shows students a pictograph depicting students' favorite animals, and verbally models how to read the information. Then, the teacher shows students another pictograph representing students' favorite colors, and asks open-ended questions about the information presented. Which of the following is most likely the teacher's intention in implementing these strategies?

    a. Developing students' mathematical communication skills
    b. Demonstrating the applications of mathematics in real-world contexts
    c. Formatively assessing students' understanding of the lesson
    d. Fostering connections between mathematics and other content areas

91. A kindergarten student has difficulty arranging numbers in ascending order. Which of the following strategies would likely best support development of this skill?

    a. Leading the class in counting songs, rhymes, and chants
    b. Encouraging rote memorization using flash cards
    c. Having the student practice representing numbers using a number chart and counting chips
    d. Incorporating counting activities into unstructured play time

92. Which of the following strategies would likely be most effective in promoting the concept of sorting objects among prekindergarten students?

    a. Asking students to compare and contrast the features of different shapes
    b. Explicitly teaching vocabulary related to similarities and differences
    c. Having students participate in a scavenger hunt in which they locate specific items
    d. Modeling putting away classroom materials in labeled bins

93. Before introducing a new geometry unit, a first-grade teacher gives each student a geoboard and asks them to think of and create as many shapes as they can using rubber bands. This activity establishes a foundation of understanding for developing which of the following mathematical skills?

    a. Partitioning shapes into halves and quarters
    b. Identifying two-dimensional shapes based on their attributes
    c. Using mathematical language to explain reasoning
    d. Comparing the attributes of two- and three-dimensional figures

94. During a math lesson, a second-grade teacher writes and solves an addition problem on the board in the following two ways:

$$34 + 58 = 92$$

$$30 + 50 = 80 \qquad 8 + 4 = 12 \qquad 80 + 12 = 92$$

By demonstrating that numbers can be added in different ways, this teacher promotes students' learning and development of which of the following skills?

a. Algebraic thinking
b. Estimation and rounding numbers to the nearest ten
c. Cardinality and sequencing
d. Data analysis and representation

95. A prekindergarten teacher wants to begin developing students' understanding of measurement. Which of the following activities would likely best demonstrate this concept?

a. Providing students with yardsticks and asking them to measure the length of the classroom
b. Demonstrating how to use various measurement tools
c. Engaging students in making a simple recipe in which ingredients must be measured
d. Explaining the difference between the metric and imperial systems

96. A kindergarten teacher shows students a jar of red, green, and blue beads. The teacher asks students to predict which color of bead is most prevalent in the jar, and records their responses on a bar graph. Which of the following developmental concepts is this strategy likely intended to support?

a. Estimation and measurement
b. Operations and algebraic thinking
c. Number sense and ordering
d. Data analysis and probability

Science

97. A first-grade teacher is demonstrating how various liquids and solids, including salt, oil, and ice, are combined with water. Which of the following questions would best promote student inquiry?

a. "Can we combine salt and water together?"
b. "Why did the ice begin to melt when it was placed in the water?"
c. "What do you think will happen if we combine oil and water?"
d. "Which substance dissolved the best in the water?"

98. A class of second-grade students is working in small groups to investigate whether music affects plant growth. Each group will be given four basil plants, and will expose two of them to music. As students begin the experiment, the teacher reminds each group to make sure that all plants receive equal amounts of sunlight and water. In doing so, this teacher reinforces which of the following concepts related to scientific learning?

a. The importance of verifiable evidence
b. How to properly follow the steps of the scientific method
c. How to accurately and consistently record observations during a scientific investigation
d. The importance of following directions when conducting an experiment

99. A kindergarten teacher is planning a unit on the characteristics of living and nonliving things in nature. Which of the following activities would be most developmentally appropriate in introducing this concept?

a. Leading a class nature walk focused on identifying living and nonliving things
b. Bringing in samples of living and nonliving things for students to observe
c. Creating a class art project using items from nature
d. Asking open-ended questions about the differences between living and nonliving things in a class discussion

100. A class of third-grade students is working in small groups to investigate the differences in pitch produced by striking glass bottles filled with varying amounts of water. In addition to scientific learning and development, such an activity is beneficial in demonstrating which of the following concepts?

   a. The characteristics of scientific inquiry
   b. The connection between scientific concepts and music
   c. The benefits of collaborative learning in strengthening concept knowledge
   d. The importance of following the scientific method when conducting an investigation

101. After giving a presentation on the characteristics of different terrestrial habitats, a first-grade teacher assigns students to work in pairs to illustrate a terrestrial habitat that includes all the necessary elements for living things to survive. As students work, the teacher wants to evaluate whether this activity is developmentally appropriate in meeting students' learning needs. Which of the following assessment approaches would be most effective?

   a. Observing students as they work, monitoring progress, and asking open-ended questions related to the assignment
   b. Collecting students' illustrations at the end of the lesson and grading them for accuracy
   c. Comparing students' work to district academic standards
   d. Assigning a self-reflection activity in which students assess their strengths and areas for improvement

102. A fourth-grade teacher is planning a lesson in which students will determine the distance a magnet must be from objects of varying weights in order to attract them. After posing the initial question, which of the following steps should the teacher have students take to properly follow the scientific method?

   a. Conduct the experiment and analyze the results.
   b. Discuss the potential outcomes of the investigation.
   c. Create a procedure and begin the experiment.
   d. Research the topic and formulate a hypothesis.

103. A prekindergarten teacher is planning a lesson on the characteristics of living things, and wants to promote students' ability to identify patterns among the features of animals of the same species. Which of the following activities would be most effective in doing so for this age group?

   a. Having students draw and label the parts of various species of animals
   b. Conducting a presentation on the life cycles of animals
   c. Showing various photographs of animals and leading a class discussion in which students compare and contrast their characteristics
   d. Bringing in a class pet and showing students how to care for it

104. A class of second-grade students is learning about the organ structures of various plants. Which scientific learning tool would best support their learning and development of this concept?

   a. A scale
   b. A microscope
   c. A reference guide on the structure of plants
   d. An observation log

105. A kindergarten teacher shows photos of several families and asks students to identify similar characteristics between them, such as hair and eye color. Such an activity introduces which of the following concepts to students of this age group?

   a. Adaptation
   b. The structure and function of living things
   c. Humans and the environment
   d. Heredity

106. A second-grade teacher is planning a unit on the basic needs of plants and animals in aquatic ecosystems. The teacher wants to incorporate a hands-on learning experience that allows students to interact with and compare different aquatic habitats, but due to their location, a field trip is not feasible. In which of the following ways could the teacher use technology to create a similar active learning experience?

a. Have students conduct online research about different aquatic habitats.
b. Create a slideshow presentation on the basic needs of plants and animals in aquatic ecosystems.
c. Have students participate in a virtual field trip in which they explore various aquatic habitats.
d. Show a documentary on the characteristics of aquatic ecosystems.

107. A prekindergarten teacher is leading an activity in which students use discarded items, such as tissue boxes, paper towel rolls, and egg cartons, to create art projects. This teacher is establishing a foundation for understanding which of the following environmental concepts?

a. Recycling as a form of waste management
b. The difference between renewable and nonrenewable resources
c. Ways in which litter contributes to pollution
d. How to distinguish between recyclable and nonrecyclable items

108. In a demonstration on the physical changes that occur when substances are heated or cooled, a first-grade teacher bakes cookies and asks students to observe what happens. After the experiment, one student asks why the cookies cannot be melted back into their original form once they have cooled. To address this question and provide clarification for the student, the teacher should review which of the following concepts related to the properties of matter?

a. The three states of matter (solid, liquid, gas).
b. Heating, melting, and cooling cause physical changes to matter.
c. Matter takes different shapes depending on its form.
d. Some physical changes to matter are reversible, and some are irreversible.

109. A prekindergarten teacher is planning instruction to develop students' foundational understanding of the properties of matter. Which of the following strategies would likely best promote curiosity and inquiry related to this concept?

a. Demonstrating the changes that occur when substances are heated or cooled
b. Providing a sensory bin that incorporates various types of matter
c. Leading a class discussion in which students compare and contrast the characteristics of different types of matter
d. Incorporating music and movement into instruction to promote student engagement

110. After completing a unit on the characteristics and processes of the water cycle, a fourth-grade teacher wants to evaluate students' understanding of the concept. Which of the following summative assessment approaches would be most developmentally appropriate for this age group?

a. Having students complete a self-reflection activity once the unit is complete
b. Administering a vocabulary quiz on key terms related to the water cycle
c. Having students work collaboratively to create a model of the water cycle
d. Assigning students to participate in a virtual field trip to various bodies of water

111. A kindergarten teacher is planning a thematic unit on the features of space. Throughout the unit, students will participate in activities such as reading various texts about space and space travel, listening to songs to learn the names of planets, and creating models of the moon, stars, sun, and planets using clay. Which of the following best describes how this instructional approach supports students' learning about objects in the solar system and universe?

    a. Integrating scientific instruction across content areas
    b. Providing multiple hands-on active learning experiences
    c. Using structured and unstructured play opportunities to strengthen learning
    d. Providing varied opportunities for students to demonstrate understanding

Health

112. According to the MyPlate model created by the USDA, children should be eating a variety of foods at each meal, with half of their plate consisting of which of the following?

    a. Dairy or a soy-based alternative
    b. Protein
    c. Fruits and vegetables
    d. Whole grains and legumes

113. In addition to physical health and development, daily exercise promotes which of the following among young children?

    a. Prosocial behaviors and creative self-expression
    b. Engagement and enthusiasm for learning
    c. Phonological processing skills
    d. Musical and artistic abilities

114. A prekindergarten teacher schedules time each day for unstructured play using the outdoor play equipment. Doing so best promotes the development of which skills related to physical fitness among this age group?

    a. Cooperative learning
    b. Gross motor skills
    c. Fine motor skills
    d. Language development and communication

115. A second-grade teacher wants to promote students' coordination of purposeful body movements. Which of the following activities would be most developmentally appropriate in achieving this goal?

    a. Having students practice throwing and catching a ball with a partner
    b. Providing students with opportunities to manipulate small objects
    c. Acting out finger plays
    d. Having students participate in interactive group games, such as kickball or follow-the-leader

116. Which of the following learning materials would be most effective in helping first-grade students develop their dexterity and strength for manipulating small objects?

    a. Outdoor play equipment, such as swings, slides, and tubes
    b. Scissors, pegboards, and puzzles
    c. Sporting equipment, such as basketballs, baseballs, and bats
    d. Labeled storage bins for sorting and classifying toys

117. A kindergarten teacher works with a group of students that have varying degrees of fine motor abilities. Which of the following strategies would be most effective in differentiating instruction to accommodate these variances and promote fine motor skill development among all students?

    a. Modifying activities to align with students' ability levels
    b. Allowing opportunities for student choice in learning activities
    c. Providing learning materials of various sizes
    d. Incorporating opportunities for both structured and unstructured play

118. In the dramatic play area of the classroom, a prekindergarten teacher includes pretend food items along with labeled bins for storage in the home kitchen. This is an example of a developmentally appropriate strategy for introducing which of the following concepts?

    a. The importance of portion control and variety in maintaining a healthy diet
    b. The idea that consuming unhealthy foods should always be avoided
    c. Categorization of foods based on taste and personal preference
    d. Identification of food groups and distinguishing between healthy and unhealthy foods

119. A physical education teacher uses a criterion-referenced assessment to measure various fitness skills among third-grade students, including strength, endurance, and flexibility. Which of the following best describes the benefit of implementing this approach?

    a. Objectively assessing students' fitness levels against a set of predetermined standards
    b. Evaluating students' overall engagement in health- and fitness-related activities
    c. Measuring students' progress in relation to one another
    d. Observing students as they apply physical fitness skills in a natural setting

120. A second-grade teacher has created an obstacle course for students to complete that includes several activities, such as walking on a balance beam, hula hooping, and jumping over hurdles. Throughout the activity, the teacher walks around to monitor students, using a checklist to evaluate students' ability to perform specific gross motor skills. This is an example of which of the following formative assessment approaches?

    a. A total-participation activity
    b. Observation
    c. Peer assessment
    d. Student self-assessment

121. When teaching young children about fire safety, it is important to review and practice:

    a. How to properly use a fire extinguisher
    b. Emergency evacuation procedures
    c. Ways to prevent fires from starting
    d. How to change batteries in a smoke detector

122. A first-grade teacher has been introducing fundamental practices of good health by having students practice basic hygiene routines throughout the school day and identifying various healthcare professionals. Which of the following additional strategies would likely best reinforce this concept?

    a. Inviting health experts into the classroom to discuss their professional roles
    b. Having students create collages of various tools used for maintaining good health
    c. Leading a class discussion on the characteristics of good and bad hygienic practices
    d. Modeling the appropriate use and storage of medicine

123. When planning physical activities for young children, which of the following must early childhood educators consider to foster positive attitudes toward exercise and movement?

    a. Differences in students' learning styles
    b. Strategies for integrating physical activity throughout the curriculum
    c. The availability and quality of necessary equipment
    d. Characteristics and abilities of students' developmental levels

124. While observing students during outdoor play time, a second-grade teacher notices that one student struggles with aim when throwing or kicking a ball. Which of the following strategies would likely best help this student improve these gross motor skills?

    a. Providing multiple materials and equipment to encourage active play
    b. Introducing the student to a variety of sport activities
    c. Having the student practice throwing and kicking toward targets of various sizes
    d. Implementing cooperative physical activities

125. Before letting young children use playground equipment, the teacher must:

    a. Schedule daily time for outdoor play
    b. Establish and review safety procedures for using outdoor play equipment
    c. Provide students with suggestions on ways to use the equipment
    d. Explain to students how using outdoor play equipment promotes physical fitness

126. In a prekindergarten classroom, several students have been absent recently due to a cold. This teachable moment could be used as an effective strategy for introducing which of the following concepts?

    a. How to recognize and avoid unsafe practices
    b. The purpose, proper use, and storage of medicine
    c. Environmental factors that impact health
    d. How infectious illnesses spread through germs

Answer Key and Explanations

Child Development, Learning, and Assessment

1. B: Behaviorism is rooted in the notion that humans are shaped by interactions with external stimuli from their environment. According to this theory, behavior can be conditioned using repeated positive and negative reinforcements, with the belief that individuals will ultimately engage in desired behaviors independently. In the classroom, teachers often use positive reinforcements such as prizes, praise, or rewards to elicit desired behavior among students, and negative reinforcements, such as loss of privileges, to discourage unwanted behaviors.

2. C: Young children learn by interacting with their environment in a hands-on setting. Learning stations provide multiple opportunities to do so, as students are encouraged to observe, explore, and engage with the world around them. This allows young children to formulate questions, test new ideas, and solve problems within their physical environment, thus developing learning experiences they can build upon. In addition, learning stations provide opportunities for structured and unstructured learning, both of which are integral in supporting the cognitive, physical, social, and emotional development of young children.

3. C: Jean Piaget believed that children pass through four distinct developmental stages, with each characterized by increasingly complex skills, abilities, and processes. According to his theory, prekindergarten students are in the preoperational stage of cognitive development. In this stage, young children typically engage in symbolic play as a means of organizing, representing, and understanding both their own thoughts and the world around them. Symbolic play is integral to promoting cognitive, social, emotional, physical, and behavioral development in preoperational children.

4. A: Initial learning experiences among young children typically occur within their family, cultural, and community environments. By self-educating to learn about the community, teachers can gain insight into their students' individual backgrounds, experiences, and needs. This will ultimately allow the teacher to develop more relevant, meaningful, and responsive learning experiences for all students. In addition, by learning more about students as individuals, teachers can begin recognizing areas in which they may have personal biases toward other groups and cultures, and work to eliminate them so as to create an inclusive, welcoming, and supportive learning environment.

5. C: Early childhood educators must understand the general cognitive, physical, social, and emotional developmental levels of their students while recognizing and adapting instruction to accommodate individual learning differences. In scaffolding instruction to align with varying abilities and needs, teachers provide the necessary support to promote learning and development for all students in a developmentally appropriate setting.

6. D: A culturally competent classroom is one in which the teacher recognizes the diversities among their individual students, and incorporates these differences accurately and respectfully throughout instruction. Reflecting students' diversities through developmentally appropriate instructional materials strengthens personal connections to make learning meaningful, relevant, and engaging for all students. This serves to deepen overall understanding, promote positive attitudes toward learning, and foster greater academic achievement.

7. C: Young children gain important cognitive, physical, social, and emotional skills by engaging in play, and therefore, it is imperative that the classroom environment support this developmental need by providing regular opportunities to do so. Developmentally appropriate instructional resources, materials, and equipment prioritize and support both structured and unstructured play, as both are necessary for creating and strengthening young children's connections to learning.

8. B: By modeling how to create a pattern using beads and providing a hands-on learning experience, the teacher implements age-appropriate and meaningful instruction. In asking open-ended questions as students work, the teacher effectively promotes inquiry and challenges students to employ logical reasoning skills to explain their choice in beads. This strategy also supports the development of students' language skills by encouraging them to elaborate upon their thought processes.

9. D: In the early childhood classroom, authentic assessments, such as observations, allow teachers to evaluate individual students' cognitive, physical, social, and emotional development in a natural setting. This allows for a more comprehensive and objective analysis of students' progress toward mastery of particular skills. The data gathered from authentic assessments is beneficial in setting goals for students based upon individual needs, skills, and abilities, as well as influencing future instructional planning.

10. A: Portfolios of students' work are beneficial in assessing individual progress and development across domains and content areas over a period of time. With this approach, the teacher can conduct an overall evaluation of the whole child, allowing the development of individualized goals for each student. While portfolios provide a holistic view of student achievement, they can be time-consuming to use effectively, and may be influenced by personal bias from the teacher.

11. D: Formative assessments provide teachers with valuable feedback throughout all stages of instruction regarding students' needs, levels of engagement, and overall understanding. This insight allows teachers to effectively differentiate, modify, and adjust instruction as necessary to improve overall effectiveness and enhance the learning experience for all students.

12. B: As students demonstrate understanding in various ways, it is important to implement multiple strategies for determining instructional effectiveness, engagement, and overall understanding. Doing so provides comprehensive feedback regarding individual and whole-class needs, allowing teachers to adjust instructional strategies and activities as necessary to support all students' success in learning.

13. D: Teachers have the professional and ethical responsibility to provide all students with a fair and equitable testing environment. As such, some students may require special accommodations to facilitate their ability to demonstrate mastery of a skill or concept. For ELL students, this entails implementing linguistic supports aligned with their levels of English language proficiency. Doing so supports these students' comprehension of testing material, allowing them to successfully complete the assessment.

14. C: Federal law mandates that students with disabilities or other special learning needs receive access to a free appropriate public education (FAPE) in the least restrictive environment. These students must be provided with accommodations or modifications to support their full participation in learning, including assessment, to the greatest possible extent. In this situation, providing the student with verbal test directions and questions is a reasonable accommodation to ensure that his or her learning disability does not interfere with the comprehension of material or ability to demonstrate understanding.

15. A: Establishing and frequently maintaining records of students' performance is integral to ensuring instructional effectiveness. Doing so allows teachers to identify areas of individual and whole-class need, and adjust instruction to improve the learning experience for all students. Using technological resources, such as online gradebooks, provides an efficient, objective, and accurate representation of student progress, thereby enhancing teachers' ability to interpret data and make informed decisions about future instruction.

16. A: Maintaining regular communication with students' families is integral to fostering the sense of partnership necessary for productive collaboration. Doing so helps to ensure that families feel informed and included in the learning and assessment process, thereby encouraging their active participation. Such a relationship allows teachers and families to effectively work together to find strategies, approaches, and resources to enhance students' learning and development.

17. C: Selecting instructional materials that reflect students' cultural and linguistic backgrounds helps create an inclusive learning environment in which all students feel respected, welcomed, and appreciated in their diversities. For English language learners, this strategy communicates that their primary language is valued as an asset for English language literacy development. Examples include incorporating texts in the students' primary language, teaching lessons that accurately portray their cultural and linguistic backgrounds, and integrating these diversities into the classroom environment, such as through posters, labels in the primary language, and decorations.

18. B: Social fluency typically develops prior to academic language proficiency among ELLs, as this style of communication is used more frequently in routine situations. Since academic language is content-specific and more complex than social language, it is often more difficult for ELL students to comprehend. Therefore, while the student likely developed social fluency by frequently communicating with peers in daily conversations on familiar topics, this style of language is not necessarily applicable in academic settings. Providing context when introducing new academic vocabulary, such as by calling upon students' background knowledge, gives ELLs a framework for reference to support comprehension and academic language acquisition.

19. A: According to Pennsylvania's PreK-12 English Language Proficiency Standards (ELPS), beginner-level ELL students are expected to understand general language related to the content area and produce common phrases or short sentences in oral communication. In asking the student to sort events from the story using pictures and a graphic organizer, the teacher recognizes the ability level of beginner ELLs by asking him to demonstrate comprehension using visual aids as linguistic supports. Further, by asking the student to describe a favorite character to a table partner, the teacher demonstrates awareness that beginner-level ELLs can typically produce short, simple sentences related to the content area.

20. B: The symptoms exhibited by the student are characteristic of attention deficit hyperactivity disorder (ADHD), a behavioral disorder that impacts one's ability to focus, sustain attention, and control impulses. ADHD also frequently impacts the development of reading comprehension skills, because in addition to impeding focus, it often affects language processing skills. According to the Individuals with Disabilities Education Act (IDEA), if a teacher suspects a student has a disability that impedes their ability to learn effectively must refer the student for an initial evaluation to determine the need for special education services.

21. D: Applying universal design for learning principles includes allowing multiple outlets for students to express and communicate information. In this situation, physical writing is time-consuming and painful for the student. By providing assistive speech-to-text technology, the teacher accommodates the student's individual learning need by providing an alternative means of expression and communication, ensuring their ability to fully participate in writing assignments.

22. B: Under the Individuals with Disabilities Education Act (IDEA), when developing an Individualized Education Program for a student, at least one of the student's general education teachers must be included on the IEP team. General education teachers are often highly attuned to the individual student's learning needs, as well as progress and development in relation to grade-level curriculum standards. Some of their responsibilities as contributors to the IEP team include providing samples of the student's work, current grades, and assessment scores. General education teachers can also provide valuable insight regarding effective accommodations and supports that can be included in the IEP, as well as contribute to the development of academic and behavioral goals.

Collaboration and Professionalism

23. D: Under the Family Educational Rights and Privacy Act (FERPA), teachers may only disclose students' educational records—including personally identifiable information—to the student's legal caregivers or in specific authorized situations. Although classroom photos may be posted online, teachers must adhere to the guidelines of FERPA when doing so. Photographs may not reveal any personally identifiable information related to students, such as names, birthdates, or identification numbers, and may not focus on an individual student. Teachers must also follow the protocols outlined by the school district regarding posting classroom photographs online.

24. A: According to the family systems theory, the family functions as a single cohesive unit, so the interactions and behaviors of one family member directly influence those of other family members. This theory also states that dynamics, patterns, and interactions within the family change as new challenges are presented, in an effort to achieve equilibrium within the unit. Therefore, if a student is suddenly exhibiting disruptive behavior, it may indicate that the family unit is out of equilibrium, causing the student to act out in school. Recognizing that the disruptive behavior is caused by disequilibrium within the family unit may help the teacher provide the support and resources necessary to address the issue.

25. B: Frequent communication with students' families is integral to establishing positive, collaborative relationships between the school and home that enhance the overall learning experience. Students come from a variety of backgrounds, living situations, and family dynamics, so the teacher must consider and accommodate the communication needs of all families. Using multiple methods of communication ensures accessibility and inclusivity for all students' families, promoting the positive relationships necessary for student development and learning.

26. B: Developing culturally competent practices in the classroom requires the teacher to recognize and work to eliminate personal biases and assumptions about other cultures. In doing so, the teacher gains appreciation for and strengthens understanding of individual students' backgrounds, beliefs, traditions, and values. This allows the teacher to make more informed decisions to design more thoughtful, relevant, and inclusive instruction that meets the needs of all students. In addition, working to develop culturally competent and globally aware teaching practices communicates to students that their diversities are valued and respected, encouraging them to adopt the same sentiment toward others and improving the overall classroom climate.

27. A: Teachers have the ethical responsibility to ensure their students' needs are met for successful learning and development. This includes helping families in need access community support resources. By providing the family with information regarding community food-assistance programs, the teacher helps ensure that the student receives the adequate nutrition necessary for healthy development and effective learning.

28. C: Professional learning communities (PLCs) are valuable resources for allowing educators to work together in building pedagogical knowledge and skills. In this space, teachers and other professionals can share knowledge, ideas, and experiences, as well as collaborate in developing strategies for meeting students' needs. By participating in a PLC, this teacher can gain insight and expertise from various professionals in the building regarding best practices for promoting students' development and learning.

29. D: The nature of the classroom climate significantly impacts the quality of student engagement and learning. The teacher must conscientiously try to establish and maintain a positive social context for students. This includes ensuring all interactions and relationships in the classroom are respectful, productive, and focused on positive communication. By allowing students to participate in the development of classroom norms and expectations, the teacher provides students with personal agency and accountability for maintaining a positive social context. In addition, by holding daily class meetings, the teacher demonstrates willingness to listen and gain understanding of their students as individuals while encouraging students to do the same among themselves. In doing so, the teacher contributes to the development of a positive social context focused on mutual respect and rapport.

30. C: Head Start is a federally funded education program designed to help close the achievement gap by providing an equitable foundation for learning and development among prekindergarten students from socioeconomically disadvantaged backgrounds. This program also provides information and resources to families to help support their children in promoting healthy development and learning.

31. B: The National Association for the Education of Young Children (NAEYC) Code of Ethical Conduct outlines professional expectations for early childhood educators regarding interactions with students, families, colleagues, and the community. This document emphasizes the importance of promoting the cognitive, physical, social, and emotional development of young children in a healthy, safe, supportive, and inclusive environment. Regarding assessment, it states that rather than relying solely on grades as a measure of student achievement, early childhood educators have the ethical responsibility to utilize a variety of information sources for evaluating student learning and development. Doing so provides teachers with a more holistic and individualized evaluation of the whole child.

32. D: Teachers have the legal and professional responsibility to ensure the safety of their students, including, when possible, outside of the classroom. If a teacher suspects that a student is being abused or neglected, the teacher is required to immediately report any suspicions to child protective services or another appropriate agency immediately, such as social services or the local police department. Information on how to access the appropriate agency is typically available in the school guidance office. In addition, the teacher must consult the district's professional code of conduct regarding procedures and expectations for informing administrators of reports of suspected student abuse or neglect.

33. A: Because teachers spend the majority of the school day with their students, they are often the first to notice individual learning needs, and therefore, serve as powerful advocates for ensuring these needs are met. In this situation, the teacher believes her student may have an undiagnosed learning disability that has not been addressed. To best advocate for this student, she must submit a referral for an initial evaluation to determine whether he meets the criteria to receive special education services. In doing so, the teacher helps ensure that appropriate measures are taken to facilitate this student's ability to learn.

34. D: Regularly seeking professional development opportunities is integral to continuously improving one's pedagogical knowledge and skills to enhance the learning experience for all students. Doing so helps teachers stay current in the field by exposing them to new pedagogical theories and practices, instructional strategies, resources, and learning materials. In this situation, a workshop would be most beneficial in helping this teacher become knowledgeable on available and relevant technology resources while providing hands-on opportunities to learn how to apply them in the classroom.

35. B: Mentor teachers in the school building are valuable resources in helping new educators develop their pedagogical knowledge, skills, and practices. Mentors are typically experienced teachers that can give insight, feedback, and suggestions regarding effective instructional strategies, approaches, and resources for meeting students' learning needs. Mentor teachers can also help new teachers navigate the school campus, and to learn the roles of other professionals in the building in supporting student learning and development.

36. C: Self-reflection is integral to continuously improving one's teaching practice, achieving professional goals, and meeting the learning and developmental needs of all students. By recording notes in a journal regarding instructional effectiveness and student engagement, the teacher can identify strengths within each lesson, as well as areas for improvement to inform future instruction. The teacher can make adjustments to instruction and implement appropriate supports to better meet students' needs and enhance the overall learning experience.

Language and Literacy Development

37. D: According to Pennsylvania's PreK-4 standards in language arts, kindergarten students can reasonably be expected to demonstrate fundamental reading comprehension, interpretation, and analysis of grade-level-appropriate works of literature. This includes using literary elements within a story to derive meaning, as well as identifying and recalling key details with prompting and support. The teacher can expect that after hearing the story read aloud and engaging in several corresponding activities, students will be able to identify the setting, characters, and major events within the work of literature. While it is important to account for individual differences in developmental levels, teachers can use academic standards as a framework for measuring student progress.

38. B: Receptive and expressive language skills are fundamental to literacy development among young children. Receptive language skills (the ability to understand and internalize language) are necessary for developing expressive language skills (the ability to accurately produce language). Both are necessary for building the background knowledge and vocabulary necessary for effective skill development in all areas of literacy, and therefore must be emphasized in the early childhood classroom. By reading aloud to students and providing explanations and visual examples, the teacher conscientiously promotes receptive language skill development. Further, in asking an open-ended question after the read-aloud, the teacher encourages expressive language skill development by prompting students to use expanded vocabulary to describe their favorite parts of the story.

39. A: Flexible grouping refers to the temporary and strategic grouping of students to address specific needs or develop particular skills in a given area. This strategy is beneficial in differentiating instruction to accommodate variances in abilities, learning styles, and developmental levels. Flexible groupings can be either homogenous, in which students are grouped with others of the same or similar abilities, or heterogenous, in which students of varying skill levels work together. In this situation, homogenous flexible groupings would help with scaffolding instruction to align with students' individual needs. This would allow the teacher to provide leveled texts according to students' levels of literacy skill development to effectively promote fluency and support reading comprehension.

40. D: Immersing young students in a literate environment is beneficial in demonstrating the application of literacy in daily life, strengthening literacy skill development and promoting academic achievement. Literacy skills are necessary for effective learning across content areas, so these skills must be taught in a variety of contexts in addition to language arts. By incorporating reading, writing, speaking, and listening opportunities into daily lessons, this teacher effectively infuses literacy throughout the curriculum to create a literate environment for students.

41. C: Phonemic awareness refers to one's ability to decipher, identify, and manipulate individual sounds within spoken words. Developing this skill in young children is integral to building phonological awareness, which is the ability to differentiate and understand words and sounds within spoken language as a whole. Activities focused on developing students' phonemic awareness, such as rhymes, songs, and alphabet games, emphasize individual sounds within words. Implementing such activities helps establish the foundation of understanding necessary for literacy skill development.

42. C: Phonemic awareness refers to one's ability to decipher, identify, and manipulate individual sounds within spoken words. This skill consists of several components, including phonemic isolation, which is the ability to distinguish individual phonemes, or sounds, within words. By asking students to identify the sound they hear at the beginning of each vocabulary word, the teacher evaluates students' phonemic awareness by asking them to demonstrate their understanding of phonemic isolation.

43. A: When planning instruction, the teacher must consider the general developmental level of students relative to their age group and recognize and accommodate individual differences in abilities and learning needs. According to Pennsylvania's PreK-4 standards for language arts, second-grade students can reasonably be expected to construct meaning from developmentally appropriate nonfiction texts, including multi-paragraph informational articles. In choosing such an article for a lesson focused on identifying main ideas, as well as supplementing new vocabulary with scaffolded definitions and examples, this teacher selects instructional materials that both align with state academic standards and meet students' developmental needs in language and literacy.

44. B: Sequencing in language arts is a reading comprehension skill that refers to one's ability to recall and arrange events from a text. If a student struggles with sequencing, the teacher must implement appropriate interventions, as development of this language skill is necessary for success in learning across content areas. For example, sequencing also applies to one's ability to follow a set of directions or steps in the correct order to solve problems; recognize cause and effect; and recall major events from history. In this situation, providing visual aids—such as graphic organizers, story maps, and pictures that correspond with events from stories—supports the student in developing this language skill. The teacher must continuously monitor this student's progress to determine if additional interventions are necessary.

45. C: Summative assessments typically occur at the end of a lesson or unit to evaluate students' level of progress toward achieving academic standards. These assessments measure students' mastery of particular skills to help inform future instruction and identify the potential need for remediation. In this situation, the teacher wants to see if students have mastered using transitional phrases to organize events in a story. Therefore, instructing students to write an original narrative as a summative assessment would be the most effective approach in evaluating their understanding of this concept.

46. C: Understanding basic concepts of print is a fundamental skill for emergent literacy development in young children. While most prekindergarten students have not yet learned to read fluently, it is still important to demonstrate the prevalence and application of printed language in daily life. This includes teaching young children about the purpose and use of printed books. Modeling how to hold a book, turn pages, read from left to right, and pointing out key characteristics, such as a book's title, cover, and author's name, develops print awareness in prekindergarten students. Doing so promotes students' understanding that books contain printed words that convey meaning, establishing a foundation for emergent literacy development.

47. C: Blending syllables is an important phonological processing skill that refers to one's ability to connect individual sounds within words. This skill is integral to developing reading comprehension skills, and therefore, it must be addressed when a student is having difficulty. In this situation, having the student practice spelling words using letter tiles, reading the words aloud, and clapping out syllables helps to strengthen awareness of how sounds work together. Such activities provide a multisensory intervention that lets the student visualize, verbalize, and physically manipulate multisyllabic blended words, promoting the development of this skill.

48. A: Phonemic substitution is a phonological awareness skill that refers to the ability to recognize the creation of a new word when one sound is replaced with another. Understanding this concept is necessary for the development of reading comprehension and spelling skills, so it must be taught explicitly. By using color-coded letter cards to spell vocabulary words and replace individual sounds, the teacher shows students how phonemic substitution is used to create new words. This strategy also supports students' recognition of the relationship between phonemic awareness and phonics, as it allows them to visualize the substitution of individual letters to produce new sounds and words.

49. B: The alphabetic principle is the understanding that each letter of the alphabet corresponds to a specific sound, and some letters can be grouped with others to produce certain sounds. Understanding the alphabetic principle is necessary for the development of reading and writing skills in young children. To prevent students from feeling overwhelmed and ensure they internalize this concept, it is important to teach and focus lessons on new letters individually or a few at a time. Doing so helps students understand and remember which sounds are produced by each letter or group of letters.

50. D: Morphemes are the smallest element of language that can convey a meaning. Morphemes and syllables are similar in that both are individual units of language. However, whereas morphemes must either carry a meaning independently or add meaning to an existing word, syllables do not necessarily do so. For example, the word "cat" is a morpheme that functions as an independent word. This is called a "free morpheme." Morphemes can also take the form of prefixes and suffixes. For example, adding "-able" to a word such as "fix" creates the word "fixable," indicating that something is able to be fixed. In the word "beautiful," the morpheme "-ful" indicates that something is described as full of beauty. The suffix "-er" refers to one who performs an action, as in the word "teacher." Prefixes and suffixes are examples of bound morphemes, as these units of language must be connected to a root word to convey meaning.

51. B: Homophones are words that sound the same when spoken aloud, but are spelled differently and have different meanings. Since homophones sound the same in spoken language, discerning between them often proves difficult for young students, particularly during reading and writing activities. However, the ability to correctly identify and use homophones is necessary for vocabulary acquisition, as well as the development of spelling, reading comprehension, and writing skills. Intervention is therefore necessary when a student is experiencing difficulty with this concept. Strategies that provide repetition, visual aids, and deeper understanding of word meanings promote students' ability to distinguish between commonly confused homophones. For example, sentence dictation exercises provide students the opportunity to practice writing homophones while reinforcing the concept through repetition. Visual aids, such as pictures to correspond with vocabulary words, promote students' ability to recognize and differentiate homophones. Teaching the morphology of vocabulary words also strengthens students' understanding of how parts of words are constructed, thus supporting their ability to distinguish between frequently confused homophones.

52. C: The term "irregular sight words" refers to high-frequency vocabulary words that are not spelled phonetically. Recognition and understanding of these words are necessary for vocabulary acquisition, as well as the development of reading comprehension, spelling, and writing skills. However, since these words cannot be sounded out using conventional rules of phonics, students must memorize them. Therefore, repetition through a variety of instructional strategies is most effective when teaching high-frequency irregular sight words. In this situation, the teacher reviews irregular sight words daily with students using multiple activities. Doing so fosters students' recognition, understanding, and retention of such words, thus promoting reading fluency as well as the development of other necessary literacy skills.

53. A: Formative assessments occur continuously throughout instruction to evaluate students' understanding and progress toward reaching academic standards. This style of assessment lets the teacher identify strategies, activities, or approaches that may need adjustment, and incorporate modifications and accommodations to better meet students' learning needs. By reviewing responses to journal prompts focused on opinion writing, the teacher can formatively assess students' mastery of this writing style, and can change instruction as necessary to enhance understanding prior to a formal assessment.

54. D: Automaticity refers to one's ability to quickly recognize and understand written words. This skill is fundamental to the development of reading fluency, and is cultivated by frequent exposure to new vocabulary, printed words, and patterns of phonics. Students that struggle with automaticity typically have trouble recognizing written words, reading at a grade-level-appropriate pace, and comprehending what they have read. Difficulty with automaticity in reading may result from numerous factors, such as limited phonics knowledge or exposure to printed language, weak decoding skills, or a learning disability. As this skill is integral to language and literacy development, struggling students must receive necessary interventions and support.

55. A: Prosody in reading refers to tone, pace, and stress placed on spoken words. Prosody does not refer to *which* individual phonemes are used in spoken words, but *how* the phonemes are used by changing the pitch, speed, and stress. This skill is a distinct measure of students' progress in reading fluency development, as it indicates their ability to recognize the relationship between written and spoken language. Reader's theaters offer an engaging learning opportunity for developing prosody in reading among young students. This activity allows them to assume the roles and act out the dialogue of characters from stories, thus encouraging them to read with increased expression while also promoting reading comprehension and fluency skills.

56. D: Independent reading, particularly among older students, is integral to vocabulary acquisition, as well as the development of reading comprehension and fluency skills. Regularly scheduling time for self-selected reading is a highly beneficial strategy in encouraging students to read independently. Doing so provides a sense of choice and autonomy over learning, as students have the opportunity to engage with texts relevant to their personal interests. Students that participate in self-selected reading are exposed to a wider range of new vocabulary across genres that may not be included in the general curriculum. In addition, this strategy motivates students to practice reading independently more often, thus promoting the development of reading comprehension and fluency skills.

57. C: The ability to analyze the structure of words is necessary for vocabulary acquisition, decoding, and ultimately, reading comprehension. This skill becomes increasingly important as older students are exposed to more complex vocabulary, as it allows them to more effectively examine the parts of unfamiliar terms to derive meaning. Hands-on learning opportunities, such as word-building games, are beneficial in allowing students to physically manipulate the components of multisyllabic words, thus strengthening structural analysis skills.

58. D: Prereading strategies enhance overall student engagement and comprehension. Activities such as anticipation guides serve to provide context, establish purpose for reading, and elicit prior knowledge to strengthen understanding, evoke interest, and make the learning experience meaningful and relevant for students. These guides typically ask students to agree or disagree with a series of statements related to the reading, and to make predictions about the text. This encourages students to actively engage with the text as they determine whether their predictions were correct, or whether their original opinions remained the same during and after reading, which promotes comprehension.

59. A: Story maps are a form of graphic organizer that provides students with a visual aid to more effectively record and recall important details from a text. This resource is versatile, and can be differentiated to align with students' grade level, as well as variances in literacy skills. Story maps can be completed independently, and help students identify key components of a text, thus promoting reading comprehension and the ability to retell stories by recalling major details.

60. C: Critical analysis skills are necessary for effectively reading, analyzing, and interpreting texts across genres and content areas. The ability to read critically enhances students' overall connection to and comprehension of a text, so it must be taught explicitly. In this situation, the teacher is asking students to engage in a close reading of an informational text by marking it with various symbols as they read. This strategy helps students focus intently on the text, promoting their ability to think critically about it and ultimately strengthening their understanding of the information presented.

61. B: Diagnostic assessments are administered prior to beginning a new unit of instruction, and can take several forms, such as pretests, anticipation guides, or surveys. These assessments contain new material from the upcoming unit, and provide teachers with valuable information on students' background knowledge and level of understanding prior to beginning instruction. Teachers can use this feedback to guide the planning process, as it allows them to identify areas of whole-class and individual strength and need to implement the most effective strategies, supports, and accommodations for promoting student success. Diagnostic assessments are also beneficial in allowing teachers to identify areas of misconception to clarify prior to instruction, avoiding the need for later remediation.

62. C: Acquisition and comprehension of academic language is a common challenge among young children. Early language development typically occurs in familiar settings, and reflects children's daily interactions and experiences, whereas academic language is content-specific, often more complex in nature, and therefore harder to understand. However, this skill is necessary for literacy development and success in learning across subject areas. In this situation, the teacher implements before-, during-, and after-reading strategies to promote understanding of the academic language students will encounter in the informational text. The teacher contextualizes new vocabulary by providing definitions and examples before students read the text, creating a framework for increased comprehension. By having students complete guided summary frames as they engage with the text, the teacher encourages close reading that promotes students' ability to summarize, and therefore, demonstrate understanding, of what they have read. Additionally, in instructing students to discuss their summaries with a partner, the teacher encourages students to practice using academic language, thus strengthening their comprehension of its meaning.

63. D: Recognizing the characteristics and functions of English grammatical conventions is important for reading comprehension development. Further, modeling to students how these patterns apply to spoken language is necessary for fostering reading fluency and expressive language skills. By pausing between sentences, changing intonation, and correlating inflection with variances in punctuation within the text, the teacher effectively models the relationship between English grammatical patterns in written and spoken language.

64. A: Implementing activities to promote students' oral language skills is integral to establishing a foundation for literacy development and academic achievement across content areas. Teaching prekindergarten students to listen responsively enhances a variety of skills, including receptive language, communication, and problem-solving. Incorporating listening games that include simple, multi-step directions provides young children with the opportunity to practice this skill in an engaging and developmentally-appropriate setting. When implementing such activities, teachers must ensure directions are clear, concise, and limited to only a few steps, so as not to distract, confuse, or overwhelm students.

65. C: While individual children develop oral language skills at different rates, early childhood students can reasonably be expected to communicate clearly and intelligibly when speaking. Difficulties with enunciation impede clear communication, and therefore, struggling students would benefit from individualized instruction focused on the foundations of phonics patterns. Such an intervention should include a variety of activities, such as having the student practice individual letter and word sounds with a focus on areas of difficulty, as well as reading aloud rhymes, familiar texts, and sentences that incorporate words the student has trouble enunciating. Students that continue to struggle may require a more intensive intervention, such as working with a speech and language pathologist.

66. B: Graphic organizers are highly beneficial in providing students with a visual aid when gathering and organizing ideas prior to beginning a writing assignment. These resources are versatile, as they can be differentiated to accommodate a range of purposes and student needs. In this situation, a graphic organizer such as a story map would allow students to more effectively establish a situation, introduce a narrator and characters, as well as arrange their narratives with a sequence of events that has a definite beginning, middle, and end. Using graphic organizers as a pre-writing activity ultimately promotes the development of students' writing skills, as it allows for more organized and coherent fictional narratives.

Social Studies

67. B: Teaching young children that organizations have leaders with specific roles establishes the foundation necessary to begin understanding this idea on a larger scale. In this situation, identifying and discussing the roles of authority figures within the school building demonstrates how an organization is comprised of leaders that work together to ensure its proper function. Placing this concept in a familiar context increases its relevancy for students, thus strengthening their understanding and ability to apply it to more complex organizations, such as the three branches of government.

68. A: Young children internalize new concepts most effectively when provided with a variety of hands-on, relevant, and interactive learning opportunities. The teacher's awareness of this notion is evident throughout the activities selected for a unit on markets and economic systems. By following a field trip to the grocery store with a classroom market activity, the teacher provides varied and active learning experiences to foster engagement and exploration of how the concept being taught applies to daily life. Further, by incorporating such activities as planning a budget and using pretend money, the teacher establishes cross-curricular connections between social studies and math for strengthened overall understanding.

69. D: All students learn and process new information differently, so it is important to incorporate multiple and varied opportunities for them to do so. Differentiating instruction allows teachers to appeal to variances in learning styles, individual needs, and preferences to create an accessible, engaging experience for all students. Learning stations are an effective strategy for achieving this, as they incorporate several activities focused on different strengths, interests, and abilities. In this lesson, the teacher includes both intrapersonal and interpersonal learning opportunities, as well as activities that appeal to auditory and kinesthetic learners, to provide differentiation.

70. C: Summative assessments are typically administered at the end of a lesson or unit to measure students' progress toward achieving academic standards. Such assessments can take several forms, including written exams, essays, or project-based learning opportunities. Project-based summative assessments provide flexibility and student choice in how students demonstrate understanding, as these assessments can be designed to accommodate variances in learning styles, needs, and interests. By using a project-based summative assessment at the end of this unit, the teacher provides an authentic opportunity for students to apply their learning in a relevant, meaningful way for strengthened overall understanding.

71. B: Actively engaging students in public service projects is an effective strategy for promoting the development of civic values, as well as an understanding of their roles and responsibilities in the community. Doing so should begin in early childhood, and should provide hands-on opportunities to serve others in a meaningful way, establishing a foundation for increased awareness of how individuals in a community work together to support one another. By organizing a class food drive, this teacher provides such an opportunity. By encouraging students to participate in a project that will directly benefit members of the community, the project promotes values that contribute to the development of civic competence.

72. D: Incorporating digital resources into instruction creates relevant and engaging learning opportunities. For social studies, it strengthens students' connections to topics covered in the curriculum by providing realistic visuals that enhance exploration and foster inquiry. By selecting an online satellite map as a resource, the teacher provides students with an authentic, interactive learning experience that promotes exploration and inquiry while supporting their learning in using and interpreting maps.

73. C: Developing students' understanding of their state's history promotes further inquiry and exploration while strengthening their connection to the community in which they live. Such development includes promoting students' awareness of the significance of slogans, symbols, and mottos that represent their state. Using authentic historical examples helps to increase relevancy, as it demonstrates where they appear in real-world situations. Therefore, a lesson in which students identify state slogans, mottos, and symbols from photographs, artifacts, documents, and items from events in the state would be the best approach in fostering students' understanding of this concept.

74. A: Understanding opportunity cost, or the notion that making one choice typically requires sacrificing the potential benefits of another, is important for developing economic literacy. Effectively weighing opportunity costs requires individuals to make well-thought-out choices, so instructional activities related to this concept should incorporate opportunities for students to practice doing so. Implementing a collaborative think-aloud activity would allow students to work through the decision-making process by verbalizing the advantages and disadvantages of their choices with a classmate. Such an activity would serve to enhance students' understanding of the idea that choices have consequences while strengthening their ability to make informed decisions.

Arts and Humanities

75. C: Gross motor skills refer to the ability to engage in movements that require the coordinated use of large muscle groups. Such movements include running, jumping, kicking, and waving one's arms. By prekindergarten, most young children have developed a variety of gross motor skills. Teachers can enhance this development by incorporating activities that promote students' sense of coordination between their bodies and actions. For example, integrating movement and dance into musical activities encourages young children to engage in large-muscle movements, promoting the development of gross motor skills.

76. D: Positive reinforcement of artistic expression among young children is integral to fostering creative development. Therefore, teachers must be cognizant of remarks, comments, or questions toward children's artwork to ensure all students feel valued and empowered in their artistic endeavors. Doing so encourages students to continue engaging in artistic expression while building confidence in their skills. By asking open-ended, but targeted questions and demonstrating genuine positive interest in their responses, teachers can objectively prompt students to discuss their art without fear of judgement.

77. B: Allowing multiple opportunities for both structured and unstructured dramatic play offers significant benefits for whole-child development, so it must be incorporated in the early childhood classroom. Doing so promotes creative development and self-expression as students assume and act out various roles. In addition, through dramatic play, students can explore, process, and organize new information to strengthen their understanding of the world around them. Dramatic play also supports development of young children's linguistic and interpersonal skills, as it provides opportunities to communicate with one another, work together, as well as develop problem-solving and conflict-resolution skills. By providing students with various costumes and props, this teacher demonstrates understanding of the importance and benefits of incorporating dramatic play into the classroom at this developmental stage.

78. B: When art materials are readily accessible, plentiful, and varied, students are more likely to use them for self-expression. This includes ensuring materials are within students' reach, consist of several mediums and resources for artistic creation, and implemented throughout the curriculum. In doing so, teachers can provide opportunities for creative expression and development that appeal to students of varying interests and artistic abilities.

79. A: Artistic expression is personal to each individual, so teachers should typically refrain from formal evaluation of ability, especially in the early childhood classroom. Doing so allows students the freedom and flexibility to fully engage in the artistic process in a way that is relevant to their interests, promoting confidence for further exploration and creative development. It is possible, however, to monitor individual progress in artistic ability over time by collecting samples of students' artwork to create personalized portfolios. This approach would allow the teacher to monitor each student's progress in the arts throughout the school year while avoiding a formal assessment of skill.

80. C: Music education offers significant benefits for early childhood development across domains. It is important that daily music instruction is incorporated into the curriculum, both as its own subject and throughout content areas. To effectively integrate music into the classroom, early childhood educators must be able to recognize some basic musical elements. Doing so is necessary for designing and implementing instructional strategies, activities, and learning experiences that foster students' understanding of musical concepts and promote whole-child development. Some examples of basic musical elements include, but are not limited to:

Rhythm: the pattern of sounds or beats that make up a piece of music
Melody: the progression of rhythmic sounds or beats that form a tune
Harmony: the sound created when multiple notes are played simultaneously
Timbre: the tone quality of an individual musical note
Texture: how individual components of a musical piece work together to create a whole composition
Form: the overall structure of a piece of music

---

81. D: Cross-curricular activities enhance students' understanding of new information. Specifically, by integrating arts and humanities across content areas, teachers can strengthen students' connections to learning and promote creative development while demonstrating how the arts and humanities are applicable in all aspects of life. In a scientific lesson about the life cycle of plants, providing opportunities for students to engage in music and artistic expression is an effective strategy for incorporating arts and humanities into cross-curricular learning.

Mathematics

82. D: Mathematical skills build upon one another. To learn advanced ideas, young children must first master basic mathematical concepts. For example, before learning how to tell time, which requires abstract thinking, students must first be able to recognize and count numbers up to 60. This foundational knowledge will be beneficial as students learn to read both an analog and digital clock, count upward, and recognize the progression of time.

83. C: When teaching foundational mathematical skills to early childhood students, it is important to recognize the characteristics and abilities of their cognitive developmental levels. Prekindergarten students are in the preoperational stage of cognitive development and have not yet acquired concrete thinking skills. The ability to understand conservation—the idea that altering the appearance of something does not change the quantity—does not develop until the concrete operational stage of development. Therefore, when asked which group of unit cubes contained more, students were unable to recognize that both groups consisted of eight cubes. Rather, they selected the group that visually appeared larger.

84. C: Young children develop foundational mathematical skills, such as problem-solving, most effectively when given opportunities to apply them in a variety of situations. Early childhood educators should strive to integrate mathematical concepts throughout all areas of the curriculum. Doing so helps establish the foundation necessary for students to develop more advanced mathematical skills, and demonstrates how these skills apply across content areas. By selecting students to pass out art materials and ensure that all classmates receive the same quantity of supplies, this teacher encourages these students to engage in problem-solving, strengthening their development of this skill.

85. A: Early childhood students internalize new mathematical concepts best through concrete experiences in which learning occurs through the physical senses. Providing students with manipulatives during mathematics instruction that they can use to touch, work with, and visualize new ideas, promotes development of concept knowledge. In this lesson, base-ten blocks would be most effective in allowing students to physically arrange and manipulate two-digit numbers to determine place value, strengthening their overall understanding.

86. B: Cross-curricular instruction strengthens students' understanding of content knowledge while demonstrating its applications in various contexts. By integrating mathematical concepts throughout the curriculum, teachers foster students' ability to recognize how these concepts transfer to other subject areas. By asking students to create original mosaics, this teacher promotes students' ability to draw and create two-dimensional shapes while demonstrating connections between the mathematics and art curriculum.

87. B: Diagnostic tests are typically administered prior to beginning a new unit of instruction. These assessments can be either formal or informal, and they provide teachers with feedback regarding students' background knowledge and level of understanding prior to instruction. Teachers can use the data interpreted from diagnostic tests to guide instructional planning, as it lets them identify areas of need for the whole class, as well as individual strengths and levels of need to provide adequate differentiation, accommodations, and supports. By administering a pretest prior to a unit on equivalent fractions, this teacher can more effectively group students based on ability to scaffold instruction and meet individual learning needs.

88. D: Formal benchmark assessments are administered periodically throughout the school year, and are intended to provide feedback regarding students' progress in meeting district and state academic standards in a given content area. The data from these assessments is used for a variety of purposes, including determining student readiness for the next grade level, evaluating instructional effectiveness, identifying potential need for remediation, and guiding teachers in the planning process. In this situation, administering a benchmark assessment at the end of the first semester will give the teacher insight regarding whole-class and individual students' strengths and needs. This will allow the teacher to make any necessary adjustments to instructional strategies, activities, accommodations, and supports to most effectively meet students' learning needs as they progress through the school year.

89. C: Learning becomes more relevant and meaningful when students are aware of its applications in real-world contexts, as this demonstrates how concepts learned in class can be used in daily life. This strengthens students' connections to learning, fostering deeper understanding of concept knowledge. By leading students around the school building to identify shapes learned during a geometry lesson, this teacher effectively demonstrates the applications of mathematics in real-world contexts by showing students where they appear in a familiar environment.

90. A: Mathematical communication skills are necessary for students to understand their own thinking in relation to mathematics, explain their reasoning to others, and strengthen concept knowledge. Development of this skill builds the foundation of understanding necessary to apply the same thinking patterns to other, more advanced mathematical concepts. By asking open-ended questions during mathematics instruction, teachers encourage students to verbalize and work through their thinking processes, promoting the use of mathematical communication and fostering greater overall understanding.

91. C: Ordering refers to the ability to correctly arrange a series of numbers, either by ones or by periodic intervals, in ascending or descending order. This pre-numeracy skill is necessary for developing understanding of a range of foundational mathematical concepts, so it must be addressed when a student is having difficulty. Having students who struggle in this area practice representing numbers using a chart and counting chips provides a hands-on opportunity to physically manipulate and visualize the difference between numbers. This strategy supports the development of understanding of cardinality, and ultimately, how to correctly order numbers.

92. D: Developing young children's ability to sort objects is necessary to help them understand the world around them, and it promotes a range of skills, including logical reasoning, classification, and categorization. Therefore, early childhood educators must model this skill in a variety of situations, such as in putting classroom materials away in designated bins. Labeling the bins with words and visual aids to indicate where different items belong reinforces the concept, strengthening students' understanding of how to correctly sort classroom materials when putting them away.

93. B: Providing young children with learning materials that allow them to physically manipulate and visualize new mathematical concepts establishes the foundation of understanding to develop more advanced skills. Using geoboards, this teacher effectively creates a hands-on learning experience in which students can actively explore and experiment with new shapes. This strategy also provides context for learning by calling on students' prior knowledge of shapes, further creating a foundation for understanding that will enhance students' skill development in identifying two-dimensional shapes.

94. A: Understanding algebraic concepts requires abstract thinking skills that must be developed in early childhood. Doing so provides students with a foundation of understanding that can be expanded and applied to more advanced mathematical concepts. Such development includes teaching young children to identify patterns and relationships among numbers, as well as different ways in which numbers and equations can be represented. By showing students how to solve the same addition problem in both standard and expanded form, this teacher demonstrates that numbers can be added in different ways by recognizing relationships between them, thus promoting algebraic thinking skills.

95. C: Introducing the concept of measurement through familiar activities, such as cooking, supports development of young children's foundational understanding that attributes can be quantified. This strategy allows students to make connections to and expand upon prior knowledge for more effective learning. In this situation, engaging students in making a simple recipe in which ingredients are measured provides a hands-on activity that introduces measurement in a relevant context, supporting their development and learning of this concept.

96. D: Teaching young children to make predictions is an effective strategy for supporting their learning and development related to probability, as it encourages students to consider the likelihood of potential outcomes.

236

This establishes a foundation of understanding that can later be applied to more advanced mathematical situations that involve determining probability. Further, representing students' predictions using a bar graph promotes the understanding that information can be quantified and represented in visual form, which supports learning and development in data analysis.

Science

97. C: Promoting student inquiry through open-ended questions fosters students' natural curiosity for exploration, investigation, and problem-solving. Through inquiry, young children gain a deeper understanding of how scientific principles apply to the world around them. By asking what might happen if oil and water are combined, students are prompted to use critical thinking skills as they consider various potential outcomes, encouraging active engagement and promoting inquiry.

98. A: Teaching young children to rely on verifiable evidence is a foundational skill for scientific learning, as it emphasizes the importance of supporting one's own claims using valid data, as well as determining the credibility of other investigations. By reminding students to ensure that all plants receive equal amounts of sunlight and water, this teacher reinforces the concept of establishing a control variable to produce verifiable evidence from their investigation. Developing this skill ultimately strengthens students' ability to explain the results of investigations and apply logical reasoning skills, both to scientific learning and across content areas.

99. A: Scientific learning and development are best supported when young children are provided with hands-on learning experiences that promote their natural curiosity. Such activities allow for active exploration in which students use their physical senses for investigation and inquiry, fostering engagement and strengthening understanding of how scientific concepts apply to the world around them. By leading a class nature walk to introduce the characteristics of living and nonliving things, students have the opportunity to physically touch, smell, observe, and listen as they begin exploring the characteristics of living and nonliving things in nature. This ultimately places the new concept in a relevant and meaningful context for young students, providing a framework for greater understanding when the unit begins.

100. B: Students' learning and development are enhanced across content areas when they know how concepts from one subject area apply to another. Demonstrating cross-curricular relationships increases the relevancy of scientific instruction, fostering students' connections and understanding of how science is present in everyday life. In this situation, students are investigating differences in pitch when glass bottles are filled with varying amounts of water. Such an experiment demonstrates the factors that influence sound while promoting students' ability to recognize the connection between science and music, strengthening their knowledge in both content areas.

101. A: To promote learning and development in science, teachers must ensure that instructional strategies, activities, and assessments align with students' cognitive abilities. Doing so is important for establishing the foundation of scientific understanding necessary to encourage students' sense of inquiry, curiosity, and exploration, and to ultimately grasp more advanced concepts. Formative assessments allow teachers to determine the developmental appropriateness of instruction as students actively engage in learning, giving immediate feedback on their level of understanding, engagement, and need. This feedback lets teachers adjust, modify, and differentiate learning to better align with students' abilities. By observing students as they work, monitoring progress, and asking open-ended questions, this teacher can formatively assess the effectiveness of instruction to make any necessary changes for enhancing scientific learning and understanding.

102. D: Effective science instruction emphasizes following the scientific method when conducting investigations. Teaching this skill develops students' ability to thoughtfully engage in scientific inquiry, apply logical reasoning, and conduct a valid experiment that produces reliable results. In addition, this skill helps students understand the nature and construction of scientific knowledge, as it promotes their ability to distinguish between fact and belief. To follow the scientific method, one must first pose a question to investigate, gather information about the topic, and formulate a hypothesis regarding potential outcomes. A procedure to test the hypothesis must then be developed, and data must be gathered throughout the experiment. After data is analyzed, a conclusion is formed based on repeated results. Therefore, after posing the initial question for this investigation, the teacher should have students research the topic and formulate a hypothesis for experimentation.

103. C: Demonstrating the unifying concepts of science through developmentally appropriate activities is essential for developing young children's understanding of how scientific principles apply to the world around them. In this situation, the teacher wants to promote students' ability to identify the unifying concept of patterns related to characteristics of animals within the same species. Showing photos of various animals, and leading a class discussion in which students compare and contrast their physical characteristics, fosters their ability to recognize patterns among animals of the same species. Such an activity establishes a foundation of understanding that will allow students to identify patterns in other contexts, promoting their ability to make thoughtful predictions when engaging in scientific inquiry.

104. B: Scientific learning and development are best supported when young children are provided with opportunities that allow for active exploration. This includes incorporating realistic and developmentally appropriate scientific tools for students to use when investigating a new concept. Doing so creates a learning environment that fosters students' natural curiosity and inquiry, and reinforces the notion that in science, specific tools are used for gathering information. In addition, this strategy increases the relevancy of learning by placing it in a real-world context, as students have the opportunity to work with the same tools as scientists. Letting second-grade students investigate the organ structure of plants using microscopes provides such a hands-on learning experience, promoting engagement, exploration, and deeper understanding.

105. D: Scientific instruction must be placed in a developmentally appropriate context to foster student understanding. Doing so is necessary for providing young children with a framework for reference that can ultimately apply to more advanced scientific concepts. In this situation, showing photographs of families and asking kindergarten students to identify similar characteristics introduces the complex topic of heredity using a familiar context. This strategy uses a developmentally appropriate approach to support students' understanding that individuals within the same family often share physical traits. Establishing this foundation of knowledge promotes students' learning and development of more advanced topics related to heredity, such as how physical traits are passed from parent to offspring, and how this concept applies to plants and animals.

106. C: Conducting field trips to reinforce classroom instruction gives students hands-on opportunities to interact with and explore scientific concepts in a natural setting. This increases the relevancy of learning while fostering students' natural sense of inquiry. However, physical field trips may not always be possible, and can sometimes be limited in scope. Virtual field trips can provide similar interactive learning experiences. For this unit specifically, leading students in a virtual field trip allows them to explore and compare the characteristics of aquatic ecosystems in various locations, thus providing an active learning experience that expands their understanding of the concept.

107. A: Teaching young children how to repurpose discarded items shows the concept of recycling as a form of waste management. Doing so demonstrates in a developmentally appropriate context how waste is generated, and how individuals can reduce it to protect the environment. Integrating this concept into daily activities, such as art projects, develops students' understanding of how recycling contributes to managing waste, while encouraging their sense of personal responsibility toward caring for the environment.

108. D: When learning about the physical changes that occur to substances when heated or cooled, students should recognize that some changes are reversible, but others are not. This is essential to understanding that physical changes resulting from chemical reactions may produce entirely new substances. After the student asks why the cookies could not be melted back to their original state, reviewing this concept would support the understanding that baking cookie dough is an irreversible cause-and-effect process.

109. B: Sensory play activities are highly valuable in providing young children with hands-on learning experiences. Such activities promote students' natural sense of inquiry and curiosity for scientific learning, as they encourage the exploration of new concepts through the physical senses. Further, sensory play experiences often lend themselves to unstructured learning opportunities that allow young children to investigate, manipulate, observe, and test out ideas in a natural setting. A sensory bin with varying types of materials fosters inquiry among prekindergarten students when introducing the physical properties of matter. Students can actively explore different shapes, colors, sizes, and textures of materials, thus establishing a foundation for understanding that matter exists in multiple forms.

110. C: Summative assessments are assessments that take place at the end of a unit to assess mastery of concepts. These are distinct from formative assessments, which take place alongside instruction and can be used to modify the curriculum while students are still learning. Effective summative assessments allow students to demonstrate understanding of a concept in a manner that aligns with their developmental levels, characteristics, and capabilities. When summative assessments are developmentally appropriate, teachers can more accurately assess students' mastery of learning targets as they progress through the curriculum, and identify any potential need for remediation. Fourth-grade students are in the concrete operational stage of development, so summative assessments that incorporate logical reasoning skills, physical manipulation and exploration, and collaborative learning, are most effective. A collaborative project-based summative assessment, such as creating a physical model of the water cycle, is therefore most appropriate in letting students of this age group demonstrate their understanding.

111. A: Thematic units refer to instructional activities across the curriculum that focus on a particular topic. In the early childhood classroom, this approach allows students to explore a new concept in-depth by engaging in various related learning activities. Regarding scientific learning and development, thematic units strengthen understanding by integrating new concepts into daily learning activities while demonstrating the connection between science and other content areas. In this thematic unit, students will explore the features of space by participating in literacy, art, and music activities.

Health

112. C: Healthy nutrition is essential to young children's overall wellness and development across domains. As such, in addition to emphasizing the importance of exercise and movement, health education must also focus on teaching the components of a balanced diet, including variation, portioning, and moderation. Doing so establishes a foundation of knowledge for students to make informed and healthy dietary choices throughout their lives. The MyPlate model from the USDA should be used when teaching this concept, as it provides a visual graphic that demonstrates healthy food portioning and variation. According to MyPlate, each meal should include a variety of food groups, with half of the plate consisting of fruits and vegetables.

113. A: Children that are physically healthy are more capable of engaging in and enjoying activities that involve movement, social interaction, and creative self-expression. The importance of daily exercise must be emphasized in the early childhood classroom, and opportunities for both structured and unstructured movement must be incorporated throughout all areas of learning. Doing so promotes the development of both the gross and fine motor skills necessary for healthy physical growth. Children that regularly engage in physical activities are more likely to develop prosocial behaviors, as such activities foster opportunities for positive communication, cooperation, and problem-solving. In addition, incorporating physical activity into the classroom is beneficial in creating a learning environment that supports creative self-expression, as students are encouraged to explore feelings, thoughts, and ideas through movement.

114. B: Gross motor skills refer to the ability to engage in large-muscle movements that incorporate use of the whole body, such as running, throwing, kicking, climbing, and jumping. These skills are necessary for healthy physical development, so activities that promote them should be integrated into daily learning experiences in the early childhood classroom. Young children learn most effectively through play, providing multiple opportunities to do so is important for allowing them to explore movement and develop coordination between their bodies and actions. Outdoor play equipment, such as slides, swings, tubes, and stairs, encourages young children to engage in large-muscle movements that promote gross motor skill development.

115. D: Second-grade students can reasonably be expected to have the gross motor skills necessary to participate in a variety of games that require physical activity. Students of this age are developing an increased sense of control over their bodies, and thus benefit from active learning opportunities that allow them to practice coordinated large-muscle movements. In addition, second-grade students have reached the collaborative play stage of development. As such, they can meaningfully participate in, benefit from, and often prefer organized cooperative learning experiences that involve larger groups of students. Interactive group games, such as kickball or follow-the-leader, can best facilitate this preferred learning style while promoting second-grade students' coordination of purposeful body movements.

116. B: Dexterity is a fine motor skill that refers to one's ease of movement, specifically in the hands and fingers. This important self-help skill is necessary for performing a variety of tasks, so early childhood educators should use multiple activities and learning materials to promote its development. Letting young children physically use and manipulate small objects is an effective strategy for achieving this goal. For example, cutting out shapes with scissors, playing with pegboards, and doing puzzles that include several small pieces, are activities that support students' development of dexterity and muscle strength.

117. C: While it is important to be aware of the characteristics and abilities associated with students' developmental levels, early childhood educators must also recognize and accommodate individual differences to promote learning for all students. Upon reaching kindergarten, most children have acquired a range of fine motor capabilities. However, individual students will inevitably possess varying degrees of these skills. Fine motor skills refer to hand and finger movements, so providing tools of varying sizes—such as pencils, crayons, paintbrushes, and scissors—is an effective strategy for differentiating instruction to align with individual abilities while promoting development for all students.

118. D: When introducing new concepts related to physical health in the early childhood classroom, teachers must use strategies, activities, and learning materials that are appropriate to students' developmental levels. Doing so promotes increased understanding by presenting new information in a way that aligns with students' cognitive abilities, establishing a foundation of knowledge that will contribute to making healthy choices throughout life. Prekindergarten students learn primarily through play, as it allows them to explore and process new concepts through hands-on experiences. Specifically, dramatic play gives young children the space and opportunity to apply their learning in real-world situations. By incorporating pretend foods and labeled storage bins in the kitchen area of the classroom, students can begin categorizing them based upon type. This teacher has created a developmentally appropriate setting for introducing the concept of identifying various food groups, and ultimately, distinguishing between healthy and unhealthy foods.

119. A: Criterion-referenced assessments measure students' progress in relation to a set of predetermined standards. This approach gives teachers objective feedback regarding students' fitness levels to determine areas of individual and whole-class strength and level of need. In physical education, criterion-referenced assessments can help teachers identify skills that require greater emphasis, allowing them to design instructional activities that better promote development in specific areas related to motor development and health.

120. B: Formatively assessing students' gross motor skill development as they engage in physical activities lets teachers continuously identify areas of individual and whole-class strength and need. Such assessments provide immediate feedback that can be used to make necessary adjustments to physical activities, and to guide future planning to better meet students' needs in promoting motor development and health. In addition, formatively assessing students' physical progress can help teachers identify potential delays related to gross motor skills that may require further evaluation or intervention. In this situation, the teacher uses a checklist while observing students as they complete an obstacle course that targets specific gross motor skills. This approach lets the teacher evaluate students' abilities in a natural setting, providing a more objective representation of their gross motor skill development.

121. B: Comprehensive health education includes teaching young children how to protect their physical safety by recognizing and responding appropriately to dangerous situations. This includes establishing, reviewing, and practicing evacuation procedures for emergency situations, such as a fire. When teaching fire safety, continuously reviewing and practicing these procedures helps ensure all students know how to quickly and safely vacate the premises to avoid potential injury. Evacuation procedures should be reinforced both at school and at home, and should include mapping a route, establishing a rally point, and teaching students to identify signs of fire or smoke in adjacent rooms.

122. A: Young children learn more effectively when new concepts are placed in real-world contexts, as this fosters personal connections that strengthen overall understanding. When introducing the fundamental practices of good health, such concrete learning experiences emphasize the importance of healthy and hygienic habits to overall wellness in a way that is developmentally appropriate. Most first-grade students have already had personal experiences with various healthcare professionals, such as doctors, dentists, and nurses. Having these individuals visit the classroom to discuss their roles in-depth reinforces the concepts of good health practices, encouraging students to adopt them.

123. D: Fostering positive attitudes toward physical activity among young children is beneficial in building a foundation for making healthy choices throughout life. Exercise and movement should be encouraged in the early childhood classroom and integrated throughout the curriculum. In addition, teachers must mindfully select and implement activities that are developmentally appropriate to students' age group. This includes recognizing the characteristics and abilities relative to students' physical, cognitive, social, and emotional developmental levels. Such awareness helps teachers ensure that all students can fully participate in and enjoy physical activities, promoting positive attitudes toward them. Activities that are too complex may discourage students, whereas activities that are too simple for a given age group likely will not stimulate interest.

124. C: Gross motor skills are integral to maintaining a healthy level of physical fitness, as well as performing a variety of tasks that require large-muscle movement. By second grade, most students can reasonably be expected to aim with a degree of accuracy when throwing or kicking a ball toward a target. Struggling students benefit from additional practice through focused activities that target these gross motor skills. In this situation, having the student practice throwing and kicking a ball toward targets of various sizes is an effective strategy for helping him improve on these abilities.

125. B: Allowing students to use outdoor play equipment offers significant benefits for gross motor skill development and overall physical fitness. However, an important component of health and fitness education is teaching young children to recognize and avoid unsafe practices to protect their physical safety. Before letting students use outdoor playground equipment, teachers must first establish and review expectations and procedures for doing so. This helps ensure that all students know how to use the equipment safely and appropriately to avoid injury.

126. D: Harnessing unplanned teachable moments is often an effective strategy for placing learning in a real-world context for greater understanding. In this situation, students likely noticed that several of their classmates were absent. The teacher could use this opportunity to discuss how infectious illnesses spread through germs, as well as actions students can take to avoid sickness. This concept could be reinforced by reading books about specific illnesses and doing hands-on activities to demonstrate the spread of germs.

PECT Practice Test #2

Child Development, Learning, and Assessment

1. A first-grade teacher is planning a lesson focused on recalling the main idea and key details from informational texts. Which of the following strategies should this teacher use to align learning with students' zone of proximal development as they learn this new concept?

    a. Flexible grouping
    b. Formative assessments
    c. Differentiated instruction
    d. Scaffolding

2. One of the most important factors influencing the quality of learning and development among young children is:

    a. Background knowledge and experiences
    b. Adequate health and nutrition
    c. Intrinsic motivation
    d. Parental involvement in the education program

3. A second-grade teacher is planning a science lesson on the water cycle that will include several unfamiliar vocabulary terms. Based on typical progressions of linguistic development, this teacher can reasonably expect that students can do which of the following when introduced to the new vocabulary?

    a. Ask questions about meaning and utilize new terms in various contexts
    b. Accurately guess meaning based on context clues
    c. Pronounce new, complex vocabulary without difficulty
    d. Identify prefixes and suffixes to derive meaning

4. In the art center of a kindergarten classroom, the teacher has included multiple tools of varying sizes, such as pencils, paintbrushes, and crayons. This strategy is likely intended to promote students' development of which of the following?

    a. Gross motor skills
    b. Artistic expression
    c. Fine motor skills
    d. Locomotor skills

5. A prekindergarten teacher has just completed a science lesson on changes in seasons and weather conditions. Which of the following strategies would likely best help students internalize this new concept based on their cognitive developmental level?

    a. Having students practice writing vocabulary terms associated with seasons and weather patterns
    b. Incorporating various types of seasonal clothing into the dramatic play area
    c. Make accurate predictions about weather conditions
    d. Leading a class discussion on the effects of climate change on weather and seasons

6. A second-grade teacher is planning a unit on place value. Which of the following steps would help this teacher ensure that instruction, learning activities, and classroom assessments throughout the unit are developmentally appropriate and challenging for all students?

a. Reviewing students' standardized assessment scores in mathematics from the previous school year
b. Conducting an interest inventory to determine students' preferred methods of learning
c. Referring to district or state academic standards for expectations regarding student performance in second-grade mathematics
d. Differentiating instructional strategies to appeal to all learning styles

7. In order to establish an inclusive, respectful, and supportive classroom environment, it is important that teachers first do which of the following?

a. Recognize and eliminate personal biases toward other groups
b. Differentiate instruction to appeal to varying learning styles
c. Understand students' learning needs relative to their developmental levels
d. Establish and maintain communication with students' families

8. A second-grade teacher has decorated the classroom with a word wall, labels, a bulletin board, and a class calendar. This teacher has also created a classroom library that includes several leveled texts of varying genres for students to utilize. This is an example of which of the following strategies for promoting the learning and development of language and literacy skills for all students?

a. Providing opportunities for student choice in learning
b. Modifying instruction to align with varying abilities
c. Creating a print-rich environment
d. Scaffolding learning activities

9. A third-grade teacher works with a group of students that have a diverse range of backgrounds, experiences, and needs. At the beginning of the year, this teacher attends back-to-school night, and plans to maintain communication with students' families throughout the year by making phone calls, sending emails, and updating a weekly class newsletter. Which of the following best describes how doing so will benefit this teacher's overall instructional effectiveness?

a. Students will be more inclined to follow classroom expectations.
b. Family members will be able to contribute to curriculum planning.
c. The teacher will easily be able to document interactions with students' families.
d. The teacher will be able to create more culturally, linguistically, and developmentally responsive instruction.

10. Prior to the start of the school year, kindergarteners are given a screening test on various skills across developmental domains. Such an exam is intended to provide teachers with data-based feedback on which of the following?

a. Student readiness and individual learning needs
b. Differences in learning styles
c. The appropriateness of state academic standards
d. Individual students' aptitudes across subject areas

11. After a unit on decimals, a fourth-grade teacher uses a criterion-referenced assessment to evaluate students' mastery of learning objectives. This assessment approach helps this teacher do which of the following?

a. Compare student progress in relation to grade-level peers
b. Determine students' level of prior knowledge
c. Objectively measure student performance to identify individual achievement and learning needs
d. Evaluate student engagement and understanding throughout instruction

12. Which of the following best describes one way that Pennsylvania's English Language Proficiency Standards (ELPS) help teachers design appropriate and effective content assessment for English language learners?

    a. Providing teachers with ideas for content-based assessment strategies
    b. Emphasizing the importance of students' primary language in English language acquisition
    c. Determining the level of linguistic support necessary based on students' level of English language proficiency
    d. Finding alternatives to traditional classroom assessments

13. A third-grade teacher uses an analytic rubric while evaluating students' explanatory essays. Doing so helps this teacher avoids which of the following?

    a. Taking too long to provide students with feedback
    b. Assessment bias
    c. Inaccurate scoring
    d. Providing irrelevant feedback

14. After completing each unit in social studies, a second-grade teacher typically administers a multiple-choice exam to evaluate student understanding. Which of the following assessment approaches would be more effective in identifying individual needs and supporting the development of all students?

    a. Focusing primarily on formative assessments
    b. Compiling examples of student work to include in a portfolio
    c. Utilizing different assessment strategies throughout instruction
    d. Having students self-reflect on their level of understanding

15. Using technological resources for maintaining records of student performance, such as online gradebooks and data spreadsheets, helps teachers do which of the following?

    a. Stay current on pedagogical developments in assessment
    b. Differentiate instructional strategies to meet students' learning needs
    c. Align classroom assessments with state academic standards
    d. Efficiently and accurately collect, analyze, and interpret data regarding student performance

16. A first-grade teacher wants to include students' families as active participants in the assessment of their children's learning and development. Which of the following strategies would likely best achieve this goal?

    a. Communicating information about curriculum, assignments, and important updates through a class newsletter
    b. Providing families with resources to use at home to prepare their children for upcoming assessments
    c. Using a variety of communication methods to meet all families' needs
    d. Sending students home with weekly progress reports

17. A first-grade teacher works with a group of primarily native Spanish-speaking students, many of whom are identified as English language learners. In the classroom, this teacher incorporates students' native language into instruction by labeling items in both English and Spanish, including Spanish texts in the class library, and teaching Spanish vocabulary words that correspond to daily lessons. Which of the following best describes the benefit of this strategy?

    a. Promoting bilingual immersion for all students
    b. Creating an inclusive environment that recognizes the importance of students' primary language in English language acquisition
    c. Providing English language learners with the opportunity to learn in their preferred language
    d. Scaffolding instruction to align with varying levels of English language proficiency

18. A student in a fourth-grade class struggles with reading comprehension and writing. This student reads at a much slower pace than classmates, and when writing, often misspells high-frequency words and writes several letters backwards. This student has been receiving Response to Intervention (RTI) services to improve literacy skills, but the teacher has noticed minimal progress. Based upon this information, the teacher has the professional responsibility to do which of the following?

    a. Refer the student for an initial evaluation with the school special education department.
    b. Contact the students' parents to address concerns.
    c. Consult grade-level colleagues for instructional strategies that may benefit the student.
    d. Offer this student extra tutoring sessions before and after school hours.

19. A fourth-grade student with medically diagnosed attention deficit hyperactivity disorder (ADHD) often becomes overwhelmed and struggles to focus on lengthy reading passages. Which of the following accommodations would best support the student's ability to fully engage in reading assignments?

    a. Preferential seating toward the front of the room
    b. Providing audio recordings of reading passages
    c. Reducing the length of reading assignments and providing enlarged font
    d. Chunking the texts and providing extra time for processing

20. A fourth-grade student identified as an English language learner has recently enrolled in a new school. Previously, this student moved around frequently in his home country, and as a result, received minimal formal education. Which of the following best explains how this may slow this student's learning of English?

    a. The student is not accustomed to attending formal school.
    b. The student was not exposed to English at an early age.
    c. Minimal formal education resulted in underdeveloped literacy skills in the primary language.
    d. Formal education is not valued as highly in the student's culture.

21. A kindergarten teacher has noticed that one student tends to avoid eye contact when speaking, engages in repetitive hand gestures, and becomes agitated by loud noises in the classroom. The student also struggles with various grade-level-appropriate skills, such as grasping writing utensils, using scissors, and zipping a coat. These characteristics may be indicative of which of the following?

    a. A learning disability that impacts the development of self-help skills
    b. Potential neglect at home
    c. A linguistic developmental delay
    d. A developmental disorder that affects progression across domains

22. A third-grade teacher works with students of varying needs and learning abilities, including English language learners. For an upcoming math unit on fractions, which of the following instructional approaches would be most effective in making learning accessible to all students?

    a. Incorporating digital resources to promote engagement
    b. Beginning the new unit by reviewing previously learned material
    c. Presenting new information through a variety of mediums
    d. Aligning instructional activities with grade-level district academic standards

Collaboration and Professionalism

23. A second-grade student who is typically outgoing has been withdrawn and agitated in class lately. After contacting home, the teacher learned that the student's parents have recently separated. According to the family systems theory, which of the following best explains why this likely caused the student's recent change in behavior?

    a. The student experienced negative interactions with parents.
    b. There has been disequilibrium in the family unit.
    c. The student is spending more time alone.
    d. There has been less emphasis on education at home.

24. A third-grade student has recently transferred to a new school. Under the Family Educational Rights and Privacy Act, the new school has the right to request access to which of the following student information?

    a. Previous education records
    b. Extracurricular activities and community involvement
    c. Learning style and preferences
    d. Parents' highest level of education

25. The primary purpose of Title I, Part A of the Elementary and Secondary Education Act is to:

    a. Provide academic support to students with learning disabilities.
    b. Provide additional support to students from low-income families.
    c. Fund the development of parent education programs.
    d. Establish partnerships between schools and families.

26. A third-grade teacher is having difficulty sustaining students' attention and interest. In which of the following ways might the grade-level department chairperson be able to help this teacher better meet students' needs to promote engagement?

    a. Calling parents and guardians to invoke family engagement in the students' education
    b. Rewriting classroom procedures and expectations to reduce distractions
    c. Offering guidance on instructional strategies, approaches, and activities
    d. Providing lesson materials to differentiate instruction

27. A fourth-grade teacher wants to ensure students are aware of their academic progress. The teacher posts students' assessment scores on the classroom bulletin board next to student identification numbers. This method of communicating grades violates which of the following?

    a. IDEA
    b. ESSA
    c. FERPA
    d. ESEA

28. A new first-grade teacher works with several English language learners who have varying degrees of proficiency. Each week, she meets with the school ESL teacher to review weekly lesson plans. Which of the following best describes the benefit of this collaboration for promoting learning and development among ELL students?

    a. Gaining insight into these students' backgrounds and experiences
    b. Developing strategies to integrate students' primary language into instruction
    c. Promoting academic achievement while facilitating English language acquisition
    d. Learning the difference between academic and social language acquisition

29. Each month, an elementary school hosts a parent-teacher association meeting in which families are invited to discuss the education program. Which of the following best describes how these meetings promote student learning and development?

   a. Maintaining communication through a variety of means
   b. Ensuring families are aware of classroom expectations
   c. Providing families with access to community support resources
   d. Establishing a collaborative partnership between the school and students' families

30. A fourth-grade student has recently begun exhibiting at-risk behaviors in class, such as failure to complete or turn in assignments, declining grades, and hostility toward peers. Upon contacting the student's parents, the teacher learned that the family is experiencing homelessness. Which of the following professionals in the school building would be most helpful in connecting this family to the appropriate community support resources?

   a. The grade-level vice principal
   b. The school special education teacher
   c. The school principal
   d. The school pupil personnel worker

31. A group of second-grade students informed their teacher that during physical education class, only boys were allowed to participate in a basketball game. Upon learning this, the teacher has the professional responsibility to do which of the following to protect students' rights?

   a. Notify the school administration of the students' claims
   b. Meet with the physical education teacher to determine whether the claims are true
   c. Refer the students to the school guidance counselor
   d. Suggest that the administration conduct a walkthrough observation of the next physical education class

32. According to Lev Vygotsky's sociocultural theory, which of the following best describes why a student's culture impacts his or her learning and development?

   a. Learning and cognitive development are intrinsic
   b. Learning and development occur primarily through interactions with individuals in one's immediate environment
   c. Different cultures place varying degrees of emphasis on education
   d. Language barriers may impact the rate at which students learn

33. A second-grade teacher works with a diverse group of students and wants to begin the school year by establishing a positive social context for learning. Which of the following strategies would be most effective?

   a. Having students complete interest inventories about their learning styles
   b. Reviewing students' assessment scores from the previous school year
   c. Encouraging students to share elements of their cultural backgrounds with the class
   d. Implementing Positive Behavioral Interventions and Supports (PBIS) strategies

34. A second-grade teacher believes she could improve students' learning experience with updated textbooks and new technology equipment in the classroom. Which of the following steps would be most effective in advocating for better resources to meet students' learning needs?

   a. Meeting with the school administration to discuss how new learning materials would benefit students
   b. Starting a donation fund among grade-level colleagues to pay for new textbooks and technology equipment
   c. Asking students' families to provide the new learning materials
   d. Consulting the school library and media specialist for suggestions regarding alternatives to new textbooks and technology equipment

35. During a standardized assessment in English language arts, a third-grade student tells the teacher he is unsure how to answer one of the questions. According to Pennsylvania's Code of Professional Practice and Conduct for Educators, she may NOT:

    a. Refuse to help the student with the test question
    b. Suggest the student skip the test question
    c. Implement additional supports at her own discretion
    d. Provide unauthorized assistance to the student during the test

36. A new first-grade teacher wants to collaborate with other grade-level educators to develop instructional practices, strategies, and activities to best meet her students' learning needs. Which of the following would be best?

    a. Working with the school mentor teacher
    b. Enrolling in online classes related to early childhood education
    c. Participating in an online community for first-grade educators
    d. Attending district in-service meetings

Language and Literacy Development

37. A second-grade teacher is planning a unit on analyzing informational texts. Based on the Pennsylvania English language arts standards for second grade, which of the following activities would best align with expectations for student performance at this grade level?

    a. Recognizing and labeling feeling words within the text
    b. Answering "who," "what," "how," and "why" questions about the text
    c. Making inferences based on the author's use of literary devices
    d. Connecting illustrations to the text

38. A first-grade teacher reviews high-frequency sight words with students each day by having them recite the words aloud from the class word wall, trace them on dotted lines, and practice writing the words independently. These strategies are likely intended to develop which of the following skills?

    a. Phonemic awareness
    b. Text comprehension
    c. Orthographic processing
    d. Phonological processing

39. Each week, a kindergarten teacher introduces a new short-vowel sound. To practice, the teacher implements letter games that incorporate movement, chooses books to read aloud that focus on the new sound, and has students recite it along with corresponding CVC words. These activities are beneficial in building which of the following emergent literacy skills?

    a. Phonics
    b. Receptive language
    c. Reading comprehension
    d. Orthographic processing

40. Which of the following best describes how immersing students in a print-rich environment contributes to language and literacy development?

    a. Differentiating literacy instruction to appeal to various learning styles
    b. Encouraging students to interact with a variety of literacy materials
    c. Providing multiple opportunities for self-selected reading
    d. Reflecting students' diversities in literacy instruction

41. A third-grade teacher wants to develop a community of readers by fostering connections between the literacy curriculum and students' lives. Which of the following strategies would best achieve this goal?

a. Offering students a choice in activities related to literacy instruction
b. Providing daily opportunities for self-selected reading
c. Immersing students in a print-rich environment
d. Incorporating literacy materials that reflect students' diversities into the curriculum

42. To practice decoding skills, a first-grade teacher has students clap out each sound of multisyllabic words. Which of the following additional strategies would best promote the development of this skill for children in this age group?

a. Exposing students to new multisyllabic words in a variety of contexts
b. Having students cut and paste letters to form multisyllabic words
c. Using a semantic map to demonstrate the features of new multisyllabic words
d. Having students identify the prefixes and suffixes of multisyllabic words

43. Labeling items throughout the classroom with words and corresponding images is an effective strategy for promoting prekindergarten students' ability to:

a. Understand the purpose of written language
b. Read written text from left to right
c. Describe the connections between pictures and words
d. Identify and name objects

44. A kindergarten teacher has noticed that one student is struggling with sight word recognition and decoding skills, and is beginning to fall behind the rest of the class. The teacher is concerned that this may impede the student's development of reading comprehension skills. Which of the following interventions would be most appropriate in this situation?

a. Providing individual instruction with a reading resource teacher
b. Implementing Response to Intervention (RTI) services
c. Contacting the student's parents to address the concerns
d. Developing an Individualized Education Program (IEP) to address the student's learning needs

45. A fourth-grade teacher is planning a multi-day unit in which students will write a short research essay on a topic of their choosing. Students will first brainstorm topics using a graphic organizer, and, after a demonstration, will gather relevant supporting evidence for their topics using color-coded notecards. Students will then create an outline of their essay and begin a rough draft, which will be peer-edited prior to writing the final version. By incorporating these activities into the unit, the teacher is planning to guide students through which of the following?

a. Strategies for editing writing using language conventions
b. A formative assessment of students' writing skills
c. Foundational steps of the research process
d. How to use transitional words and phrases to manage the sequence of events

46. A third-grade teacher has noticed that a student often skips words or guesses them incorrectly when reading aloud. When writing, the student often uses inventive spelling, particularly for complex words. The student would likely benefit from intervention to develop which of the following skills?

a. Listening responsively to spoken language
b. Initiating and responding appropriately in conversations
c. Irregular sight word recognition
d. Decoding and encoding

47. A kindergarten teacher wants to determine students' readiness for grade-level language arts instruction at the beginning of the school year. Which of the following assessment approaches would likely be most effective?

   a. Conducting a screening assessment focused on foundational literacy skills
   b. Observing students as they engage in both structured and unstructured play
   c. Reviewing students' prekindergarten portfolios
   d. Administering a diagnostic exam focused on the first unit of instruction

48. A second-grade teacher gives each student a list of familiar vocabulary words and asks them to circle the ones that are misspelled. In doing so, this teacher is assessing which of the following skills?

   a. Word association
   b. Phonological processing
   c. Phonemic awareness
   d. Orthographic processing

49. A prekindergarten teacher has decorated the classroom with brightly colored posters, signs, and charts, and frequently refers to them throughout the school day. This strategy supports the development of which of the following emergent literacy skills?

   a. Letter recognition
   b. Word association
   c. Print awareness
   d. Phonological awareness

50. Which of the following words does NOT contain a digraph?

   a. Doing
   b. Wait
   c. Reaching
   d. Quit

51. A second-grade teacher is planning a unit in which students will read and analyze a work of grade-level fictional literature. Prior to introducing the text, the teacher administers a reading comprehension preassessment. Which of the following best describes how the teacher can use the feedback from this assessment to plan instruction?

   a. Planning activities aligned with students' learning styles
   b. Grouping students based on reading ability
   c. Choosing texts based on students' interests
   d. Planning formative assessments to measure student progress throughout the unit

52. A kindergarten teacher is reviewing CVC words with students using letter tiles. After students read each word aloud, the teacher removes the first letter and asks them to recite the remaining sound. This activity is an example of which of the following instructional strategies to promote phonemic awareness?

   a. Phoneme substitution
   b. Phoneme isolation
   c. Decoding
   d. Phoneme deletion

53. A first-grade student often leaves out the ending sounds when reading high-frequency sight words aloud. Which of the following strategies would best help this student improve her decoding skills?

   a. Having the student practice sounding out words using letter tiles
   b. Incorporating rhyming games and songs into instruction
   c. Giving the student a list of spelling words to practice each week
   d. Having the student trace and practice writing high-frequency sight words

54. After reading an informational text, a third-grade teacher has students write a short opinion piece using sentence frames to guide their responses. This strategy is likely intended to develop students' understanding and use of:

   a. Nonverbal communication
   b. Context clues
   c. Academic language
   d. High-frequency sight words

55. A kindergarten teacher is planning to introduce students to word families. A beneficial concept to teach first would be:

   a. Automaticity
   b. Semantics analysis
   c. Onset and rime
   d. Prosody

56. A second-grade teacher is working with a student individually on reading aloud. While reading from a short passage, the teacher tells the student to follow along with the text using his index finger. This strategy is likely intended to develop which of the following skills?

   a. Prosodic reading
   b. Accuracy and rate
   c. Blending and segmenting
   d. Word recognition

57. A first-grade teacher is using direct instruction to introduce multiple-meaning words to students. Which of the following additional strategies would reinforce this concept?

   a. Having students complete sentence dictation exercises
   b. Displaying new vocabulary in the classroom with corresponding images
   c. Having students practice segmenting the new words
   d. Implementing word-building activities using letter tiles

58. A third-grade teacher is preparing to introduce an informational text to students. As a prereading strategy, the teacher reads a portion of the text aloud to the class and pauses at unfamiliar vocabulary. The teacher then asks students to identify surrounding words that may indicate examples, synonyms, antonyms, or definitions of the new words. This strategy is likely intended to develop which of the following skills?

   a. Contextual analysis
   b. Structural analysis
   c. Phonological processing
   d. Decoding and encoding

59. After having students read an informational text on the life cycle of plants, a third-grade teacher noticed that some individuals struggled to understand key vocabulary in the passage. Which of the following strategies would likely best help these students improve their comprehension?

a. Assigning comprehension questions corresponding to the text
b. Having students complete a KWL chart
c. Demonstrating how to look up unfamiliar vocabulary in the dictionary
d. Having students create a semantic map

60. While reading a work of fictional literature, a third-grade teacher asks students to circle words that describe the main character in order to determine the character's motives throughout the story. This strategy is likely intended to develop which of the following skills?

a. Literal reading comprehension
b. Inferential reading comprehension
c. Critical reading comprehension
d. Evaluative reading comprehension

61. During a writing activity, a kindergarten teacher prompts students to spell unfamiliar words phonetically. This practice encourages students to use which of the following?

a. Orthographic processing skills
b. Inventive spelling
c. Pre-communicative spelling
d. Decoding skills

62. A prekindergarten teacher uses a combination of verbal cues and nonverbal gestures to signal various transitions in the classroom throughout the school day. This strategy is beneficial in developing students' speaking and listening skills because it:

a. Provides multiple means of understanding
b. Aligns communication with students' developmental levels
c. Demonstrates that communication occurs in a variety of ways
d. Strengthens their understanding of parts of speech and types of sentences

63. A third-grade teacher is planning a unit on identifying and writing compound sentences. Which of the following instructional strategies would best support students' understanding of this concept?

a. Creating a word wall with a list of common conjunctions
b. Asking students to identify compound sentences in grade-level reading passages
c. Implementing sentence-dictation exercises
d. Having students practice the concept using sentence-building strips

64. A fourth-grade teacher is planning a unit in which students will write narrative essays, and wants to focus on developing students' ability to establish a clear beginning, middle, and end. Which of the following prewriting strategies would be most effective?

a. Having students complete a story map
b. Demonstrating how to gather supporting evidence
c. Asking students to brainstorm topics for their narratives
d. Conducting a lesson on transitional words and phrases

65. After a reading fluency check, a first-grade teacher has noticed that a student is struggling to distinguish between open and closed syllables when reading aloud. Which of the following interventions would likely best support the student's development of this skill?

    a. Reviewing how to blend and segment syllables
    b. Having the student sound out words letter by letter
    c. Providing direct instruction on the beginning, middle, and final phonemes in words
    d. Having the student practice forming words with letter tiles and reading them aloud

66. A kindergarten teacher wants to promote students' ability to retell a fictional story in sequential order. Which of the following activities would be most effective in achieving this goal with students of this age group?

    a. Providing students with a story map to fill out as they read
    b. Having students sort events from the story using picture cards
    c. Modeling how to identify transitional words and phrases in the text
    d. Having students arrange sentences from the story in the order in which they happened

Social Studies

67. After completing a unit on continuity and change over time, a second-grade teacher wants to evaluate students' ability to use timelines for recording events. Which of the following assessment approaches would be most effective in achieving this goal with students of this age group?

    a. Observing students as they sequence events from a fictional story
    b. Assigning students to write a biographical essay about a prominent historical figure
    c. Having students create an autobiographical timeline
    d. Having students identify past, present, and future events on a classroom calendar

68. A third-grade teacher is planning a unit on the characteristics of different freshwater and saltwater bodies. Which of the following accompanying activities would best connect this topic to social studies?

    a. Leading a class discussion on how hurricanes, tsunamis, and floods impact the environment and human activities
    b. Having students complete a research project on how proximity to water bodies influenced human settlement patterns
    c. Creating a Venn diagram to compare and contrast the characteristics of saltwater and freshwater bodies
    d. Instructing students to identify rural, suburban, and urban locations on a map

69. After completing a social studies unit on the election process, a second-grade teacher has students fill out secret ballots to vote on which review game to play before the summative assessment. This strategy promotes students' sense of:

    a. Leadership and social responsibility
    b. Moral imperative to follow classroom procedures
    c. Respect for diverse opinions and perspectives
    d. Democratic ideals and civic duties

70. A fourth-grade teacher is planning a lesson in which students will read and interact with a famous speech by Franklin D. Roosevelt. Prior to beginning the unit, the teacher temporarily groups students based on reading ability. This is an example of which of the following strategies for differentiating instruction?

a. Flexible grouping
b. Heterogeneous grouping
c. Student-choice grouping
d. Random grouping

71. At the beginning of each school day, a kindergarten teacher reviews the monthly calendar with students. The teacher labels days of the week as "yesterday," "today," and "tomorrow," and asks students to identify important events throughout the month. This strategy is beneficial in developing students' sense of which foundational concept related to social studies?

a. How to differentiate between fact and opinion about important events
b. Personal responsibility when working with a group
c. Time, continuity, and change
d. The importance of structure and routine to the function of an organization

72. A first-grade teacher has just completed a lesson on cardinal directions. Which of the following instructional activities would be most appropriate for allowing students of this age group to practice using this skill?

a. Using written directions to draw landmarks on a town map
b. Placing pictures of household items in the correct location on a floor plan template
c. Using an online satellite map to locate various physical and man-made landmarks
d. Comparing and contrasting the features of different types of maps

73. A third-grade teacher wants to implement technology into an upcoming lesson to increase students' awareness and understanding of important buildings, monuments, and statues related to Pennsylvania's history. Which of the following online activities would be most effective in achieving this goal?

a. A slideshow presentation focused on major events in Pennsylvania's history
b. A video clip made by a local historian about important buildings, monuments, and statues in Pennsylvania
c. An online flash card game in which students review the names of major cities in Pennsylvania
d. An online scavenger hunt in which students locate and learn about important buildings, monuments, and statues in Pennsylvania

74. A fourth-grade teacher uses a classroom token economy in which students can redeem tickets earned for positive behavior in exchange for various prizes. The most sought-after prizes require more tickets, whereas less desired items cost less. This strategy promotes students' understanding of which of the following concepts?

a. Supply and demand
b. Scarcity and choice
c. Limited resources
d. Profits and losses

Arts and Humanities

75. A kindergarten teacher strives to promote students' creative self-expression by exposing them to a variety of art materials. In the classroom, students have access to artistic materials throughout the school day, and the teacher integrates arts and humanities into multiple subject areas. Which of the following additional strategies would be effective in achieving this goal?

    a. Rotating art materials to provide students with a variety of experiences
    b. Modeling the appropriate use and care of art materials
    c. Practicing vocabulary related to visual arts
    d. Asking open-ended questions about students' artwork

76. When teaching the basic elements of visual arts, early childhood educators should demonstrate familiarity with which of the following?

    a. Proportion, hue, intensity, and value
    b. Pattern, dimension, value, medium, and balance
    c. Color, line, shape, form, and texture
    d. Primary, secondary, warm, and cool colors

77. While informally observing students during an unstructured art activity, a prekindergarten teacher noticed that one student struggled to grasp crayons, pencils, and markers. Which of the following strategies for differentiation could this teacher implement to meet this student's needs?

    a. Offer the student alternative materials to use during art time.
    b. Provide direct instruction on how to properly hold art materials.
    c. Allow the student extra time to work on art projects.
    d. Provide art materials of various sizes.

78. A fourth-grade teacher has assigned an art project in which students will apply their knowledge of acute, right, and obtuse angles to create a realistic drawing of a city. This strategy promotes students' understanding of which of the following concepts?

    a. The importance of accuracy when creating artistic representations
    b. The connection between mathematics and the arts
    c. How to properly scale a drawing to size
    d. The relationship between basic elements of the visual arts

79. Each day during music time, a first-grade teacher leads the class in singing songs that incorporate group movement and dance. Which of the following additional learning materials would promote students' sense of spatial and kinesthetic awareness?

    a. A variety of musical instruments
    b. Props such as hula hoops, ribbons, and sticks
    c. A metronome for keeping time
    d. Visual examples of various dance movements

80. A kindergarten teacher has just completed a social studies lesson on the role of firefighters, police officers, and emergency service workers in the community. Which of the following activities would best incorporate the arts and humanities to reinforce students' understanding of these roles?

    a. Showing students various images of individuals performing these roles
    b. Having students create drawings of various service workers in the community
    c. Incorporating movement into songs about community service workers
    d. Providing clothing, materials, and props for students to act out these roles

81. During an unstructured art activity, a second-grade teacher walks around to informally observe students' progress. The teacher notices that one student is using paints to create a work of art. Which of the following questions should this teacher ask to promote further exploration and inquiry?
    a. "What made you think of this idea?"
    b. "Why did you choose these colors for your project?"
    c. "Why don't you try adding some warmer colors to your project?"
    d. "What do you think would happen if you mixed red and blue?"

Mathematics

82. A second-grade teacher is planning a unit on adding and subtracting numbers up to 1,000. Prior to beginning the unit, the teacher administers a diagnostic assessment focused on content and skills from the upcoming unit. Which of the following foundational concepts should this teacher include on the assessment?
    a. Comparing three-digit numbers
    b. Order of operations
    c. Place value
    d. Creating and extending patterns

83. A fourth-grade teacher is planning a lesson in which students will use a variety of recycled materials to create a vehicle that can propel itself forward. This teacher is incorporating which of the following into instruction?
    a. Academic language
    b. Accelerated math
    c. Scaffolded instruction
    d. The STEAM model

84. For a lesson on basic multiplication facts, a third-grade teacher provides each student with an individual whiteboard and manipulatives. During the lesson, the teacher shows several problems on the board for students to solve using their manipulatives, and asks them to write their answers on the whiteboards to hold up when they're finished. This activity is an example of which of the following formative assessment approaches?
    a. Total participation techniques
    b. Informal observation
    c. Think-pair-share
    d. Student self-assessment

85. A prekindergarten teacher provides each student with a set of counting chips as they practice learning to count to ten. As students count each number aloud, the teacher instructs them to move a chip from one side of their desk to the other. This strategy is likely intended to help students do which of the following as they develop this pre-numeracy skill?
    a. Name numerals up to ten
    b. Compare numbers between one and ten
    c. Recognize and identify numerals
    d. Keep track of counting

86. A fourth-grade teacher is planning a unit on adding fractions with unlike denominators and wants to incorporate activities that align with students' varying skills, needs, and ability levels. Which of the following strategies would be most effective in scaffolding instruction to achieve this goal?

a. Reviewing flash cards that include problems with varying levels of difficulty
b. Having students play an online game in which they solve increasingly complex problems
c. Providing manipulatives for students to use as they engage in practice activities
d. Implementing total participation techniques to encourage participation

87. A second-grade teacher wants to promote students' ability to tell time to the nearest five minutes using an analog clock. Which of the following strategies would best support students' development of this skill?

a. Showing images of analog clocks corresponding to the time of events on the daily class schedule
b. Using unit cubes to help students learn to skip count by fives and tens
c. Reviewing addition and subtraction skills to help students determine elapsed time
d. Introducing digital clocks first to teach the general concept of telling time

88. A third-grade teacher displays the following word problem on the projector screen:

Sam went to a bake sale with $10.00. At the bake sale, he purchased two cookies for $1.25 each and a muffin for $2.30. Then, he bought a cupcake for his friend Julie for $1.75. How much money did Sam spend in total? How much money does he have left after the bake sale?

Which of the following instructional strategies would best help students solve this problem?

a. Representing the bake sale items Sam purchased on a pictograph
b. Reviewing how to skip count by fives and tens
c. Providing students with pretend paper money and plastic coins
d. Including a word bank with relevant mathematical language

89. In a prekindergarten classroom, the teacher has labeled each station of the play area with a number. Students' desks are also labeled by number, and a number line is posted on the front wall of the room. At the beginning of each school day, the teacher reviews the date on the class calendar and counts how many students are present. These strategies promote students' learning and development of:

a. Cardinality
b. Number sense
c. Sorting and classifying
d. Ordering

90. A kindergarten teacher wants to begin developing students' ability to think algebraically throughout a unit on adding numbers up to ten. Which of the following strategies would be most effective in achieving this goal?

a. Providing both verbal and written directions on how to add numbers up to ten
b. Modeling how to finger count when adding two numbers
c. Introducing expressions concretely, pictorially, then abstractly
d. Demonstrating where the concept of addition is applicable in real-world situations

91. A third-grade student is having difficulty with the notion that fractions represent parts of a whole. Which of the following learning materials would best support the student's understanding of this concept?

a. A geoboard
b. Base-ten blocks
c. Unit cubes
d. Pattern blocks

92. During unstructured play time, a kindergarten teacher asks a group of students in the block area to arrange the blocks from largest to smallest. This is likely intended to promote students' early development of which of the following foundational skills related to mathematics?

a. Measurement
b. Geometric awareness
c. Pattern recognition
d. Sequencing

93. As a group of fourth-grade students work independently to practice solving division problems, the teacher walks around and asks questions to check for understanding. Which of the following questions would best promote the development of students' mathematical communication skills?

a. "What answer did you get for that problem?"
b. "Can you explain how you got this answer?"
c. "What step did you take first to solve that problem?"
d. "What strategy can you use to check your answers?"

94. A third-grade teacher places the following equation on the board and asks students to estimate the answer:

$$143 + 227 + 96 =$$

Students must already have which of the following skills in order to estimate properly?

a. Representing equations in multiple ways
b. Skip counting by fives and tens
c. Comparing three-digit numbers
d. Rounding numbers to the nearest ten and hundred

95. After conducting a survey on students' favorite seasons, a first-grade teacher tallies up responses on the board. Then, the teacher provides students with a bar graph template and instructs them to color in the appropriate number of spaces to correspond with how many students prefer each season. This strategy is likely intended to develop students' understanding of which of the following?

a. When to use estimation versus calculation
b. The fact that changing an object's appearance does not alter the quantity
c. The idea that data can be represented in multiple ways
d. How to make reasonable predictions in math

96. A prekindergarten teacher notices a group of students building a block tower in the play area of the classroom. Which of the following strategies would best promote their sense of geometric awareness during this activity?

a. Prompting the students to guess the height of the tower
b. Having the students create a drawing of their tower before taking it down
c. Asking the students open-ended questions about their process
d. Encouraging the students to build another, identical tower

Science

97. Each week, a kindergarten teacher assigns a different student to be the class weather reporter. This student looks outside and describes the weather for the rest of the class. Afterward, the teacher records the student's daily report on a class weather chart. These activities encourage students to do which of the following?

a. Make observations about their environment to identify patterns and make predictions
b. Identify the effects of climate change on daily weather patterns
c. Predict how animals will adapt to changes in temperature
d. Select appropriate articles of clothing for each type of weather

98. A second-grade class is reading a text on plants and animals that have gone extinct. As they read, students circle clue words using different colors to indicate whether various statements throughout the text are facts or opinions. This strategy begins to develop students' understanding of:

a. How to create a testable hypothesis
b. The connection between language arts and science
c. The importance of verifiable evidence
d. How to analyze and interpret a nonfiction text

99. During a unit on matter and energy, a class of second-grade students will conduct an investigation to determine which method is most effective in changing a solid to a liquid. Prior to beginning the experiment, the teacher wants to develop students' ability to formulate scientific hypotheses. Which of the following strategies would be most effective in achieving this goal?

a. Reviewing the concept of cause and effect
b. Conducting an example experiment for students to observe
c. Having students conduct online research about the properties of matter
d. Providing students with sentence frames to create "if then" statements

100. A fourth-grade teacher is planning a science unit on agricultural systems and wants to integrate elements from the social studies curriculum. Which of the following activities would best demonstrate the connection between these disciplines?

a. Conducting a lesson on the life cycles of plants and animals
b. Having students complete a research project in which they investigate the agricultural practices involved in making their favorite foods
c. Showing video clips on various agricultural systems and practices
d. Demonstrating how geographic location influenced the development of civilizations

101. A third-grade teacher is planning a unit on forces of motion in which students will work in pairs to investigate the speed at which marbles of varying sizes and weights roll down a ramp. Prior to introducing the unit, the teacher administered a diagnostic exam and identified a few students that will likely need additional support. Which of the following strategies should this teacher implement during the investigation portion of the unit to ensure these students can learn effectively?

a. Provide these students with a graphic organizer to fill out during the investigation.
b. Strategically pair these students with others that can provide scaffolding.
c. Check frequently for understanding throughout the investigation.
d. Have these students complete self-reflection activities at the end of each lesson during the unit.

102. A second-grade teacher works with students of varying interests, skills, and abilities. After completing a unit on the life cycle of animals, this teacher plans to use a project-based approach to evaluate overall understanding. How could the teacher best differentiate this assessment to accommodate all students' learning needs?

a. Implementing a flexible deadline for completing the project
b. Allowing students to choose their groups
c. Providing a variety of materials for students to utilize
d. Creating a project menu to allow for student choice

103. In a prekindergarten classroom, students are creating bird feeders using recycled materials and seeds. The teacher plans to hang the feeders outside and allow students to observe as birds come to eat the seeds. This activity is likely intended to introduce which of the following scientific concepts?

a. The life cycle of animals
b. The difference between living and nonliving things
c. The basic needs of animals
d. The fact that animals grow and change over time

104. A kindergarten teacher is planning a unit on changes that can occur in matter. During one of the lessons, the teacher plans to demonstrate that water takes the shape of its container by having students work in groups to observe what happens when water is transferred between a cup, bowl, and tray. This unit and lesson activity support development of students' understanding of which unifying concept related to scientific learning?

a. Constancy and change
b. Form and function
c. Systems and order
d. Measurement and equilibrium

105. A first-grade teacher is preparing a lesson in which students will work in groups to investigate what happens when food coloring is added to different forms of liquids. At each group, the teacher has placed a bin with measuring spoons, cups, a funnel, and a magnifying class. Providing these items develops students' understanding of:

a. The connection between science and other disciplines
b. How to follow the steps of the scientific method
c. The purpose of scientific tools and when to use them
d. The proper care, handling, and storage of scientific tools

106. A first-grade teacher is planning a unit on genetics, and would like to integrate art into the science curriculum to introduce this concept. Which of the following activities would be most developmentally appropriate for students of this age group?

a. Leading a class nature walk and having students draw the plants they observe
b. Having students create a family tree
c. Playing a matching game in which students match animals with their offspring
d. Having students use clay to create models of different species of animals

107. During a field trip to a local recycling center, a group of kindergarten students learned that mixing recyclable materials prevents some items from getting recycled. To reinforce this concept in the classroom, the teacher should:

a. Have students conduct an experiment to demonstrate the impacts of litter on the environment.
b. Show examples of recyclable and nonrecyclable materials.
c. Assign an art project that incorporates recyclable materials.
d. Place labeled recycle bins in the classroom.

108. During a lesson on seasonal changes, a fourth-grade student asks the teacher why there is less sunlight during the winter months. Which of the following activities could this teacher implement to best help the student investigate and understand this concept?

a. Creating a three-dimensional model of the Earth's revolution around the Sun
b. Building a diorama of the Earth's position in relation to other planets
c. Constructing an outdoor sundial using recycled materials
d. Having the student keep a daily log of sunrise and sunset times

109. A second-grade teacher is planning a project in which students will plant seeds in containers and then cover some of them with plastic bottles that have been cut in half. This activity is likely intended to begin developing students' understanding of which concept related to agriculture?

a. Plants and animals need food to survive.
b. Recycling materials for agricultural purposes helps reduce waste.
c. There is a relationship between the greenhouse effect and food production.
d. Agricultural practices vary depending on the crop.

110. A first-grade teacher is planning a lesson in which students will identify and compare the features of different earth materials, including soil, rock, pebbles, and clay. Which of the following activities would best promote students' sense of inquiry about this concept?

a. Showing students pictures of different types of earth materials
b. Having students conduct online research about the characteristics of different earth materials
c. Asking open-ended questions about why earth materials take different forms
d. Having students search for and identify different earth materials on the school campus

111. A third-grade teacher is conducting a multi-day unit in which students investigate the effects of combining different substances. As they work, students record their thoughts, processes, and observations in a journal. After each class, the teacher reads through students' journals and provides them with feedback to use the next day. This is an example of which of the following assessment approaches?

a. Formative
b. Observation
c. Summative
d. Norm-referenced

Health

112. A first-grade teacher is conducting a lesson on segmenting multisyllabic words. Which of the following activities could this teacher incorporate into the lesson to promote students' gross motor skill development?

a. Having students practice writing multisyllabic words on dotted-line paper
b. Including a song in which students clap and stomp out the syllables of words
c. Having students count syllables on their fingers
d. Implementing a word-building activity using magnetic letter tiles

113. One of the most significant factors that may influence young children's nutrition, physical health, and overall development is:

a. Cultural background
b. Parents' highest level of education
c. Socioeconomic status
d. Genetic history

114. A third-grade teacher is preparing a project in which students will plan a meal consisting of healthy choices from each food group. Prior to beginning this project, the teacher wants to build students' knowledge of the nutritional benefits of consuming a variety of foods. Which of the following activities could this teacher implement to effectively develop their understanding of this concept?

    a. A sorting game in which students categorize foods based on their food group
    b. Having students explore the MyPlate website
    c. A class discussion on why the food pyramid is no longer used
    d. Having students keep a log of the foods they eat in a day

115. In a kindergarten classroom, the teacher asks students to cover their hands in glitter and move around the room to shake hands with their peers. By implementing this activity, the teacher most likely intends to promote students' understanding of which of the following concepts?

    a. Prosocial behaviors and positive communication skills
    b. Environmental factors that can affect health
    c. Identifying the signs of illness
    d. How quickly germs can spread

116. A first-grade teacher often looks for fun, engaging opportunities to incorporate and encourage movement throughout the curriculum. Also, this teacher often discusses ways she enjoys exercising, and has decorated the classroom with posters that promote healthy lifestyles, exercise, and good nutrition. She is doing which of the following to promote health and physical fitness?

    a. Modeling a positive attitude toward health and physical fitness
    b. Presenting health and wellness education in a variety of ways
    c. Incorporating kinesthetic components into instruction
    d. Demonstrating that physical exercise can take place in different contexts

117. While on a class nature walk, a group of first-grade students encountered a bee nest. The teacher directed students away from the nest, and explained that bee nests should be avoided because bee stings could be harmful. This teachable moment helped students understand which of the following concepts?

    a. Environmental factors that can impact health and safety
    b. Healthy and unhealthy behaviors
    c. How to identify harmful substances
    d. The importance of following basic safety rules

118. A physical education teacher is planning a fitness assessment for a group of fourth-grade students with a wide range of skills, abilities, and interests. The assessment will include four activity stations to measure students' strength, endurance, flexibility, and agility. Which of the following additional strategies could this teacher use to best differentiate the assessment in order to meet all students' needs?

    a. Allow students the option to complete the activities with a partner.
    b. Provide multiple activity options at each station.
    c. Avoid using formal grading for the assessment.
    d. Create a paper-based assessment as an alternative assignment.

119. A second-grade teacher wants to improve students' fine motor skills by developing their ability to utilize tools with control and skill to perform specific tasks. Which of the following activities would be most developmentally appropriate in achieving this goal for students of this age group?

    a. Having students practice grasping drinking cups during meal and snack times
    b. Implementing activities that require a pincer grasp
    c. Encouraging students to practice self-help skills, such as zipping coats and tying shoes
    d. Introducing the concept of typing on a keyboard

120. A physical education teacher is preparing a unit on basketball, and plans to differentiate instruction by grouping students based on ability level. Prior to beginning the unit, the teacher has students participate in a skills test and uses a checklist to evaluate their ability to perform gross motor skills related to the sport. This is an example of which type of assessment approach?

a. Diagnostic
b. Formative
c. Summative
d. Observation

121. In a kindergarten classroom, students are threading beads of various sizes onto a string. This is an example of a developmentally appropriate activity for students to practice which of the following perceptual awareness skills?

a. Temporal awareness
b. Pattern recognition
c. Hand-eye coordination
d. Spatial awareness

122. A second-grade teacher has invited an emergency responder into the classroom to speak with students about when and how to make 911 calls in an emergency. Which follow-up activity could best reinforce this concept?

a. Conducting emergency evacuation drills
b. Leading a class discussion to differentiate emergency and non-emergency scenarios
c. Establishing safety rules for the classroom and discussing their purpose
d. Reviewing environmental risk factors that may cause physical harm

123. During a lesson on the dangers of using harmful substances, a third-grade teacher has students role-play several scenarios in which they are offered drugs and alcohol. This activity develops students' ability to do which of the following?

a. Recognize that drugs and alcohol are damaging to overall health.
b. Understand that medicine is intended only to treat illnesses.
c. Practice basic refusal skills in a variety of situations.
d. Identify what constitutes a drug.

124. By second grade, most students can reasonably be expected to perform which of the following tasks in relation to fine motor development?

a. Use knitting needles to create basic patterns
b. Use tools, with assistance to complete classroom jobs
c. Engage in self-help skills independently
d. Practice using a variety of stringed instruments with accuracy

125. Each day, a kindergarten teacher begins class by leading students in a variety of simple yoga poses. This activity supports students' development of:

a. Locomotor skills
b. Fine motor skills
c. Non-locomotor skills
d. Gross motor skills

126. To protect students' physical safety before allowing them to utilize an outdoor playground, teachers must first ensure that all equipment is:

a. Varied to support differences in student ability
b. Used only for structured play activities
c. Accessible to all students
d. Clean, functional, and the appropriate size

Answer Key and Explanations

Child Development, Learning, and Assessment

1. D: The zone of proximal development (ZPD) is a concept developed by Lev Vygotsky to refer to one's ability to perform a given task with the assistance of a more experienced or knowledgeable individual. This is the second of three stages of learning outlined by Vygotsky, with the first referring to that which one cannot achieve even with assistance, and the ultimate being what one can do independently. Vygotsky proposed that if individuals are provided with adequate support while in the ZPD, they will ultimately be able to perform new tasks independently. This theory helps teachers understand how to appropriately scaffold instruction to align with students' abilities and provide necessary guidance as they learn new concepts. In this situation, scaffolds such as graphic organizers, visual aids, or chunked reading passages would be effective in supporting students in their ZPD as they learn to recall the main idea and key details of informational texts.

2. B: The quality of health and nutrition significantly impacts nearly all aspects of learning and development among young children. These factors contribute to students' energy levels, ability to focus and sustain attention in class, working memory, and emotional regulation. Further, adequate health and nutrition are necessary for proper long-term cognitive, physical, social, and emotional development. Teaching young children about the importance of nutrition and maintaining a healthy lifestyle establishes a foundation for encouraging healthy choices throughout life. In addition, teachers must know how to recognize when students' health and nutritional needs are not being met so as to provide the appropriate support and resources.

3. A: While individual students acquire language at varying rates, teachers can design effective instruction based upon knowledge of the typical progressions of linguistic development relative to students' age group. By second grade, students generally have an expansive vocabulary of about 10,000 words or more, and can identify unfamiliar terms. Further, children in this age group can typically ask for clarification and participate in discussions on the meaning of new words, and can use them in various contexts. When presenting new vocabulary about the water cycle, this teacher can reasonably expect students to ask questions about the meaning of unfamiliar words and use them in a variety of situations.

4. C: Fine motor skills are purposeful, coordinated small-muscle movements, specifically using the fingers, hands, and wrists. These skills are needed for a variety of daily tasks, so early childhood educators must offer several materials and activities to develop them. While individual children progress at varying rates, most kindergarten students can reasonably be expected to begin using tools such as pencils, crayons, and paintbrushes with a degree of purpose and control. By incorporating these materials of varying sizes into the art section of the classroom, this teacher effectively promotes students' mastery of fine motor skills while recognizing and accommodating individual ability levels.

5. B: Young children learn most effectively through play, it is important that early childhood educators incorporate several structured and unstructured opportunities to do so. Specifically, dramatic play provides a natural, hands-on setting for young children to organize, represent, and understand their learning as it applies to the world around them. After a lesson on changes in seasons and weather conditions, incorporating various types of seasonal clothing into the dramatic play area would best reinforce this new concept. Doing so would strengthen students' personal connections to learning to promote internalization, and help them understand how clothing choices correspond to changes in seasons and weather.

6. C: State and district academic standards give teachers an important framework for reference regarding expectations for student progress relative to their grade level. When planning a unit, referring to these standards helps ensure that instruction, learning activities, and classroom assessments are aligned. Doing so helps teachers plan developmentally appropriate, meaningful, and challenging learning experiences that adequately prepare students for academic success.

7. A: The nature of the classroom atmosphere significantly impacts the overall quality of learning. Students are more likely to achieve academic success when they feel included, respected, and supported in their learning environment. Establishing such a classroom requires that teachers communicate and model appreciation for students' differences. To do so authentically, teachers must first recognize and work to eliminate any personal biases toward other groups. This includes differences in race, religion, culture, and gender, as well as students' abilities. Doing so will help teachers recognize students as individuals, value their diversities, and encourage students to adopt the same sentiment toward one another. In addition to creating an overall welcoming environment, eliminating personal biases allows teachers to design more effective instruction aligned with students' individual needs to provide a challenging and educationally focused learning experience.

8. C: Print-rich environments promote language and literacy skill development among young children of all proficiency levels, including English language learners and students with learning disabilities. Such an environment exposes students to and encourages them to interact with a variety of print materials, promoting acquisition and retention while demonstrating the applications of literacy in daily life. Further, a print-rich environment aligns learning with students' individual needs, as teachers can provide materials to accommodate a wide range of skill levels. By incorporating a word wall, labels, bulletin board, and calendar, as well as a classroom library with leveled texts, this teacher effectively creates a print-rich environment that is accessible and enriching for all students.

9. D: Establishing and maintaining frequent communication with students' families is essential to planning instruction that is responsive to all students' backgrounds, experiences, and needs. Doing so creates the sentiment that family members are considered equal participants in the education program, and encourages them to share information relevant to their children's needs to help teachers plan more effective instruction. Communicating with students' families provides teachers with valuable insight into the diverse range of cultures, languages, beliefs, and individual abilities that exist within their classroom. By attending back-to-school night and maintaining communication with family members through a variety of means, this teacher will gain a greater understanding of students' needs to create more developmentally, linguistically, and culturally responsive instruction.

10. A: Screening tests are typically administered prior to the beginning of the school year to determine students' level of overall readiness for learning the grade-level curriculum. These tests measure students' abilities across developmental domains, and give teachers data-based feedback to make informed instructional decisions throughout the school year. Screening tests allow teachers to identify individual learning needs and implement appropriate instructional strategies, supports, and accommodations to ensure all students can learn effectively.

11. C: Criterion-referenced assessments are used to evaluate individual student progress in relation to a set of predetermined standards. These assessments typically have a set score that students must earn to indicate mastery of learning objectives. This approach helps prevent assessment bias, as it provides teachers with objective and data-based—and therefore, more accurate—feedback on student achievement. Criterion-referenced assessments allow teachers to identify individual student learning needs to adjust instructional strategies, practices, and supports as necessary, as well as determine the need for potential remediation.

12. C: The Pennsylvania English Language Proficiency Standards for English language learners PreK-12 outline performance indicators for ELL students at varying stages of language acquisition. These standards provide teachers with a framework for reference regarding expectations for student performance, as well as strategies for linguistic support relative to proficiency level. Referring to these standards is integral to planning appropriate and equitable content assessments for ELLs that promote English language acquisition while providing the degree of linguistic support necessary to facilitate achievement of academic standards.

13. B: Teachers have the ethical and professional responsibility to provide a fair assessment of students' academic progress. As such, it is important to maintain impartiality when evaluating students' work. This includes avoiding bias regarding culture, race, gender, or skill level, as well as any preconceived assumptions about individual students' abilities. However, at times, teachers may inadvertently experience unconscious bias that may impact their ability to provide an objective assessment. An effective strategy for avoiding assessment bias—particularly when assignments, such as essays, lend themselves to subjectivity—is to use a rubric with predetermined performance indicators. Specifically, an analytic rubric allows teachers to numerically evaluate student work in relation to several criteria, helping to provide a fair, accurate, and objective assessment.

14. C: Young children learn and demonstrate understanding in multiple ways. As such, it is important to utilize multiple performance indicators to measure student progress toward achieving learning objectives. This includes administering assessments at all stages of the learning process to evaluate student understanding. Doing so gives teachers more accurate, comprehensive feedback regarding individual learning needs, letting them adjust instructional strategies, activities, and supports as necessary to promote development for all students.

15. D: Teachers have the professional responsibility to establish and frequently maintain records of students' progress toward achieving academic standards. Utilizing technological resources, such as online gradebooks or data spreadsheets, is highly beneficial in increasing the efficiency and accuracy of this process. Such tools allow teachers to quantify student performance, thus allowing for an objective analysis and interpretation of data. This provides teachers with an accurate representation of student progress and individual needs so they can adjust instruction as necessary and implement appropriate supports to promote learning and development for all students.

16. B: Establishing, developing, and sustaining productive assessment partnerships with families enhances the overall learning experience and student achievement. To do so, teachers must include family members as equal and active participants in the assessment process. Often, family members are unsure how to contribute to their children's learning and development. By providing resources to utilize at home, such as study guides or review materials for upcoming assessments, teachers help foster the sense of inclusion necessary for an effective partnership.

17. B: Incorporating students' cultural and linguistic diversities into instruction is an important part of creating an inclusive environment in which all students feel safe and supported to engage in learning. For ELL students specifically, this strategy also fosters positive attitudes toward learning English, as it communicates that their primary language is valued and respected in the classroom. Further, incorporating students' native language into instruction promotes English language acquisition, as many foundational literacy skills from one's first language are often transferable to subsequent languages.

18. A: Under the Individuals with Disabilities Education Act (IDEA), teachers that suspect a student may have a learning disability are required to refer the student for an initial evaluation to determine the need for special education services. Doing so is integral to creating an equitable environment in which all students receive the necessary support to learn effectively. In this situation, the fact that the student in question continues to struggle with reading comprehension and writing skills despite receiving RTI services may be indicative of a potential learning disability. Upon noticing the student's lack of progress, this teacher would have the professional responsibility to refer the student for an initial evaluation with the school special education department.

19. D: Students with learning disabilities often require special accommodations to support their individual needs. Accommodations typically do not alter what the student is expected to learn, but facilitate their ability to do so effectively in an equitable environment. Students diagnosed with attention deficit hyperactivity disorder (ADHD) often struggle to focus in class, and may easily become overwhelmed by lengthy assignments. Chunking long reading passages into smaller, more manageable parts, and giving extra time for processing, would help this student sustain attention while reducing feelings of being overwhelmed. These accommodations would ensure that the student is provided with the support necessary to fully engage in learning without reducing academic expectations.

20. C: The degree of literacy skill development in the primary language contributes significantly to the rate of second-language acquisition. Many foundational literacy concepts are transferable from the primary language to subsequent ones, so those with strong skills in this area typically experience greater success and accelerated proficiency development when learning a second language. Since this student received minimal previous formal education, his literacy skills in the primary language are likely underdeveloped, which will likely hinder English language acquisition.

21. D: While all students progress at individual rates, certain atypical patterns may be indicative of a developmental delay. In this situation, the student's symptoms are characteristic of autism spectrum disorder (ASD). This is a developmental condition that can cause a range of delays across domains. Upon noticing that this student displays atypical behaviors, the teacher must refer the student for an initial evaluation to determine the need for special education services. Doing so will help ensure that this student receives the support necessary to learn effectively.

22. C: Applying universal design principles to instruction helps ensure that learning opportunities are equitable and accessible to all students, including those with learning disabilities and those who are English language learners. This approach emphasizes the importance of implementing various methods for engagement, representation, action, and expression of information to meet students' diverse needs in the classroom. In this situation, the teacher could incorporate universal design principles by introducing the new unit on fractions through a variety of mediums. This could be achieved by incorporating such accommodations as visual representations, audio and video clips, and assistive technology as necessary. Doing so would create an inclusive classroom environment in which all student needs are met to promote success in learning.

Collaboration and Professionalism

23. B: The family systems theory states that the family exists as a cohesive unit that strives to achieve equilibrium through the interactions, relationships, and dynamics of the individuals within it. According to this theory, family members directly influence one another, and a sudden shift in dynamics will cause disequilibrium that may worsen their behavior. In this situation, the separation of the student's parents disrupted the dynamics of the family system. As seen through the lens of the family systems theory, this event caused disequilibrium, which caused the change in the student's behavior.

24. A: According to the Family Educational Rights and Privacy Act (FERPA), schools may not disclose information related to students' education records without written permission from the student's parents, guardians, or legal caregivers. This extends to the student's academic, medical, and behavior records, as well as any other personally identifiable information. However, in certain situations—such as when the student enrolls in a new school—schools may release this information without prior consent from the student's designated caregivers. Upon transfer, the new school has the right to request access to the student's previous education records.

25. B: Title I, Part A is a federally funded program intended to help close the achievement gap for economically disadvantaged students. This program allocates more financial assistance to schools with a high percentage of students from low-income households to provide the support necessary to facilitate equitable learning opportunities. Funds may be used to provide learning materials and resources, additional staff, intervention programs, and staff development opportunities. In addition, Title I funds may be used to give families access to resources and education to further support their children's learning and development.

26. C: Each professional in the school building serves an important role in meeting students' learning needs. Consulting and collaborating with these professionals is essential to a positive, productive environment that fosters student learning and development. Department chairs act as leaders among their grade-level or subject-area colleagues. These experienced individuals are valuable resources for their team, as they can offer suggestions, resources, and mentoring on ways to improve one's teaching practice. By consulting the department chair, this teacher can gain insight into effective instructional strategies, approaches, and activities to more effectively meet their students' diverse needs and promote engagement in the classroom.

27. C: Teachers have the legal and professional responsibility to protect the confidentiality of their students. According to the Family Educational Rights and Privacy Act (FERPA), any information related to students' education records, including personally identifiable information, may only be disclosed to parents, guardians, or legal caregivers. In education, personally identifiable information refers to anything that may reveal students' identities, such as names, birth dates, or student identification numbers. In this situation, the teacher reveals both academic records and personally identifiable information by displaying students' assessment scores next to their identification numbers, violating their right to privacy under FERPA.

28. C: Collaborating with other professionals in the school building helps teachers develop effective instructional strategies, approaches, and supports that meet students' diverse needs to promote learning and development. The English as a second language (ESL) specialist works with students whose native language is not English. These professionals are familiar with the nuances of second language acquisition, as well as the needs and abilities of individual English language learners in the school building. The ESL specialist can offer guidance on which linguistic supports will best promote student learning, as well as strategies for incorporating students' language objectives into instruction. By reviewing weekly lesson plans with the school ESL specialist, this teacher can effectively develop and implement strategies for supporting English language acquisition among her ELL students while providing the supports necessary to facilitate academic achievement.

29. D: Students achieve greater academic success when schools and families work together to promote learning and development. It is important to provide frequent opportunities for schools and families to collaborate as equal partners in the education program. Doing so communicates the sentiment that their contributions are valued, encouraging further participation in their children's learning. Holding monthly parent-teacher association meetings provides families with the space to meaningfully share thoughts, ideas, and concerns, and contribute to decisions related to the education program, fostering a positive, collaborative partnership that enhances students' overall learning experience.

30. D: Connecting families to the appropriate community support resources is necessary to ensure students' needs are met for successful learning and development. Schools typically have a pupil personnel worker (PPW) on staff to address and provide support for circumstances that may impede students' ability to learn. These professionals act as liaisons between schools, families, and the community, and can link families to a range of community support resources to address a variety of needs. In this situation, the school PPW could help direct this family toward resources such as social service programs related to homelessness, food banks, and counseling for the student and family.

31. A: Under federal law, teachers have the legal and professional responsibility to ensure all students receive fair and equal access to learning opportunities. Schools may not discriminate against students for any reason, including race, ethnicity, religion, gender, or sexual orientation. Based on the claims of these students, the physical education teacher may be discriminating against the female students in class by not allowing them to participate in basketball games. Upon hearing this information, this teacher must report the claims to the school administration. Doing so will allow the administration to investigate and properly address the issue, protecting students' right to learn.

32. B: Lev Vygotsky proposed that learning and development occur through interactions with individuals in one's immediate environment. For young children, therefore, most early learning experiences take place within the family and community setting prior to beginning school. As values, behaviors, beliefs, and interactions vary among cultures, the nature of learning and development among children will also differ. Teachers must be aware of these differences, as well as the role of family and culture in learning and development, so as to design cross-culturally competent instruction.

33. D: The social context of the classroom significantly impacts students' attitudes toward learning and overall achievement. Teachers must make efforts to ensure that all interactions, behaviors, and relationships in the classroom are positive, respectful, and focused on productive learning. Implementing Positive Behavioral Interventions and Supports (PBIS) in the classroom is an effective strategy for establishing such a social context. This three-tiered framework is intended to promote desired behavior among students through increasingly intensive interventions and supports. First-tier strategies are typically applied to all students, such as implementing classroom behavioral expectations, praising positive behavior, and implementing reward systems. Second-tier interventions support small groups of students, and may include communication with students' families, implementing a daily check-in system, or revising behavioral expectations. Tier-three interventions focus on individual students that continuously exhibit negative behaviors, and include specialized supports such as counseling, behavior contracts, and behavior intervention plans (BIPs). In this situation, the teacher should first implement tier-one supports, such as praising desired behavior and creating classroom expectations, to establish a positive social context at the beginning of the year. This teacher should consistently implement these strategies throughout the year to maintain a positive, productive learning environment.

34. A: Advocating for students' needs is integral to ensuring they have the resources and support necessary for academic achievement. This includes ensuring that all students have the materials and equipment necessary to reach their full learning potential. To best advocate for better textbooks and technology equipment in this situation, the teacher should begin by meeting with the school administration to discuss her concerns and ideas. In doing so, the teacher can explain why the new learning materials would benefit students, and potentially influence decision-making on budgeting for the education program.

35. D: Standardized assessments are intended to provide objective feedback regarding students' progress in reaching state and district academic standards. The results of these tests are used for a variety of purposes related to the education program, such as curriculum planning, student placement, and resource allocation. Teachers therefore have the ethical responsibility to adhere to their state and district's code of conduct regarding practices related to standardized assessments. According to Pennsylvania's Code of Professional Practice and Conduct for Educators, teachers may not provide unauthorized assistance to students during these assessments. In this situation, the teacher may be able to reread assessment directions aloud, but may not offer any information that would allow students to infer the answer to specific test questions.

36. C: Collaboration with other grade-level colleagues is essential to continuously developing one's pedagogical knowledge and skills. Numerous online resources are available to facilitate such collaboration, such as online communities focused on teaching specific grade levels. In this space, teachers from different locations and levels of experience can interact to share thoughts, ideas, and experiences within the realm of education. By participating in an online community of first-grade educators, this teacher can build on others' diverse range of experiences and learn best practices, instructional strategies, and activities for meeting students' learning needs.

Language and Literacy Development

37. B: The Pennsylvania PreK-4 learning standards for English language arts outline expectations for student performance at each grade level, and should be used as a framework for planning instruction, lesson activities, and classroom assessments. According to these standards, second-grade students can reasonably be expected to use details from a grade-level informational text to answer specific questions. This includes correctly responding to "who," "what," "how," and "why" questions.

38. C: Orthographic processing skills are the ability to recognize and recall written words. These skills are necessary for the development of reading and writing fluency, as they are foundational for decoding both familiar and unfamiliar words, as well as using proper spelling and punctuation conventions. Activities to promote orthographic processing skills should include multiple opportunities for students to use and visualize words in written form, such as by tracing and writing sight words and reciting them aloud from a word wall.

Such activities help students internalize the spelling, pronunciation, and meaning of new vocabulary, thus building writing and reading comprehension skills.

39. A: Explicit phonics instruction is essential for developing foundational reading and writing literacy skills among young children. Phonics is the ability to recognize which sounds are made by individual letters or groups of letters, and is therefore necessary to decode, comprehend, and produce entire written words. Many beginner-level sight words, such as consonant-vowel-consonant (CVC) words, are easy to spell and include short-vowel sounds, so using them to introduce phonics promotes word recognition and retention. Further, reviewing short-vowel sounds through varied repetition and kinesthetic activities helps young children internalize the concept of phonics to build literacy skills.

40. B: Immersing young children in a print-rich classroom environment exposes them to a variety of language and literacy materials to promote early skill development. Such an environment may include such components as a vocabulary word wall, labels, bulletin boards, a writing center, and a classroom library containing texts of varying genres and levels of complexity. In a print-rich classroom, students are encouraged to interact with literacy materials in a variety of contexts. This helps to build foundational knowledge while demonstrating the prevalence of literacy in everyday life, strengthening students' connections to learning and fostering positive attitudes toward literacy.

41. D: Students achieve more when they are able to make personal connections to the curriculum through relevant, meaningful learning experiences. For literacy instruction specifically, this includes incorporating materials into the curriculum that reflect students' diverse backgrounds, cultures, and experiences. Doing so helps to create an inclusive learning environment that contributes to developing a community of readers. When students can see themselves represented in literacy materials, they are able to establish personal connections, fostering positive attitudes and encouraging active participation in learning.

42. B: Decoding is the ability to recognize and pronounce written language by correctly sounding out the letters within words. Selecting age-appropriate learning materials is important in designing instruction that builds this emergent literacy skill to ultimately promote reading comprehension and fluency. Young children learn best through active, hands-on learning experiences, implementing kinesthetic activities in literacy instruction helps to strengthen connections and increase retention. In this situation, having students cut and paste letters to create multisyllabic words allows them to physically interact with learning materials, promoting their understanding of letter-sound relationships to build decoding skills.

43. D: Learning to name and identify objects is an essential component of speech and language development. This concept should be integrated throughout all areas of the early childhood curriculum. Strategies that promote receptive language skills, such as labeling items in the classroom with words and corresponding images, help young children learn the names of objects around them. This provides consistent exposure to vocabulary in a variety of contexts to reinforce understanding and increase retention.

44. B: Response to Intervention (RTI) is a three-tiered model intended to provide students that struggle in a particular content area with additional support. Each tier consists of increasingly intensive services designed to develop students' skills to a grade-appropriate level. Tier-one RTI services are generally applied to all students to promote universal understanding and achievement. Students that continue to have difficulty are typically referred for tier-two RTI services, in which they receive small-group instruction outside the classroom to develop their skills in the given subject area. Tier-three services are directed toward individual students in need of significant support. In this situation, the student likely has not responded to the tier-one interventions applied to the whole class, and therefore would benefit from receiving tier-two RTI services.

45. C: Guiding students through the foundational steps of the research process should begin in early elementary school. Doing so promotes writing skill development while establishing a foundation for success across content areas. In this situation, the teacher plans to guide students through the steps of the research process with each activity. Having students brainstorm topics will help them narrow their essay's focus.

Demonstrating how to gather evidence shows students how to effectively support their writing topics with relevant information. Assigning students to create outlines prior to beginning rough drafts will help them organize their writing, while peer-editing will help them refine it. These activities for each stage of the research process will help students produce clear, coherent, and organized essays while promoting writing skill development.

46. D: In phonics, decoding refers to one's ability to recognize and correctly pronounce sounds produced by written letters and words. Encoding refers to one's ability to identify and produce written letters and words to correspond to the sounds of spoken language. These skills are reciprocal, and both are imperative for literacy development across domains, as they directly contribute to students' reading comprehension, writing, and oral language abilities. In this situation, the student shows deficiencies with both decoding and encoding, and therefore would benefit from more support to develop these skills.

47. A: Screening assessments are typically administered at the beginning of the school year to determine students' level of readiness to participate in grade-level instruction in a particular content area. These assessments provide teachers with valuable feedback on students' prior knowledge, abilities, and skills so teachers can prepare instruction that aligns with their developmental levels and individual needs. Screening assessments can be conducted either formally or informally, and generally include the curriculum that will be covered throughout the school year. In this situation, conducting a universal screening test focused on foundational literacy skills will help this teacher select appropriate learning materials, implement necessary supports, and differentiate instruction to promote success for all students.

48. D: Orthographic processing skills encompass the ability to recognize and recall written words, as well as implement conventions related to writing, including spelling, punctuation, and capitalization. Students with strong orthographic processing skills are able to visually identify when a word is spelled incorrectly because of their understanding of the parts of words. In this situation, by asking students to circle misspelled words from a list of familiar vocabulary, the teacher is assessing students' orthographic processing skills in relation to writing conventions.

49. C: Print awareness is the understanding of the prevalence of printed language in everyday life, as well as the recognition that printed words and letters convey meaning. Understanding this basic concept of print is foundational in emergent literacy skill development, so it must be emphasized in the early childhood classroom. Surrounding young children with multiple examples of environmental print, such as posters, signs, and charts, demonstrates the existence and purpose of printed language to begin building print awareness.

50. A: A digraph is the combination of two letters to create a single phoneme. These combinations may consist of vowels, consonants, or a combination of both, but must only produce one syllable. Digraphs are common in English, so identifying and recognizing the sounds they produce is fundamental in building word recognition and reading comprehension skills. Common examples of digraphs include "ch," "qu," "ai," "sh," and "th." While "oi" can also be a digraph in some cases, in a word such as "doing," the letters "o" and "i" are pronounced as two syllables, so it is not a digraph.

51. B: Diagnostic assessments are typically administered prior to a new unit of instruction. These assessments can take several forms, such as preassessments, anticipation guides, or surveys, and are intended to provide teachers with feedback on students' background knowledge, abilities, and level of understanding in relation to the upcoming unit. Teachers can use this feedback to guide the planning process, as it allows them to identify areas of student need to implement appropriate strategies, supports, and accommodations. For English language arts, this can include using preassessment data to group students based on reading ability. Doing so will help the teacher scaffold instruction to ensure learning aligns with students' needs to be successful throughout the unit.

52. D: Phoneme deletion is an instructional activity in which students practice sounding out parts of words after one phoneme, or sound, has been removed. This strategy develops students' sense of phonemic awareness, or the ability to distinguish individual sounds in spoken words or parts of words. Building phonemic awareness is foundational for emergent literacy skill development, as it contributes to phonological awareness, which is the ability to differentiate and understand words and sounds in spoken language as a whole.

53. A: The ability to isolate individual phonemes is essential to building the degree of phonemic awareness necessary for oral language and reading comprehension development. While activities such as rhyming games, chants, and songs help young children acquire this skill, such activities often present new words in their entirety, which proves difficult for some students. When decoding high-frequency sight words, students may recognize and correctly pronounce the root of the word, but often ignore modifiers such as prefixes or suffixes, leading to errors in pronunciation. Having struggling students practice sounding out words using letter tiles lets them visualize and physically manipulate each letter, strengthening their understanding of letter-sound relationships.

54. C: Academic language is language used primarily in the realm of education. Its complexity and content-specific nature often make it difficult for young children to acquire, comprehend, and use correctly. However, academic language is a necessary component to literacy skill development and achievement across content areas. Sentence frames are an effective tool for guiding students as they learn to use this unfamiliar vocabulary. This strategy contextualizes and scaffolds learning by prompting students to fill in blanks as they craft written responses, supporting their understanding of how to use academic language.

55. C: Word families are words that are spelled and pronounced similarly. For example, the words "brain," "rain," "stain," and "train" all share the "-ain" ending, and therefore belong to the same word family. Introducing word families using the concept of onset and rime—the beginning and ending sounds of a syllable—familiarizes students with the different parts of words. The onset is the initial consonant that begins the syllable, and the rime consists of the remaining vowels and consonants. Teaching this concept first contributes to developing the phonological awareness skills necessary for decoding written language. Doing so helps students identify words in the same word family while promoting vocabulary acquisition, word recognition, and ultimately, reading comprehension skills.

56. B: Accuracy and rate are essential components to building reading fluency. Accuracy is the ability to read and comprehend text with minimal errors, and rate is the speed at which one reads. Typically, as accuracy improves, rate also increases. Having students physically track text using their finger when reading is an effective strategy for developing both these skills. Doing so enhances students' ability to focus on individual words as they read while incorporating a kinesthetic element to strengthen connections as they develop reading comprehension skills.

57. B: Developing students' range of vocabulary is essential to building reading comprehension skills. This includes teaching students that some words in English may have multiple meanings. Homonyms are words that are spelled and pronounced the same, but have different meanings, such as "right," "left," "bat," and "well." Providing consistent reminders of the various meanings of such words helps students internalize this difficult concept to promote retention and deepen their understanding of new vocabulary. After introducing homonyms to students through direct instruction, displaying the new vocabulary with corresponding images would give students a visual reference to reinforce the multiple meanings of these words.

58. A: Contextual analysis skills, or the ability to look for clues within a text to decipher the meaning of unfamiliar words, are essential to vocabulary acquisition and reading comprehension. Examples of context clues include synonyms, antonyms, examples, or definitions that are embedded throughout the text and indicate the meaning of the new word. Teaching students to locate and use these clues helps them learn to make educated guesses regarding the meaning of unfamiliar terms, which increases vocabulary and improves reading comprehension skills.

59. D: Vocabulary acquisition is a necessary component in the development of reading comprehension skills. When engaging with a new text, students may struggle to understand unfamiliar terms, impeding their ability to comprehend the text as a whole. Semantic mapping is an analysis strategy intended to help students develop word-learning skills by having them categorize the features of new vocabulary using a graphic organizer. This activity allows students to visualize the characteristics of and relationship between new words associated with a particular concept, thus strengthening overall understanding, and ultimately, reading comprehension. In this situation, having students complete a semantic map of words associated with the life cycle of plants would be beneficial in improving their comprehension of the informational text.

60. B: Reading comprehension refers to one's ability to read and understand a text. This skill can be categorized into three levels with increasing degrees of complexity. Literal reading comprehension refers to the ability to read and understand the basic meaning of words and sentences in a text. Inferential reading comprehension requires individuals to employ higher-order thinking skills by using contextual clues to determine what is implied by the author's use of literary techniques. Evaluative, or critical, reading comprehension occurs when readers connect a text to their own background knowledge and experiences to formulate personal thoughts and opinions on what they have read. In this situation, the teacher asks students to circle descriptive language that may indicate the motives of the main character. Students are tasked with using evidence from the text to support their thoughts and ideas about this topic, promoting the development of inferential reading comprehension skills.

61. B: Inventive spelling occurs when students employ their knowledge of letter-sound relationships to spell unfamiliar words. As spelling development occurs in stages, it is important to recognize that many young children will rely on inventive spelling as they begin learning to write. Encouraging this practice has students use their sense of phonemic awareness to sound out new words, ultimately improving their spelling abilities. However, the teacher must correct misspelled words to ensure proper development. Students that continue to use inventive spelling past the normal developmental stage may require additional support and intervention.

62. C: Helping young children understand that communication can occur in different ways, including both verbally and nonverbally, is an important component of developing their speaking and listening skills. Verbal communication refers to spoken language, volume, and intonation, whereas nonverbal communication includes such elements as eye contact, gestures, physical distance, and body language. Incorporating both forms of communication into the classroom for different purposes helps students learn to listen and respond appropriately in a variety of contexts. Further, this strategy supports students' oral language development, as accompanying verbal communication with nonverbal cues strengthens their understanding of its meaning.

63. D: Compound sentences occur when two independent clauses are joined by a conjunction, such as "and" or "but." This concept builds on students' knowledge of simple sentences, which consist of only one independent clause. Teaching the components and formation of compound sentences is important in developing students' ability to write on a more complex level, as well as their understanding of the characteristics and functions of the English language. Introducing compound sentences using kinesthetic materials, such as sentence-building strips, allows students to explore this concept in a hands-on learning setting. This strategy allows students to physically construct sentences using independent clauses and conjunctions, strengthening their understanding.

64. A: Effective writing includes a clear beginning, middle, and end. Teaching students this important skill is essential to developing their ability to write clearly and for a variety of purposes. As young children learn to express themselves in writing, particularly in narrative form, they may find it difficult to organize their thoughts in such a way. Story maps are a versatile form of graphic organizer that can be used as a prewriting activity to help students organize the events of their narrative pieces. This resource provides students with a visual aid to better arrange their ideas into a distinct beginning, middle, and end, improving the clarity and organization of their writing.

65. D: Distinguishing between syllable types is essential to developing the decoding skills necessary to facilitate reading comprehension, spelling, and writing abilities. Closed syllables are ones that include the short vowel sound followed by a consonant, whereas open syllables end with a long vowel sound. Students that struggle to recognize the difference will likely require additional support to ensure proper literacy development. Having these students practice forming words with letter tiles and reading them aloud provides a multisensory approach to develop this skill. This activity allows students to visualize, verbalize, and physically manipulate letters to strengthen their understanding of the different sounds produced by these two syllable types.

66. B: In language arts, sequencing refers to one's ability to recall and retell events of a text in the order in which they occurred. Teaching this important skill is essential to promoting success across content areas, as it contributes to the development of reading comprehension and writing, as well as the ability to understand and respond appropriately to directions. By kindergarten, students can reasonably be expected to retell the major events of a fictional work of literature in the order in which they occurred using visual aids as support. In this situation, having students sort events from the story using picture cards would most effectively promote their sequencing abilities.

Social Studies

67. C: Authentic summative assessments provide students with relevant and meaningful opportunities to demonstrate what they have learned. This assessment approach places learning in a familiar and real-world context, fostering students' personal connections for greater understanding. By second grade, students can reasonably be expected to create and use simple timelines to record events, including from their own lives. An autobiographical timeline project provides students with a personalized, engaging, and grade-level-appropriate learning opportunity to demonstrate their knowledge of how to sequence events chronologically.

68. B: Cross-curricular opportunities enrich instruction by demonstrating the relevance of learning in various contexts to strengthen students' understanding across content areas. When social studies is incorporated into other subject areas, students can explore its prevalence and application in daily life. In this situation, incorporating elements of social studies into a science unit on saltwater and freshwater bodies helps students understand the characteristics of different water resources, as well as how physical geography impacts human life. With exploratory activities such as a research project, students can learn how proximity to different bodies of water influenced human settlement patterns, and ultimately, other aspects of civilization, such as agriculture, diet, and commerce.

69. D: Young children learn best when provided with opportunities to actively participate in the process. For social studies instruction, such opportunities apply learning in real-world contexts, making it relevant and meaningful. In this situation, allowing students to vote on which review game to play promotes their understanding of the significance of voting as a civic duty to uphold democratic ideals and influence decisions related to the group as a whole. Further, in accompanying a unit on the election process with this activity, the teacher reinforces content-area material while developing students' sense of civic responsibility and their role in a democratic society.

70. A: Differentiating instruction is necessary to provide students of varying needs, abilities, skills, and preferences with equitable and engaging opportunities to participate in learning. Differentiated instruction takes several forms, and should occur throughout all stages of instruction. In this situation, the teacher plans to differentiate a lesson on a speech made by Franklin D. Roosevelt by implementing flexible grouping based on students' reading ability. Flexible grouping is the temporary grouping of students to accommodate specific learning needs in a given area. This strategy will allow the teacher to incorporate the appropriate scaffolds, such as chunking or modifying the text, to ensure all students have the supports necessary to learn effectively.

71. C: Teaching young children the notion of time, continuity, and change is necessary to develop their understanding of foundational concepts related to social studies, such as cause and effect, as well as how to accurately situate, recall, and make connections between historical events. Doing so should take place in a developmentally appropriate, familiar, and applicable context to ensure understanding. In this situation, labeling the days of the week as "yesterday," "today," and "tomorrow," as well has having students locate various events on a monthly calendar, shows how time functions in their daily lives. This strategy helps students begin to understand that time is linear and events happen chronologically, developing their sense of time, continuity, and change.

72. A: Providing young children with hands-on experiences to practice skills related to social studies strengthens their internalization of foundational concepts necessary for continued success in learning. Doing so helps establish a framework for reference that students can apply when learning increasingly complex topics in the content area. The ability to use cardinal directions, for example, is necessary for describing the locations of places and regions, as well as understanding more complex ideas related to geographic literacy, such as spatial awareness, latitude, longitude, and time zones. In this situation, having students use written directions to physically draw landmarks on a town map allows them to visualize cardinal directions in a hands-on, developmentally appropriate learning setting.

73. D: Incorporating digital resources into instruction creates an engaging learning experience in which students can interact with the curriculum in a meaningful way. In this situation, an online scavenger hunt on elements of Pennsylvania's history encourages a sense of inquiry, interest, and exploration about the subject. Such an activity increases the relevance of learning, as it lets students view and learn more about important buildings, monuments, and statues located in Pennsylvania in a realistic setting, thus strengthening their understanding of and connection to their community's history.

74. A: Understanding the concept of supply and demand—the notion that the availability of and desire for a product influences its price—is important for developing economic literacy. This skill is necessary for grasping increasingly complex topics, such as economic interdependence, price determination, and market competition. Students learn this foundational concept most effectively when provided with opportunities to interact with it in a relevant and meaningful way. By requiring more tickets for sought-after prizes, this teacher incorporates supply and demand into the classroom token economy in a real-world, applicable context to promote student understanding.

Arts and Humanities

75. A: Providing young children with a variety of artistic experiences is essential to promoting exploration, interest in the arts, and creative development. This includes teaching students to use a range of mediums, including paints, pencils, three-dimensional materials, and age-appropriate digital tools. While art materials should be accessible throughout the school day, it is also important to rotate which materials are available, to provide rich and varied experiences. Doing so provides exposure to multiple outlets for creative expression, allowing students to engage in the artistic process in a way that best suits their interests while promoting their ability to use a variety of materials when creating a work of art.

76. C: Teaching students to identify, describe, and apply basic elements of visual arts establishes the foundation for building artistic knowledge and creative development. Doing so helps students improve their own skills as they learn to manipulate these elements while fostering their ability to recognize, analyze, and interpret techniques in others' works of art. To design and implement effective learning experiences that incorporate the visual arts, early childhood educators must be familiar with the following basic elements:

- **Color**: the degree of hue, value, and intensity represented in the visual elements of a work of art
- **Line**: marks in a work of art that convey shape, movement, direction, and emotion
- **Shape**: two-dimensional objects in a work of art
- **Form**: three-dimensional shapes and objects in a work of art
- **Texture**: elements in a work of art that convey physical feeling

77. D: While formal evaluation of artistic ability is not typically advised in the early childhood classroom, conducting informal observational assessments attunes teachers to differences in students' learning styles, abilities, developmental levels, and needs. Feedback from such informal assessments allows teachers to adjust, modify, and implement supports to ensure all students can learn effectively. Doing so promotes positive learning experiences that encourage continued interest and exploration in the arts and humanities. By conducting an informal observational assessment, this teacher identified a student with a specific need, which means she can address it properly. In this situation, the student appears to have not yet developed the fine motor skills necessary to grasp certain artistic materials. Incorporating art materials of various sizes will provide the differentiation necessary to ensure that unstructured art time is aligned with this student's level of fine motor skill development, facilitating the student's full participation in learning.

78. B: Integrating the arts and humanities into other disciplines strengthens students' content knowledge while promoting creative development. Further, providing such cross-curricular learning activities illustrates the connection between the arts and other subject areas, increasing relevance by demonstrating their prevalence in everyday life. By having students apply their knowledge of acute, obtuse, and right angles to draw a realistic impression of a city, this teacher facilitates students' ability to make connections between art and mathematics. In doing so, this teacher fosters greater understanding of both disciplines by demonstrating how concepts learned in each content area can be applied to one another.

79. B: Incorporating music into daily learning experiences promotes development across domains, including students' ability to express themselves creatively. Further, incorporating group movement and dance activities into music instruction develops students' sense of spatial and kinesthetic awareness. Kinesthetic awareness is the understanding of how one's body moves, whereas spatial awareness is the awareness of one's body in relation to other individuals or objects. Through group movement and dance, students develop a greater understanding of how their bodies move, both individually and in relation to their environment, ultimately promoting the development of purposeful, coordinated movements. Providing students with physical props during these activities, such as hula hoops, ribbons, or sticks, enhances the development of these skills, as it encourages students to physically manipulate objects with purposeful awareness as they move within the group.

80. D: Incorporating opportunities for dramatic play into the early childhood classroom is essential to promoting students' ability to creatively express thoughts, ideas, and feelings as they make sense of the world around them. Through dramatic play, young children can imitate people, objects, animals, and scenarios observed in real-life experiences to organize, process, and develop a deeper understanding of their environment. After a lesson on the roles of firefighters, police officers, and emergency service workers, providing items for students to act out these roles in a dramatic play situation would reinforce their understanding.

81. D: Learning experiences in the arts and humanities should foster student inquiry and exploration. As students engage in the artistic process, they should be encouraged to take risks, test new ideas, and create new solutions to problems. Doing so promotes students' creative development and artistic ability while fostering continued interest in the arts. Asking students open-ended questions as they create works of arts promotes such exploration and inquiry. This strategy communicates genuine interest in students' artwork while instilling confidence to try new methods and explore potential outcomes. In this situation, asking the student what she thinks would happen if red and blue were mixed prompts her to try a new technique and build on her creative skills.

Mathematics

82. C: Before introducing a new concept in mathematics, it is important to determine whether students have developed a solid understanding of related fundamental concepts. Doing so ensures that students have the foundation of knowledge necessary to grasp increasingly complex concepts, problems, and methods. Administering diagnostic exams before a new unit of instruction gives teachers insight on students' level of background knowledge related to new material. The feedback provided from such assessments allows teachers to address areas of student need, clarify misconceptions, and identify any potential need for remediation to facilitate all students' ability to learn effectively. In this situation, students must have mastered the concept of place value in order to properly understand how to add and subtract numbers up to 1,000. This skill serves as an important framework for reference on how to set up addition and subtraction problems with two- and three-digit numbers, work within the appropriate columns, and regroup as necessary. Including this concept on a diagnostic test will help ensure students are fully prepared for success in learning when the new unit begins.

83. D: STEAM activities refer to those which simultaneously incorporate elements of science, technology, engineering, art, and math. Such multidisciplinary activities enrich learning by promoting higher-order skills such as critical thinking, problem-solving, and creativity while demonstrating the connection between content areas. For math instruction, STEAM activities highlight the prevalence of mathematical concepts in daily life, strengthening students' real-world connections to learning for greater understanding. In this activity, the teacher integrates all components of STEAM to provide a rich and multifaceted learning experience. Students will explore the properties of force and motion by creating a vehicle that can propel itself forward. Further, by using recycled materials to plan, design, and build the vehicle, students will employ concepts related to technology, engineering, and art. Math is involved because students will need problem-solving strategies to build a functional vehicle, and to calculate the amount of force required to propel it forward based on its weight.

84. A: Total participation techniques are whole-class activities in which students are prompted to actively participate in the learning experience. Such activities are intended to promote student engagement, strengthen understanding, and serve as a valuable formative assessment tool for teachers. By having students hold up their answers to multiplication problems on individual whiteboards, this teacher can quickly and formatively evaluate students' understanding. This strategy will provide the teacher with the feedback necessary to make adjustments throughout instruction, implement supports, and identify areas that may need reteaching to better meet students' learning needs.

85. D: Learning to keep track while counting is an important pre-numeracy skill that supports the ability to understand such concepts as ascending and descending order, cardinality, and one-to-one correspondence. When teaching prekindergarten children to count to ten, providing manipulatives such as counting chips creates an active, hands-on learning experience to support students in developing this skill. This strategy provides a kinesthetic element to learning by allowing students to physically move individual chips as they learn to count to ten, as well as a visual aid to help them keep track of how far they have counted.

86. B: Scaffolding math instruction is essential to ensuring all students are supported as they develop the foundational skills necessary for grasping increasingly advanced concepts. Doing so aligns instruction to students' individual needs, skills, and abilities while promoting their learning and development in math. Having students play an online game in which they solve fraction problems that gradually increase in difficulty is highly effective in accommodating a range of needs in the classroom. This strategy allows students to build knowledge based on their current abilities, work at their own pace, and develop greater understanding as they work with increasingly complex problems.

87. A: Young children learn effectively when new mathematical concepts are placed in familiar, real-world contexts. This strategy fosters personal connections to learning, as students can see where it is relevant and applicable in their own lives. Showing images of analog clocks helps students internalize how to read them by providing a visual reference of how various times appear. Further, this concept is reinforced by corresponding each image to the time of each event on the class schedule. Doing so connects the idea of telling time with analog clocks to an immediately recognizable situation, making learning meaningful and promoting students' learning and development of this skill.

88. C: Learning to count money requires that students apply knowledge of several learned concepts, including addition and subtraction, skip counting, decimals, and the value of each denomination. Creating hands-on learning experiences supports students' ability to integrate these ideas when developing this new skill. By providing students with paper money and plastic coins as they work through this word problem, the teacher adds a visual and kinesthetic component to instruction that promotes students' understanding of how to count, add, and subtract money. This strategy will allow students to physically manipulate the various denominations of money as they work while providing a visual reference to keep track of their counting. Further, using representations of actual currency adds a realistic element to solving the problem, increasing relevance and strengthening students' personal connections to learning for greater success.

89. B: Number sense refers to a variety of early numeracy skills, including number recognition, counting, comparing numbers, and the ability to use mathematical language. Developing students' number sense is essential to establishing a foundation for understanding fundamental concepts in mathematics, so it must be emphasized in the early childhood classroom. Placing numbers in multiple contexts provides students with frequent and varied exposures to numbers throughout the school day. Doing so familiarizes students with numbers, how to use them, and what they can represent. By labeling the play area and students' desks with numerals, posting a number line in the classroom, and reviewing numbers with the whole class, this teacher demonstrates the prevalence of numbers in everyday life, promoting students' number sense.

90. C: Promoting students' ability to think algebraically in early elementary school establishes a foundation for thinking abstractly when working with increasingly advanced mathematical concepts. To achieve this, teachers should introduce math experiences gradually as students develop mastery. This method allows young children to progress through increasingly complex levels of algebraic thinking as they learn, while also demonstrating that the same expression can be presented in multiple ways. When introducing a new mathematical concept, teachers should begin by doing so concretely, then pictorially, and ultimately, in abstract terms. For example, in this situation, the teacher could begin by having students work with manipulatives as they solve addition problems, then present the equation using pictures of familiar objects, and eventually, show them only the numerical equation. Doing so helps students learn how to think algebraically when approaching new mathematical concepts.

91. D: The idea that fractions represent parts of a whole can be difficult for young children to grasp initially, as it requires a degree of abstract thinking. Incorporating manipulatives, such as pattern blocks, can help promote understanding for struggling students by adding a concrete element to learning. Pattern block sets are typically composed of squares, equilateral triangles, hexagons, rhombuses, and trapezoids, and are often used to demonstrate that shapes can be divided into equal parts. This resource allows students to visualize and physically manipulate shapes into equal parts, strengthening their understanding that fractions represent parts of a whole.

92. A: Understanding the concept of measurement is essential to developing skills across subject areas and in multiple real-world situations. Further, introducing measurement in early childhood establishes the foundation of understanding necessary for students to grasp increasingly complex topics, such as volume, height, weight, and mass. To introduce this idea, teachers should begin with the notion that some objects are larger or smaller than others, which prompts students to recognize differences in size. By asking students to arrange blocks from largest to smallest, this teacher encourages them to notice the size of each block and sort them accordingly, promoting early development of measurement skills.

93. B: Mathematical communication skills are the ability to speak and write effectively using mathematical terms. This includes using mathematical language to discuss one's thoughts, reasoning, and problem-solving strategies. Mathematical communication skills are necessary for developing and building on concept knowledge, as they promote students' understanding of their own thinking, connections between mathematical ideas, and ability to verbalize their processes. In this situation, asking students how they got a particular answer prompts them to consider their own reasoning and explain each step of their problem-solving strategy, promoting mathematical communication skills.

94. D: Teaching students strategies for estimation is beneficial in developing their mental computational skills, ability to make predictions, and understanding of reasonableness in terms of mathematical thinking. The ability to round numbers is an essential skill when working with estimation, as it allows students to simplify large numbers to quickly approximate an answer with a relative degree of accuracy. In this situation, students must be familiar with how to round numbers to the nearest ten and hundred in order to produce a valid estimation of the answer.

95. C: Teaching students to analyze and interpret data is essential in fostering their ability to identify patterns and relationships, compare information, and make informed predictions. This includes demonstrating that data results can be represented in multiple ways, such as bar graphs, pictographs, line plots, pie charts, or tally marks. Developing students' understanding of this concept is necessary to help them learn to analyze and interpret data in various formats, as well as determine when each one is most applicable. By having students create a bar graph based on tally marks to represent students' favorite seasons, this teacher demonstrates two ways that the same data can be presented.

96. B: Geometric awareness is the fundamental understanding of shapes, their characteristics, and their relationship to space. This includes recognizing the attributes of two- and three-dimensional shapes, differentiating between them, and describing their position and location in the environment. Teaching this skill in early childhood is essential to promoting students' spatial awareness, ability to grasp increasingly advanced mathematical concepts, and algebraic thinking and problem-solving skills. Encouraging young children to engage in geometric play, such as having them use blocks to build a tower, fosters an early sense of geometric awareness. Teachers can further enhance this development by asking students to create a drawing of their block tower before taking it down. Doing so prompts students to translate the physical form of their block tower into a drawing, promoting geometric awareness by encouraging them to focus on specific characteristics of each shape and their relationship to one another within the tower.

Science

97. A: Young children are naturally inclined to make observations about the world around them as they learn, process, organize, and test new ideas. Creating learning opportunities in which students are encouraged to do so promotes learning and development in science by fostering their inherent sense of curiosity, inquiry, and exploration. By selecting students each week to conduct a daily weather report and recording it on a class weather chart, this teacher prompts students to think scientifically about this concept by asking them to make observations about the natural environment to identify patterns and make predictions.

98. C: The ability to distinguish between fact and opinion is essential for learning and development across content areas, as well as in a variety of real-world contexts. For scientific learning, developing this skill helps instill the notion that science is rooted in fact, as well as the importance of seeking and producing verifiable evidence. Teaching students to distinguish between facts and opinions promotes their ability to support their own claims using valid data and determine the credibility of others' findings when engaging in scientific inquiry. In this situation, the teacher establishes the foundation for understanding the importance of verifiable evidence by first teaching students to distinguish between facts and opinions as they read through a text.

99. D: In science, a hypothesis is a testable prediction about the outcome of an experiment. These statements describe the intended effect of the independent variable on the dependent variable, and are the foundation of scientific investigations. Teaching young children to write an effective hypothesis is fundamental in developing their ability to follow the scientific method, so it must be taught explicitly. Giving students sentence frames to construct "if then" statements effectively introduces and develops this skill. Doing so guides students' writing to help them clearly express the cause-and-effect relationship between the variables in their experiment.

100. B: Integrating science into other disciplines strengthens students' understanding of learning across subject areas while highlighting the prevalence of scientific concepts in a variety of contexts. This makes science instruction relevant and meaningful to students as they begin to recognize situations in which their learning is applicable in daily life. In this situation, the teacher wants to highlight the relationship between scientific practices involved in agricultural systems, food production, and how it impacts the daily lives of people. By accompanying this science unit with a project in which students investigate the agricultural practices involved in making their favorite foods, the teacher creates an engaging, personalized learning opportunity that promotes understanding of the concept from both a scientific and social studies perspective. Through this activity, students can explore the interconnection between agricultural systems and the processes, individuals, and economics involved in producing their favorite foods.

101. B: Scaffolding science instruction helps to ensure that students of varying needs, skill levels, and abilities receive the support necessary to succeed in all stages of the learning process. Scaffolds can be implemented in a number of ways to accommodate a variety of learning situations. Many science activities incorporate hands-on, collaborative investigations, so strategic pairing scaffolds learning to facilitate all students' participation in the process. This strategy allows students who may need extra help to build upon the knowledge, skills, and understanding of their partners to promote their own learning and development in science.

102. D: Differentiating science instruction, particularly during project-based activities, is essential to fostering students' natural sense of curiosity and inquiry. Doing so aligns learning to students' varying interests, abilities, and skills to promote engagement and active participation. Science instruction should be differentiated throughout all stages of the learning process, including the assessment of content knowledge. By offering a choice in assessment using a project menu, this teacher can accommodate a range of needs in the classroom while ensuring all students are evaluated on the same criteria. This strategy would allow for flexibility in demonstration of understanding to promote learning and development in science for all students.

103. C: Introducing new concepts in science using active learning opportunities to promote exploration, creativity, and observation fosters students' natural sense of curiosity in the early childhood classroom. Doing so strengthens students' connections to learning by encouraging them to ask questions and test ideas, and helping them process new information. By having students create bird feeders to hang outside and observe, this teacher uses a hands-on learning approach to introduce the concept that animals have basic needs. This strategy will encourage students to watch as birds come to eat from the feeders they created, establishing a real-world foundation for understanding that living animals require food for survival.

104. A: Effective instructional planning in science is based on a set of central unifying themes within the field. This promotes student learning and development in science by establishing a foundation for understanding increasingly complex ideas while demonstrating the connections between scientific concepts. In this situation, students will learn that liquid takes the shape of its container by transferring water from a cup to a bowl, and then to a tray, thus developing a fundamental understanding of the law of conservation of matter. This law applies to the unifying concept of constancy and change; it states that although matter can change shape and form, its quantity remains constant.

105. C: Supporting students' learning and development in science includes helping them understand the purpose of scientific tools and when to use them. It is important to provide students with a variety of tools, materials, and equipment to promote active exploration and inquiry as they begin learning the steps of the scientific process. Doing so develops students' awareness that scientists use specific equipment to conduct investigations, gather information, and produce valid results. By giving each group a bin with various tools for conducting the experiment, this teacher encourages students to select which item will be most useful in gathering information, promoting their understanding of the purpose and uses of scientific equipment.

106. B: Introducing scientific concepts through developmentally appropriate practices is essential to establishing the foundation necessary for students to grasp increasingly complex ideas. Doing so promotes engagement and understanding by fostering students' natural sense of curiosity, exploration, and inquiry in a setting aligned with their interests and abilities. Young children internalize new scientific concepts most effectively when provided with active, relevant, and hands-on learning opportunities that foster personal connections to learning. This notion is strengthened by incorporating other disciplines, such as art, into science instruction. By first grade, most students can reasonably be expected to understand basic relationships between family members. Introducing the concept of genetics by having students create a family tree places learning in a personalized, project-based, and cross-curricular setting. This developmentally appropriate activity will ultimately strengthen students' understanding of genetics by allowing them to visualize similarities between their own family members, introducing the idea that individuals within the same family often share similar traits.

107. D: Placing new concepts in a relevant, meaningful context promotes scientific learning and development among young children. Doing so lets students recognize the real-world implications of their learning as it applies to their own lives, fostering personal connections for greater understanding. In this situation, placing labeled recycling bins in the classroom demonstrates to students how they can use concepts learned on the field trip in everyday situations. This strategy encourages students to incorporate recycling into their daily routines while simultaneously prompting them to classify recyclables by material to promote appropriate recycling practices.

108. A: Developing students' understanding of the causes of seasonal changes requires them to have a foundational awareness that the Earth revolves around the Sun on a tilted axis. This understanding helps students recognize that as the Earth revolves around the Sun over the course of a year, its axis points either toward or away from the Sun, causing varying degrees of sunlight. When learning about the causes of seasonal changes, young children may have difficulty comprehending how the Earth's position relative to the Sun affects the amount of sunlight they experience throughout the year. Young children build connections to learning through hands-on, project-based experiences, so having this student create a three-dimensional model of the Earth's revolution around the Sun would let the student investigate and gain clarification about this concept.

109. C: As young children begin learning about agricultural systems, food production, and its relationship to the environment, it is important that they also learn about the implications of the greenhouse effect. The greenhouse effect is a phenomenon in which certain gases in the atmosphere, including carbon dioxide, water vapor, methane, and nitrous oxide, trap heat and humidity. While an excess of these gases is harmful, the greenhouse effect is necessary for the growth of plants, so it can be beneficial for agriculture and food production. The greenhouse effect can be created by forming an enclosure in which plants can harness sunlight, but gases are not released into the atmosphere. This allows for plant growth throughout the year in a variety of climates and locations. Providing active, hands-on learning experiences is most effective in developing students' understanding of this concept in the early childhood classroom. By having students plant seeds and cover only some of them with a plastic bottle that has been cut in half, students can observe and compare how greenhouse gases affect plant growth. This will ultimately establish a foundation for understanding the relationship between the greenhouse effect and food production.

110. D: Scientific learning and development are best supported when young children are provided with opportunities that facilitate their natural inclination to observe and interact with the world around them. Such activities foster students' inherent sense of inquiry, as they are encouraged to use their physical senses to actively explore, investigate, and make discoveries as they build understanding of new concepts. In this situation, having students search for and identify different earth materials around the school campus would promote such inquiry by prompting students to physically interact with their immediate environment. In doing so, students would learn where these materials can be found in a natural setting, and would have the opportunity to observe, touch, and compare differences between them, thus strengthening their overall connection to learning.

111. A: During scientific exploration, asking students to record their thoughts and findings in a journal promotes inquiry and problem-solving skills. This strategy prompts students to reflect on their own thinking processes, work through problems, ask questions, and devise creative solutions. Further, having students keep observation journals can become a valuable formative assessment tool throughout instruction. By reading through these journals and providing feedback during the investigation, this teacher can gain insight into students' level of understanding, guide their process, and adjust instruction as necessary to support scientific learning and development.

Health

112. B: Gross motor skills refer to one's ability to engage in purposeful, coordinated large-muscle movements that incorporate the whole body, such as running, jumping, climbing, clapping, and stomping. These skills are essential to healthy physical development, so activities that incorporate such movements should be integrated throughout all areas of instruction in the early childhood classroom. By including a song in which students clap and stomp out syllables, and incorporating it into a language and literacy lesson on segmenting words, this teacher can strengthen students' understanding of the concept while promoting gross motor skill development.

113. C: Socioeconomic status may have significant implications on the quality of children's nutrition, physical health, and overall development. Families from low-income backgrounds often face several obstacles that may prevent access to resources and education related to adequate nutrition and health practices. This places children at greater risk for experiencing hindered development across domains, including cognitive delays, slowed physical growth, illness, and social, emotional, and behavioral issues. Further, as the foundation for nutrition, health, and fitness practices are often instilled in early childhood, those from socioeconomically disadvantaged backgrounds may be less likely to adopt healthy practices as they develop. If it is suspected that a student is in such a situation, it is important to refer the family to school- and community-based resources that can provide assistance.

114. B: The MyPlate website was created by the United States Department of Agriculture (USDA) to provide education and resources related to nutrition, health, and well-being at every stage of development. This visual and interactive website includes an array of information on the different food groups, portioning, and the nutritional benefits of consuming a variety of healthy foods. Having students explore the MyPlate website before beginning a meal-planning project would provide an active learning experience that establishes a framework for reference on how to make healthy food choices, as well as how these choices impact overall health and wellness. This would help students thoughtfully consider and make informed decisions about the foods they choose to include in their project.

115. D: An important component of health and wellness education is promoting students' understanding of how maintaining good hygiene helps to avoid illness. Instilling this concept in early childhood establishes a foundation for encouraging students to adopt good hygiene practices into their daily routines throughout life. Providing young children with active, hands-on experiences to teach the importance of hygiene demonstrates its relevance to increase students' understanding and connections to learning. In this activity, the glitter symbolizes germs. As students shake hands with one another, the glitter will transfer and stick to their hands, exemplifying how quickly illness-causing germs can spread. Further, as glitter is difficult to remove without proper handwashing, this activity shows how this basic hygiene routine helps avoid illness and maintain good health.

116. A: Modeling is a powerful instructional strategy in the early childhood classroom, as young children learn by imitating the actions, behaviors, and beliefs of adults in their immediate environment. Modeling a positive attitude and good practices related to health and physical fitness is essential to encouraging young children to adopt the same sentiment. Doing so helps to establish a foundation for students to engage in habits to maintain their own health, fitness, and well-being throughout their lives. In this situation, the teacher effectively models such a positive attitude by discussing her own exercise routines, incorporating movement into the classroom, and creating a learning environment that promotes health and physical fitness.

117. A: Teaching young children about healthy lifestyle choices and practices includes teaching them how to stay safe in the natural environment. This includes helping students learn to recognize and avoid environmental factors that can impact health and safety, such as harmful plants, animals, and insects. Using unplanned teachable moments strengthens students' understanding of this concept by placing it in an immediately applicable context. In this situation, the bees presented an environmental risk to students' physical safety. By telling them to avoid the bees and explaining that bee stings are harmful, this teacher effectively used this moment to provide students with a real-world example of how to identify potential dangers while outside in nature.

118. B: Promoting positive attitudes and confidence toward physical fitness and health requires that instruction, learning activities, and assessments are differentiated to align with students' individual needs. This includes providing students with a variety of options for physical activity. Doing so helps ensure that all students can participate in exercise and physical movement in a way that best suits their skill level, ability, and personal interests, encouraging their active participation. By providing multiple activity options at each station for students to demonstrate their strength, endurance, flexibility, and agility, this teacher can effectively differentiate the assessment to accommodate and engage all students.

119. D: Activities to develop students' fine motor skills are essential to helping them learn to perform a variety of daily tasks, including using tools with skill and control for specific purposes. When planning such activities, it is important to consider and align learning with students' developmental levels to promote engagement and confidence while providing the appropriate amount of challenge for skill building. By second grade, most students can reasonably be expected to possess a range of fine motor skills, and can begin engaging in increasingly complex tasks for greater development. Further, students in this age group learn most effectively through hands-on learning experiences in which they can physically manipulate learning materials. Introducing the concept of typing on a keyboard would provide these students with such an active learning opportunity while developing their dexterity and hand-eye coordination as they learn to correctly navigate a keyboard to type words.

120. A: While it is important to be aware of general expectations regarding gross motor skill development for each age group, early childhood educators must also understand that individual students will progress at different rates. When planning fitness instruction, recognizing these differences helps teachers implement the necessary supports, accommodations, and modifications to align learning with students' needs. Doing so promotes skill development while fostering students' confidence and positive attitudes toward physical activity. Diagnostic assessments are typically conducted prior to beginning a unit of instruction, and can be used to identify individual students' skill levels, abilities, and needs so as to differentiate learning accordingly. In this situation, performing a diagnostic skills test prior to beginning a unit on basketball will provide the teacher with insight into students' level of gross motor skill development so they can be placed in the appropriate groups.

121. C: Perceptual awareness skills are those which enable individuals to integrate sensory and physical motor skills in order to interact with the environment. This includes recognizing one's body and movements in relation to space, time, and direction. An example of a perceptual awareness skill is hand-eye coordination, which is the ability to use vision when performing activities that require controlled hand movements. This skill is essential for performing an array of daily tasks, engaging in physical activities, and learning to write. While hand-eye coordination is often acquired naturally as young children interact with the world around them, it is also important to provide multiple hands-on opportunities for developing this skill. Activities such as threading beads of various sizes allows students to practice using sight to guide their hands in purposeful movements, promoting the development of hand-eye coordination.

122. B: Teaching students to protect their physical safety by recognizing and responding appropriately to emergencies is an essential component of health and wellness education. This includes knowing the purpose of 911 calls in emergencies and how to make them. When teaching this concept, it is important to develop students' awareness of what constitutes an emergency to ensure they understand what to do in different situations. In following a visit by an emergency responder with a class discussion to differentiate emergency and non-emergency scenarios, this teacher can reinforce students' understanding of when it is appropriate to call 911.

123. C: Promoting healthy lifestyle choices among young children includes teaching them to identify and avoid unhealthy behaviors. Teachers must educate students about the negative impacts that drugs and alcohol have on overall health and well-being. Students must also be made aware that they will likely encounter instances in which harmful substances are present, and learn strategies for refusing them. In having students role-play scenarios in which they are offered drugs or alcohol, this teacher develops their ability to practice basic refusal skills by placing learning in a real-world context. As young children learn most effectively through play, so this activity provides a developmentally appropriate context for building strategies to avoid harmful substances and engage in healthy behaviors.

124. C: While individual children will acquire fine motor skills at varying rates, it is important to be aware of the characteristics, skills, and abilities associated with each developmental level. This understanding can help teachers implement age-appropriate activities to support fine motor skill development, as well as identify potential delays. By second grade, most students can reasonably be expected to grasp and manipulate small objects and tools for performing specific tasks. This includes independently engaging in self-help skills, such as tying shoes, zipping coats, and fastening buttons. Students who cannot perform these tasks independently by second grade may require further assessment of their fine motor skill development.

125. C: Non-locomotor skills are the ability to engage in gross (or large) movements of the body that are *not* used for propelling the body from place to place. Examples of such skills include bending, twisting, swaying, and stretching. Non-locomotor skills are an important component of overall physical fitness and health, as they contribute to building strength, balance, stamina, and flexibility. To promote development of these skills in the early childhood classroom, non-locomotor movements should be incorporated into daily learning experiences. By beginning each school day with yoga, this teacher prompts students to engage in a variety of stationary whole-body movements, supporting their development of non-locomotor skills.

126. D: Protecting students' health and safety requires that teachers follow specific precautions and guidelines related to physical activities. This includes making sure that all outdoor play equipment is clean, functional, and the appropriate size for students' developmental levels before allowing them to use it. Doing so is necessary to prevent injury and illness so as to provide them with a suitable, age-appropriate outdoor environment that promotes physical activity, learning, and motor skill development.

PECT Practice Test #3

To take this additional PECT practice test, visit our bonus page:
mometrix.com/bonus948/pectprek4

SCAN HERE

How to Overcome Test Anxiety

Just the thought of taking a test is enough to make most people a little nervous. A test is an important event that can have a long-term impact on your future, so it's important to take it seriously and it's natural to feel anxious about performing well. But just because anxiety is normal, that doesn't mean that it's helpful in test taking, or that you should simply accept it as part of your life. Anxiety can have a variety of effects. These effects can be mild, like making you feel slightly nervous, or severe, like blocking your ability to focus or remember even a simple detail.

If you experience test anxiety—whether severe or mild—it's important to know how to beat it. To discover this, first you need to understand what causes test anxiety.

Causes of Test Anxiety

While we often think of anxiety as an uncontrollable emotional state, it can actually be caused by simple, practical things. One of the most common causes of test anxiety is that a person does not feel adequately prepared for their test. This feeling can be the result of many different issues such as poor study habits or lack of organization, but the most common culprit is time management. Starting to study too late, failing to organize your study time to cover all of the material, or being distracted while you study will mean that you're not well prepared for the test. This may lead to cramming the night before, which will cause you to be physically and mentally exhausted for the test. Poor time management also contributes to feelings of stress, fear, and hopelessness as you realize you are not well prepared but don't know what to do about it.

Other times, test anxiety is not related to your preparation for the test but comes from unresolved fear. This may be a past failure on a test, or poor performance on tests in general. It may come from comparing yourself to others who seem to be performing better or from the stress of living up to expectations. Anxiety may be driven by fears of the future—how failure on this test would affect your educational and career goals. These fears are often completely irrational, but they can still negatively impact your test performance.

Elements of Test Anxiety

As mentioned earlier, test anxiety is considered to be an emotional state, but it has physical and mental components as well. Sometimes you may not even realize that you are suffering from test anxiety until you notice the physical symptoms. These can include trembling hands, rapid heartbeat, sweating, nausea, and tense muscles. Extreme anxiety may lead to fainting or vomiting. Obviously, any of these symptoms can have a negative impact on testing. It is important to recognize them as soon as they begin to occur so that you can address the problem before it damages your performance.

The mental components of test anxiety include trouble focusing and inability to remember learned information. During a test, your mind is on high alert, which can help you recall information and stay focused for an extended period of time. However, anxiety interferes with your mind's natural processes, causing you to blank out, even on the questions you know well. The strain of testing during anxiety makes it difficult to stay focused, especially on a test that may take several hours. Extreme anxiety can take a huge mental toll, making it difficult not only to recall test information but even to understand the test questions or pull your thoughts together.

Effects of Test Anxiety

Test anxiety is like a disease—if left untreated, it will get progressively worse. Anxiety leads to poor performance, and this reinforces the feelings of fear and failure, which in turn lead to poor performances on subsequent tests. It can grow from a mild nervousness to a crippling condition. If allowed to progress, test anxiety can have a big impact on your schooling, and consequently on your future.

Test anxiety can spread to other parts of your life. Anxiety on tests can become anxiety in any stressful situation, and blanking on a test can turn into panicking in a job situation. But fortunately, you don't have to let anxiety rule your testing and determine your grades. There are a number of relatively simple steps you can take to move past anxiety and function normally on a test and in the rest of life.

Physical Steps for Beating Test Anxiety

While test anxiety is a serious problem, the good news is that it can be overcome. It doesn't have to control your ability to think and remember information. While it may take time, you can begin taking steps today to beat anxiety.

Just as your first hint that you may be struggling with anxiety comes from the physical symptoms, the first step to treating it is also physical. Rest is crucial for having a clear, strong mind. If you are tired, it is much easier to give in to anxiety. But if you establish good sleep habits, your body and mind will be ready to perform optimally, without the strain of exhaustion. Additionally, sleeping well helps you to retain information better, so you're more likely to recall the answers when you see the test questions.

Getting good sleep means more than going to bed on time. It's important to allow your brain time to relax. Take study breaks from time to time so it doesn't get overworked, and don't study right before bed. Take time to rest your mind before trying to rest your body, or you may find it difficult to fall asleep.

Along with sleep, other aspects of physical health are important in preparing for a test. Good nutrition is vital for good brain function. Sugary foods and drinks may give a burst of energy but this burst is followed by a crash, both physically and emotionally. Instead, fuel your body with protein and vitamin-rich foods.

Also, drink plenty of water. Dehydration can lead to headaches and exhaustion, especially if your brain is already under stress from the rigors of the test. Particularly if your test is a long one, drink water during the breaks. And if possible, take an energy-boosting snack to eat between sections.

Along with sleep and diet, a third important part of physical health is exercise. Maintaining a steady workout schedule is helpful, but even taking 5-minute study breaks to walk can help get your blood pumping faster and clear your head. Exercise also releases endorphins, which contribute to a positive feeling and can help combat test anxiety.

When you nurture your physical health, you are also contributing to your mental health. If your body is healthy, your mind is much more likely to be healthy as well. So take time to rest, nourish your body with healthy food and water, and get moving as much as possible. Taking these physical steps will make you stronger and more able to take the mental steps necessary to overcome test anxiety.

Mental Steps for Beating Test Anxiety

Working on the mental side of test anxiety can be more challenging, but as with the physical side, there are clear steps you can take to overcome it. As mentioned earlier, test anxiety often stems from lack of preparation, so the obvious solution is to prepare for the test. Effective studying may be the most important weapon you have for beating test anxiety, but you can and should employ several other mental tools to combat fear.

First, boost your confidence by reminding yourself of past success—tests or projects that you aced. If you're putting as much effort into preparing for this test as you did for those, there's no reason you should expect to fail here. Work hard to prepare; then trust your preparation.

Second, surround yourself with encouraging people. It can be helpful to find a study group, but be sure that the people you're around will encourage a positive attitude. If you spend time with others who are anxious or cynical, this will only contribute to your own anxiety. Look for others who are motivated to study hard from a desire to succeed, not from a fear of failure.

Third, reward yourself. A test is physically and mentally tiring, even without anxiety, and it can be helpful to have something to look forward to. Plan an activity following the test, regardless of the outcome, such as going to a movie or getting ice cream.

When you are taking the test, if you find yourself beginning to feel anxious, remind yourself that you know the material. Visualize successfully completing the test. Then take a few deep, relaxing breaths and return to it. Work through the questions carefully but with confidence, knowing that you are capable of succeeding.

Developing a healthy mental approach to test taking will also aid in other areas of life. Test anxiety affects more than just the actual test—it can be damaging to your mental health and even contribute to depression. It's important to beat test anxiety before it becomes a problem for more than testing.

Study Strategy

Being prepared for the test is necessary to combat anxiety, but what does being prepared look like? You may study for hours on end and still not feel prepared. What you need is a strategy for test prep. The next few pages outline our recommended steps to help you plan out and conquer the challenge of preparation.

STEP 1: SCOPE OUT THE TEST

Learn everything you can about the format (multiple choice, essay, etc.) and what will be on the test. Gather any study materials, course outlines, or sample exams that may be available. Not only will this help you to prepare, but knowing what to expect can help to alleviate test anxiety.

STEP 2: MAP OUT THE MATERIAL

Look through the textbook or study guide and make note of how many chapters or sections it has. Then divide these over the time you have. For example, if a book has 15 chapters and you have five days to study, you need to cover three chapters each day. Even better, if you have the time, leave an extra day at the end for overall review after you have gone through the material in depth.

If time is limited, you may need to prioritize the material. Look through it and make note of which sections you think you already have a good grasp on, and which need review. While you are studying, skim quickly through the familiar sections and take more time on the challenging parts. Write out your plan so you don't get lost as you go. Having a written plan also helps you feel more in control of the study, so anxiety is less likely to arise from feeling overwhelmed at the amount to cover.

STEP 3: GATHER YOUR TOOLS

Decide what study method works best for you. Do you prefer to highlight in the book as you study and then go back over the highlighted portions? Or do you type out notes of the important information? Or is it helpful to make flashcards that you can carry with you? Assemble the pens, index cards, highlighters, post-it notes, and any other materials you may need so you won't be distracted by getting up to find things while you study.

If you're having a hard time retaining the information or organizing your notes, experiment with different methods. For example, try color-coding by subject with colored pens, highlighters, or post-it notes. If you learn better by hearing, try recording yourself reading your notes so you can listen while in the car, working out, or simply sitting at your desk. Ask a friend to quiz you from your flashcards, or try teaching someone the material to solidify it in your mind.

STEP 4: CREATE YOUR ENVIRONMENT

It's important to avoid distractions while you study. This includes both the obvious distractions like visitors and the subtle distractions like an uncomfortable chair (or a too-comfortable couch that makes you want to fall asleep). Set up the best study environment possible: good lighting and a comfortable work area. If background music helps you focus, you may want to turn it on, but otherwise keep the room quiet. If you are using a computer to take notes, be sure you don't have any other windows open, especially applications like social media, games, or anything else that could distract you. Silence your phone and turn off notifications. Be sure to keep water close by so you stay hydrated while you study (but avoid unhealthy drinks and snacks).

Also, take into account the best time of day to study. Are you freshest first thing in the morning? Try to set aside some time then to work through the material. Is your mind clearer in the afternoon or evening? Schedule your study session then. Another method is to study at the same time of day that you will take the test, so that your brain gets used to working on the material at that time and will be ready to focus at test time.

STEP 5: STUDY!

Once you have done all the study preparation, it's time to settle into the actual studying. Sit down, take a few moments to settle your mind so you can focus, and begin to follow your study plan. Don't give in to distractions or let yourself procrastinate. This is your time to prepare so you'll be ready to fearlessly approach the test. Make the most of the time and stay focused.

Of course, you don't want to burn out. If you study too long you may find that you're not retaining the information very well. Take regular study breaks. For example, taking five minutes out of every hour to walk briskly, breathing deeply and swinging your arms, can help your mind stay fresh.

As you get to the end of each chapter or section, it's a good idea to do a quick review. Remind yourself of what you learned and work on any difficult parts. When you feel that you've mastered the material, move on to the next part. At the end of your study session, briefly skim through your notes again.

But while review is helpful, cramming last minute is NOT. If at all possible, work ahead so that you won't need to fit all your study into the last day. Cramming overloads your brain with more information than it can process and retain, and your tired mind may struggle to recall even previously learned information when it is overwhelmed with last-minute study. Also, the urgent nature of cramming and the stress placed on your brain contribute to anxiety. You'll be more likely to go to the test feeling unprepared and having trouble thinking clearly.

So don't cram, and don't stay up late before the test, even just to review your notes at a leisurely pace. Your brain needs rest more than it needs to go over the information again. In fact, plan to finish your studies by noon or early afternoon the day before the test. Give your brain the rest of the day to relax or focus on other things, and get a good night's sleep. Then you will be fresh for the test and better able to recall what you've studied.

STEP 6: TAKE A PRACTICE TEST

Many courses offer sample tests, either online or in the study materials. This is an excellent resource to check whether you have mastered the material, as well as to prepare for the test format and environment.

Check the test format ahead of time: the number of questions, the type (multiple choice, free response, etc.), and the time limit. Then create a plan for working through them. For example, if you have 30 minutes to take a 60-question test, your limit is 30 seconds per question. Spend less time on the questions you know well so that you can take more time on the difficult ones.

If you have time to take several practice tests, take the first one open book, with no time limit. Work through the questions at your own pace and make sure you fully understand them. Gradually work up to taking a test under test conditions: sit at a desk with all study materials put away and set a timer. Pace yourself to make sure you finish the test with time to spare and go back to check your answers if you have time.

After each test, check your answers. On the questions you missed, be sure you understand why you missed them. Did you misread the question (tests can use tricky wording)? Did you forget the information? Or was it something you hadn't learned? Go back and study any shaky areas that the practice tests reveal.

Taking these tests not only helps with your grade, but also aids in combating test anxiety. If you're already used to the test conditions, you're less likely to worry about it, and working through tests until you're scoring well gives you a confidence boost. Go through the practice tests until you feel comfortable, and then you can go into the test knowing that you're ready for it.

Test Tips

On test day, you should be confident, knowing that you've prepared well and are ready to answer the questions. But aside from preparation, there are several test day strategies you can employ to maximize your performance.

First, as stated before, get a good night's sleep the night before the test (and for several nights before that, if possible). Go into the test with a fresh, alert mind rather than staying up late to study.

Try not to change too much about your normal routine on the day of the test. It's important to eat a nutritious breakfast, but if you normally don't eat breakfast at all, consider eating just a protein bar. If you're a coffee drinker, go ahead and have your normal coffee. Just make sure you time it so that the caffeine doesn't wear off right in the middle of your test. Avoid sugary beverages, and drink enough water to stay hydrated but not so much that you need a restroom break 10 minutes into the test. If your test isn't first thing in the morning, consider going for a walk or doing a light workout before the test to get your blood flowing.

Allow yourself enough time to get ready, and leave for the test with plenty of time to spare so you won't have the anxiety of scrambling to arrive in time. Another reason to be early is to select a good seat. It's helpful to sit away from doors and windows, which can be distracting. Find a good seat, get out your supplies, and settle your mind before the test begins.

When the test begins, start by going over the instructions carefully, even if you already know what to expect. Make sure you avoid any careless mistakes by following the directions.

Then begin working through the questions, pacing yourself as you've practiced. If you're not sure on an answer, don't spend too much time on it, and don't let it shake your confidence. Either skip it and come back later, or eliminate as many wrong answers as possible and guess among the remaining ones. Don't dwell on these questions as you continue—put them out of your mind and focus on what lies ahead.

Be sure to read all of the answer choices, even if you're sure the first one is the right answer. Sometimes you'll find a better one if you keep reading. But don't second-guess yourself if you do immediately know the answer. Your gut instinct is usually right. Don't let test anxiety rob you of the information you know.

If you have time at the end of the test (and if the test format allows), go back and review your answers. Be cautious about changing any, since your first instinct tends to be correct, but make sure you didn't misread any of the questions or accidentally mark the wrong answer choice. Look over any you skipped and make an educated guess.

At the end, leave the test feeling confident. You've done your best, so don't waste time worrying about your performance or wishing you could change anything. Instead, celebrate the successful completion of this test. And finally, use this test to learn how to deal with anxiety even better next time.

> **Review Video: <u>Test Anxiety</u>**
> Visit mometrix.com/academy and enter code: 100340

Important Qualification

Not all anxiety is created equal. If your test anxiety is causing major issues in your life beyond the classroom or testing center, or if you are experiencing troubling physical symptoms related to your anxiety, it may be a sign of a serious physiological or psychological condition. If this sounds like your situation, we strongly encourage you to seek professional help.

Additional Bonus Material

Due to our efforts to try to keep this book to a manageable length, we've created a link that will give you access to all of your additional bonus material:

mometrix.com/bonus948/pectprek4